OTHER BOOKS BY ELLIN DODGE

You Are Your First Name

Win the Lottery!

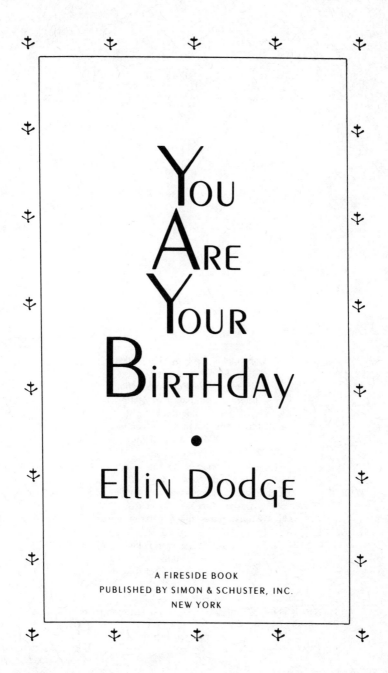

You Are Your Birthday

•

Ellin Dodge

A FIRESIDE BOOK
PUBLISHED BY SIMON & SCHUSTER, INC.
NEW YORK

A Fireside Book
Published by Simon & Schuster, Inc.
Simon & Schuster Building
Rockefeller Center
1230 Avenue of the Americas
New York, New York 10020
FIRESIDE and colophon are registered trademarks of Simon & Schuster, Inc.
Designed by Karolina Harris
Manufactured in the United States of America
1   3   5   7   9   10   8   6   4   2
Library of Congress Cataloging in Publication Data
Dodge, Ellin.
You are your birthday.

"A Fireside book."
1. Fortune-telling by birthdays.   2. Symbolism of numbers.   I. Title.
BF1891.B54D63   1986   133.3'354   86-10051
ISBN: 0-671-61091-0

This book is dedicated
to Ivy Robyn Dodge,
born on September 29,
and to Jeffrey David Dodge,
born on October 25.
I am so proud of you both!
With gratitude for the happiest
and most rewarding
birth days of my life.
With love, from your mother
—THE AUTHOR

ACKNOWLEDGMENTS

My deepest appreciation to design-engineer, computer whiz, and kindred spirit Harold W. "Skipper" Pearce, Jr., of Phoenix, Arizona, who turned an Apple IIe into a mainframe.

To Betty Flores, a lady who wears many hats. For birthday research in this book she wore a journalist's fedora. For keeping Bill, my dad, Freddy, my Yorky, and our Phoenix household-office running smoothly, she wore her "flunky" hat. For being helpful in all kinds of weather, she wore her umbrella hat and never let it rain on my parade. For the record, Betty—thank you.

Special thanks to my agent, Ellen Levine, who, I am delighted to discover, is a good sport and enjoys surprises as much as I do.

My Fireside editor, Barbara Gess, made this two-title year a treasure and a pleasure. At a welcoming Fireside, kindred spirits are sought but not always available. How fortunate I have been to work with you.

Thanks also to Fireside's dynamic Cathy Hemming and Simon and Schuster's elegant Julia Knickerbocker, who both made me think that it was déjà vu when we met . . . and Jennifer Kittridge, I know how hard you tried.

To clients, friends and readers who have waited for me to return calls and letters, thank you for your patience and encouragement during the six months that this book progressed and deadlined. Happy birthday, you all are wonderful!

CONTENTS

INTRODUCTION

Is it coincidental that the number of a day of birth is personally revealing? Not to a numerologist. *You Are Your Birthday* explains your options, as seen through the eyes of numerology. This book was written in the hope that you will note the similarities in the lives of people who are born on the same day.

When the word spread that I wanted to know how people felt about celebrating—or not celebrating—a birthday, varying degrees of enthusiasm, yawning and candor greeted the question. Numerology doesn't ask for astrology's generalized sun sign; it is specific. I asked for the exact month and day of birth. Vibes rolled in that indicated the question was opening up a can of worms. The answers received were typical of the personalities indicated by numerology's birthday synopsis.

Attitudes vary. Some have a sheepish attitude toward birthdays. If you skipped from twenty-seven to thirty-six, thirty-six to forty-five or think that anything over fifty is between you and your urologist or gynecologist, you probably have a traditional number 2, 4, 6 or 8 lurking in your birthdate. On the other hand, if you have a 1, 3 or 5 in your birthdate, like Shirley MacLaine, Betty Ford and Cary Grant, you probably look twenty years younger than you are and don't mind being publicly honest about your age.

It seems that birthdays are very private affairs. I get a New-Year's-resolution-time feeling as birthdays approach. Not young enough to greet them eagerly as Christmas or old enough to awaken thinking "Thank you, Lord, for another day," this mid-life perfectionist reviews the entire past, present and future. That's about par for an October 7 personality.

Easygoing, George Burns celebrates his January 20 birthday. One imagines that he is just glad to wake to find he's looking up at the sun—not down, shining on us. My eighty-three-year-old detail-conscious father shrugs off a November 2 birthday cake with, "We don't have enough fire insurance for this." Songstress Jo Sullivan Loesser says, "I never think about my birthday. But every year I take five years off my age; and get away with it for a while." She's on my team! Birthdays are party time. The only number that should be mentioned is the hour that guests are expected to arrive. Jo's typical

August 28 approach indicates her need for privacy, her individuality and her philosophical style of chutzpah.

Since birth *day* numbers add insights and shed light on personality, while the *month* number indicates experiences only, the combination of the two reveals the inconsistencies of a person's public image and the child within. Pulitzer prizewinner David Mamet, a November 30 birthday boy, commentator on society, unconventional college professor, known for his down-to-earth style of people watching and writing, said it for the numbers of his birthday when he commented, "I love my birthday because people give me things."

Typical of the unpretentious, May 12 born, secure in her unique philosophy and birthright but in all ways questioning, Academy Award nominee—and David's wife—Lindsay Crouse Mamet said, "My birthday; what is so rare as a day in May—beats me." Lindsay Crouse and David Mamet, who share the same root number 3 in their day of birth, are enthusiastic about life. To them, birthdays mean anticipating goodies. The imaginative, youthful, friendly Mamets revel in the fairytale quality of birthdays. Their birthdays invite gifts, awards and attention. People born with a 3, 12, 21 or 30 birth day should be aware of their dreams and update them regularly. Those dreams are bound to come true—if a time limit is not placed upon them—because of the number 3's extraordinary ability to create colorful mind pictures.

While doing research for this book, I was fascinated to learn that spouse compatibility is predictable by birthday numbers too. Joanne Woodward (born 2/27) and Paul Newman (born 1/26), whose marriage has withstood Hollywood hoopla and domestic East Coast realities, have the same combination of birthday numbers as do long-married Jayne Meadows (born 9/27) and Steve Allen (born 12/26).

The Newmans and the Allens *month*-of-birth numbers differ, which indicates that they had different childhood desires and experiences. Their day-of-birth numbers indicate that the lower number will stretch and the higher number has a more mature philosophy in mid-life. The common denominator first digit provides compatibility, and the different second digit adds unknowns that stimulate growth. It seems that couples do stay together when birthday numbers are only one digit apart.

Numerologists know that people, universally, are attracted to other people whose birthday numbers are the same or so completely opposite—and therefore challenging—that they pursue the unknown qualities offered by the relationship. The results of too much sameness may produce boredom; it does not always lead to long-term partnerships.

The Smothers brothers, Dick (born 11/20) and Tommy (born 2/2), were partners until they approached late years. Their months and days of birth share the numerological symbol 2, the number of benefits from partnership, cooperation and musical aptitude. Their years of birth, which are different, indicate a change after mid-life. As they approached the changing point in their late forties, they began to express themselves individually. But the day-of-birth number 2, common to both brothers, is a *lifetime* personality indicator. So the Smothers brothers will continue to want the advantages of a close, easygoing alliance. Both Dick and Tom Smothers feel better when they have companionship and are at their best when they are involved in an intimate, loving relationship.

Wish we may, wish we might, birthdays come and go. It's better to live through them, at any age. Every birthday begins a new learning adventure, if you accept it as such. Your birthdate numbers will help you understand your personality and will reveal the types of experiences you'll meet in life. How you cope with the challenges of numerology's eye openers is up to you. If this book serves you well, you may agree—*You Are Your Birthday* and it is wonderful!

HOW TO USE THIS BOOK

You can use this book to **change your expectations, identify personality extremes** and, if you are willing to work to balance the personality challenges and use self-awareness and self-discipline, you can **clarify your options, balance your compulsive tendencies** and **increase your productivity.**

This book can alter your expectations because it encourages self-understanding, identifies the mistakes that you have made repeatedly and offers suggestions for changing the ways you cope with people and experiences that numerology foretells for your life.

Here's how to make the best use of this book.

1. Look up your birthday in the Numerology Birthday Calendar (pages 49–416).

2. Look up the individual descriptions of your month, day, year and practical growth numbers in the Do-It-Yourself section (pages 21–43). These interpretations may be positive or negative. If you are not comfortable with the descriptions, look to the opposite meaning of the interpretations given.

3. Look up your challenge number in the Do-It-Yourself section (pages 36–43). This description will give you important information about your personality extremes and will help you plan your own luck.

4. Look up your birthstone meaning (pages 44–48).

The combined analysis of these personal descriptions will reflect the entire numerological picture of your personality and future.

But don't expect this book to solve your problems. Expect it to reflect their origin, confirm them and explain why you attract them. *You Are Your Birthday* offers a glimpse into your childhood and productive years—and suggests options for changing your attitudes, your self-image and your direction.

1

Numerology and Your Birthday

Numerology is a mystical arithmetic system that reveals character, personality and experience through the sensible progressions of numbers. Some of the numbers most closely associated with you are those of your birthday. These numbers symbolically describe the form, order, beauty, unity and elegant arrangement of your progress through life. In a very real sense, you are your birthday.

DO YOU SEE THE COINCIDENCES?

If February 22 is your birthday, you are an extremist where rules and traditions are concerned. Ted Kennedy, George Washington and Robert Baden-Powell, Boys Scouts founder, share February 22 birthdays and a sense of responsibility to build better family, community and world environments.

Born in September? You've come a long way from your roots. Clan founder Joseph Kennedy, merchant J. C. Penney and magnificent Swedish film great Greta Garbo—all September babies—traveled far in cultural ways. They stretched their birthright to reach a broad scope, polished the quality of their own lives and made outstanding contributions. People born in the ninth month, September, learn from experience how to set an example that beautifies, improves tastes and awakens quality consciousness.

Youthful enthusiasms, charming talents and fiery relationships increase after your late twenties if you're born on the twenty-third of any month. Life will be a sensual, unconventional and unpredictable adventure for you. Male sex symbol Douglas Fairbanks, female sex symbol Joan Collins and much-married Mickey Rooney were all born on the twenty-third. Empress Josephine; Edward, the twentieth-century Duke of Windsor who gave up the throne of England for the woman he loved; and Akihito, crown prince of Japan, all share untraditional royal memoirs as well as number 23 birthdays. Astronomer and foreteller Nostradamus; mesmerizer Anton Mesmer; and space age engineer Werner von Braun were all catalysts for change and non-routine life-stylers. Their number 23 birthday experiences exposed them to situations and people beyond their expectations and attracted influential family or associates. Their energetic minds helped them thrive on challenging uprootings.

DO YOU GET THE PICTURE?

When you look up the birthdays of yourself and your friends in the *You Are Your Birthday* pages and relate them to the pictures painted and the notables listed, you will understand the ways in which birthdays are revealing. Think about the lives of the public figures listed with each birthday. You may be familiar with them through history books or newspaper headlines. It is astonishing how many similarities you will find in their lives and the lives of your family, friends and business associates born on the same day.

WHAT IS NUMEROLOGY?

Throughout history, mighty explorers, dictators and religious leaders have "listened to the numbers." The ancients gave meanings to cumulative number symbols as far back as precivilization and the cave clans. Later the Chinese, Hindus, Egyptians, Hebrews, Phoenicians and sophisticated Greeks used ancient methods to assign cause and effect to alphabets, language and cumulative number symbols.

Civilizations have been lost, but the intellect, science, opinion and sense of numerology, which takes idea to ideal, lived in the theosophy of Greek mathematician Pythagoras. Originally a means to measure mundane nature and the immaterial, its documentations now irretrievably lost, the number system as divined by Pythagoras was intended to invite all men to commune with the gods. In ancient civilizations the numbers that were used to symbolize man's spiritual progression from pure selfishness to selflessness were systematized and called by the name numerology.

Moses, Julius Caesar and the Greek father of geometry Pythagoras interpreted types of people and experiences and planned their ambitions, forecasting with numerology. These men were highly intuitive and dynamic. Years ago, when I discovered numerology and leaned how many of the greats of history used it, I realized it must be a system worth trying.

I have learned—and hope you will, too—that there are unknowns in life that require an open mind. Society's greatest business and professional achievers trust their "sixth sense." Numerology is the outgrowth of people's attempts to organize "sixth sensing" and "feeling vibrations" into a system.

Vibrations, or "vibes," are acceptable unseen sensings that, in daily conversational descriptions, explain the cold shivers we feel when approaching a situation that is surprisingly threatening. The word *vibes* is also used to describe a sexy turn-on or turn-off. Vibes are the basis for the numerology system divined by Pythagoras back in the sixth century B.C.

PYTHAGORAS, FATHER OF NUMBERS

Pythagoras, a philosopher, astronomer and teacher, established the diatonic scale by which we still tune a piano today. He traveled the world, the same Eastern path that Jesus traveled, to bring other cultures back to the Greeks. In Greece he became part of the old Mystery Schools spoken of in the writings of Plato, Cicero and Apuleius.

In the sixth and seventh centuries before Christ, all life was based upon religious ceremony. Priests jealously guarded the secrets that kept them above the masses. The divine numerical "globe" that was substituted for the sacrifices of animals and other harmful acts used to appease the gods was the foundation for the university established by Pythagoras. Unfortunately, this "globe," described as a sphere, ring or circle containing letters and numbers, has been forever lost. But disciples of Pythagoras passed the word and wrote in a medical text of a "circle made up of letters and numbers" that was comprised of character traits and personality definitions.

Modern numerology has expanded upon the original globe. Throughout the years contributions have been made by philosophers and scholars. Numerology adapts itself to foreign languages and various types of birthdate recordings. However, the system is essentially the same today as the one established by Pythagoras.

PYTHAGORAS'S NUMBER THEORY

Pythagoras, the founder of the numbers system, believed that the numbers 1 through 9 led to perfection, symbolized by the number 10. When you read the number meanings that follow, you will understand how the numbers 1 through 9 evolve.

We begin with 1, an idea that grows in a predictable, step-by-step progression.

Number 2 symbolizes that idea reaching out, being received by others and getting the cooperation needed to continue its growth.

The number 3 brings the idea to others for inspection and approval.

Number 4 brings the idea to practical application and corrects impracticalities.

Number 5 adds promotion and exposure to public opinion. Five, the central number, opens the door for unexpected pluses or minuses. Here the idea makes the transition from an individual concept to a community awareness.

Number 6 is the symbol for group participation and community responsibility. It broadens the concept to serve a larger purpose.

Number 7 is the symbol for debugging, questioning and perfecting the idea technically until it can be brought to a major material result.

Number 8 stands for stamina, mental and physical organization, and practical power. It brings body, mind and spirit together to produce tangible results. Ideas come to form through the planning, work and structure applied during the influence of a number 8.

Number 9 polishes, develops the skills necessary to bring the idea to a broad marketplace and concludes the process.

This process relates to everything we do. Ambitions grow through the activities or experiences indicated by the number meanings. The stages of growth during the nine months of pregnancy and the final perfection of the fetus in the ninth month are a prime example of the evolution of the numbers 1 through 9. The birth of the child begins a new life a few days after the conclusion of the ninth month. The child, a new concept, starts the cycles of life at its birth—the tenth month. In numerology number 10 becomes a number 1 when we add 1 + 0, which results in a 1. The pregnancy ended in a number 9 month—9 the number of endings. Life begins in a number 1—the number of beginnings.

2
·
Do-It-Yourself
Birthday Numbers

THE BASICS

Numerology has a basic rule: all double numbers are added together and reduced to a single number by adding from left to right.

- EXAMPLE: $45 = 4 + 5 = 9$
  $34 = 3 + 4 = 7$
  28 is tricky.
  It calls for double action.
  $28 = 2 + 8 = 10;$
  reduce again to end up with a single number:
  $10 = 1 + 0 = 1;$
  so a 28 becomes a 1 in numerology.

You Are Your Birthday is based upon the month and day of birth numbers. The month and day of birth numbers are added, subtracted and analyzed to explain the complexities of character and life experience indicated by the number meanings of the birthday.

The **month-of-birth number** indicates your early life—childhood exposures, preteen fantasies and teenage experimentations, and influences of the family. Academic, commercial and spiritual intentions also relate to the month-of-birth influence. The month-of-birth number is the training ground indicator. It governs the time in life when we have not yet begun our best work or experienced total productivity.

The **day-of-birth number** reveals the experiences of the productivity cycle. Productivity begins at approximately twenty-eight years of age, lasts for three nine-year evolvements for a total of twenty-seven years, and we enter our wisdom cycle at approximately fifty-six years of age.

The productivity cycle begins our maturity and provides experiences that establish a practical foundation for the final third of our lives. During the mid-life productivity cycle, lifetime social contacts and career choices firm up.

The **year-of-birth number** indicates the wisdom cycle, which begins at approximately fifty-six years of age. These are the years when we are most self-expressive because we use all the four number ingredients of our birth year.

The **practical growth number** works together with the month number, before age twenty-eight, to set your expectations and goals for a lifetime.

Some of us experience a lifetime of immature judgments, remain antisocial or change careers or spouses with the seasons. Numerology incorporates our reactions, compulsions and obsessions by subtracting the month-of-birth number from the day-of-birth number (whichever is the smaller from the larger). This simple subtraction, related to the youth cycle, results in your **challenge number**. It explains the extremes to which we will go when emotionally triggered by people and experiences, indicated by the number resulting from the subtraction.

Childhood programming often limits goals and ambitions. Whether we are capable of reaching our potential during the productivity cycle depends upon youth cycle environments, exposures and expectations, which are indicated by the numbers of the month and day of birth individually and in combination.

If this is beginning to seem complicated, don't worry. That's why *You Are Your Birthday* was written.

Just remember that it is not only what is forecast as an incoming experience that produces an accurate profile. Our expectations, based upon childhood experiences or teachings, govern the way we will cope with the experience presented to us.

If you expect to take the lead and be a winner, you will do it. If you have been programmed to support authoritative people, you will not seize the opportunities offered to be creative and to direct others.

If you understand the meanings of your birthday numbers, you are in a better position to make decisions and steer the course of a successful, happy life. So let's get started!

YOUR MONTH NUMBER

The months are given numbers according to their position in the calendar.

January = 1,
   individuality
February = 2,
   sensitivity
March = 3, self-
   expression
April = 4,
   practicality
May = 5,
   restlessness
June = 6,
   responsibility

July = 7,
   introspection
August = 8,
   financial or
   material
   concentration
September = 9,
   cultural
   expansion
October = (10) 1
   individuality and
   empathy for
   others combined

November = (11) 2
   sensitivity
   combined with
   individuality and
   inventiveness
December = (12) 3
   self-expression
   combined with
   individuality and
   sensitivity.

The definitions of the month numbers reflect early exposures that influence childhood and youthful expectations for the future.

Month Number Meanings

JANUARY

1

January children are individuals. The circumstances surrounding them from infancy through the late twenties breed independence. They may be loners; however, they develop inner resources. Number 1 is synonymous with ego; the "I." People born in January want to be number 1 and, as tots, usually suffer the indignities of dependence upon their elders, the authority figures. Since they are born to be in leadership, a sense of repression or isolation may prevail until they have the resources to stand on their own.

Activity, creativity, originality, leadership, independence and courage are key words for January children. These character traits are developed during the nurturing first cycle of life and are reinforced by types of people, circumstances and environments.

Those who are January born are keenly aware of paternal or assertive personalities and relate strongly to them. They are the inventors of the future who become indispensable leaders or associates to leaders, because they learn to make decisions for themselves when life's exposures set them up to be accountable for their own actions.

FEBRUARY

2

February children need attention, because they are sensitive. The circumstances surrounding them in infancy through the late twenties demand their cooperation and dependence upon a modest attitude. They may be spoiled or neglected, but they are keenly aware of their personal feelings and relationships. Number 2 is synonymous with the necessity to appreciate and apply diplomacy; partnerships and intimate contacts prevail throughout the nurturing years. Since February children relate on an emotional level, they are sensitive to the feelings of others and often react to the repression of their independence with chronic allergies, physical maladies and/or the suppression of communication. They react inwardly to frustration when surrounded by individuals and circumstances that insist upon adaptability, obedience and interdependency.

Gentleness, friendliness, consideration, detail consciousness, charm and closeness are the key words for February children. These character traits are developed during the nurturing first cycle of life and are reinforced by types of people, circumstances and environments.

February-born people are the diplomats of the future who become the glue that holds families, businesses or nations together. They learn to work with and for others and to guard their own and the secrets of others, and rarely serve driving personal ambitions.

MARCH

3

March children are sociable and self-expressive. The circumstances surrounding them in infancy through the late twenties breed imagination. They may be attractive physically and/or gifted with talent, personality and humor. During the nurturing process, females and siblings may cause them to suffer personality highs and lows due to petty jealousies. March babes may have Cinderella or Shirley Temple memories, but when reflecting upon disappointments or failures, they find a way to bounce back and create a happy ending. Since they are born to give and attract beauty, to entertain and be entertained and to inspire and be an inspiration, a sense of optimism prevails.

March born are the game players of the future; the people who learned early in life to appreciate toys, laughter and social contact. Responsibilities come second to the expression of talents, pleasures and love of life in youth. They latch on to maturity gradually.

APRIL

4

April children are orderly. The circumstances surrounding them in infancy through the late twenties breed common sense. They may be conventional, economy oriented, practical and desirous of security; however, they grow to express their creative personal ideals. Since they are born to be materially constructive, their talents are highly structured and practiced in youth. Our most determined pianists, ice skaters and athletes are April babes.

Self-discipline, devotion, endurance, exactitude, organization and conservatism are the key words for April children. These character traits are developed during the nurturing first cycle of life and are reinforced by types of people, circumstances and environments.

Those who are April born are the administrators, managers and builders of the future because they learn to work, develop a conscience and conscientiousness and respond with a willingness to do whatever must be done to obtain a goal.

MAY

5

May children are restless. The circumstances surrounding them in infancy through the late twenties breed untraditional ambitions. They may be free of routine, unencumbered by conventions or constantly uprooted. As a result of uncertainty or insecurity, they develop resilience, adaptability and cleverness. In some way May born do not conform to the norm. Number 5 is synonymous with freedom; the quest to taste all that life has to offer entices them.

Too often May children are unable to cope with their sexuality and sensuality, or they feel guilty about their impulsive actions or experimentations. However, a unique or charming personality is the result of the variety of experiences offered to the May born.

Mental curiosity, life experience, adventure, versatility, sexual magnetism and enthusiasm for everything that is new and progressive are the key words for May children. These character traits are developed during the nurturing first cycle of life and are reinforced by types of people, circumstances and environments.

May born are the swashbucklers of the future, the catalysts that unsettle the traditional, inspire youthful enthusiasms and shake up nations. They are the promoters, politicians and sex symbols in youth and may seem to be irresponsible youngsters. They break the rules, push for change and move on to new adventures when others try to conventionalize their offbeat actions.

JUNE

6

June children are domestically rooted. The circumstances surrounding them in infancy through the late twenties breed responsibility. They may be home, neighborhood and family oriented, unable to completely individualize. Number 6 is synonymous with service to others. People born in June may be surrounded by love, protection and sociability; however, the personal adjustments required in order to assume positions of trust within the clan are restricting. Since June babies are born to recognize convention, express beauty and excel through the educational forms of communications, they carry the burden of community awareness and rarely lose their strong sense of justice for all.

Love, sympathy, conscientiousness, musical talent, domesticity and harmonious relationships are the key words for June children. These character traits are developed during the nurturing first cycle of life and are reinforced by types of people, circumstances and environments.

June born are the protector-educators of the future who center their personalities when giving guidance or service to others. They are artistic and emotional and have strong personal ideals, which closely relate to family and home duties early in life.

JULY

7

July children are introspective. The circumstances surrounding them in infancy through the late twenties breed a need for privacy. They may be investigative, questioning and impractical. Number 7 is synonymous with quality consciousness. People born in July may reject manual labor and seek spiritual, scientific or technical interests to satisfy a drive for authority and wisdom. A natural reserve and aloofness from earthy realities often repels intimacy for those who are July born. They are never conspicuous. Since July babies are apt to ask why grass is green, why the sky is blue or why their pet knows when Daddy is coming home before he rings the bell—while Mommy's preparing dinner—the child may not get a satisfactory answer. If that is the general rule, the babe represses its intellect and is labeled the silent type. July tots, teens and adults may be a trial to understand.

Technicality, good taste, intellectualism, quiet, peace, unflappability and emotional reserve are the key words for July children. These character traits are developed during the nurturing first cycle of life and are reinforced by types of people, circumstances and environments.

July-born people are the perfectionist-professionals of the future who speak with authority or not at all. They are often judged to be loners, "snooty," or opinionated. They speak up when they have decided opinions. They should specialize, be born rich or strive for academic credits if they wish to be commercially competitive. Number 7, the July child, must attract worldly possessions or power; money flies away if it is greedily pursued.

AUGUST

8

August children are exposed to affluence and/or influential people and are involved with establishment realities. Rich or poor, number-8 born aim to be better off than their parents. As adults, these children never lose their drive or appreciation and expectation for the things that money and power imply. There is a presence, an assumption of control or executive authority that will forever give the impression of status. They may aim to be professional athletes, class presidents or entrepreneur lemonade vendors because their environments breed ambition, vision and imagination.

Authority, organization, self-reliance, stamina, discrimination and ability to join body, mind and spirit are the key words for August children. These character traits are developed during the nurturing first cycle of life and are reinforced by types of people, circumstances and environments.

August-born babes employ good humor, dignity and energy to rise above the crowd. They are the executives, benefactors and self-assured risk takers of the future who thrive on practical ventures.

SEPTEMBER

9

September children are born with wisdom. The circumstances surrounding them in infancy through the late twenties demand common sense and emotional understanding far beyond their years. They are precocious. The number 9 is one step below perfection of spirit, and September born have the birthright to heal bodies, minds and souls. Our most charitable, creatively talented and magnetic leaders have September's romance with life and nobility of purpose. Too often the early years are lonely and emotionally anxious for the child that is exposed to people and situations that demand tolerance, empathy and unquestioning love.

High-level communication talents, empathy for all, cultural expansion, material-emotional-spiritual generosity, education, healing and brotherly love are the key words for September children. These character traits are developed during this nurturing first cycle of life and are reinforced by types of people, circumstances and environments.

September born are creatively self-expressive and inspirational. They travel physically, intellectually and spiritually far from their roots to share their experiences with family, community, groups, corporations or, if they have reached a high level of skill and performance, the world.

OCTOBER

10/1

October children combine the creativity of January born with a talent for inspiring others to express their individuality, leadership and ambition. The circumstances surrounding them in infancy through the late twenties breed a strong sense of worldly comradeship and self-confidence. They may be very influential; however, until they relate and communicate their unique ideals to serve or improve the quality of life for others, complete attainment is withheld. Number 10 is synonymous with constant change and the progressive aspirations.

Changes in fortune, ideas, goals, courage, daring, pioneering and mental creativity are the key words for October children. These character traits are developed during the nurturing first cycle of life and are reinforced by types of people, circumstances and environments.

The October born are the designers of the future who romantically desire to teach or preach peace, brotherly love and diplomacy. They have the focus on ego of the January born, because both are inspired by the number 1, but October's children are less self-absorbed.

NOVEMBER

11/2

November children generate creative energy and are passionate extremists. The circumstances surrounding them in infancy through the late twenties breed a personality that holds itself above and beyond the conventions of society. Our greatest diplomats and most infamous gangsters are November born. They may be impulsive, impatient, individualistic and sensitive; however, their need for supportive partnership or group alliances forces constant compromise and choices, which ignite their tempers and boil their emotions. November, the eleventh month, $(11 = 1 + 1 = 2)$, and February, the second calendar month, share the number 2 character traits, and both have a need for intimacy, comfort and accumulation. November born have exaggerated personal beliefs and ideals that attract their peers, and they wouldn't have it any other way. Number 11 is synonymous with martyrdom, evangelistic energy and immateriality. When reduced to its mundane self, the number 2, November babes are inclined to be modest, easygoing and thoughtful of others.

Inspiration, service, foresight, compassion, decisions and responsiveness are the key words for November children. They are bent upon achieving their dreams, appear impractical and are often misunderstood tots and teens who turn out to be late bloomers. Often, November's sense of the exquisite makes them feel different, and they become disillusioned into fulfilling the ambitions of others.

November born enlighten, inspire, uplift and attract what they need. They achieve expertise when reaching out to sense the needs of others. They may be tested emotionally until they channel their creative nervous energy to a specific goal that is in harmony with established procedures.

DECEMBER

1 2 / 3

December children are courageous, sensitive and self-expressive. The circumstances surrounding them in infancy through the late twenties breed creative independence, perseverance and social consciousness. They may be one of a kind and have a unique philosophy in respect to their own lives. Number 12, December's numerical place in the calendar, combines the individuality of the 1, the seriousness of the 2 and the charming looks and/or personality of the 3 $(12 = 1 + 2 = 3)$.

Artistic, expressive, attractive, independent, adaptable and optimistic are the key words for December children. These character traits are developed during the nurturing first cycle of life and are reinforced by types of people, circumstances and environments.

December born crack the whip in creative society and aim to finish the variety of projects that they start. They are givers who expect a return on the investment of their leadership. While expressing themselves intellectually, emotionally and morally, they attract rewards in human relationships but not without personal sacrifice and/or financial problems.

YOUR DAY NUMBER

The day-of-birth number describes the types of people and experiences that will indicate turning points in the destiny from approximately twenty-eight to fifty-six years of age. The environment, motivation and influence that this number creates on a personality and character are briefly outlined here. To deepen understanding of lifelong opportunities, the preceding month-of-birth description should be analyzed along with the day.

Born on the —

First   Motivation is for accomplishment. Environment is conducive to self-reliance. Influences are stimulating, progressive and innovative.

Second   Motivation is for harmony. Environment is conducive to partnerships. Influences are inspirational, helpful and emotional.

Third   Motivation is for self-expression. Environment is conducive to social activity. Influences are youthful, fashionable and imaginative.

Fourth   Motivation is for stability. Environment is conducive to conventional relationships. Influences are constructive, dependable and practical.

Fifth   Motivation is for autonomy. Environment is conducive to experimentation. Influences are unconventional, nonconfining and liberal.

Sixth   Motivation is for responsibility. Environment is conducive to expressing personal ideals. Influences are clannish, instructional and comforting.

Seventh   Motivation is for perfection. Environment is conducive to investigation. Influences are dispassionate, cultural and technical-scientific-spiritual.

Eighth   Motivation is for material success. Environment is conducive to expansion. Influences are productive, affluent and influential.

Ninth   Motivation is for quality and skill. Environment is conducive to reaching a broad scope of people and emotional experiences. Influences are humanitarian, artistic and romantic.

Tenth   Motivation is for independent leadership. Environment is conducive to regulating power. Influences are prime movers, pioneers and loners.

Eleventh   Motivation is for uniqueness. Environment is conducive to zealous enthusiasms. Influences are intuitional, inventive and attract notoriety.

Twelfth   Motivation is for emotional outlets. Environment is conducive to geniality. Influences are artistic, nonconformist and transforming.

Thirteenth   Motivation is for invulnerability. Environment is conducive to traditional ambitions. Influences are domestic, purposeful and varied.

Fourteenth   Motivation is for satisfying curiosity. Environment is conducive to learning from experience. Influences are sensual, competitive and conventional.

Fifteenth   Motivation is for family-community responsiveness. Environment is protective. Influences are kindly, reciprocal and rational.

Sixteenth   Motivation is for self-communion. Environment is conducive to overthrowing erroneous beliefs. Influences are specialized, introspective and intuitive.

Seventeenth   Motivation is for tangible results. Environment is conducive to overcoming obstacles. Influences are executive, intellectual and advancing.

Eighteenth   Motivation is for personal integrity. Environment is conducive to recognition. Influences are accomplished, valiant and eccentric.

Nineteenth   Motivation is for self-assertion. Environment is conducive to contentment. Influences are impulsive, energetic and liberating.

Twentieth   Motivation is for alternative decisions. Environment is conducive to developing artistry. Influences are illuminating, powerful and community conscious.

Twenty-First   Motivation is for individualism within partnership. Environment is conducive to developing talents. Influences are buoyant, companionable and inventive.

Twenty-Second   Motivation is for solving practical problems. Environment is conducive to taking responsibility and having the power to handle it. Influences are futuristic, managerial and possessive.

Twenty-Third   Motivation is for travel and variety. Environment is conducive to business and sports. Influences are questionable, unsettling and challenging.

Twenty-Fourth   Motivation is for controlling social contacts and resulting peace of mind. Environment is conducive to favors from older or influential associations. Influences are structured, personalized and inherited.

Twenty-Fifth   Motivation is for specialized, tireless work. Environment is conducive to inner searching and enlightenment. Influences are skeptical, legalistic and authoritative.

Twenty-Sixth Motivation is for prominence. Environment is conducive to giving impression of prosperity. Influences are democratic, materially minded and family-community conscious.

Twenty-Seventh Motivation is for inspiring others as a power behind the throne. Environment is conducive to combining intellect and emotions to improve the quality of life. Influences are privileged, empathetic and straight-shooting.

Twenty-Eighth Motivation is for cooperation, leadership and accomplishment. Environment is conducive to self-reliance; being self-made or controlling inherited power . . . or both. Influences are aggressive, changeable and creative.

Twenty-Ninth Motivation is for duality of desires: To provide intimate and universal service. Environment is conducive to business and invention. Influences are evangelistic, practical and sociable.

Thirtieth Motivation is for power through art, using words and giving social service. Environment is conducive to developing skilled forms of self-expression and attracting rewards via charismatic personality. Influences are domestic, traditional and culturally polished.

Thirty-First Motivation is for overcoming mundane antagonists and organizing projects effectively. Environment is conducive to utilizing high energy. Influences are dramatic, forceful and trendy.

YOUR YEAR NUMBER

The birth year number describes the life cycle called wisdom. This cycle generally begins at age fifty-six and stays with us for the rest of our lives. These are the years of our greatest self-expression, when we reap the rewards or suffer the consequences of our youth and productivity cycles. On this second time around you should have the nerve to follow your first instincts. Past life experiences are stepping stones that offer mobility to your schemes for instigating major long-term goals. This is the time for progressive changes.

Athletes Ted Williams, Bobby Riggs and Phil Rizzuto broke their traditional life-styles in their mid-fifties and changed direction after enjoying successful careers. Betty Ford, a dancer in youth, a support system for her husband during her productivity cycle years, had a rebirth during her mid-forties after making public her addiction to liquor. She has been an inspiration in her wisdom cycle. Alan King, Arlene Dahl, William Redfield, George Plimpton, Sidney Poitier and Roger Moore are just a few other examples of people who have turned their later years to invigorating new challenges.

The wisdom cycle is your golden time to be self-reliant, creative and mentally active. Go for it!

Use the chart that follows to find your year-of-birth number. For an interpretation of the meaning of that number, refer to the number definitions given in the practical growth number section (page 34). This information, along with the descriptions of your month and day numbers, will give you an overview of the opportunities and experiences you can expect to meet throughout your entire life cycle.

YEAR-OF-BIRTH NUMBER								
YEAR	1900	2000	YEAR	1900	2000	YEAR	1900	2000
00	1	2	34	8	9	67	5	6
01	2	3	35	9	1	68	6	7
02	3	4	36	1	2	69	7	8
03	4	5	37	2	3	70	8	9
04	5	6	38	3	4	71	9	1
05	6	7	39	4	5	72	1	2
06	7	8	40	5	6	73	2	3
07	8	9	41	6	7	74	3	4
08	9	1	42	7	8	75	4	5
09	1	2	43	8	9	76	5	6
10	2	3	44	9	1	77	6	7
11	3	4	45	1	2	78	7	8
12	4	5	46	2	3	79	8	9
13	5	6	47	3	4	80	9	1
14	6	7	48	4	5	81	1	2
15	7	8	49	5	6	82	2	3
16	8	9	50	6	7	83	3	4
17	9	1	51	7	8	84	4	5
18	1	2	52	8	9	85	5	6
19	2	3	53	9	1	86	6	7
20	3	4	54	1	2	87	7	8
21	4	5	55	2	3	88	8	9
22	5	6	56	3	4	89	9	1
23	6	7	57	4	5	90	1	2
24	7	8	58	5	6	91	2	3
25	8	9	59	6	7	92	3	4
26	9	1	60	7	8	93	4	5
27	1	2	61	8	9	94	5	6
28	2	3	62	9	1	95	6	7
29	3	4	63	1	2	96	7	8

YEAR-OF-BIRTH NUMBER

Year	1900	2000	Year	1900	2000	Year	1900	2000
30	4	5	64	2	3	97	8	9
31	5	6	65	3	4	98	9	1
32	6	7	66	4	5	99	1	2
33	7	8						

YOUR PRACTICAL GROWTH NUMBER

Combine the month-of-birth number and the day-of-birth number to find the practical opportunities for the years prior to age fifty-six. This number combines the aspects of both the month and day numbers to give a broader scope to the first part of life, including your youth and productivity cycles.

All double numbers are reduced to a single number. When you add month and day to a sum of two numbers, add the two resulting numbers to reduce to a single number.

Months are given a number according to their placement in the calendar.

January = 1
February = 2
March = 3
April = 4
May = 5
June = 6
July = 7
August = 8
September = 9
October = 1 (10 = 1 + 0 = 1)
November = 2 (11 = 1 + 1 = 2)
December = 3 (12 = 1 + 2 = 3)

Add the month number to the day number and reduce to a single number by adding from left to right.

- EXAMPLE: March 14
  March = 3
  3 + 14 = 17
  Reduce to a single number
  1 + 7 = 8
  THE PRACTICAL GROWTH NUMBER for March 14 is 8.

- EXAMPLE: August 25
  August = 8
  8 + 25 = 33
  Reduce to a single number.
  3 + 3 = 6
  THE PRACTICAL GROWTH NUMBER for August 25 is 6.

Read the **practical growth number** meanings that follow to find the combination of people and experiences that are offered when the influence of the month-of-birth number is combined with the influence of the day-of-birth number.

Practical Growth Number Meanings

---

1 Expect to meet people and experiences that help you instigate fresh ideas, require independent decisions and actions and spark long-term goals. This time span requires courage, self-assertion and self-reliance. The ego, creative talents and leadership are the focus. Marriage is favorable if independence is established.

2 Expect to meet people and experiences that are detail conscious, friendly and nonaggressive. Tact, diplomacy and a willingness to be modest, humble and kindly are required of you. This time span demands patience. It will be difficult to make firm decisions or draw long-standing conclusions. Sensitive, intimate relationships are in focus. A receptive time for marriage and partnerships.

3 Expect to meet people and experiences that are charming, self-expressive and imaginative. Humor, beauty and all forms of artistic talent are open to you. Friends, mail, phone, fashion, travel, gifts and compliments keep communications high and responsibilities low. Getting attention is the focus. Love of people, animals and life are in focus. A happy time for marriage.

4 Expect to meet people and experiences that keep you down to earth, practical and routined. Self-discipline, work and organization govern this time span. Material accumulation, conventional values and the use of common sense are in focus. A time for traditional ambitions that include marriage.

5 Expect to meet people and experiences that are unconventional, changeable and surprising. Sensuality, physical experimentation and learning from experience are in focus. Restlessness, curiosity, travel, speculation and short-term interests or opportunities are offered by this time span when plans are made and unexpectedly altered. Affairs of the heart flourish, but marriages have little staying power.

6 Expect to meet people and experiences that require a mature approach. Responsible, family-oriented, socially conscious people offer you a chance to assume positions of trust. You depend upon others, and they depend upon you. Peace or disharmony in groups or families is in focus during this time span that builds strong personal ideals and standards. A favorable time for marriage.

7 Expect to meet people who are introspective, analytical and more interested in quality than quantity. Money is not in focus; education, spirituality and selectivity are nurtured. Material or commercial experiences are slowed, and the desire to observe, investigate, develop expertise and stay aloof from mundane realities is the key to using this time span wisely. This is a time when privacy is necessary, physical intimacy is uncomfortable and marriage is not favored.

8 Expect to meet people who are businesslike, self-made and striving for material power. Affluence, influence and physical stamina are in focus. Experiences to bring body, mind and spirit together to achieve goals are offered. The focus is upon aiming high, executive wheeling and dealing or delegating authority. A time span to get the best, or the most, out of yourself and everyone else. You reap whatever you sow. Marriage is favorable if the spouse is wealthy or influential or if financial security and ambitions are established.

9 Expect to meet people and experiences that offer cultural growth, a broader philosophy and humanitarian interests. Empathy, compassion and selflessness are in focus. This is a time span that attracts notables and develops talents geared to produce a quality and skill of performance. Emotions run high and low, priorities are sorted constantly and projects come to conclusions. Nothing fresh or original begins. The scope broadens and you receive recognition for past accomplishments. Not a favorable time for marriage.

YOUR CHALLENGE NUMBER

Challenges can tip the scales of personality from positive to negative and various degrees in between. They are the extreme responses, the flashes of inappropriate anger and overreactions to people and experiences. When we become obsessed with an idea, attitude or opinion or become compulsive in our activities, we are challenging the balance in our personalities. If things appear to be stubbornly black or white, and the gray areas of compromise or a brighter tomorrow elude us, a challenge may be in effect.

Numerology identifies the challenges by number.

When your challenge number is identical to your month, day, or practical growth number, the triggering of your challenges will be more active during the time span associated with that number. If the challenge number is different, the challenges will happen less frequently and will be less apparent.

(Birth number relates to youth, day number to mid-life, practical growth number to the combined time spans of youth and mid-life.)

Nothing is written in granite. We have choice and may meet our challenges with awareness and apply self-discipline to change nonproductive behavior. It takes time for a challenge to take effect. It requires equal time to recognize that there is a pattern. Time and patience are necessary in order to apply discipline. Additional time is needed to give our new reactions a chance to be received by people. People need time to digest and give us feedback. When the attitudes of others change for the better and fewer disappointments or emotional upheavals arise, you sense that your personality extremes or challenges are leveling off.

The following challenge number descriptions explain the extremes for each number and offer positive attitudes and actions that answer the challenge. You will probably identify how the meaning affects your personality. We switch from one extreme to the other. Usually we reflect upon an overreaction and go to the other extreme to avoid making the same blunder.

Challenges, based on emotional ordeals, begin with childhood. Our response to a challenge is like a bull's reaction to a red cape. It is a conditioned reflex. Emotions are not founded upon mature intellectual assessments or logic. When we are overwhelmed, insecure or intimidated, the child within breaks through the layers of self-preservation that we formed as we grew up.

Challenge numbers, when understood and harnessed, are tools to help you relax with the people and experiences you encounter. It is the way you rise or fall to an occasion that accounts for good or bad luck. You make your own luck by planning realistically and coping appropriately with each day.

Numerology opens the door to understanding what the future holds. You are in control. You select which options to take, and you are accountable for your actions. Fate takes over only when you let go of the reins and give your challenges their head. The choice is yours.

Find Your Challenge Number

Subtract the smaller from the larger number of the month and day to find the *challenge number.*

- EXAMPLE: July 4 birthday
  July = 7
  7 − 4 = 3
  THE CHALLENGE NUMBER for July 4 is 3.

- EXAMPLE: October 23
  October = 1
  23 = 2 + 3 = 5 (numerology reduces all double numbers to a single number by adding from left to right)
  5 − 1 = 4
  THE CHALLENGE NUMBER for October 23 is 4.

- EXAMPLE: December 3
  December = 3 (Twelfth month, 1 + 2 = 3)
  3 − 3 = 0
  THE CHALLENGE NUMBER for December 3 is 0.

Challenge Number Meanings

1—EGO—Independence, Aggressiveness, Creativity

You may turn this challenge into a positive by patiently assessing your independent ambitions and applying your creativity and self-determination. Impatience is your project for improvement. Nobody deserves the best more than you do. However, your ideas or desires must be received and understood before you will get anyone else to take an action to support your action. If your idea is not acceptable to others, they need a conversational pause to reflect upon a reasonable reply.

Be careful to avoid speaking hurriedly and breaking into another's sentence. Wait a minute. Let another comprehend, then decide whether to accept or reject a proposal that you make. Don't speak up quickly, then rescind the request, anticipating rejection. Don't get angry because your words are not met with a burst of immediate acceptance. Don't break off an interaction when another appears to be unable to comprehend the point that you are attempting to make. Tapping your finger or your foot to indicate that you are annoyed at being kept waiting is the obvious symptom of impatience. The subtle ways that a lack of patience shows up in everyday living are difficult to identify and control.

Get the little things you need by expressing your likes and dislikes on a daily basis. Do not think you are being kind to anyone by keeping your personal preferences to yourself. If others think you are content, they will repeatedly try to please you by giving the things or responses that appear, to them, to make you happy. When you change your behavior, then you will be able to see the changes in others.

Your leadership and authority are often challenged. You want control over others, or you imagine that they control you. Suppress the desire to have everything instantly and the belief that submitting to the will of others will sustain their love. They'll love you all the more for not getting frustrated and angry at inappropriate times.

You will find that your creative juices flow when it's time to be decisive. A mature understanding of when to be firm, not stubborn, will balance your tendencies to be too forceful or too submissive; to be too bossy or too accommodating; too determined to win, no holds barred—or too sure that you will lose—projecting the vibes of defeat. You will balance this challenge if you are aware that you have the right to accept or reject anything that this book says.

2—PERSONALIZED SENSITIVITY—Detail Consciousness

You may turn this challenge into a positive by tempering your emotional reactions, maintaining a broad-scoped philosophy and showing a willingness to be cooperative when others assert themselves.

People who are picky, self-centered or insensitive may irritate you to the extreme emotional reaction of depression. Searching out the reason behind another's action, with an intellectual approach, will help you perceive the incident in its proper perspective. People who have the number 2 challenge's positive aspects (a practical gift for details, collecting data, friends and little treasures) tend to make emotional mountains out of molehills and think that every comment is shot at them. What appears to you to be a petty slight may have been meant as a friendly observation.

When you hear someone say, "I hate blue shirts" and you happen to be wearing one, do not imagine that the words are a direct criticism. You may be too self-conscious, modest, or shy.

In intimate relationships, are you too willful or too weak? Do you imagine problems before they occur? Are you inclined to be too weepy or too dry? Are you using your superior emotional responsiveness, intuition and sensitivity as assets or liabilities? A less personalized attitude should alter your perception.

3—SELF-EXPRESSION—Communication and Imagination

You may turn this challenge into a positive by enjoying the lighter side of life; by allowing people to share your personality, talents, humor, charm and game-playing joy in living. Are you communicating your desire for friendship? Do you understand that your attitude toward surface values, your self-image and superficiality are extreme?

Do you talk too much or too little? If you refuse to talk for a while, bottle up your dramatic reactions and then finally share your thoughts, you may speak—nonstop—for an entire day. You may find yourself using the mail, the phone, or fashions to an extreme, or you may completely ignore the need for personal communications.

Your own or the suspected exaggeration or lying of others makes you unable to experience trust. You accept the face value without sensing the depth or breadth of a statement or person and use your imagination to place someone on a pedestal. When you discover average variations, you lose the facility to trust the person or situation and refuse to believe that what you hear is the truth. The number 3 challenge means acting too mature or too childish.

You can alleviate this challenge by developing a mature attitude toward recreation, love and responsibility and by guarding against becoming too sophomoric or too stuffy. By concentrating your time, money and talents, and by using a subtle approach to attracting attention, you can turn the often extravagant, naive, charming and up-to-date number 3 personality into a social success.

4—MATERIAL RESULTS—Practicality, Reality, Work

You may turn this challenge into a positive by using common sense, organizing your priorities and being prudent. To safeguard the future, avoid having too much or too little structure, being rigid or rule breaking and becoming too conventional or too disorganized. Pay attention to the down-to-earth doers and be economical without becoming tacky. Take time for a break and aim not to overdo work-aholic tendencies. Balance this challenge the way you would balance your checkbook.

5—FREEDOM—Sex and the Senses, the Unconventional

You may turn this challenge into a positive by adapting to surprises, allowing new enthusiasms to flower and not obsessing about sex or intellect. The freedom to let go or hold on to people and interests may be an obsession. You may be compulsive and not know when to change and when to hang in to get the meat out of a relationship or experience. Imbalance thrives on your restlessness. Your curiosity breeds incautious commitments and actions, like sticking your hand into the fire to see what hot feels like. To combat these challenges to your happiness, you should learn from past experiences, take advice from more conventional thinkers or believe what you read in books.

Number 5 is the number of the swashbuckler, entrepreneur and sensationalist. Your allure for the physical senses or lack of concern with bodily sensations may be balanced by not becoming too busy or too bored, too enduring or too changing and too responsible or too irresponsible. Expect the unexpected, and don't be afraid to be a noncomformist. Don't deny a reasonable focus on sex. Don't fear the unknown to a point of immobility or fly off into relationships, jobs and places without investigation: Either course is overwhelming. Accidents happen when rushing, but accidents open the door to transitions. Enduring commitments are difficult but not impossible. To balance the discontentment of this challenge, guard against impulsivity, reckless speculations and their opposite—the fear of taking chances.

6—PERSONAL IDEALISM—Responsibility, Pride, Family

You may change this challenge into a positive by allowing others to set their own standards and by not assuming too much responsibility. Family, community and business ties may consume your personal time and energy to the point that you run from the obligations for which you have volunteered. You may become too self-righteous, intolerant or domineering while assuming the burdens of others, or you may refuse to relate to the problems of your intimates. You may deny yourself to keep unanimity, or you may become the self-sacrificing drone that cries out for sympathy and attention while jealously creating disharmony. A reasonable tolerance for another's weakness (try a tease, joke or lighthearted hug!) and taking yourself less seriously bring balance to this overbearing and emotionally draining challenge.

7—SELF-DECEPTION—Isolation, Faith, Investigation

You may turn this challenge into a positive by getting down to earth, questioning and allowing yourself and humankind to be vulnerable. You swing between mundane earthiness and aristocratic aloofness in this challenge to your self-confidence. You may be too guarded or intellectually insecure or fear that you lack polish. On the other hand, you may be gullible, authoritarian and pretentious. You have a sense of inadequacy that forces you to demand perfection from yourself and the universe. To expect that dreams of perfection may be realized on a day-to-day basis results in distrust, disillusionment and the realization of only a modicum of the success you anticipated. You are unable to build self-confidence and faith in others if you constantly find fault with your own judgments and look to others for the "right" answers. To balance this challenge, put aside your escapist tendencies and accept life with all its imperfections.

8—MATERIALISM AND POWER—Efficiency, Stamina

You may turn this challenge into a positive by carefully considering your reasons for accumulating money, power and possessions and for disregarding the importance of organizing body, mind and spirit to achieve material ambitions. This challenge may cause impatience with less physically or mentally self-disciplined people. You may be overly ambitious and resort to unscrupulousness. Organization, efficiency and conventional material symbols may be your gods, or you may show disrespect for the Establishment. If material gain for emotional reasons is behind dogged determination to outfox the establishment, it's time to remember that the pleasure should be in the work itself and not in the result alone. If you are thorough and self-reliant and can discriminate between workaholic compulsions and a real desire to put an occasional thrust of power into practical goals, you will not be obsessed with the need for money, misuse power or resort to cruel, unjust dictatorship. Guard against acquiring a false set of values and harboring the fear of limited freedom due to a lack of money or power.

9—Nonexistent

It is not numerically possible to arrive at 9 for a challenge number.

0—UNDERSTANDING EMOTIONS—Romanticism, Principles

You may turn this challenge into a positive by recognizing the breadth of human emotions—yours and others. Try to understand the beauty, culture and philosophy of all races, creeds and nationalities and to give more than lip service to the words *tolerance, empathy* and *unselfishness.* You know what to do to help yourself and others, but just knowing where things may go wrong, philosophizing about solutions or expounding your theories will not break the barriers to emotional responsiveness. You may obsessively give your all or nothing. You expect love to feed a family, you expect constant compassion, you expect loyalty to the death from everyone you meet. The other extreme is to coldly detach from emotional contacts: not to allow yourself to trust or to expect personal considerations. Rid yourself of these unrealistic expectations or you'll live in a constant state of disappointment.

The party is over for a marriage when the spouse with a number 0 challenge decides that his or her self-denial is not appreciated. Loyalty to an extreme or cold detachment are the most obvious reactions. To sustain your own personality, you must maintain balance—for self-identity is lost in empathy or service, the ego will cry out for recognition in frustration and anger. The natural inclination is to let go of the pain and end the commitment. In your desire to find emotional rewards, you may forget the romance, understanding, and nobility the two of you once shared, and you may instigate new allegiances. But you cannot end and begin at one time, and you make a mistake when you do not recall the past, sort priorities to correct misconceptions and skillfully add a dimension to improve the situation. The person with a number 0 challenge cries and feels the emotions of a character in a movie but often misses the suffering in his or her own family. This is a rare challenge, but it is easily overcome when you realize you have the ability to cut off emotional stress and get in touch with your real feelings. Wisdom is the key word for this challenge, as you must choose whether to bring out the inherent qualities of "an old soul" or to retreat into immaturity.

How to Get Results and Balance the Challenge

The best way to balance obsessive or compulsive attitudes is to sleep on your decisions. When you wake up the next day you will be under the influence of the new number for that day and have a fresh perspective. Here are ten steps to reaching for and realizing your expectations.

1. Read your birthday page.
2. Sleep on the information offered. Read it again.
3. Read your separate month, day, year and practical growth number descriptions.
4. Sleep on the information offered. Read them again.
5. Read your challenge number description. Identify which side of the challenge is operating at the moment.
6. Select an expectation to work on. Ask yourself why you haven't reached your goal. If you have not reached out for your expectation, ask yourself why not. Decide to get what you expect, and be sure you really want it, for you will surely get what you visualize.
7. Sleep on your expectation and either reaffirm or discard your desire when you awaken. If you wish to continue, identify your positive and negative feelings. Ask yourself if or where you are placing blame and feeling anger or frustration. List your options, check the list for facts and be sure that it is comprised of realistic choices. If you were not reacting emotionally, your list will be concise, to the point and factual. If it is wordy, larded with adjectives and based upon deception, mischief making, cruelty, cowardice, pessimism, overtrustfulness, self-effacement or just plain bad temper, scrap it and begin again. Complete a list, select the most feasible option and visualize a plan of action.
8. Read your birthday description again to decide if your expectation seems premature, appropriate for the character and experiences of the moment or nostalgic. If your expectation is appropriate, begin your plan of action.
9. Do not set time limits or become impatient. Allow for life's inconsistencies and delays and the reactions of others. Prepare to deal with success; don't push it away habitually.
10. After sleeping on all the previous steps, reread your birthday page. You will be able to apply more practical solutions to your problems.

3

.

YOUR

BIRTHSTONE

Birthstones are symbols for the month of a person's birth. The ancients believed that they influenced the personality of the wearer and invited good luck. During the Middle Ages the stones were selected to ward off evil. During the 1700s Poland spread the word to other European countries and to the United States. It's difficult to believe that a stone can affect a person's life; however, inanimate objects have vibes too and send out a message to attract a companionable person or experience—perhaps that's what the ancients perceived. Jewelers the world over follow the birthstone lists, and almost everyone has received a birthday gift that includes his or her birthstone.

The following month and birthstone definitions reflect the system used and explained in depth in *You Are Your First Name.**

JANUARY

Point of view is independent, creative and intellectual.
Expresses nobility, polish and skill.
Goes to extremes when too aristocratic or too earthy.

Birthstone: **Garnet**
Point of view is mystical, intuitive and probing.
Expresses sensitivity, inspiration and elitist ideas.
Goes to extremes when too intricate or too plain.

FEBRUARY

Point of view is hospitable, compassionate and intuitional.
Expresses domesticity, personal idealism and love.
Goes to extremes when too skeptical or too gullible.

Birthstone: **Amethyst**
Point of view is self-reliant, inventive and intellectual.
Expresses security, versatility and sex appeal.
Goes to extremes when too faceted or too unpatterned.

MARCH

Point of view is reconstructive, practical and physical.
Expresses aloofness, secrecy and mental analysis.
Goes to extremes when too powerful or too weak.

Birthstone: **Aquamarine**
Point of view is distinctive, courageous and self-conscious.
Expresses individuality, positiveness and dominance.
Goes to extremes when too unconventional or too traditional.

APRIL

Point of view is changeable, active and independent.
Expresses fluctuations, vitality and indecision.
Goes to extremes when too sprinkled or too concentrated.

Birthstone: **Diamond**
Point of view is anchoring, materialistic and practical.
Expresses love, responsibility and personal idealism.
Goes to extremes when too measured or too unlimited.

MAY

Point of view is regenerative, constructive and fair.
Expresses beauty, variety and illusion.
Goes to extremes when too lazy or too materially active.

Birthstone: **Emerald**
Point of view is exciting, daring and impulsive.
Expresses competitiveness, determination and ambition.
Goes to extremes when too dramatic or too unexpressive.

JUNE

Point of view is aspiring, creative and projecting.
Expresses sensuality, expansiveness, speculation.
Goes to extremes when too cautious or too impulsive.

Birthstone: **Pearl**
Point of view is perfecting, aristocratic and faithful.
Expresses authority, dignity and composition.
Goes to extremes when too adorned or too underdeveloped.

JULY

Point of view is aspiring, creative and projecting.
Expresses sensuality, expansiveness and speculation.
Goes to extremes when too lazy or too materially active.

Birthstone: **Ruby**
Point of view is intense, tolerant and restorative.
Expresses beauty, variety and advancement.
Goes to extremes when too pretentious or too inelegant.

AUGUST

Point of view is independent, active and creative.
Expresses strength, materialism and determination.
Goes to extremes when too sensitive or too uncaring.

Birthstone: **Peridot**
Point of view is aristocratic, inspirational and aloof.
Expresses harmony, love and sympathy.
Goes to extremes when too petty or too magnificent.

SEPTEMBER

Point of view is reflective, ambitious and amassing.
Expresses confidence, methodology and production.
Goes to extremes when too empathetic or too unfeeling.

Birthstone: **Sapphire**
Point of view is reflective, ambitious and amassing.
Expresses discrimination, inspiration and illusion.
Goes to extremes when too conventional or too untraditional.

OCTOBER

Point of view is parental, persevering and emotional.
Expresses growth, honesty and intelligence.
Goes to extremes when too empathetic or too unfeeling.

Birthstone: **Opal**
Point of view is parental, persevering and emotional.
Expresses research, mystery and distinction.
Goes to extremes when too colorful or too washed out.

NOVEMBER

Point of view is sensual, competitive and adventurous.
Expresses confidence, orderliness and substance.
Goes to extremes when too empathetic or too uncaring.

Birthstone: **Topaz**
Point of view is tender, responsive and indecisive.
Expresses sympathy, generosity and attainment.
Goes to extremes when too self-confident or too stressful.

DECEMBER

Point of view is practical, determined and down to earth.
Expresses creativity, independence and aspiration.
Goes to extremes when too empathetic or too uncaring.

Birthstone: **Turquoise**
Point of view is sensitive, detailed and receptive.
Expresses recognition, reflection and psychic development.
Goes to extremes when too variable or too unchanging.

*You Are Your First Name, a dictionary of over one thousand five hundred names as described by numerology, includes instructions to do it yourself and letter-number definitions. A Fireside Book, Simon & Schuster, reprinted October 1985.

4

•

The Numerology Birthday Calendar

JANUARY

· 1 ·

"Physician, heal thyself"—you'll find that you are your own best medicine. Expect security, respect and responsibilities. Understand that if you do not make a fortune or attract attention, it is due to your own childhood programming to be unobtrusive and your resulting lack of expectations. If you feel like a loner, perhaps you are a bit ahead mentally, but not as courageous as you could be.

Family, although sensitive, cannot provide stability. You have initiative, and are progressive. However, your first career choice may have to be delayed or forgotten due to practical reasons. Relationships are turbulent, and if you wait too long to marry, you may not take the plunge. You need a liberal education and feel the futility of emotional responses. You are frustrated and never pleased with yourself.

You want knowledge and do not realize that you were born wise. Use your ESP. You do not trust your intuition, and that's too bad. You have independent questions and diagnoses but are not focused upon popular issues. Throughout life you will tolerate ignorance and should be determined to aim for a profession. At worst you do well in business, lead less daring followers wisely and create a unique and respected life-style.

A childhood emotion triggers unnecessary financial fears and, imagined or real, they may prevail over your willingness to take a chance on a career change. A dynamic older woman crosses your path; you see yourself reflected in her. She is a test and a teacher. Stand on your own two feet. Dare to be different. No need to feel, "If I were king." You may be magnificent just being a knight to remember.

• OTHER JANUARY 1 BIRTHDAYS

Dana Andrews	1909
Charles Bickford	1889
Marcus Tullius Cicero	106 B.C.
Xavier Cugat	1900
Yuri Erigorovich	1927
William Fox	1879
Barry Goldwater	1909
Hank Greenberg	1911
Ernest Hollings	1922
J. Edgar Hoover	1895
Frank Langella	1946
Terry Moore	1932
James Oglethorpe	1697
Betsy Ross	1752
J. D. Salinger	1919

JANUARY

· **2** ·

It's lonely at the top, and even lonelier on the way down if you insist upon instant gratification. Patience is not your prime virtue. Understand if you don't win 'em all, you win more than you allow yourself to recognize. But how could you build your ego when, as a child, you were loaded to the gills with adult decisions and responsibilities? Your frustrations may be the result of unrealistic family expectations or ambitions, which cause you to blossom later, in your thirties, in response to the tender sharing of an alter ego.

It takes a very special someone to help you overcome your inclinations to emulate males who heavy-handedly assert or inappropriately submit while expounding their personal philosophies. If you were misdirected or outshouted as a babe, you may reflect your insecurity as a bully. A dedicated, stubborn teacher or spiritual leader surfaces mid-life and offers your restless mind a skillful and knowledgeable outlet. You respond to your chosen mentors and mellow like a fine wine.

You want beauty, ease, comfort, friendships and warmth in exchange for your willingness to give affection in your twenties. You want the things that money can buy, but not as a loner. Love affairs prove to be expensive, and you question your desire to marry at all.

Your late thirties and forties find you tuned to a new school of thought that attracts responsibilities and respect. Later in your life, health improves as you become less of a renegade, more of a teacher. You are apt to relax into a new life-style. You find your consort, emotional security and self-esteem near the water.

• OTHER JANUARY 2 BIRTHDAYS

Isaac Asimov	1920
St. Ignatius Loyola	1492
Roger Miller	1936
Julius La Rosa	1930
Ann Southern	1912
Joseph Stalin	1880
Renata Tibaldi	1922
Vera Zorina	1917

JANUARY

· 3 ·

When you seek the limelight, someone is sure to crop up with tangible memories of you with braces on your teeth. You'd do best to remember Oscar Wilde's observation, "Always forgive your enemies—nothing annoys them so much." It takes all your childhood practical training, sense of humor and independence to temper your super sensitivity, but you get to it—eventually.

You're blessed with charm, talent and the ability to attract money after age twenty-eight. Mama and friends get you everywhere, including a disappointing long-term commitment. Marriage doesn't allow for independent ego objectives or time for the variety of interests that you have; it is disappointing, but love is the essence of your security. You make adjustments and reinforce your optimism with the same intensity you give to all your interests. You make the best of most bargains—eventually.

Your earliest female relationships stay in focus throughout your lifetime. Too much childhood mother-smothering or inattentiveness delays your maturity. You keep waiting or following the leader until you identify your heart's desire—eventually.

Immaturity is overcome by material accomplishments in youth, but opposition from aristocratic, perfectionist intellectuals who point up your drawbacks continually adds to your chronic health and emotional problems. You must keep busy and avoid making mountains out of molehills. After thirty you attract attention, but a work-related problem challenging your leadership abilities alters your course. You cease to be a jack of all trades, find imaginative companionship and stop saying, "eventually, I'll . . ."

• OTHER JANUARY 3 BIRTHDAYS

Maxene Andrews	1918
Victor Borge	1909
Marion Davies	1897
Betty Furness	1916
Ray Milland	1908
Pola Negri	1897
Zasu Pitts	1898
Henriette Sontag	1806
Steven Stills	1945
Anna May Wong	1907

JANUARY

·4·

"You must have been a beautiful baby"—changeable, ambitious and intuitive, too. Your childhood is unconventional, and your success at school is dependent upon the instructor's ability to provide a challenging pace. Home-based emotional upheavals, unsettled finances and dissatisfaction spark your drive for self-improvement. Assessing career choices is difficult, and you are too close-mouthed about personal affairs to learn from others.

Too often you hide talents or lose personal objectives in the interest of love or material security. Your siblings and mother, or grandmother in association with your mother, are the root of a lack of social graces or self-esteem established in childhood. You tend to try to escape through early marriage or secret adventures. You do better to use your imagination constructively in investigative work and accept the fact that life just isn't always fair.

You will stabilize after age twenty-eight and find fellowship in a mundane, structured and down-to-earth environment. Be aware of superficial judgments. You tend to take things too literally or worry too much about the impossible. You're a hard worker and will do well in real estate or building trades and, with an education, excel in the military or government work.

How you do enjoy a good conspiracy! Don't clam up or oversell, lie to yourself and others or place too much stress on facades. Golden opportunities after age thirty-six will not be lost when you reflect and learn from past experiences. Later life offers relief from petty jealousies, enthusiasms and contentment. You remain a beautiful baby with a toy box filled with treasures.

• OTHER JANUARY 4 BIRTHDAYS

Thomas Beckett	1119
Louis Braille	1806
Grace Bumbry	1937
Dyan Cannon	1937
William Colby	1920
Everett Dirksen	1896
Jacob Grimm	1785
Sir Isaac Newton	1643
Floyd Patterson	1935
Barbara Rush	1927
Don Shula	1930
Jane Wyman	1914

JANUARY **·5·** It's all in the family and the family is all. Rules, regulations and traditions fight your unconventional opportunities, and you live too closely to the rules or break them with a passion. You were toilet trained with a whip!

Love, music and a venerable oldster can set you straight. In your thirties be willing to be different and you'll be handling large sums of money mid-life.

Choose your course without fearing financial insecurity. You may be tagged the family eccentric for your ideas, workaholic tendencies or disdain for tradition. When the results of your labors improve the quality of life for others, you achieve your potential because you sense what the public wants.

You're ambitious, attract changes and are apt to marry young. You will always meet polished, skilled entrepreneurs who open doors to your self-confidence. Envy is a problem you have to overcome repeatedly. Older men assist your climb. Establish goals and stick to them—destiny will bring needed transitions and you will evolve effortlessly.

In your forties you attract detail-oriented associates who assume petty burdens and free you to focus upon practical investments. You find, as sensual curiosity is dulled, that travel or speculations prove disappointing. You have fewer emotional upheavals as you get older. Your own home, friendly neighbors and humanitarian interests are more important to your well-being than money or power. You feel less nervous when you cease to equate love and sex. If you consider yourself peculiar for your personal idealism, you live your later years as a skeptical loner.

• OTHER JANUARY 5 BIRTHDAYS

Konrad Adenauer	1876
Alvin Ailey	1931
Jean-Pierre Aumont	1909
Diane Keaton	1946
Walter Mondale	1928
Zebulon Pike	1779

JANUARY

·6·

If you cannot get all the affection that you crave or attract the applause you feel you deserve, examine your snobbish background. Understand that generous gifts will not buy love. Sexual attraction wanes with financial pressures. Flashy shows for glitzy, free-spending friends end in self-depreciation. Stick to the successful women who provoke your ambitions and help you hide until your ship comes in.

Childhood affections were limited, but you treasure and protect family to accommodate your pride, and you have to work at it. Ups and downs in finance, health and relationships are evident during your twenties. Insecurities stem from your desire for closeness and freedom in marriage and friendships. If you're narrow-minded and tight-fisted with money for practical necessities and put up a flashy front, you'll never find solid ground. Tame your curiosity; it's better to invest in your home, take the long-term security and avoid speculative investments.

You're superstitious. Mid-life finds you with dramatic pressures and responsibilities, but an inheritance or family protector saves the day—knock on wood—and for unknown reasons, when you least expect it, you're a big shot again. If you took time to analyze yourself, you would find that you worked, assumed obligations and cultivated an education from your experiences.

You want opulence, comfort and authority. Get an education early. If prethirties challenges don't unsettle your plans, your natural healing abilities should be supported with expertise. Theater arts provide a career or hobby that keeps you company later in life. Overall happiness comes from service, not money.

· OTHER JANUARY 6 BIRTHDAYS

Joey Adams	1911
Bonnie Franklin	1944
Thomas Gray	1717
Louis Harris	1921
Johann Kepler	1572
Tom Mix	1880
Sun Myung Moon	1920
Sam Rayburn	1882
Carl Sandburg	1878
Earl Scruggs	1924
Danny Thomas	1914
Early Wynn	1920
Loretta Young	1913

JANUARY

· 7 ·

"Hail to the Chief"—and a twenty-one-gun salute to your ability to lead with concern for the good of all. You don't require the uniforms—just sense the needs of your superiors or associates, wait until others expose their cards and silently take over.

You were defensive as a youth, too much was expected of you, and you were perceived as a go-fer. Sic 'em; you're a tiger in mid-life, when a wealthy, aristocratic, ambitious man respects your trustworthy executive abilities and starts your legalistic mind on its rise to the pleasure of making money and living well.

Education is a necessity for uncontested success; fight for it. Water travel has a special meaning for you. Opportunities come and go to make use of your childhood respect for the people and things related to boats or the sea. Maintain your belief in preventive medicine, partnerships and upgrading benefits for the less powerful. Later life brings a lighter, more sociable, active and commanding life-style, but you must understand that you have power. The sooner you stop relating happiness and blessings to love and stop assuming responsibilities and bearing burdens for a partner, the sooner you will cease to live beyond your means. You lose by feeling subservient. You win as a secret power, recognized as a faithful lover, teacher and counselor.

You can have it all in your fifties. After your personal idealism balances to allow for the frailties of humanity, you will understand your power to be a philanthropic, refined, invulnerable diplomat. Do not work to justify money. Work to live.

• OTHER JANUARY 7 BIRTHDAYS

Charles Addams	1912
Orval Faubus	1910
Millard Fillmore	1800
Vincent Gardenia	1922
Kenny Loggins	1948
St. Bernadette of Lourdes	1844
Butterfly McQueen	1911
Adolph Zukor	1873

JANUARY

· 8 ·

"You've come a long way, baby." It's time to accept yourself and the rest of us for what we are . . . just human. Secrets of the past are not worth hanging on to after all you've been through. It's lonely to be wise beyond your years, but wisdom is lasting; you evolve to become noble and attract notables, to overcome obstacles and to gain leadership and status.

Childhood was too challenging. After age twenty-eight, affluent, influential, physically strong associations help you to forget loneliness, disillusionment and feeling powerless to help or change the emotional upheavals of youth. You are old before your time; too soon burdened with responsibilities and delays which are made less painful by a youthful mother or an understanding sister.

If you forgo get-rich-quick schemes, and instead get an education to gain self-confidence, you will hold on to money that comes your way before age thirty-six. Positive thinking and adaptability will save you from a life-style of manual labor, although you always make your work pay off. Mental pursuits and expertise lighten your neurotic tendencies to beat yourself over the head for not being perfect. In childhood you weren't perfect, but who is?

You may be dominating or dominated—nothing in between. Love causes conflict and could interfere with a balanced health regimen or ambitions. Avoid bigotry. Commercialize on the arts to overcome loneliness. If you don't feel appreciated for the sacrifices you make in the name of love, gain prominence by associating with the psychics and intellectuals who later surround you.

• OTHER JANUARY 8 BIRTHDAYS

Little Anthony	1940
Shirley Bassey	1937
David Bowie	1947
Hans Von Bülow	19??
Frank Nelson Doubleday	1862
José Ferrer	1912
Bill Graham	1931
W. M. Kiplinger	1891
Yvette Mimieux	1941
Elvis Presley	1935
Soupy Sales	1926
Larry Storch	1925

JANUARY

·**9**·

You'll never be the same once you recognize yourself. Giving for love; sacrificing for family; forgoing pleasure for an education—who are you? You'll deny yourself freedom or face disillusionment before you meet the one man who comes to your rescue. Take heart; you've got scars to prove that you're entitled to success.

Worthy ambitions make use of your knack for routine, efficiency and control later in life; don't become discouraged. You're a great lover and a noble friend, and you attract notables after age twenty-eight. You grow culturally, and travel to serve major causes. Try government agencies, merchandising or politics as an outlet for your brotherly love, stamina and dedication. After age fifty-six, home and hearth look good and you are finally able to ingest wisdom instead of just doling it out.

Athletics or business tempt you to overexertion or compulsive drive. You are, no doubt, self-made. People do not help you, and you're the first one to say, "God helps those who help themselves." Intuition is on your side. ESP and healing come naturally when you find yourself rebuilding your life repeatedly. Stay away from labor for the sake of using energy; your mind will atrophy if you don't work it. If you find yourself losing ambition, get out of the rut or face the dullest of existences. You have a choice mid-life to broaden your scope or drone away in the survival rut.

Go for it! A person foreign to your background will throw you a life preserver when you're drowning in self-pity. You will go a long way after you think you are tired. Hang in to win.

- OTHER JANUARY 9 BIRTHDAYS

Joan Baez	1941
George Balanchine	1904
Simone de Beauvoir	1908
Rudolph Bing	1902
Gracie Fields	1898
Fernando Lamas	1915
Gypsy Rose Lee	1914
Richard Nixon	1913
Bart Starr	1934
Susannah York	1942
Chic Young	1901

JANUARY
· 10 ·

You'll never get anything without paying the piper. Compose a song that you like hearing and whistle it continually. Work, duty and traditions are the tunes to carry during your quest for security, artistic expression and prestige. Marriage or love is nice but better if your mate has a good background and/or money.

You know how to solve your own problems. When emotions run high you know that you suffer the tortures of the damned, therefore you philosophically ease yourself into a material reward to lighten the burden. You are too empathetic or too selfish and are not always sure of the true values in people and life experience. Tangibles are important to you—maybe too important.

Childhood is easier than maturity. Your family, teachers, and community love you and, if you are assertive, the contacts you make in youth serve you well in your later ambitions. If you become too dependent upon partnership, your creativity is limited because your progress is delayed. Aim to look beneath the surface and be decisive. You care about what everyone thinks. Be good to yourself first; you'll attract notables who are creative.

Self-discipline is the key to peace of mind. Be realistic. You want recognition and you fear being left out. You're an original; put your inventions to work. When you trust the creative, independent, active woman whose ambitions and talents help to direct your expenditures, your untraditional concepts bring financial rewards. Your mid-forties find you making an advantageous, radical twist in life-style. You'll love your work. In your later years you are active, comfortable and independent.

· OTHER JANUARY 10 BIRTHDAYS

Ray Bolger	1904
Donald Brooks	1928
Francis X. Bushman	1883
Charles Cornwallis	1739
George Foreman	1949
Al Goldstein	1936
Paul Henreid	1908
Willie McCovey	1938
Giselle McKenzie	1927
Sherrill Milnes	1935
Sal Mineo	1939
Johnny Ray	1927
Rod Stewart	1945
Galina Ulanova	1910
Andreas Vesalius	1515

JANUARY

• 11 •

George Bernard Shaw's one-liner, "I often quote myself; it adds spice to my conversation," should seem comfortable to you. Other people can be very disappointing. Every time you speculate, you have problems. When you look for guidance or lean on friends or family, the bottom drops out. The men in your life have added burdens and expense. Finally you recognize the need for female assistance. A generous, empathetic, conscientious woman employee or associate gets you out of a hole. She is a humanitarian who widens your horizons and shows you the way to take the challenges of responsibility in your stride.

To avoid business or labor disputes, be fair, not crafty. You attract petty, chronic physical problems when you bring emotions to your job. High nervous energy internalizes; you benefit from the holistic school of medicine. Doubt attracts disappointment; stop and think, but once you make a decision, hang in. Self-understanding is most difficult until mid-life, when you get out of your self-made rut.

You are asked to be unselfish without getting a just reward, and that discomfort makes you too serious. Take a lighter look at yourself and stop living for tomorrow. Listen to professionals in your immediate surroundings; follow through and you won't have to cover up impulsive judgments. Be patient. Your ship comes in without traveling on or living near the water.

Trust yourself; stay close to home later in life, benefit from long-term real estate investments and stroke your ego. Ignore the opinions of others where your inventive nature is concerned. Worry not lest you become a bland conversationalist.

• OTHER JANUARY 11 BIRTHDAYS

Eva Le Gallienne	1899
Bobby Goldsboro	1941
Alexander Hamilton	1757
William James	1842
William Proxmire	1915
Charles Stuart	1721
Rod Taylor	1930

JANUARY

· 12 ·

It requires a great deal of strength to decide what to do. But you're not lazy or afraid of work once your ambitions are clear. Expect to see and need tangible results and to surround yourself with practical people in youth. Creative talents pay off well when you feel needed and follow your personal philosophy. Be decisive. Mama doesn't always know what is best for you.

People applaud your down-to-earth directives and charming delivery. You're multifaceted and have a choice of self-expressive business careers. Social contacts attract love, money and recognition. You have a variety of interests throughout life and would do well writing about your experiences. Life is a drama; your curiosity is dimmed only by unjustified sensitivities to the shortcomings of intimates. Your self-criticism and search for improvement are based upon childhood memories of a close relationship with an opinionated and adored mother. Your ability to stick with it was nurtured during your early years. Because you have diagnostic intuition, you benefit from affluent friends and attract rewards through your ability to suggest remedies. Finances improve mid-life.

You should be free to work alone, along creative lines, to attract the easy way to success. During mid-life you try too hard. Don't lose sight of your need for intimacy in love, your expressions of joy in living and your yearning for travel. You are a trendsetter who needs approval. Don't compromise your wisdom to be tolerant of deviations from the norm. You'll get rich returns for your personality, talents and charity. Aim high.

• OTHER JANUARY 12 BIRTHDAYS

Bernadine Dohrn	1942
Hermann Goering	1893
Patsy Kelly	1910
Jack London	1876
Luise Rainer	1910
Paul Revere	1735
Tex Ritter	1906
John Singer Sargent	1856
Swami Vivekananda	1863

JANUARY · **13** · Childhood is troubled, unconventional and unreliable, and you're not too sure who your friends are. Changes, travel or ups and downs with money prevail until productive males note your willingness to work. If you droop to self-pity, your speculations do not bring in the male contacts that teach you how to make and hold on to money. You may become physically drained and introverted. Try to maintain friendships; friends offer you choices. Don't allow interference or family jealousy to alter your desire for the good life.

Due to emotionalizing over hardship, you are a late bloomer. Your mother, grandmother or siblings stunt your social growth, and bitterness may result. Mid-life may be limiting and the compensations unstable due to handicaps of childhood. A strong interest in parapsychology or the occult opens new channels for self-realization in your late forties, and the door is opened to learning from the past. In your early fifties you satisfy your curiosity, relate to the mystical and mellow.

You talk too much or too little. When you exaggerate, you lose your self-respect. Others find you attractive, but it's difficult for you to believe that you are desired for yourself alone. You're able to be decisive, if you're angry. Try not to scatter your interests when you're at peace with your intimates.

Your life is like a baseball game, when you're only as good as the last hit or miss. Branch Rickey knew that "problems are the price you pay for progress." Eventually you learn that nothing is eternal. Each step is a fresh upswing for progress. Forget the last game and play ball!

• OTHER JANUARY 13 BIRTHDAYS

Horatio Alger	1834
Alfred Fuller	1885
Charles Nelson Reilly	1931
Robert Stack	1919
Sophie Tucker	1884
Gwen Verdon	1925

JANUARY

·14·

Doing nothing makes you tired. You are rebellious, restless and ambitious in a conventional childhood. New enthusiasms seek channels for power, money and the comforts that status attracts. You may destroy your dreams of the perfect mate if you allow sex and romance to come second to a lofty life-style. Marriage for position and a need for prestige motivate you early in life. You choose associates for their intellect but keep a tight rein on their autonomy.

You're a rule maker or a rule breaker...all in a good cause— your success. You expect your spouse to sparkle in society and hold a good-paying job. You expect to hear opinions but rarely rely upon anyone but yourself. Young people influence your thinking and up-to-date ideas spark your progress mid-life.

You manipulate and press Lady Luck, with your eye on the bottom line production figures, demanding a return on investments in employees, friendships and domestic relationships. From your late twenties to mid-fifties, life is hectic, but you maintain enduring commitments. If you have learned the lessons of disciplined work early and dedicate yourself to self-improvement, you will not squander money in a foolish fetish to find bargains. You get what you pay for.

Experience is your best teacher as you gain maturity. Your fifties are exciting and challenging because of encounters that are foreign to your childhood expectations. A home near or on the water is a haven but not a retirement castle. Poverty is your greatest fear and security is your master. Aim to remember your staunch supporters; they will always rescue you.

* OTHER JANUARY 14 BIRTHDAYS

Cecil Beaton	1904
William Bendix	1906
Julian Bond	1940
Faye Dunaway	1941
Marjoe Gortner	1945
King Richard II	1367
Jack Jones	1938
John dos Passos	1896
Jean de Reszke	1850
Hal Roach	1892
Andy Rooney	1919
Albert Schweitzer	1875
Tom Tryon	1926

JANUARY

· **15** ·

Which is your most consuming problem, money or sex? The answer lies in learning that your best bets do not come with a focus on the material. You need education, specialization and/or educational travels to open your eyes. When you "know," you will teach and provide life's cultural treasures and a wealth of knowledge. Until then, you must work.

Childhood relationships are not to your tastes, and leaving the security of family seems right in the circumstances. You may regret impatience and impulsivity in later years as your choice of friends and lovers proves to be unstable. Legal matters—leases, contracts or agreements—are cloudy and mistakes are made. You are not suited to early life partnerships—if you're a male, you respond to domination; if you're a female, you need to respect the male authority figure, to an extreme. A late-in-life love is apt to be more conducive to material security, position and gaining through travel. Surprises become less overwhelming when you are careful.

You're either the vestal virgin or a swinger without conscience in youth. Your early thirties bring control to your sensual quests and questioning. Your strong opinions get you into trouble and you choose a mate who adds to your burdens.

An intellectual—therapist, lawyer or spiritual guide—may be helpful when your funds are tied up at mid-life. Don't try to be a good samaritan; you're not geared to nursing the sick. You do well to follow your hunches and be flexible. Take a chance on a well-traveled, assertive woman who exerts a strong influence after you reach the age of forty. Opt for a job with growth potential, and subdue your money-consciousness; a large inheritance is possible.

• OTHER JANUARY 15 BIRTHDAYS

King Saud of Saudi Arabia	1902
St. Joan of Arc	1412
Lloyd Bridges	1913
Robert C. Byrd	1918
Franz Grellparzer	1791
Maurice Herzog	1919
Thomas Hoving	1931
Martin Luther King, Jr.	1929
Gene Krupa	1909
Gamal Abdul Nassar	1918
Margaret O'Brien	1937
Aristotle Onassis	1906
Duc de Saint-Simon	1675
Maria Schell	1926
Edward Tetler	1908

JANUARY
· 16 ·
You may start as a deckhand, but you'll soon own the ship. Responsibility, reason and reserve are the three R's that help you realize your ambitions. You're all business in youth, a specialist at mid-life and you realize your intellectual, creative communications talents in later years.

Friendships are easily made and lost in early life, as is your first love. Home, family and social obligations build a firm set of personal ideals that are hard to shake. Mid-life softens your emotional reactions and brings out an aloofness and secretiveness that do not dull your charm or attractive personality. You may be a health nut and take your interest in preventive medicine to professional levels. However, your respect for money, your businesslike approach and your concern for quality consciousness are the mainstays of your life-style.

Mental challenges and people who offer them appeal to you. In youth, marriage is a necessity to your self-image, while you may marry later in life for intellectual stimulation. Friendships change as you travel physically and spiritually. Your profession should be lasting, and dedication to hobbies may bring added success later in life. You prefer serenity and are not prone to rocking the boat. If you outgrow your mate or partner you won't make the first move until the monotony and stagnation cause you to imagine that your brain is beginning to atrophy.

After age fifty writing, music and genteel people with exquisite taste attract you. A naval career or seaside hideaway provides you with inner security. In doubt? Try it, you'll like it.

• OTHER JANUARY 16 BIRTHDAYS

Fulgencio Batista	1901
Dizzy Dean	1911
A. J. Foyt	1935
Marilyn Horne	1934
Alexander Knox	1907
Pilar Lorengar	1933
Ethel Merman	1908
Nicola Piccini	1728

JANUARY

· 17 ·

You can handle anything and make it pay—anything that doesn't relate to your emotions. You are wise beyond your years as a youngster and go—and grow— far from your birthright. Independence, courage and the ability to manipulate in times of trouble add to your drive for cultural advancement. Relax, you're probably due for an inheritance and have a knack for turning a loss into a win.

A wealthy or influential woman takes an interest in you mid-life. You marry early to get the best of the crop and may choose a mate that promotes your ambitions. Youth may include feelings of secretiveness or difficult-to-diagnose problems that recede in mid-years. You may develop a skeptical approach that is difficult to change. You drive for perfection and are best when working alone or in an executive capacity.

Mid-life finds you a closet spiritual seeker, and your interest in psychic phenomena is cloaked in a traditional display and doubt. It is uncomfortable for you to accept unorthodox or "foreign" interests. If you cannot touch, taste, smell, spend or hear it—there's gotta be a gimmick. However, your desire to investigate and question is triggered; then you cannot draw conclusions and stick to beliefs that are traditional and acceptable.

Your first instinct is to do the appropriate thing and avoid complications; disillusionment and loneliness as a child stifle your emotional displays. You have a long memory for the hard times and are self-protective. Unlike your early years, later life finds you close to home, maintaining the status quo.

• OTHER JANUARY 17 BIRTHDAYS

Muhammad Ali	1942
Anne Brontë	1820
Al Capone	1899
Anton Chekhov	1860
Thomas Dooley	1927
Benjamin Franklin	1706
Joe Frazier	1944
David Lloyd George	1863
Frank Hogan	1902
James Earl Jones	1931
Shari Lewis	1934
Sheree North	1933
Mack Sennett	1880
Moira Shearer	1926
Konstantin Stanislavsky	1863
Nick Taylor	1948

JANUARY **·18·** The bigger the better; whether it's giving or getting. You love display and attract notables in your pursuit of brain power. Childhood makes financial, emotional and accidental demands upon you. Family life requires that you think for yourself, and you develop petty fears that must be alleviated by material tokens throughout your lifetime.

Due to childhood lack of material security, you are too impatient for "big deals," become a joiner and seek out influential protectors. If a "fix" can be put in, you're the first to suggest wheeling and dealing. Counseling is your forte; problem solving and healing come naturally, but there is a strain over money mid-life that should not have occurred. You need advice yourself where investments are concerned, until a late-in-life love provides a heaven-sent kindred spirit.

You're unsure of your strength and may become mercenary or power hungry. Stamina, efficiency and determination may be misused, and the beauty of your aspects for reaping whatever you sow may be lost in a tendency to control and dominate. You will always be protected by your sense of brotherly love and the empathy for humanity that you established as a somewhat deprived youngster. Aim to be less fearful and mistrusting. Take responsibility for the welfare of others less able to overcome difficulties. You have a sharp outlook, attract helpful admirers and do not have to be bullish to protect your own interests.

Retirement is not for you. Your mid-fifties find a wider scope for business interests and pleasure in traveling to return to a comfortable, opulent nest, feathered with romantic love.

• OTHER JANUARY 18 BIRTHDAYS

Cary Grant	1904
Oliver Hardy	1892
Danny Kaye	1913
A. A. Milne	1882
Daniel Webster	1782

JANUARY

· 19 ·

By helping someone else, you become strong. Childhood aggressive or male influences and the responsibilities thrust upon you by family circumstances can make or break you. You are very open and seem to learn by osmosis. Youthful challenges have a lifetime effect upon your philosophy.

Your independence and leadership qualities are top-notch, but you seem to be attracted to less assertive, ambitious and creative lovers. You are selective about everything but your mates and confuse yourself and friends. It's important to your emotional balance that you expand your cultural horizons and be true to your unique philosophy. You give when others take and take when giving seems in order . . . get thee to a university and persist in broadening your education.

Your thirty-seventh year points to a new direction: You get out of the kitchen and into the mainstream. There's a major change in lifestyle, and expectations for happiness are greatly improved. You gain the respect of your peers for your wisdom and ability to instill or renew the joy of living in others.

Mail, phone and all forms of self-expression keep you busy. A sensitive, gentle, supportive female helps you to establish your own shop, consulting business or land investments. Mid-life health problems pass quickly and stop your impatient pace long enough for you to rethink your personal goals. At first insight this delay seems dreadful, but you realize your superior capacity for survival. You gain a depth of understanding for the suffering of others, which attracts you to contribute your energy to a charitable work, just when you need to find a retirement activity.

- OTHER JANUARY 19 BIRTHDAYS

Desi Arnaz, Jr.	1953
Paul Cézanne	1839
Oveta Culp Hobby	1905
Janis Joplin	1943
Robert E. Lee	1807
Guy Madison	1922
Victor Mature	1916
Dolly Parton	1946
Edgar Allan Poe	1809
John Raitt	1917
Jean Stapleton	1923
Fritz Weaver	1926

JANUARY
·20·

It's love or financial security; they are elusive individually and refuse to coexist. You relinquish creativity for love and work, work, work for security in your own home. Changes are frequent, interests are scattered and there is a naive relationship to leases or contracts that put you off on shaky footing before your twenty-seventh year. You are too impatient, take people at face value and attract leaners or bullies in your haste to control your destiny.

Every time you turn around, decisions have to be made. You drain emotionally at each turning point. You may have to rebuild your life-style more than a few times before you learn how to adapt to change. Expect to nurture a child or lover until a change at age forty-six brings a chance to be a support system for others and receive ample remuneration. Concentrated effort is required for you to attain serenity. You take gambles until the unpleasant consequences outweigh the excitement.

Partnership is beneficial if you don't submit yourself to drudgery. Your ego is tender, and arguments cause you to fear that all love is lost; you refuse to assert yourself until you burst with frustration and anger. Stop hiding your personal desires and feeling like a weakling. The peace of mind you seek will come when you stop vacillating as you try to please everyone—except yourself—and you begin to reveal your ambitions. It's not envy that you feel; you're inhibited.

Success may be delayed if you don't loosen up. You are an inspiration to the work force or service groups. Fame comes your way when your sympathetic nature is allowed free expression.

· OTHER JANUARY 20 BIRTHDAYS

Edwin "Buzz" Aldrin, Jr.	1930
Joy Adamson	1910
Leon Ames	1903
George Burns	1896
Shelley Fabares	1944
Frederico Fellini	1920
Lorenzo Lamas	1958
Mario Lanza	1921
Hugh Marlowe	1911
Patricia Neal	1926
Joan Rivers	1937

JANUARY
·21·

Diamonds are a girl's best friend, and boys enjoy them at the ball park too. You do well to make a game of life and forgo self-pity. Friends will get you everywhere.

Health, wealth and happiness depend upon congeniality, creative self-expression and love. You attract involvements with the opposite sex and may flirt your way to problems with a jealous lover—or two or three or four. Learn the rules of fair play, avoid the temptation to steal a base or two and obey the coach.

If you are nurtured to respect authority and are trained early to self-discipline, you'll hit homers at every turn at bat. Mother and the family environment have a strong influence on you. Aim to recognize major issues and strive not to be picky. You will fall prey to chronic allergies, emotionally induced rashes or be a finicky eater until you realize that all eyes are not upon you. Mid-life releases you from the negativity and personalized sensitivity you were subjected to as a youngster.

You cannot escape from reality. Life is not a bowl of pitless cherries, and you will have to be patient to accumulate financial freedom. Money is important to you for the beautiful clothes, home furnishings and adult toys it can buy. You've been gifted with charm, personality and bedroom eyes. Your voice is unforgettable. Gifts of communication are your security. Strive to support your talents educationally; money will flow to you.

You are fond of children, animals and dote upon loved ones. Loss, illness or disloyalty may devastate you mid-life, but you find your way to spiritual uplift or seek a just cause to serve. Inactivity is deadly to your nature. Plan for a busy retirement.

• OTHER JANUARY 21 BIRTHDAYS

Ethan Allen	1738
Robby Benson	1955
Mac Davis	1942
Christian Dior	1905
Placido Domingo	1941
Henri Duparc	1848
John Charles Fremont	1813
Benny Hill	1925
Stonewall Jackson	1824
J. Carroll Naish	1900
Jack Nicklaus	1940
Telly Savalas	1924
Paul Scofield	1922

JANUARY
·22·
Travel far and wide but don't forget the voyager within. You'll emulate a female taskmaster who drives your social self-esteem into the ground. That's your childhood sampling, and you punish others with your silence as you were shown a tight-lipped reprimand. Appearances are deemed to be important, too, and you strive to look attractive, surround yourself with bright personalities and dutifully assume family responsibilities long past the appropriate time.

Before your thirty-seventh birthday Lady Luck is full of surprises. Thereafter, you are able to use your imagination for practical purposes, real estate investments and traditional plans. You have the soul of a practical idealist; dynamic!

Travel is always a treasure trove of new enthusiasms and you may be drawn to politics, entertainment or advertising to satisfy your need for a variety of interests. However, your best business bets are found where practice makes perfect and a structure prevails. Make changes, but plan carefully.

You come down to earth and begin to use common sense when financial limitations crop up mid-life. You are a workaholic and may divide yourself between legislative or government projects that bring your ESP talents to benefit a mass market. Although you were bred to marry in the family tradition, an unconventional intimate relationship beckons and is lasting. You dislike uprooting after age forty and decide to reside far from home base.

Superficial values vanish; you become more creative and responsible and devote time, in an advisory capacity, to community welfare projects as you grow older. You master your fate.

• OTHER JANUARY 22 BIRTHDAYS

Ray Anthony	1922
Linda Blair	1959
Lord Byron	1738
Constance Collier	1880
D. W. Griffith	1875
Piper Laurie	1932
U Thant	1909
John Winthrop	1588

JANUARY
·23·
How you manage to be a nonconformist/conformist and get away with appearing conventional is your mystery. The sacrifices you make for security dull your adventurous, energetic, independent talents. You may have been accused of selfishness in childhood. The family need for group harmony was disturbed by your independent desire for your own funds. Money gave you the freedom when your activities were organized: you are the catalyst that alters future deals.

Throughout your lifetime you will want precise definitions, directions and regulations clarified—to be sure that you are not misunderstood. You were bred to "do the right thing," but really aren't eager to take on the accountability of marriage. You're torn between marrying an older secure person, for money, or working. Anything mundane is a bore, and yet you delude yourself repeatedly by making practical commitments or accepting menial work. Once obligated, you remain in a rut.

A musical career is attractive, but you are too self-limiting and may aim for any education for appearance's sake. What a waste! Experience is your teacher; work at each new enthusiasm. Why aim to fit into a mold? You are fortunate to have platonic friends who try to guide you when the unexpected happens. Loss of control throws you. You try to wait out problems. Take the bull by the horns. You are a survivor!

Early years present a need to work; you have burdens. Mid-life ambitions are overthrown by a female relative. Pursue your interests later in life. You inherit or provide yourself with a steady income. Don't expect to relax; you must remain useful.

• OTHER JANUARY 23 BIRTHDAYS

Dan Duryea	1907
Sergei Eisenstein	1898
Gil Gerard	1943
John Hancock	1737
Ernie Kovacs	1919
Edouard Manet	1832
Jeanne Moreau	1928
Chita Rivera	1933
Randolph Scott	1903
Stendahl	1783

JANUARY
·**24**·

What a cool cat you are. Hiding all that enthusiasm, curiosity and intelligence attracts the wrong people. You are self-sufficient. Why depend upon others or look for partners when you are more adaptable, clever and self-confident on your own.

Mid-life love, responsibilities and family treasures add to your financial security. In youth you have time for privacy; make the most of your experiences without becoming jaded. After age thirty your time won't be your own. Community politics, family involvements and the welfare of others should concern you. You enjoy the drama and are a magnet for other people's troubles. Expect applause for your efforts to be a good companion, helpmate and friend.

An opulent home; good smells in the kitchen; comfortable, down-filled club chairs and beautiful abundance everywhere can be yours. You want to be proud of your life-style. Be faithful, fair and adapt to another's ideals. Money, emotional security and the aristocratic good taste that you find comforting are yours for being the mainstay of the family and a pillar of your society.

What do you have to sacrifice for all this good stuff? Nothing, if you don't become dependent upon others being dependent upon you. Maintain your artistic interests, curiosity and spirit of adventure. Men may make problems in business or reject domination. Learn to handle your own freedom and the rights of others to be free. Don't become a martyr.

You find your self-sufficiency unexpectedly. Travel is not good for your peace of mind. Stay near home and direct others.

• OTHER JANUARY 24 BIRTHDAYS

Ernest Borgnine	1917
Neil Diamond	1941
Frederick the Great	1712
Mary Lou Retton	1968
Oral Roberts	1918
Maria Tallchief	1925
Sharon Tate	1943
Edith Wharton	1862
Estelle Winwood	1883

JANUARY **·25·** If you think you've experienced déjà vu, answered a question before it was asked or just followed your feelings and were right—don't compromise your principles or ambitions—the mystical aspects of your destiny are working with you. Money will come and go, but once you meet established persons who recognize your communications talents and intellect, you are protected. Let go of family security or dependency upon a woman. Owing to nervous energy, you do more than one thing at a time and make them pay.

Childhood demands independence, and if your curiosity is denied, leave home early. Adventure calls, and the family is oppressive, demanding and undependable. You resent parental attitudes but find a way to keep the peace. You marry too young or hang on to a dependent love and finally extricate yourself.

You are at your best if you have an education or speciality midlife. The mail, phone, computer are always at your fingertips, and social involvements provide a forum for your concerned opinions. Watch spending and credit card limits; follow your instinct to stay out of debt. You cannot gamble. Investigate before you make a business commitment or marry.

Once you are involved, it is difficult for you to let go. Extricating yourself from obligations is costly and emotionally draining; marriage particularly, because it involves children and requires integrity to maintain or break up. Family burdens ease by your late thirties, after you find your expertise or professionalism. You are your best promoter; beware of flattery.

Later you travel, are secure professionally and demand 101 percent from yourself and life.

• OTHER JANUARY 25 BIRTHDAYS

Benedict Arnold	1741
Robert Burns	1759
Mildred Dunnock	1906
Dean Jones	1935
W. Somerset Maugham	1874
Edwin Newman	1919
Virginia Woolf	1882

JANUARY
·**26**·

No matter how many possessions you have, they will never satisfy your intellectual hunger. Knowledge is the food to stave off loneliness—fears of practical and emotional poverty. Too much mother love or too little affection as a tot is the cause of your personal isolation. You depend upon your mind; it is your security blanket or the banana peel that slips you up.

You want authority and autonomy; not an easy trick for a child. You demand love and are aloof when response is expected. Sex is not the solution to providing feelings of love. You search in the wrong areas in your youth. Male business partnership is disastrous and you learn to work alone. Lawyers add to problems. You realize that money or power aren't problem-solvers that you imagined them to be when you vacillate, gamble and lose.

Mid-life has heartaches when a lover proves to be unworthy. You do best to forgive and forget or you suffer emotional drains. You take risks for tangibles. Property investments tie you down and aren't worth the sacrifice of your freedom. You do better as an investment counselor than an investor.

A library filled with books that you haven't read may provide the facade of affluence. You learn that the results of your work prove to be reward enough; you build faith. Phony displays are self-defeating. Forget escapist moods—dreams of buried treasure. You gain security when you are employed by admiring professionals.

Finances are inconsistent mid-life and stabilize when you learn patience and persistence. Late years are spent away from your original neighborhood. An ocean voyage changes your life and causes you to pull up stakes and settle far from your roots.

· OTHER JANUARY 26 BIRTHDAYS

Angela Davis	1944
Jules Feiffer	1929
Jimmy Van Heusen	1913
Eartha Kitt	1928
Douglas MacArthur	1880
Paul Newman	1925
William Redfield	1927
Maria Trapp	1905
Roger Vadim	1928

JANUARY

·27·

Inspiration, ambition and progress fill your prophetic dreams. You must follow your inventive ideals and expect the nobility of your purpose to attract money, love and fortunate partnerships. Childhood is a friendly experience and offers education and preparation to become an excellent parent. Athletics or a job are important in youth, as are thoughts of love. You're romantic; early marriage is attractive to you.

You should be self-made and dislike the petty details. Work hard and you'll grow far from your birthright into a cultural paradise. Shirk your traditional responsibilities, be selfish, fail to follow your love of education and you'll find life dull; teeming with uninspirational people. You need a worthwhile purpose. If you decide to work in the field of medicine or counseling, look into natural aspects of healing the body and the mind. You're not a technician. Emotional responsiveness increases your polish and skill of performance. You find that mid-life demands a spirit of brotherly love, additional study and consistency. Focus on broadening your fields of interest.

Money should not be a problem. You may donate it or use it to entertain friends or support your artistic interests. Earning is not a problem; you work hard and want the pleasure of living generously and graciously. Take yourself seriously. Be careful, and don't expect that those near and dear to you know how much you love them unless you take time to show your tenderness.

Late years may not fulfill the promises you made to yourself of globe-trotting or writing your novel. Reflect; life's been good, if you've rowed your own boat and ignored the blisters.

• OTHER JANUARY 27 BIRTHDAYS

Mikhail Baryshnikov	1948
Lewis Carroll	1832
Troy Donahue	1938
Samuel Gompers	1850
William Randolph Hearst	1908
Skitch Henderson	1918
Jerome Kern	1885
Wolfgang Amadeus Mozart	1756
Donna Reed	1921

JANUARY

·**28**·

You have to take risks to win. Before you run toward a goal, know what you want and be prepared to lose. Decisions are difficult for you. Impatience is your enemy, yet you have wisdom beyond your years. Your high energy, creativity and emotional responsiveness need to find a direction in youth. When you find your way to succeeding in a creative field, you cease to feel itchy and restless. You'll be a winner when you establish your own philosophy and expertise.

You are capable of submerging your personality into the life of your lover and hating yourself for losing your individuality. Changing home and direction will not alter your personality extremes. After age thirty, find a career in the theater or government and take a full-charge position. Avoid letting your temper take you over when you get paranoid. Find outlets among people with your interests. Aim to stop suffering; make contacts and stick to your guns. Remember, all saints live a hell on earth. Sacrifice will only bring you discontentment.

Your forties are intense. Money and notable people add incentive for you to reach the top in your profession. Why you become secretive is a mystery, but you want power after you gain financial freedom and go for it through charitable works. You may attract a following of elitists or cultists who emulate your distinctive style later in life.

At any stage of your life, education is a good bet. Success may come through law, politics or journalism. The confusion you felt as a child is best forgotten. Don't dwell upon the past; your viewpoint narrows and shrinks your potential.

• OTHER JANUARY 28 BIRTHDAYS

Alan Alda	1936
Colette	1873
Corky Laing	1948
Jackson Pollock	1912
Arthur Rubenstein	1886
Susan Sontag	1933

JANUARY
·29·
You can stroke people with words and, like F. Scott Fitzgerald, share your extraordinary point of view. You know you are meant to do something special and attract followers with that glint in your eye, the sparkle of your ideas and your direct approach. Impatient as you are for the moment of recognition, don't let compromise or escapist unrealities alter your course.

Never say never. Think it out. Problem parents and grandparents cannot drown your youthful imagination. Educational advantages would spurt your growth, but even when you are unbalanced by financial concerns, you live as an elitist. Money—the freedom and power that it provides—draws you to hard work. You never stay with a job that you dislike. It's a struggle after you leave home to assume the burdens of family and community.

In your thirties a male offers a chance to show responsibility and reap the rewards of your willingness to apply yourself to a routined life-style. Partners and lovers have an important role in your creative success. Be selective in your choice of mates. They may be a blessing or a burden in legal matters.

You always seem to anticipate events and finally realize that you have the gift of vision. You buy clothes that become popular styles a few years later—after you've tired of them. You have a unique philosophy that attracts followers, and through their willingness to be supportive, you are able to help them.

Don't live with fear. Stroke yourself; your forties are secured by money, beneficial travels and a sense of fulfillment. You are meant to be an inspiration and to spread the word.

• OTHER JANUARY 29 BIRTHDAYS

Clara Bow	1905
Paddy Chayefsky	1923
W. C. Fields	1880
John Forsythe	1918
Germaine Greer	1935
Noel Harrison	1936
William McKinley	1843
John D. Rockefeller, Jr.	1874
Katharine Ross	1943
Tom Selleck	19??
Moche Joseph Spiegel, Jr.	1901

JANUARY **·30·** Find your calling and expect to be a magnetic leader with abilities to mobilize divergent groups of people. Your enemies are stubbornness, pettiness and dictatorship. Friends are drawn to your wisdom, high motives and dedication to obligations.

In youth a hard-driving, kindly mother sets the stage for your insecurities. Intimate relationships prove disappointing, and the seeds of a lifelong desire to help less fortunates are sown. Marriage is not a sensual focus; it provides a friendly support system and team player for your ambitions.

Duty calls in mid-life and your self-confidence is challenged repeatedly. Affluent and powerful people related to unions, governments or big business alternately applaud and chastise your activities. Your undertakings involve ways and means to help less educated or innovative sections of society. Money is not your problem; your status or positioning creates confusion in relationships.

Be independent. Few people have the aspirations that you have to improve situations and regulations. Critics abound when you take the lead. Partnerships should not compromise you, but a philosophical kindred spirit is an ally and a discomfort throughout your adult life. Don't allow your sensitive nature to try to solve everyday problems when emotions are taxed.

You require stamina and a thick skin. It isn't easy, but you relate to an intimate love years after you make your mark. Later years offer travel, diversions and sunshine. Trials and tribulations do not abate. However, your self-discipline, training and determination win you affection, applause and awards.

* OTHER JANUARY 30 BIRTHDAYS

Carol Channing	1921
Gene Hackman	1931
John Ireland	1915
Winnie Ruth Judd	1905
Dorothy Malone	1925
Dick Martin	1922
Harold Prince	1928
Vanessa Redgrave	1937
Franklin D. Roosevelt	1882
Boris Spassky	1937
James Watt	1736
David Wayne	1914

JANUARY

· 3 1 ·

You're really a pussycat; cuddly and playful, why show your claws to get your way? Dramatic, attractive, energetic and intensely competitive talents support the pride you have in yourself. You're a fighter with extravagant ideas and tastes. The world is your pet mouse if you stop trying to trap and play games to prove your points.

Early years found you the ugly duckling or the graceful swan of the family. Too much approval or too much criticism left you undecided in youth as to how to show love. The foundation of your nature requires an adjustment to overcompensating or understating the importance of friendship. When you find someone to talk to, you find a lover, friend and the only intimate sharing you allow. Words are your dearest resource or your staunchest enemy until your emotions stop governing your mind.

Mid-life brings out your personal convictions, buoyancy and desire to construct a meaningful career in the arts or business. Opportunities to triumph over fast-paced, unconventional, accident-prone youthful experiences surface. You meet the one person, probably male, who exerts a lifelong influence. A love based upon intellect and reason surfaces to give you the choice and chance to have the courage of your convictions and master your ambitions.

You are independent, resilient and a worker, but must not pussyfoot around means of self-expression or you will be insecure until after age thirty-seven. Later years offer business, home and marital stability if you have paid your debts, unstintingly acknowledged responsibilities and weren't catty.

• OTHER JANUARY 31 BIRTHDAYS

Tallulah Bankhead	1903
Eddie Cantor	1892
Joanne Drew	1923
James Franciscus	1934
Zane Grey	1875
Mario Lanza	1921
Norman Mailer	1923
Garry Moore	1915
Anna Pavlova	1882
Suzanne Pleshette	1937
Jackie Robinson	1919
Franz Shubert	1797
Jean Simmons	1929

FEBRUARY **· 1 ·** Humility, modesty and dignity are your calling cards as you enter life sensing that knowledge is power. People and large corporations are the keys to overcoming the sensitivities you acquired as part of a matriarchy. In youth older women help if you want a good education or subsidize your artistic ambitions. You must make an effort to be progressive or your duties will envelop your elevated standards and you will compromise yourself into a marriage of convenience. You may marry more than once.

Mid-life you benefit from friendships with strong males. You are more comfortable with individualistic men and become part of a group of loners. Each of these pioneers leaves a regal heritage that stems from and communicates his response to the principles of brotherly love. Each is a king, and you travel among your peers after age twenty-eight.

Money is not your master. You attract security from birth, and although influential contacts, gifts and honors come your way, there is heartache from illness, loss of a loved one or lack of opportunity to be a free spirit. After your forties a reliable, devoted love becomes your counselor and friend. Stress must be avoided after age fifty and usually is relieved by travel and the joy of teaching or inspiring subordinates or associates.

Take charge of your options. Late years are delicious if you make the right choices. Establish an artistic or scientific channeling before age thirty. When personal identity is not clearly defined before mid-life, you will not receive your rightful rewards of friendship, experience and love. Valet or lord of the manor? Listen for a different drummer and make your own music.

• OTHER FEBRUARY 1 BIRTHDAYS

John Canaday	1907
Don Everly	1937
John Ford	1895
Clark Gable	1901
Victor Herbert	1859
Hildegarde	1906
S. J. Perelman	1904
Jessica Savitch	1948

FEBRUARY Time is friendly when you're willing to alter your traditional approach. You learn that the expedient deci-
· 2 · sion is not necessarily the best for emotional serenity.
Childhood demands wisdom, maturity and compas-
sion. Financial security comes only through your willingness to form
intimate relationships, actively change and enlarge your scope.

The secretiveness and loneliness you feel as a child ease away
mid-life. The ambitious changes you made in your twenties pay off
when you meet a philosophical, polished, noble kindred spirit. Partnerships or alliances are continually offered. Until a career choice
is made, you take any job to get by or seek a marriage for convenience. Either course brings on martyrdom.

During your productive years—age twenty-eight to fifty-five—
you are best suited to using your investigative natural instincts. Your
philosophy, musical talents and sensitive concern for human nature
should be structured. Business and home vie for first place mid-life,
and you find that the petty attitudes of others and your own en-
viousness cause stress.

If it seems that sacrifices are constantly delaying your realizing
your ambitions, use your natural ability to be the intermediary between opposing opinions to attract recognition. You are less apt to
feel emotionally insecure or deprived when you are making a contribution. You invite celebrity before you're age thirty-six.

Late years demand that you be honest with yourself and more
straightforward. You will attract money, security and opportunities
for travel as logic prevails and unmellowed, emotional, secretive
judgments decline. Let go and you'll enjoy.

• OTHER FEBRUARY 2 BIRTHDAYS

Francis Bacon	1561
Shelley Berman	1926
James Dickey	1923
Farrah Fawcett	1947
Anne Fogarty	1919
Eddy Foy	1905
Stan Getz	1927
Gale Gordon	1906
Jascha Heifetz	1901
James Joyce	1882
Fritz Kreisler	1875
Ayn Rand	1905
Alphonse Rothschild	1827
Tom Smothers	1937
Elaine Stritch	1928

FEBRUARY
· **3** ·

Express yourself, be a star and let the ups and downs of youth pass into the realm of valuable experiences. Childhood uncertainties teach you to do your homework and place importance on the technical aspects of your untraditional ideas. Charm, talent and imagination need an outlet, and you race toward sensual experimentations for companionship and stimulation.

Youth is a hunt-and-peck, taste-and-move-on, bittersweet training ground for your inability to know when to change direction and when to hang in for stability. You need freedom.

You resent being told how and what to do, but you ask for frustration in your twenties when you attach yourself to an older man or an assertive woman. Mid-life offers a variety of affluent associations; you are able to let go of a creatively restricting relationship. Curiosity and an eagerness to learn bring you into a monied crowd, and your restlessness should be satisfied. If you concentrate, consistently work and only change mental stimulations, your forties are made secure by the support of friendly, imaginative, attractive associates.

Friends help you do the detail work and financial planning. Don't flit like a butterfly from one interesting idea or person to another. Use your ability to sense public interest for profit. Conservative types will consider you strange. Be aware of your vulnerability where your individualism is concerned. Position yourself in a career related to communications and let social contacts work for you.

Late years are tamer. You maintain your equilibrium, status and sparkle to hear your applause to the final curtain.

• OTHER FEBRUARY 3 BIRTHDAYS

Joey Bishop	1918
Peggy Ann Garner	1932
Horace Greeley	1811
Felix Mendelssohn	1809
Mabel Mercer	1900
James Michener	1907
Bibi Osterwald	1920
Norman Rockwell	1894
Gertrude Stein	1874
Fran Tarkenton	1940

FEBRUARY

·4·

Off you go into the wild blue yonder to take the challenges of responsibility. Hard work and the burdens of intimate relationships are offset by practical rewards. You want to reach the heights but must wait until mid-life to individualize. Family demands require interactions that put you in positions of trust that cannot be declined. Education may have to wait, but is a must. Public service, theater and government tempt you.

Talents find a structure mid-life and your childhood longing for tenderness finds an outlet. How you love to give and want to see the fruits of your generosity . . . but your sympathy always seems to cost money. You make it when you travel for profit. People are drawn to your comforting counsel and you discover that you are a natural healer, teacher and showman.

Sensitivity may be your downfall. All the world's a stage but you require top billing to a fault. Accept the times when you can't pick up the check. Hiding out until you're in the chips again activates your youthful programming to be self-depreciating. You tend to be self-conscious or puffed with pride. Your need for association with the P. T. Barnums of the world makes you appear to be a snob when you can't afford the ballyhoo. Money is an up-and-down affair that leads you to become less generous and more self-protective as you grow older.

Late years see you courting disappointment in marriage and requiring less intimacy. A dynamic woman helps you stretch skills, build real estate investments and organize objectives. Aim for prestige, but don't blame superstition for your success or failure. You are born with wisdom; share the wealth.

• OTHER FEBRUARY 4 BIRTHDAYS

Conrad Bain	1923
Alice Cooper	1948
Betty Friedan	1921
Eddie Foy, Jr.	1905
Charles A. Lindbergh	1902
Ida Lupino	1918

FEBRUARY

· 5 ·

The question is not whether you are a success, but whether you really understand how severely childhood expectations have programmed you to expect perfection. Your most productive happenings come as surprises and have no point of reference in your modest youth. Too much satisfaction leads you to failure. Too extreme a focus upon superficial values dulls social acceptance. Too many irons in the fire scatter your productivity.

You're on the defensive before you are attacked and look up to intellectual mentors. You are aloof from displays of emotion and deeply moved to love. Childhood offered a second-class citizenship, while mid-life provides the grit for learning from experience. You could, with a quality, not quantity, value system, shine in the world of finance, charity and the law.

You need a specialty. Money finds you when you speak with authority. The limelight may not attract you, but a need to have a cultured, gentle and beautiful life-style provides the motivation for your ambitions. You're either an extreme introvert or a natural ham. Communications extremes keep you fashionably up to date or sneering at jet-set antics. You benefit from a kinship with the water, and travel attracts solid friendships and social contacts. Mid-life finds you a diplomatic loner with a touch of class and a talent for promotions or politics. Your greatest strengths are your intuition and faith.

Late years find you spiritual, comfortable and investigative. You've got a personal credo, influence over others and attract notables. Love, sex and money will never be problems if you avoid impracticality and living above your means.

• OTHER FEBRUARY 5 BIRTHDAYS

Hank Aaron	1934
Red Buttons	1919
John Carradine	1906
Belle Starr	1810
Roger Staubach	1942
Adlai Stevenson	1900

FEBRUARY

·6·

Neither a borrower nor a lender be . . . you lean toward get-rich-quick schemes or care little for tangible assets. Fortunately, optimistic, imaginative, colorful people get you off to a good start. If you ignore your inclination to point a finger at their easygoing attitudes, you maintain helpful social relationships into mid-life. They are your key to a successful foundation. After age twenty-eight you become too serious for your own good.

Family and community concerns are never far from your mind. Money and a strain for status symbols make you a workaholic manager. You are a giver and suffer from a lack of appreciation. Freedom to explore the world is denied you, but a loving household and opulent life-style more than make up for staying close to home. Music, art and education are attractive to you. Peace is your heart's desire as you enter late years and you aim for cultural attainments. You may finally stop trying to change the world to suit your enthusiasms.

Avoid losing your individuality to the domination of a strong female after age thirty-six. Your sixth sense warns of a loss of personal ethics. Your concern for justice is tested. Establish your politics and hang in. You have a responsibility to adjust your desires for the general good. Don't bend the rules in the name of sweet charity. Be decisive, not dictatorial. Your mental powers tune up as you open emotionally.

Later years will be disappointing if you have lacked initiative in youth. However, with love as motivation, your stubborn determination will work to your advantage at any age.

• OTHER FEBRUARY 6 BIRTHDAYS

Eva Braun	1912
Tom Brokaw	1940
Aaron Burr	1756
Natalie Cole	1950
Mamie Van Doren	1933
Fabian	1943
Mike Farrell	1942
Louis Nizer	1902
Ronald Wilson Reagan	1911
Babe Ruth	1895
Rip Torn	1931
François Truffaut	1932

FEBRUARY

·7·

Have one for your baby, one more for the road and cool your restless search for perfection. Music, travel and challenges are the keys to your introvert/extrovert nature. Your youth takes you far from the nesting space to a broader cultural horizon. Surprises titillate and frighten you. By the time you reach the age of twenty-nine, your drive for self-improvement, dissatisfaction with your surroundings and impulsivity have caused high nervous tension for you and your family. A cheatin' love affair puts you on the road again.

Childhood male relationships demand some sacrifices from you and you're a "good kid"—willing to take a backseat or to back away from educational aspirations. A lack of money or understanding from the family causes you to become disillusioned. You look for love, romance and sensual experiences in the wrong places and with the wrong people. Youth is emotionally untraditional. Love affairs are compulsive and problematic.

Mid-life offers help from a foreign-born male who has a better financial background or innate business sense than you do. You find a noble, aristocratic, authorative friend with the talent to heal or counsel. A partnership, with you as a support system, develops. Tact, diplomacy and careful investigation improve your status. Take the time to concentrate on one interest and you attract notable achievers, financial security and community respect before you're age fifty-four.

Later years offer the educational opportunities that you wanted in youth. Your major lifetime project has been to fight frustration. Fulfillment comes through your love of progress.

• OTHER FEBRUARY 7 BIRTHDAYS

Eubie Blake	1883
Eddie Bracken	1920
Keefe Brasselle	1923
Buster Crabbe	1908
John Deene	1804
Charles Dickens	1812
Sinclair Lewis	1885

FEBRUARY **·8·** Bring body, mind and spirit together and you'll have the stamina to take on all comers. Business and the arts have purpose for your intuitive ESP. If you are unsuccessful, blame it on your inability to take a direct course of action at the prompting of the family. Idle hands are not for you. Assume your responsibilities, work and you will prosper. Your projects for self-improvement are based upon your intolerance of people who do not live up to your personal standards and the emotional upheavals that result from your disappointments.

Childhood provides strong family and community ties. You have teachers. Don't cling to kitchen table philosophies; aim to expand social contacts. Mid-life prospects dip back to early relationships for support and status. Look at the depth of character in your personal relationships; surface judgments sour and slow your advancement if you are shallow. The financial security and influential life-style you build enable you to donate to worthy causes and be counted as an acknowledged humanitarian.

You want everyone to feel comforted and you take pleasure in receiving recognition. Childhood taught you to be independent, progressive and ambitious. Mid-life draws upon your leadership abilities, communications skills and tendencies to delegate authority. Large corporations value your personality and character; strive for executive positions. After age forty-six, career changes occur owing to the futuristic vision of an innovative woman from your past. Don't be too critical of yourself. You are appreciated and will travel in later years.

• OTHER FEBRUARY 8 BIRTHDAYS

Gary Coleman	1968
James Dean	1931
Dame Edith Evans	1888
Betty Field	1918
Ted Koppel	1940
Jack Lemmon	1925
Ray Middleton	1907
Henry Roth	1906
John Ruskin	1819
William Sherman	1820
Lana Turner	1920
Jules Verne	1828
King Vidor	1895

FEBRUARY

· 9 ·

Calm down and make up your mind. You feel secretive, sensitive and fear loneliness when the world is your oyster. Your fears of poverty are unfounded and create a heavy emotional burden. Let go of the disillusionments of childhood. Your judgment and erroneous ideas tripped you up. People nurture your cultural growth mid-life but the subtle tones of skepticism that you reveal do not encourage cooperation when you need money in youth. Your best bet is to adapt yourself to the power of positive thinking and establishing practical self-control.

Your mind governs your health, financial judgments and ambitions. When impulsivity overrules mental analysis mid-life, it's due to a too personal attitude that is based upon romantic notions. Childhood cannot offer opportunity to meet the expansive drives you have to pursue noble purposes. After age thirty-six, a partnership with a vigorous woman—not just any woman—will enable you to be self-expressive and to prosper.

Speculations, carelessness and irresponsibility are the seeds of escapist tendencies that may trip you up. Be fair to fellow workers or employees. You get caught when you cheat. When you are steadfast and dedicated, your self-confidence attracts the authority figures, notables and perfectionists who keep you away from ill-considered mundane labors. Cultural growth comes with age, and you will travel far from your roots mid-life. People need you, and you respond to their emotions.

Later life offers opportunity for introspection. You are at your best staying close to home, curbing your temper and contributing your unique talents in a communications profession.

• OTHER FEBRUARY 9 BIRTHDAYS

Heather Angel	1909
Ronald Colman	1891
Mia Farrow	1945
Kathryn Grayson	1923
William Henry Harrison	1773
Carole King	1941
Carmen Miranda	1909
Roger Mudd	1928
Thomas Paine	1737
Dean Rusk	1909
Ernest Tubb	1914
Bill Veeck	1914
Peggy Wood	1892

FEBRUARY

·10·

Friends will get you everywhere. Expect that everyone from school chums to the extraordinary people you attract while traveling late in life will crop up with jobs, gifts and the answers to your prayers. Dare to be different. You can be adaptable, modest and entertaining without being bored or becoming dull. Be your own boss and resist the temptation to follow the leader.

You need encouragement to individualize as a youngster but should charge ahead independently mid-life. Hobbies are important for your emotional stability. In your desire to keep the peace you often sacrifice inventiveness to collecting toys or game playing. A childhood male influence alternately stifles your ambitions or goads you to make inappropriate changes. Women are more sympathetic, encouraging and optimistic. You receive money and tenderness from a gentle female when you take steps to improve yourself mid-life.

You are too impatient. Wait for a reply to your question before deciding that the answer is no. You are too critical of yourself, have too much pride and often think you are losing face when, in fact, you are just allowing people to receive the new thought that you present. Between the ages of twenty-eight and fifty-six, you must relax or the opportunity for domination in your field may slip away.

The opportunities to develop artistic talents, a sense of humor and your knack with words bring you in contact with the public. Financial progress is based upon satisfying your need to lead and direct after maturity. Late years find you catching up on a variety of interests and having influence over others.

• OTHER FEBRUARY 10 BIRTHDAYS

Larry Adler	1914
Dame Judith Anderson	1898
Jimmy Durante	1893
Roberta Flack	1939
Joyce Grenfell	1910
Lon Chaney, Jr.	1906
Charles Lamb	1775
Leontyne Price	1927
Mark Spitz	1950
Robert Wagner	1930

FEBRUARY

· 11 ·

You're a late bloomer but you won't be disappointed or submerge your personality late in life. Childhood is lonely. You have wisdom beyond your years and the scars to show for the creative limitations exacted through your conventional environment. Through emotional upheaval, you learn to feel for others, and this special sensitivity seeds your ability to leave a lasting image. Don't pity yourself for an unsettled youth; take your work-hard approach to serve a humanitarian cause. Rewards are spiritual, and until your early fifties, you only tap your potential.

Expect to marry for love, make unselfish contributions to children and take a mature attitude to serving family, community and the golden age group. Traditions, common sense and a down-to-earth practicality have been ingrained in you from youth. Apply yourself; use tact and detail-consciousness and avoid petty reactions to imagined disloyalties. You tend to be overly generous and then show resentment when your good nature is assumed.

Your high-strung nervousness is the result of your dramatic imagination and you always seem to be making decisions. Allow for the earthiness of most humans, and although you feel a bit above the crowd, don't let tendencies to be an elitist place your ambitions on too high a pedestal. Expectations may be illusory.

Your destiny requires that you fight mercenary ideas and understand that you attract what you need through intuition, not intellect. Late years attract the unconventional and you finally take a "never say die" approach and discover yourself.

• OTHER FEBRUARY 11 BIRTHDAYS

Lloyd Bentsen	1921
Thomas Alva Edison	1847
King Farouk of Egypt	1920
Eva Gabor	1925
Conrad Janis	1928
Virginia Johnson	1925
Tina Louise	1934
Joseph Mankiewicz	1909
Mary Quant	1934
Burt Reynolds	1936
Kim Stanley	1925

FEBRUARY

· **12** ·

Your unorthodox approach, gift of gab and wisdom in youth project you to surround yourself with beauty. Love may come in second to the practical profits you attract with an impressive presence. Childhood established a pattern for your ambition to live a comfortable life, and friends get you everywhere you want to go.

A strong male influence in childhood sets the stage for your leadership abilities. You were a good child who broke out to establish independence and find frustration when surrounded by aggressive, assertive, changeable types of people. Creative people need you and you need an outlet for your self-expression; be careful not to let public opinion dull your artistic talents. Remember that there is one thing worse than being talked about, and that is not being noticed at all.

Mid-life finds you in a communications field. People are your source and trigger your sense of drama; your charm and wit should carry weight in business. You are an extremist. Having learned from experience—finding the flames of love often too hot to handle—you choose to rise above mundane values. You attract affluent young associates who tout your generosity to spite your regal attitude. You'll never get old in spirit or let the grass grow under your feet if you keep up your concentration. Too much diversification or speculation may be your downfall. Take a firm grasp on education or follow self-improvement techniques before age thirty-six to reap a harvest of travel and challenging activity after fifty.

Later years confirm your early suspicions that boredom was the greatest threat to your health, prestige and security.

• OTHER FEBRUARY 12 BIRTHDAYS

Joe Don Baker	1936
Judy Blume	1938
Omar Bradley	1893
Charles Darwin	1809
Joe Garagiola	1926
Lorne Greene	1915
Nell Gwyn	1560
John L. Lewis	1880
Abraham Lincoln	1809
Alice Roosevelt Longworth	1884
Ted Mack	1904
Forrest Tucker	1919
Franco Zeffirelli	1923

FEBRUARY If you see your obligations with a dash of resentment,
your recipe for life will lack spice. Family and com-
· 13 · munity are the basic ingredients that make you stew.
Add a dollop of patience, sympathy and tenderness,
and your restlessness won't cause you to boil over. You may need
to simmer for a while to adjust to the peppery pinches and to set
the table before you serve a well-balanced meal. If you have difficulty
deciding what you are prepared to spend or decline to seize the
options offered in a proven cookbook, life will be filled with pot-
luck dinners.

Childhood and youth do not offer serenity. You want the security
offered by the family but chance losing future affluence through a
lack of self-esteem. Taking a supportive position or listening to the
advice of concerned, wise and experienced teachers both attracts
and repels you. Intimate relationships in love or business find you
emotionally responsive when you should be objective and using
practical judgment when sentiment should be your guide.

Time is wasted on chronic problems, indecisiveness and a lack
of trust until a worldly wise, efficient, prominent woman becomes
your tutor. Later years reap financial rewards, but mid-life finds you
working hard for everything you want or need. A real estate investment is lucky, and if you take a speculative attitude for a fast
transfer, you can upgrade your social status.

Late years provide a supermarket stocked with love, a chance to
satisfy gourmet tastes. Travel the shelves, forget yourself and feed
the hungry that come to your table. Bargain ingredients have never
worked for you. Expect to pay manufacturer's list prices and enjoy.

• OTHER FEBRUARY 13 BIRTHDAYS

Patty Berg	1918
Stockard Channing	1944
Eileen Farrell	1920
Tennessee Ernie Ford	1919
Carol Lynley	1942
Kim Novak	1933
George Segal	1936
Bess Truman	1885

FEBRUARY

· 14 ·

Cupid's arrows are tipped with platinum and your regal tastes enjoy their perfection. Opportunity knocks and youth carefully prepares you to expect the best and opens the door to a whirlwind mid-life. Theater, promotional schemes and mysticism are the gems that decorate the sheath that covers a critical longbow that you carry to your late years. It is your expertise, developed in youth, that will unleash your most precious missiles.

Speak up to attract your targets. Hiding talents, beauty and cleverness under a bush conceals you from marksmen. Stay still long enough to attract the money and intellect you need to decorate your life-style. Be prepared to fall in love—probably marry young—but without establishing a sound friendship in intimacy, you court disillusionment.

Trust is a must for your security. Silent withdrawal and taking a tactful stance work for youthful encounters in business and love. Your secretiveness breeds a reserve in you, and only your innate charm attracts the wise female who sets you to making changes. True love may come late and after a try or two.

You are an entrepreneur and make your own luck. Friends are powerful forces in your financial ambitions. However, the cooperation that you receive is earned by your uncanny awareness of how and when to focus upon your ESP.

You work well with the opposite sex. Don't go on overkill talking, letting the cat out of the bag. In later years you check your restlessness with a variety of hobbies and fashionable enthusiasms. Shoot straight from the heart and look expensive. You'll grow old secured by good taste and well-traveled wisdom.

• OTHER FEBRUARY 14 BIRTHDAYS

Mel Allen	1913
Jack Benny	1894
Carl Bernstein	1944
Hugh Downs	1921
Florence Henderson	1934
Jimmy Hoffa	1913
James Pike	1913
Thelma Ritter	1905
Paul Tsongas	1941

FEBRUARY

· 15 ·

There is more to life than material treasures. As you grow from training in youth that places ambition above love, circumstances teach you to expect help from intimates when you are most needy. Family pride is a matter of concern throughout your life, and you stand to gain through inheritance of money, community respect or loving protection due to your background.

You are generous and enjoy attracting attention for humanitarian gestures and opulence in your life-style. You can be tenacious— dedicated to work, practicality and orderliness—or, under emotional stress, run from the creatively self-limiting guidelines that you have imposed upon yourself.

Mid-life you are too serious, self-examining and enmeshed in self-imposed responsibilities or the burdens placed upon your energetic shoulders. You ask for advice but find yourself a doubter and play the devil's advocate to defeat your own purposes. You attract noteworthy people, and the limelight shines on your creative talent for teaching and calculating your moves based upon your gift for observing mistakes made by others.

You fail to penetrate the surface too often and create a false set of values until a woman, with practical perceptions and expensive tastes, insists that you learn to laugh at your own and the idiosyncrasies of others. Childhood kept you under wraps. Later years are less enclosing and bring the bargains you enjoy getting, the security you need and the liabilities of leadership.

Your community follows your example while inwardly you question yourself. You finally accept life's imperfect truths.

• OTHER FEBRUARY 15 BIRTHDAYS

Susan B. Anthony	1820
Harold Arlen	1905
John Barrymore	1882
Claire Bloom	1931
Harvey Korman	1927
Kevin McCarthy	1914
Cyrus McCormick	1809
Cesar Romero	1907
James Schlesinger	1929
Leonard Woodcock	1911

FEBRUARY

· 16 ·

Life is one growth experience after another. Your ideas, loves and hopes for perfection undergo changes until you build faith in yourself. In childhood you learn only from experimentation. In mid-life you alter your ambitions when you learn to stop taking emotional and financial gambles. In later life you learn not to fear loneliness and poverty to the point of sacrificing your need for privacy, perfection and the truth as you see it.

Childhood sets the stage for coping with surprising people and events. However, you find it difficult to learn from experience because you refuse to look back. Youth exposes you to a broader scope, and you grow far from your birthright. You learn to let go of the dominating influences that hampered your intellect, but you cannot concentrate on yourself. Legal problems in love and business arise because you are inclined to overestimate yourself or the experts you seek out. Slow down and question your own motives and those of your associates. You're self-critical, a good professional critic, but you get hooked on the debating game and fail to practically apply your own observations.

The payoff is too important to you. Take the time to dig into intuitive misgivings to avoid paying the piper. You look for influential supporters and strive to keep a "godfather" in your back pocket. Money, reputation and loves require skillful handling or you fall from your pedestal repeatedly. Later years will be successful but you cannot withdraw from society, travel far from home or stop fighting for the rights of the underdog.

• OTHER FEBRUARY 16 BIRTHDAYS

PATTY ANDREWS	1920
BRIAN BEDFORD	1935
EDGAR BERGEN	1903
SONNY BONO	1940
KATHARINE CORNELL	1898
GEORGE F. KENNAN	1904
CHRISTOPHER MARLOWE	1564
CHESTER MORRIS	1901

FEBRUARY
· 17 ·

Finding the solution to practical problems is second nature and financial success, influential friends and a first-class ticket to life are yours when you aim high. Childhood taught you humility, diplomacy and social responsibility. Mid-life finds opportunity for your originality, executive ability and professionalism. Later years are peaceful. The slow-down finds an outlet for philanthropic pursuits, hobbies and new uses for your love of material accomplishment.

Childhood sets the stage for coping with surprising people and events. However, you find it difficult to learn from experience because you refuse to look back. Youth exposes you to a broader scope, and you grow far from your birthright. You learn to let go of the dominating influences that hampered your intellect, but you cannot concentrate on yourself. Legal problems in love and business arise because you are inclined to overestimate yourself or the experts you seek out. Slow down and question your own motives and those of your associates. You're self-critical, a good professional critic, but you get hooked on the debating game and fail to practically apply your own observations.

Dig deeply to find your feelings. Surface accomplishments come easily because your are a mental person, and the need for practical purpose in your life seems obvious to you and to others. You have stamina and overcome pressures, but you fall short when it comes to finding relaxing diversions. Be still, don't grab the reins and take charge when there is nothing to challenge you for the moment. Your need for outward shows of approval causes a lack of sensitivity: no need to bully; aim to mellow as you ripen. You have nobility.

• OTHER FEBRUARY 17 BIRTHDAYS

Marian Anderson	1902
Red Barber	1908
Alan Bates	1934
Jim Brown	1936
Hal Holbrook	1925
Arthur Kennedy	1914
Chaim Potok	1929
Margaret Truman	1924
Montgomery Ward	1843

FEBRUARY

· 18 ·

After age thirty-five you attract the expansive opportunities you desire as a youngster. During mid-life you have freedom to travel, to investigate other cultures and to upgrade your talent for social service. You want to be paid for your good works. Youth teaches you to keep secrets, collect input and avoid getting into legal battles. Lawyers are your nemesis. Expect to make sacrifices before you get the message.

Academic, spiritual or technical training is too important or lacks priority in youth. Until you reach your thirties you feel a lack of self-confidence, owing to a secret longing relating to a frustrating childhood experience. A menial job, lost love or incautious risk-taking delay your material progress. Impulsive gestures, accidents or misplaced confidence in loved ones require time and energy until you're nearly fifty. Once a concentrated effort is made to improve the lot in life for others, a change takes place. Focus turns to balancing emotional stress and financial ambitions.

Dreams provide the answer to self-analysis when all else fails. You never rest and are solving your own and the problems that pass through the swinging doors of your mind constantly. A waterside retreat, a collecting hobby and a sound health regimen are important to alleviating heartache in late years.

Home, as a haven, proves disappointing. Quality and perfection demand money. Without financial freedom, you attempt to escape your reality. When you have money your love life is unsteady, and when you're broke you find love. Preacher, take your own advice. Don't contemplate your navel; work to prosper.

• OTHER FEBRUARY 18 BIRTHDAYS

Helen Gurley Brown	1922
Dane Clark	1915
Bill Cullen	1920
George Kennedy	1925
Adolph Menjou	1890
Jack Palance	1920
Wallace Stegner	1909
John Warner	1927
Billy de Wolfe	1907

FEBRUARY
· 19 ·

First you accommodate, then you find your voice and take the lead. Frustrations and childish angers linger on until you are willing to show your true colors. Childhood taught you to follow the leader, but how will you hold your own in the creative environment of your mid-life, if you are not willing to have the courage of your convictions?

Childhood influences are domineering, strongly principled and selfish. Habits are drummed into your character. It's easier to agree than to face an argument. You rarely challenge authority—tell the truth—until you realize that everyone around you insists upon respect for her or his unique desires. Your values will undergo a major change mid-life, and in late years you will recall the diplomacy, tact and modesty developed in youth. Success in your chosen field depends upon the ability you have to balance inventiveness and to charm opposing idealists.

Cooperative, sensitive friends—particularly of the opposite gender—bring your self-expression, artistic talents and dramatic desire to be an innovator to your attention. Fear of failure is strong, and without a guarantee of financial security you may miss the boat. Watch out for envious co-workers or family members. Large corporations want people with your broad philosophy and sense of individuality. Strive to note your obligations to the group effort and give credit where credit is due. Overcoming obstacles is your forte; expect prominence.

A betrayal or personal sadness darkens later years, but a dedication to public service heals your wounds. You're fit, intuitive and mentally agile. Plan for an active retirement.

• OTHER FEBRUARY 19 BIRTHDAYS

Louis Calhern	1895
John Frankenheimer	1930
Sir Cedric Hardwicke	1893
Stan Kenton	1912
Lee Marvin	1924
Merle Oberon	1911
George Rose	1920

FEBRUARY

·20·

You may have a reputation for patience because you are too lazy, unrealistic or caught up in fulfilling a lover's dreams to begin anything. You have rhythm, musical talent and the childhood discipline to plan, practice and fashion a notable life-style. Traditional guidelines and a not-too-extraordinary beginning change as you realize your power as an energy force in group, civic or political administration. Be realistic and your financial picture will be clear.

Childhood found you too wise for your peers and too young to form intimate relationships with grown-ups. Lonely? Precocious? Frustrated? You need not feel unable to relate to others' emotional problems if you follow your inborn philosophy. Recognition is found through pitching in, allowing yourself to act upon your intuitive problem-solving techniques and to help when you're needed without reliving past disappointments. Don't stand aloof from your own emotional reactions or those that surround you. At your best you are an example for others; at your worst, you are a formidable enemy.

Temper your temper. You'll never get anything without working cooperatively. Use your down-to-earth background mid-life to find a direction and hang in. Family depends upon you, and the obligations are real. Emotional stress reacts on your body, mind and talents. Memories of a strong mother, rigid methods and fluctuating finances in youth bring on difficult-to-blueprint emotional points of reference. You have a fabulous imagination; stimulate your creative juices. If you let go of the past, late years bring travel, success and the joy of loving.

• OTHER FEBRUARY 20 BIRTHDAYS

Robert Altman	1925
Amanda Blake	1931
John Daly	1914
Sandy Duncan	1946
Jennifer O'Neill	1949
Sidney Poitier	1924
Buffy Ste. Marie	1941
Nancy Wilson	1937

FEBRUARY

·21·

If a career choice is difficult, seek out professional testing. Scattering interests mid-life is the result of emulating a childhood friend who took responsibility too seriously. If you follow your penchant for beauty, artistry and fashion, life may be child's play, based upon your vow not be chained to obligations. However, you may never grow up.

After age thirty life can be a bowl of cherries, but not without spending effort to get material rewards. Later life brings inheritance or security, accompanied by uncomfortable details to clean up. All conclusions in youth are drawn from unsettling experiences. You are well prepared to take on responsibilities in mid-life because you stuck your fingers in the fire as a youth. You know how blistering restlessness can be. Guard against unleashing resentment of family responsibility. You'll pass up opportunities or cause delays by emotionalizing.

Assertive males challenge your individuality, and as a maturing adult, you cannot expect to have control over everyone or every aspect of life. You must get work projects going early. Promises, contracts and handshake agreements require detailed examination. Fear of failure hinders your ambitions, activities and concentration into your forties—a misguided youth is no excuse for checking off your leadership abilities. Take a position where independence combines with artistic or sympathetic service. A career in real estate sales uses your abilities to be personable, glib and clever. Earth products are lucky for you.

Self-delusion is your personality extreme. In later years consistency attracts improved finances, travel and benefactors.

• OTHER FEBRUARY 21 BIRTHDAYS

Erma Bombeck	1927
Hubert Givenchy	1927
Sam Peckinpah	1925
Ann Sheridan	1915
Nina Simone	1933

FEBRUARY **·22·** Take hold of your own destiny. The end justifies the means. You have the opportunity to build a better mousetrap, manufacture it, profit and help others through practical, down-to-earth, constructive thinking. Your ability to command attention when you expound your theories and your talent for getting recognition from notables attracts leaners. So what? You have *chutzpah*, determination and guts. You work for tangible results.

The ability to touch greatness, leave a lasting mark and intuitively know how to correct your own and others' mistakes is possible in your lifetime. Men make unreasonable demands, jealousy prevails and you are constantly forced to rebuild assets. Marriage may drain or disappoint you due to the sacrifices it entails. You are repeatedly enticed, by circumstances, to be accommodating, to "let your cat out of the bag" and "keep your irons in the fire." You labor for love.

Mother and the family are strong childhood influences and responsibilities. Beware of an inclination to be too self-concerned, sensitive and petty. You are protective, collecting and expansive. The strong set of personal ideals within you is too demanding and emotionally unsettling. Crafty professionals cause you to begin at square one after age thirty-six. A move results in security. You become secretive. To relieve pressures, you seek youthful companions.

Late-year travels are not rewarding. Your work pace slows, you befriend less worldly neighbors and work at hobbies. Your spirit is undaunted. The challenge to seek, speak and teach universal truths remains within you. Your means are justified.

- OTHER FEBRUARY 22 BIRTHDAYS

Robert Baden-Powell	1857
Luis Buñuel	1900
Frederic Chopin	1810
Edward M. Kennedy	1932
Sheldon Leonard	1907
John Mills	1908
Edna St. Vincent Millay	1892
George Washington	1732
Robert Young	1907

FEBRUARY **· 2 3 ·** Neither an introvert nor an extrovert be . . . mid-life finds you a swinger, changing locales, loves and liabilities. Women and siblings are both your nemesis and your strength in childhood. Youth finds you establishing an identity that was challenged in childhood and caused you to marry too young or to compromise your talents. Responsibilities tax your ego and you are restless.

Social contacts, clubs and self-improvements are twenties interests. Rarely does the opportunity for conventional education knock; however, you are clever, opportunistic and enthusiastic about everything. Experience is your teacher. You dislike being in anyone's debt and must not speculate. Money is always a project. Affluent and influential people solve your problems, or you stick to a job once you find an interesting position. Only misplaced love puts your finances in the red.

You are too talkative or too withdrawn and should be in authority to feel secure. Love is based upon establishing a meaningful friendship. When trust is misplaced, intimacy denied, or disloyalty experienced, you are a formidable enemy.

Mid-life exposures place you in a managerial situation with controls far from home. Be aware that compliments may be your downfall. You need praise, rarely get it and are often swayed by flattery. Travel and unknown experiences interest you. An enticing gamble is offered. If you take the bait, you'll have to be adaptable and learn how to change horses in midstream. Your life may become a swashbuckler's adventure.

Be philosophical, diplomatic and tactful. In late years you travel, and your patience is tested by practical problems.

• OTHER FEBRUARY 23 BIRTHDAYS

Peter Fonda	1940
George Frederic Handel	1685
Cesar Ritz	1850
William Shiver	1904

FEBRUARY
·24·

You want a showy library and influential prospects and are determined to have it all. You are quiet, and allow a dominating female to chart your course. Still waters run deep. You rarely let the right hand know what the left hand is touching. Your barometer for success points to tangibles. Love, to last, should provide a foundation for your ambitions. Romance flies out the window without possibilities for power. More than one marriage is likely if you allow sensuality to take over at age thirty-two.

If you are promiscuous, your energy is misdirected. Aim for a career in social service work, or take on family duties with the same enthusiasm that you give to outside interests. Your intellect lacks the challenge it needs. Consumer-product purchases or physical competitiveness will not relieve tensions.

Contracts, leases or legal agreements create problems if you are impulsive. If you are indecisive, you miss the boat. Wait. Mid-life finds you craving an opulent home, beauty and love. Work, plan and be patient. Beware of possessiveness, envy and greed. You are self-absorbed, hold on to petty slights and suffer from champagne tastes and a beer pocketbook. Your forties offer solutions to your acquisitive nature.

Late in life, expect to move, settle down and travel. You may be surprised to find that you do not want what you thought you wanted, when you get it. One discovers that life is fair when emotions are considered, expectations are conventional and ambitions realistic. Gambles in real estate, stocks or commodities will not bring the desired results. An ocean voyage provides a sixties love, and you learn how to be good to yourself.

• OTHER FEBRUARY 24 BIRTHDAYS

James Farentino	1938
Wilhelm Grimm	1786
Winslow Homer	1836
Marjorie Main	1890
Renata Scotto	1934
Abe Vigoda	1921

FEBRUARY **·25·** Childhood is difficult, mid-life nonroutine and late years provide mental investigations, security and time for introspection. Youth provides opportunities for job and educational ambitions. Creative, often testy executive types who have made a mark show you the way to expand culturally. Impatience, impulsivity and restlessness get you into trouble. You spend your life reflecting upon the years of personal instability and making decisions based upon early experiences.

Marry young—or a younger person. After age thirty-six your need for privacy, demands of professionalism and urge to uproot make settling down domestically difficult. You observe, analyze and detail to arrive at conclusions. Partnerships make you frivolous and careless. Mid-life exposes you to major moneymaking opportunities, industries and dynamic people. You gain expertise from a male mentor who is employed in communications.

Dedication and perseverance aid your abilities. You realize your ambitions. Tap your talents for photography, computer technology and electronics. A successful career is based upon your willingness to assist others. Do not just assume the expert's role. Your attraction to polished, skillful, empathetic people in youth pays off mid-life. If your spiritual bent takes over, too much introspection and not enough action drains your self-assurance. Squelch your escapist tendencies and moodiness.

Later years should inspire a quest for knowledge. Home provides a nurturing space. You are tempted to get too comfortable. Let your legalistic mind spark new interests. You have cultivated tastes, wisdom and experience. Be charitable.

• OTHER FEBRUARY 25 BIRTHDAYS

Jim Backus	1913
Enrico Caruso	1873
Tom Courtenay	1937
John Foster Dulles	1888
Millicent Fenwick	1910
Galileo Galilei	1564
George Harrison	1943
Pierre Auguste Renoir	1841
Bobby Riggs	1918
Zeppo Marx	1901

FEBRUARY
·**26**·

Family uncertainties do not delay your success if you are willing to work. If anything, your strong personal ideals, morals and domestic standards attract the limelight. Just finish the things that you begin. Marry young or take a chance on never taking the plunge—or waiting until you find late-in-life companionship. Peace in domestic or job environment is a top priority. Humor, beauty and artistic talents must grace your life. You are ambitious, sensitive and expressive. Youth places you two steps ahead of your peers and stretching for success.

You are never sure where you stand because you expect everyone to uphold you. Most relationships cannot deal with your criticism, melodramatic jealousy or contrariness. You either change with the wind or get think-stuck. It is fortunate that you are a wise counselor and have a gift for healing minds and bodies. Your sense of responsibility, however, makes you too much a volunteer or too inclined to mind your own business. Single or married, you must have the comfort of your own home.

Business and commercial activity are foremost in mid-life. You attract partnerships. However, you should not take advice on investments. If anyone can get swindled, you can. Spend for your self-improvement, update business procedures or add promotions. Provide yourself with the best tools of your trade. Be tolerant of less efficient employees or co-workers. You are gifted with the ability to bring body, mind and spirit together to participate in sports and commerce and to achieve tangible results.

Watch your pennies. After age fifty-five companionship, travel and leisure are assured if you have saved your money.

• OTHER FEBRUARY 26 BIRTHDAYS

Robert Alda	1914
Madeleine Carroll	1906
Johnny Cash	1932
Fats Domino	1928
Jackie Gleason	1916
Betty Hutton	1921
Margaret Leighton	1922
Tony Randall	1924
Robert Taft, Jr.	1917

FEBRUARY **·27·** Impractical or unrealistic demands begin early. Ambitious elders may be a problem in childhood, and you sense that you are intended to be or do something special. You are born with the concern that you're not good enough without the perfections of an aristocratic base. Youth finds you focused upon the power of affluence, overpowered by mother or grandparents and empowered with the gifts of originality, magnetism and cultural expansion.

If you want to be happy, don't believe in miracles. Aspire to be healthy, wealthy and wise—you can have it all. Wisdom and vision are your tools. Positive expectancy guides your hand. The joy of a lifetime graced with polish and skill of performance begins in childhood and the example that you set is the well from which others dip. You play the devil's advocate too often with emotional overtones. Emotional upsets delay your intellectual growth; your ability to learn is not tested by everyone in authority.

Marriage is difficult. You want to roam free to escalate enlightenment, have a fertile companionship and home life. The responsibilities connected with your desires are burdensome and you are taxed with caring for elders, friends or a sickly spouse.

Mid-life friends come to your aid if you avoid the moodiness and melancholy associated with your fears of poverty, loneliness and not being as good as the next guy. Concentrate, work and build an impressive expertise. Be tolerant, empathetic and charitable. After a few starts and stops you will develop your ideas, receive rewards and build for security later in life.

After age forty-five expect to live a cosmopolitan life-style.

• OTHER FEBRUARY 27 BIRTHDAYS

Joan Bennett	1910
James T. Farrell	1904
Guy Mitchell	1927
Irwin Shaw	1913
Elizabeth Taylor	1932
Franchot Tone	1905
Peter De Vries	1910
Joanne Woodward	1930

FEBRUARY

·28·

Set your goals, don't speculate or trust to others and prepare to use your head to fight city hall. Your expectations are not unrealistic. If you maintain self-confidence, others will hang in as you change direction. You have a workaholic influence in childhood that tests your mettle and remains a treasure for reflection throughout life. As a youngster, you expect instant gratification, and as a youth, you remain impatient for immediate success.

Assertive males set an independent example. The challenge to your creative mind spurs you to activity early, and you look for approval in all directions. Everyone is not going to love you, particularly if you tread on their aspirations.

In your thirties duty to another slows you down and your sense of loyalty is tested. Companionship is essential to your emotional growth, material power is an ego need and your inventive nature must have outlets. Until mid-life—the fifties—your ethics are in focus, legal matters should be avoided and laboring to provide a business service is the answer to your ambitions.

If you have been assertive, have avoided impulsive investments and have persisted, your late years are not dull. New directions are inviting, and globetrotting beckons. Your marketplace expands; social and business contacts are transformed and become vivifying. The restlessness in you is satisfied by the changeable people you meet. The undependable among them pass on, if you are selective. Your life is one of personal choice. Options are offered that will inspire leaders of the future.

• OTHER FEBRUARY 28 BIRTHDAYS

Milt Caniff	1907
John B. Connally	1917
Bob Marcucci	1930
Vincente Minnelli	1913
Zero Mostel	1915
Linus Pauling	1901
Bernadette Peters	1949
Tommy Tune	1939

FEBRUARY
· 29 ·

Decisions, decisions, decisions! Right from the beginning you are betwixt and between; anxious, vague and indecisive. The key is to maintain a willingness to seek the sun. Chronic stresses slow progress, frustrations are debilitating and early life demands a mature approach.

Family burdens are heavy for a sensitive tot. Help is offered. You are strongly affected by a wise person who unintentionally attracts your dependency. The habit of leaning upon independent men who set an example that you follow is formed in youth. The creative temperament is tuned to supporting or serving another's lead.

Your foresight, imagination and elitist touches are compelling. The business world is not your oyster but financial backers seek you out. The unique quality of your ideas and the intensity of your personal idealism create problems until you are able to take a less haughty attitude. You have a desire for quality, and details both fascinate and repel you. Your thirties are a testing time when contacts are made, errors identified and loyalties established.

Mid-life brings a focus to health in business interests, personal relationships and personal emotional reactions. Radio, photography, TV or computers are tools of electricity that hold promise of leaving your lasting image. Organizational work for the elderly set will reap financial rewards and recognition if you connect with your love of history.

Late years are less uncertain and you attract an appreciative following, applause and serenity. To the end you find down-to-earth realities distasteful. Aim for tolerance.

• OTHER FEBRUARY 29 BIRTHDAYS

Arthur Franz	1920
Pepper Martin	1904
James Mitchell	1920
Michele Morgan	1920
William Wellman	1899

MARCH **· 1 ·** Life begins with expressive, attractive, imaginative people and experiences, and you must show your independence. A too loving, authoritative or inconspicuous mother is a challenge to your self-esteem. Your mind is your strength, while your emotions strain your logic. A less personal attitude is a must for the success of your creative, financial and sensual aspirations.

Love of people, life and the limelight is the cause of ambivalence between marriage and career. You need attention. You want independence. You have the option to begin an artistic study that forms the foundation for a lifetime work or you can play with a variety of interests. An older man has a strong influence upon your decisions. The relationship ends in frustration.

Traditional schooling is not as rewarding as specialized training for you. Your environment is conventional, and orderly routine, proper planning and practical financial obligations are in focus until your thirties. Changes in childhood may have caused you to have too many love affairs and transitions. Concentration mid-life will attract influential friends who become supporters for your unorthodox and inconsistent ideas. You'll keep the money that you attract if you curb your purchases of fashionable adult toys, reaffirm personal ideals and stop quibbling.

In later years a real estate investment will pull you out of any previous financial mistakes you have made. Money is not your little blue blanket. The emptiness you feel stems from an unrealistic picture of the intimacy you have missed or denied yourself. You find happiness in charitable, community-minded causes and making music for less fortunates.

• OTHER MARCH 1 BIRTHDAYS

Harry Belafonte	1927
Nicolaus Copernicus	1473
Robert Lowell	1917
Glenn Miller	1904
David Niven	1910
Pete Rozelle	1926
Dinah Shore	1917

MARCH

·2·

You learned how to win friends and influence people as a youngster and tried your hand at playing big shot. You attract attention with charm, humor and a flair for the dramatic. A youthful romance is short-lived if you cannot keep up with your curiosity. First you look for direction from assertive males and then you take the bull by the horns and crash through your twenties. You learn from experience, get scorched and have little need for formal education until mid-life.

It is difficult for you to take an aggressive stance until you are angry or frustrated in intimate relationships. Why do you forget your pride initially—act submissively—and snobbishly pounce upon your need to live beautifully in the end? If you think that your youth is filled with surprising and unconventional changes and want stability, stop putting up a fancy front. If you don't calm down by choice, after age thirty-six your life-style becomes less vibrant; people and experiences position you as a backdrop for another's creative talents, and through partnership in marriage or business, you receive protection.

Mid-life teaches you to pay attention to the little things and life may offer less sparkle, drive and opportunities for leadership. Activity is slowed, and you have time to be diplomatic, tactful and genteel. It is your own indecisiveness that will trigger change between age thirty and your mid-fifties.

In late years you may be drawn to religion, humanitarian service work or bolster your talent for artistic self-expression. You are less concerned with others and finally find yourself.

• OTHER MARCH 2 BIRTHDAYS

Desi Arnaz	1917
Sam Houston	1793
Mikhail Gorbachev	1931
Jennifer Jones	1919
Kurt Weill	1900

MARCH
· 3 ·

You can tackle just about anything if you can settle on what talent to put your energy into. People keep you busy, and the telephone seems to be an extension of your arm. Family and the neighborhood are your childhood and youthful focus. Responsibilities, changes and educational opportunities center around household comforts, music and improving circumstances for all concerned.

Marriage is based upon respect for intellect, and the happiest choice would be to a professional with an established practice. You are trustworthy and require stature in your community. The greatest threat to your emotional happiness is that you will submerge your personality to satisfy loved ones or reject your lovers' apologies, thereby creating a boundless distance that enables you to let go of your commitment. You are the soul of loyalty or a cruel adversary.

You count love, children, pets and education among your blessings as you mature. Problems will arise if education has been neglected, but money comes from a willingness to work and the desire to be surrounded by beauty. You are a volunteer and contribute time and leadership to worthy causes. You attract gifts, prizes and friendships during a vacation or seaside business trip. A home near the water will bring in profits and serenity. Life becomes more sociable and less dedicated to material ambitions after age fifty-five.

Late years are filled with recognition, family pleasures and security. You keep the promises that you made to yourself in the past and associate yourself with agencies for humanitarian reforms.

• OTHER MARCH 3 BIRTHDAYS

Alexander Graham Bell	1847
Bobby Driscoll	1937
Jean Harlow	1911
Princess Lee Radziwill	1933
Gia Scala	1936
David Schlesinger	1955

MARCH

·4·

Questioning doesn't counter faith, it supports the faithful. You are born to ask why; to investigate and seek. The church, temple or library tempt you as a child, and in their opportunities for silence and conjecture, you try to comprehend the distortions of your environment. Cheerful females perk up your days, and males dominate your ego. Your future happiness in career is based upon the concentration you put into your education. From the age of twenty-eight and throughout your life your specialty, expertise and authority bolster your basically sincere and serious character.

Youth twinkles to parties, playmates and petty passions. The friends you make stand you in good stead to the end, although you may make light of your early social contacts mid-life. You find that you have control of your own ambitions and leave behind the ego wounds of childhood. Power comes with self-confidence. You may be aloof, high-minded and all logic. Emotionally you're a pussycat and submerge your independence to loved ones, avoiding confrontations, unless you are trapped by frustrations.

Money is not a problem if you are practical. Financial problems may arise from never having had the concentration to seek the perfection of your elegent tastes. You repeatedly find yourself on the express track and forgetting that even a train stops. Whether you acknowledge the emotional ties of the past or just accept help as your due, friends are your mainstay.

Later years offer travel, intellectually stimulating people and responsibilities. You expound "brotherly love" and desire intimacy: Expect conflicts.

• OTHER MARCH 4 BIRTHDAYS

Charles Goren	1901
Chastity Bono	1969
Knute Rockne	1888
Antonio Vivaldi	1678
Charles Rudolph Walgreen	1906

MARCH
· 5 ·

Hit the road for an untraditional, changable and ambitious life-style. You'll never get old or sour: just a bit petty at times. Mother has the strongest influence on you as a child. Her attention or inattention to your needs sets the stage for your feelings of self-doubt.

Smotheringly near or distant, the female of your youth provided the emotional triggers for your feelings of discouragement. The males may cause you to seek work at an unusually early age. Eventually a male friend rescues you from a major financial difficulty and foreign markets open the door for profit from creative efforts.

Freedom is a necessity to your mental health and physical well-being. You want to see self-improvement and family benefits from the transitions you make. Your loves are deep and require dedication. Marriage may be put off until you feel that you can provide your best effort, and often your concern is not appreciated.

You will learn most from experience. Through disillusionment, impulsiveness or business pressures, you are unsettled by irritating surprises. Expect that you will never learn from books or another's experiences. You are going to test the flame to see if fire is really hot.

Your aspirations were honed to work up from Chevy to Caddy and to aim to the height of a Rolls. If you refuse to be discouraged and maintain your physical stamina to plan, work and visualize substantial results you will not allow circumstances or your emotions to limit your ambitions. Late years are secure, settled and enlightening. You get a chance to improve your mind and to perfect your ambitions.

• OTHER MARCH 5 BIRTHDAYS

Jack Cassidy	1927
Rex Harrison	1908
Eddie Hodges	1947
Blair Sabol	1947
Sylvester Stallone	1944
Dean Stockwell	1936

MARCH

·6·

Words will get you everywhere: that includes trouble. If you go on overkill talking, enlarging on the facts, or clam up, the love that you have to give and creative talents that you have to enjoy will atrophy. In childhood you're either Beauty or the Beast.

You may give too much attention to superficial values or have too little concern for social obligations. Mother and the other siblings or grandmother and mother as a team paid too much or too little attention to you. You are charming, talented, imaginative as an adult. As a child, you may go to extremes, becoming the class clown or hiding your presence under a blanket.

You express yourself best in an art form and are willing to assume responsibility and provide a service with your work. You can be a star if you refuse to take people and experiences at face value. Money will never be a problem because you insist upon a payoff for your self-expression.

Home, family and comforts are a focus in mid-life. You are a sympathetic counselor and will see your desire to heal all wounds to a conclusion. You scatter loves, hobbies and talents. Aim to finish the projects that you instigate. It gives you pleasure to teach, and you are untraditional, innovative and far-reaching when you produce a product or organize a charitable work.

Expect surprising travels in your forties. A clever woman supports your late life changes, which prove to be propitious.

• OTHER MARCH 6 BIRTHDAYS

Cyrano de Bergerac	1620
Elizabeth Barrett Browning	1806
L. Gordon Cooper	1927
Lou Costello	1908
Ring Lardner	1885
Ed McMahon	1923

MARCH

· 7 ·

No man is an island, but you need privacy to develop the creative talents introduced in youth. Childhood propelled people and experiences to your conventional doorstep and sparked your interest in fashion, the arts and sociability. Too strong a dedication to practicality or too little structure as a child makes you a workaholic or too disorganized to plan for tangible results. Mid-life you will be able to balance your dislike of accepting daily details or getting caught in a rigid routine. Late years are independent, stable and financially secure if the advice of a down-to-earth woman was heeded in your thirties.

Don't expect help from your friends—or family—or anyone. Build your independent character to refuse risks related to money or emotional dependencies. Keep your checkbook balanced and avoid the temptation to spend uncollected funds on the basis that cash is forthcoming. Conniving catches you short and it smarts.

It becomes more difficult to trust as you gain experience. As mid-life exposes you to the politics of business, you become authoritative and opinionated. Mistakes are made because you do not listen to the advice you hear. You will benefit from a commonsense female who says it like it is, helps you overcome burdens incurred by a male family member and increases your profits. Your forties provide the time span for specialization that was impossible in your uncertain twenties and thirties.

You attract what you need and are best when you do not wheel and deal. Persistence will get you recognition. Later years make you more aloof from physical activity. Your mind is a scrutinizer for the public contributions you wish to make.

• OTHER MARCH 7 BIRTHDAYS

Antony Armstrong-Jones	1930
Luther Burbank	1849
Anna Magnani	1908
Maurice Ravel	1875
Willard Scott	1934
Peter Wolf	1946

MARCH
· 8 ·

Channel your energies after age twenty-eight to the material world and maintain an elitist taste for quality. Bolstering your courage, practicing decisiveness and knowing when and what to discard as you meet the thirties changes the course of your life. Childhood's powerhouse of friendships, and the surprising variety of untraditional experiences that cause you to run from curiosity or take on more new enthusiasms than you could handle, make wheeling and dealing second nature.

Reflect upon the wasted self-insistence of youth. Learn from your experiences. When you attempt "never to do that again," with stubborn caution, the opportunity to use your entrepreneur's mental agility flies. You are expected to do something special with your life and only disciplined, consistent, realistic training prepares you to crystalize a career.

Home is important but seems dull when all your energies are applied to its maintenance. To balance your temperament and basic needs, compromise is necessary. Impulsivity will cause you to overlook the importance of maintaining relationships with the affluent and influential individuals who cross your path. Assume control, focus your direction and strive for big results as you rub shoulders with the geese that lay golden eggs.

Which way to go and how much to give up to gain the approval of partners or mates? Answer these questions; take a lifetime to ponder. Multifaceted, too busy or too bored and fiddling while your multitude of irons smolder in the ashes or flame out of control, you still attract an audience in later years. Expect change to be the only constant, and allow your ambitions free flow.

• OTHER MARCH 8 BIRTHDAYS

Carl Philipp Emanuel Bach	1714
Cyd Charisse	1923
Oliver Wendell Holmes	1841
Sam Jaffe	1898
Lynn Redgrave	1943

MARCH

· 9 ·

You are your brother's keeper. The love you have to share is put to the test in youth. Wisdom, personality and creative talents are your tools to overcome the trials of emotional relationships. One-to-one loves are disappointing or cut off unexpectedly. Family and community responsibilities are heavy, and the duties drain finances. Pleasure from exotic or romantic ideas and personal ideals is short-lived. You are destined to place the welfare of others before your own, and the rewards are often veiled. Your life has nobility of purpose.

You'll grow far from your roots and birthright. Expect to change residences, travel and expand your philosophy. The quality of your work and the extent of its helpfulness to mass markets is important to your feelings of self-esteem. Pay attention to your personal ideals—morals, ethics, standards—and let bosses, spouses and friends take care of themselves.

Your judgments, when imposed upon others, are displeasing. A critical approach attracts a lonely old age. To build an extroverted, enlightening and notable life-style after age fifty-six, stop pushing for money or ego boosters at forty. Take pleasure in a job well done, valuable service rendered and stay with the effort.

Children and parents are a major concern. Males readily cooperate with your attitudes, while women are unreliable. You take the attitude that charity begins at home. When the going gets rough, self-pity knocks. Mid-life burdens make you introspective—secretive—but they prepare you to adopt a faith that bolsters emotions and attracts serenity in late years.

• OTHER MARCH 9 BIRTHDAYS

James L. Buckley	1923
Fernando Bujones	1955
André Courrèges	1923
Raul Julia	1940
Yuri Gagarin	1934
Vyacheslav Molotov	1890
Mickey Spillane	1918
Joyce Van Patten	1934

MARCH **·10·** You are an oasis in the desert of mediocrity. Grand muftis reward your ability to change undrinkable water to champagne. You are sharp and use your mind to learn from your own and others' mistakes. Nomad tribes come together to acknowledge your uniqueness and award you an oil well. It is your sensitivity to the bedoin's ability to scout, adapt and move on to greener grazing grounds that assures your success. If you are insensitive to the need for survival techniques and products that the fickle, down-to-earth traditionals crave, you'll select the wrong camel or, because of small-mindedness, promote the value of coal over oil.

You are honest, imaginative and restless; eager for challenges, education and success. In childhood and youth you are constructive. Mid-life, you are best when assuming a position of leadership. Late years require intellectual activity as you travel, peruse, and investigate untried territories.

Marriage is a step up the ladder. You want personality and brains plus a love of home to dominate your intimate relationship. You are not one to repeat yourself or to copy another and your mind, not your emotions, triggers changes. Mid-life finds you involved with progressive and youthful people who inspire hard work and profits. You are a stickler for detail and will not tolerate wastefulness.

Love is not your mainstay. Later years are not disappointing, and you realize that your success is the product of your own efforts and any uncalculated failures the result of a subconscious desire to move on. You may be Lawrence of Arabia.

• OTHER MARCH 10 BIRTHDAYS

Barry Fitzgerald	1888
Pamela Mason	1918
James Earl Ray	1928
David Rabe	1940

MARCH

· 11 ·

When the going gets rough, relationships get you down and you're flying high—aloft, changing with each propelling headwind. Aim to carry passengers into the clouds with you. Your trips may appear to be impractical flights of fancy to the average population, but when shared with peers, your unlimited horizons focus upon elevating the expectations of future generations.

From childhood your intuition, vision and high-strung, nervous, creative energy is applied with force and determination. Impulses govern your decisions. You're quick; often too accelerated to stop to count the people you leave on the ground. The lessons of conventional routine, work and down-to-earth responsibilities set you to cruise control.

Partners who are lovers, business associates and friends are the objects of your critical maneuvers. You can suffer from incompatibility, constant discontent and fickle finances after the age of thirty-six. Money may be the root of unfulfilling labors. Mid-life problems are not the result of jet lag. They are the product of your fear of failure, losing emotional control and winging it. You grow, at this stage of life, by taking charge of your ambitious personal ideals.

In later years you hand the wheel over to a sensitive, notable female co-pilot. She attracts the prestige and affluence you have traveled from childhood to experience. You are your own and only true source of fuel when rudders are balanced. Success is offered earlier. Crash trucks stand ready to save you. Dare to chart a solo flight and expect to earn your wings.

• OTHER MARCH 11 BIRTHDAYS

Ralph Abernathy	1926
Dorothy Gish	1898
Dorothy Schiff	1903
Lawrence Welk	1903

MARCH
· 12 ·

Doctor, banker or Indian chief—speak up, set your stage and designs for a moneymaking career in the spotlight. You are an original with multifaceted talents that make you an invaluable asset to inventive people. Go for the feeling of satisfaction, and financial success follows. Strive only for money and your relaxed, humorous, charming personality loses its sunny glow. Tease, flirt, dress up to the nines to attract an early marriage. Paint your backdrop for mid-life's ambitions before age twenty-eight or the loner in you will take over.

At a cocktail party, a lunch or chatting with the neighbors, you attract business contacts, sponsorship and revenue. The responsibilities, conventions and educational focus present in your youth provide a base for your fashionable and expensive tastes. It would be wise to read a book for cultural expansion once in a while, to stimulate your mind and place value on your intellect. You are a mental and emotional person and must develop a humanitarian outlook as you enter your sixties.

Prepare in mid-life to face the challenges of bigotry and to de-personalize your opinions in order to maintain your loving personality or get lost in a disorientation of disloyalties. You give the shirt off your back or nothing at all. It's a puzzlement when you feel that you are not appreciated. Your detachments are permanent. Your attachments are all-encompassing. Your loves and hates swing the way a pendulum swings: in extreme arcs. Meet the universe with compassion, and the universe will give you everything you will need or desire.

At maturity a secure position depends upon remaining active.

• OTHER MARCH 12 BIRTHDAYS

Edward Albee	1928
Barbara Feldon	1941
Gordon MacRae	1921
Liza Minnelli	1946
Walter "Wally" Schirra	1923
James Taylor	1948

MARCH

· 13 ·

Fibber Magee's wife Molly repeatedly chided Fibber by saying, "'Taint funny, Magee" as he joked through his bungles. "M.A.S.H." gave us Hawkeye in the 1970s— the 1930s needed Fibber. The ability of these characters to find a constructive option when everything substantial fell apart eased their disillusionment when circumstances indicated a fall-to-rise and rise-to-fall pattern that got them down. You will find that building a traditionally substantial life-style requires you to plan, work, succeed—and then rebuild at a higher level when money or position changes. You are offered high physical energy and a variety of personalities to emulate. You'll use these tools mid-life.

Laughter inspires detachment from a problem. Take inspiration from self-expressive, imaginative, kindly youthful ties. Experience teaches you to fight for the things that you need and to drive a hard bargain throughout life. You are attractive, investigative and inclined to stay within your own circle. Women are helpful; men challenge your leadership. Expect to find a commercially oriented woman to point out when to take a risk and when to be cautious in your forties. There are social and material profits from this relationship.

When you feel confident, you can move mountains. Strive to bolster your ego. Ask for the personal pleasures that you give willingly. Fears of emotional and financial poverty make you cautious and skeptical later in life. You enclose your world and may miss the chance to grow culturally.

Later you keep a low profile and narrow perimeters. Travel is possible, but you prefer to manage your affairs personally.

• OTHER MARCH 13 BIRTHDAYS

Judith Evelyn	1913
L. Ron Hubbard	1911
Sammy Kaye	1910
Percival Lowell	1855
Leona Powers	1896
Hugo Wolf	1860

MARCH

· **14** ·

Develop your leadership abilities in youth and you'll organize to manage and direct commercially mid-life. Take control; partners realize that you will work to get the most out of a challenge. Everyone benefits when your childhood programming has been directed to investigate before speculating and to minimize your love of largess.

Your childhood requires parents to provide openings for self-expression or you and they get caught in the rebellion and resulting adolescent frustration. Educational opportunities are more positive when directed to artistic interests. You may be all play and no work until you get all the affection you crave.

A dominating female, no matter how subtle the smothering, may affect your choice of a mate or business partners. You want to be stroked—and stroked—and stroked or you shut down your emotional sensitivity altogether. Swing from tenderness to toughness all your days and your desire for an intimate love will be unfulfilled. When you are controlled you wallow in the closeness; when you break free you tend to control the people you love.

In mid-life you bend traditions. Unconventional and surprising people set the scene for learning experiences. Your perceptions are altered, and your thirties to fifties are entrepreneurish. Don't over-estimate your ability to tackle anything for love or money. Late years are more sensually satisfying. A late marriage brings with it the security, activity and practicality that you tried to stabilize mid-life.

• OTHER MARCH 14 BIRTHDAYS

Frank Borman	1928
Michael Caine	1933
Eugene Andrew Cernan	1934
Albert Einstein	1879
John Garfield	1913
Osa Johnson	1894
Casey Jones	1864
Quincey Jones	1933
Max Shulman	1919
Rita Tushingham	1942

MARCH
· 15 ·

The Japanese say it's easier to rule a kingdom than to regulate a family—and you know it to be true. After age thirty you set your heart and your mind to protecting your roots. Prior to accepting your chosen responsibilities, you grow far from your birthright and develop your self-expression. Practical success is offered to you after age thirty-six, but with it come the pitfalls of love and the redirection of your personal ideals.

Power and money can be all you ask from your destiny, or you may choose to stabilize after youth to overcome the influence of the male you idolized as a child. Women and the siblings in childhood set the stage for your extreme sense of responsibility. You are very set in family patterns. However, you are a charmer who attracts attention, enjoys playing devil's advocate and needs harmony in your surroundings.

Sex and sensual relationships are laced with emotional upheaval. More than one marriage would not be surprising to you or your intimates. You must learn to discriminate between love and sex—and not to judge a book by its cover. Business affairs are easier to handle. You will be able to overcome financial insecurities through real estate, community service or theatrical investments after forty. Keep abreast of educational offerings.

Late years do not offer opportunities for travel or exploration. Your talents for providing home and community improvements are best served after age fifty-five. The love of fashion, humor and artistry you displayed as a young adult revive in late years, and there is no time for selfishness. Expect to stay mentally alert and youthful, to be protected and protective.

• OTHER MARCH 15 BIRTHDAYS

Alan Bean	1932
George Brent	1904
MacDonald Carey	1913
Andrew Jackson	1767
Harry James	1916
Marjorie Merriweather Post	1887
Sly Stone	1944

MARCH
· **16** ·
Fear of loneliness and poverty guides your decision to save for your golden age. If you want to have things your way, expect to go it alone. Money will not be a problem if you perfect your skills and hang in. Your aim for financial power proves to be disappointing without the wherewithall to set yourself up as an authority. Take your opportunity for early education. Without expertise, and the respect that concentration attracts, you will not accumulate the material assets you want.

You are a workaholic or you refuse to manage your practical affairs. After age thirty lawyers and legal entanglements are a major concern. The fine print in contracts or leases repeatedly crops up to overthrow the material security that you build. Be careful to investigate the credentials of the people in relationship to the project before you decide to invest money, or you may not come up smelling like a rose. The profits that you anticipate diminish due to your hasty approach to business, sensual curiosity or your desire to savor life's embellishments.

An affair of the heart is destructive to your material security. A young person unsettles your complex life-style. Stay active and you recoup your losses. Changes are always traumatic. The value system that you establish undergoes a complete overhaul each time you become dissatisfied with your intimate relationships. Maintain versatility in business activity to alleviate the discomfort you feel when home commitments do not keep up with your intellectual capacities.

In late years you become more introspective, less speculative. After age sixty you loosen up and attract distinction.

• OTHER MARCH 16 BIRTHDAYS

Walter Cunningham	1932
Jerry Lewis	1926
James Madison	1751
Patricia Nixon	1912
Robert Rossen	1908

MARCH · 17 · Tell 'em what you're gonna' tell 'em—send out your message—and tell them what you told 'em. You are intended to make money, fly high and learn through your experiences. Preach your brand of materialism and be prepared to bounce back when you lose.

Youth does not offer the unconventional. Your inquiring mind sets a fast pace for the teens and twenties; however, the family base is solid. If you stop to think before you take on unknown quantities, business goals identified in youth will be realized mid-life. Pleasant, talented, attractive personalities cross your childhood to spark your imagination.

You are too sensual or too concerned about family responsibilities to give vent to your curiosity. When you decide to taste, you open a can of worms. Your stubborn streak dulls your fine mind, but the influence of an unconventional and forceful female puts you on a profitable business path mid-life. You attract favors, gifts and support for your independent, creative ideas and are able to exert influence on others through your persuasive methods. When you are confident, careful and intuitive, any area of concentration will bring financial rewards. You want a prominent position and the freedom that money implies. Escapist tendencies crop up when your finances are in the red.

Later in life you profit from your discomforts as a youth. You've learned from experience and frustration. Plan for late years early and set up an efficient routine for retirement or you'll be a cranky oldster. Practice what you preach . . . you will be called upon to set an example of quality versus quantity.

• OTHER MARCH 17 BIRTHDAYS

Frederick Brisson	1913
Nat "King" Cole	1919
Mercedes McCambridge	1918
Alfred Newman	1901
Rudolph Nureyev	1938
John Sebastian	1944
Monique Van Vooren	1938

MARCH

· 18 ·

You are out to beautify the world. You are multitalented and invite notables to your generous table. Your scope is limitless. When you discipline yourself to impersonalize your love of human beings and nature, expect to influence a multitude of tastes.

Youth offers social growth. Mid-life demands individualism, stamina and unselfishness. Later years will nurture your talents, and you will be inspirational to your peers. Speak up. Words are your weapons, and they provide you with a material tool that helps to buy your daily bread. The romance in your soul is displaced by practicality as time goes by.

Youth finds you money-conscious. Your obligations are heavy, and you are not able to follow your inspirations. Family and community place burdens upon you, but the guidelines set by an idealistic female early in life provide a barometer for difficult mid-life decisions. You must submit to the requirements of the group and are sheltered. Personal ambitions are placed on the shelf until you travel or seek a wider scope of education. Your ethics and standards are set in concrete as a youngster.

Mid-life places you in a service industry surrounded by people from various nations and backgrounds. You are not one to take advice, and you use your inventive and energetic mind to cope with expansive fields that require efficient administration.

All the world loves a lover and you are the best. However, marriage is not a totally fulfilling commitment. Late years are dedicated to travel and reaching out to serve humanitarian causes.

• OTHER MARCH 18 BIRTHDAYS

Samuel Botero	1945
Edgar Cayce	1877
Grover Cleveland	1837
Peter Graves	1926
Anna Held	1873
Edward Everett Horton	1887
Nicolai Rimski-Korsakov	1844
George Plimpton	1927
John Updike	1932
Amerigo Vespucci	1454

MARCH

· 19 ·

You run into a sea of emotions, to plunge and rise, when creative limitations are stormy. Your concerns belie your youthful exposures to a variety of social activities and sound practical upbringing. Childhood female relationships—the basis for your personal sensitivity, modesty and feelings of humility—placed you second to siblings or others in the family. As a youth, you find it difficult to balance your inferiority complex and your ability to control or lead your peers. In late years you are better able to put your inventive notions and individualism in the forefront. The majority of your life is spent with one face to the world and another within your four walls.

Are you a loner? To a great extent you are. However, the sense of responsibility instilled as a child hangs in to bring you to mid-life as a persevering, purposeful, empathetic adult. You have abilities that require a profession or concentrated dedication to business. Change is a necessity to your growth process, and you switch goals often.

Your sensual tastes are unconventional. Only your intimates know how different you are in a domestic relationship from the picture you present. Logic and artistry combine in you. Your mind accepts challenges, yet you aim to keep the peace and refuse to fight for your individuality at appropriate times. It is your intention to appear to respect the conventions of your neighbors and appear to be unobjectionable and nonprovocative in public.

In late years you are financially secure, active and charitable. Your life is a work of work that produces results.

• OTHER MARCH 19 BIRTHDAYS

Ursula Andress	1938
William Jennings Bryan	1860
Richard Burton (explorer)	1821
Wyatt Earp	1848
David Livingstone	1813
Moms Mabley	1894
Jo Mielziner	1901
Phyllis Newman	1935
Lynda Bird Johnson Robb	1944
John Sirica	1904
Kent Smith	1907
Irving Wallace	1916

MARCH

·20·

You're more worried about judgment day than you are about the moment. Surely the inconsistencies of your childhood have paved the way for decisive actions mid-life... or are you forever calculating the challenges of responsibility? As a child, self-insistent men or controlling women cause you to act too submissively or to react to your frustrations with inappropriate self-assertion. When you were good, you were very, very good—but when you were bad, you were horrid!

Mid-life details may get the best of you, but you have a knack for attracting protection, love and assistance from friends. You are a key person in a support group, a dance troup or an orchestra and dislike getting into the earthy side of work. Without your special brand of adhesive tape, safeguards and tender nurturing, few creative projects would get off the ground.

Your impatience is not a virtue. You rarely wait for your ideas to be received before you jump the gun—come to the conclusion that they are not acceptable—and refuse to be competitive. A short escapist spell slows progress, then you get set in your ways mid-life and attract help from co-workers, spouse or a dominating female who increases your earning potential. Overt signs of recognition are not comfortable to you. You need to be artistically self-expressive but are better suited to quietly creating copy than to waking each day to the competitive doubts and bouts of an advertising account executive.

Chronic health problems linger through your lifetime—nothing life threatening but reason to rely upon your intimates. In late years you find peace, love and consistency.

• OTHER MARCH 20 BIRTHDAYS

Jack Barry	1918
Abraham Beame	1906
Wendell Corey	1914
Larry Elgart	1922
John Ehrlichman	1925
Ray Goulding	1922
Henrik Ibsen	1824
Hal Linden	1931
Lauritz Melchior	1890
Ozzie Nelson	1907
Sir Michael Redgrave	1908
Jerry Reed	1937
Carl Reiner	1922
Frank Stanton	1908

MARCH
·21·
Family, friends and lovers provide financial security and feed your need for "roots" only if you will accommodate their life-styles and ambitions. When you establish a career choice and get the mail, phone and social relationships together that you require, the burdens of maturity are less of a load. Your ambitions are continually up for grabs. Change is a necessity, but you find it difficult to leave the positions of trust you attract in spite of unpleasant or outgrown relationships.

You are happy to leave your childhood. The memories are sprinkled with resentments. Education or an expertise are important and you find it difficult to demand the salary that you are worth until your early forties. The twenties find you feeling like a support or backdrop for others less capable. In your thirties the people in your life seem more important than ambition. They keep you interested in fashion, decorating and hobbies. The forties present a time for work.

Mid-life you set your practical foundation after a mid-forties stir-up. The risks you take are losers and you tie in with established people who help you to earn your financial and professional recognition. Early fifties connect you with a real estate profit. In late years financial security is in direct proportion to emotional balance. You need peace.

Boredom is a lifelong problem. You are tempted to slam the door on commitments. Irresponsibility is a temptation, but not for long. You exert the dramatic side of your nature and blow off steam. Humor and your clear perceptions get you through rough spots. Late years offer time for travel and new interests.

• OTHER MARCH 21 BIRTHDAYS

Peter Brooks	1925
Cesar Chavez	1927
James Coco	1929
John D. Rockefeller III	1906
Benito Juarez	1806
Modest Mussorgsky	1839
Kathleen Widdoes	1939
Florenz Zeigfeld	1869

MARCH

·22·

A pinch of perfection, a dash of self-expressive personality, blended with highly energized particles of problem-solving managerial ability, when combined and simmered, leave a memorable taste. You have the ingredients to rebuild where others fail. You have the vision to plan—the communications talents to attract listeners when you share—the physical stamina to practice what you preach—and the ability to bring your efforts to a practical result. You have responsibilities.

In childhood you have the opportunity to develop skills and attract audiences for your imaginative dramas. A woman has a controlling hand when you are a tot. She sets the pace for your high regard for authority and demand for autonomy. You attract intellectual, charming and artistic people. You are alone in a crowd and accept stimulation from both readers and writers while your values grow. Government, construction and real estate industries are the best places to begin your advancement.

Your mind is clever and your brain is quick. Love and emotional relationships are difficult. You are likely to be insecure or to make your mate feel neglected, which may result in infidelity. The early thirties and late forties may be testing times. Restlessness should be curbed to maintain a consistent life-style. Pay attention to your code of ethics and morals.

Your mid-life opportunities arise from the ashes of failed dreams of others. Power for purpose may be dispersed for positive or negative results. You have choice and may use your high nervous energy as a catalyst for philanthropy or profiteering. Be selective. Your name will be remembered.

• OTHER MARCH 22 BIRTHDAYS

Mai Britt	1936
Anthony Van Dyck	1599
Karl Malden	1914
Marcel Marceau	1923
Chico Marx	1891
William Shatner	1931
Stephen Sondheim	1930

MARCH
· 2 3 ·

Whether you take the challenges of big business or build your stamina to tax yourself participating in professional athletics, you will make waves wherever you choose to aim high.

Youth offers the opportunity to establish your material ambitions. Your mind is unquiet, restless, questioning and changable. In mid-life you realize that your enthusiasm and infectious energy, when applied to new and progressive interests, spark traditional non-movers to alter course. After age fifty-five you are less involved socially. The security, ease and mental stimulation that you need as a youngster are yours if discipline is applied to the multifaceted talents that surface in childhood.

You are a personality kid, cute, clever and resourceful. Right from day one, words are your tool for financial freedom. Domestic life is pleasant, and early marriage seems inviting. Friends bring in business contacts and you are able to earn money when you are consistent. You do not mind work. However, your dislike of conventional procedures and repetition may cause you to change goals too often. A mature approach to daily detail work, management and personal accountability will stabilize your laziness. You must keep abreast of all new and progressive methods to promote yourself wisely. Too often you revert to childish or naive pettiness and lose sight of long-term goals.

Experience pays off, although you are likely to spend to make a big splash. You are a lucky communicator. The grouchy criticizers of your youth should be forgotten. Let bygones be bygones. Direct your talents into skills and show the world who's boss. In late years you feel like a kid and should play.

• OTHER MARCH 23 BIRTHDAYS

Roger Bannister	1929
Werner von Braun	1912
Joan Crawford	1908
Regine Crespin	1927
Erich Fromm	1900
Akira Kurosawa	1910
Lee May	1943

MARCH

·**24**·

All the world's a stage—a drama with you as the star. Produce the play and take the center-stage spotlight. The more you do, the more you will want to do; the less you do, the less ambition you will have to reach your peak. You take on too many superficial interests, or you lock into a depth of concentration. You are too serious or too simple. You are too easily fooled by flattery or do not know how to take a compliment.

Practicality and self-expression join forces in youth. Your imagination flourishes in a social environment. The communication between parent and child could be more realistic. Misconceptions arise from problems being pushed under the rug or swept up too quickly. Heart and mind seem to be at odds.

Marriage is a winning proposition if your mate is bright and witty. Personality, charm and attractiveness are very important to you. Love may fly out the window when you change your goals mid-life or begin to feel that your mate is not your best friend.

After the age of thirty-six, family or community relationships are taxing to your ego needs. Your attitude is positive and willful. You find intimate relationships cloistering and inhibiting. Personal commitments and marriage are more fulfilling in later years. Early retirement is not in the cards. A real estate investment sprouts profits. When you are ready to slow your work pace, it will add importantly to your retirement income.

Throughout life you enlarge your joys and sorrows. Steer clear of depression. Your imagination should be coupled with observation. You benefit from a major change after age fifty. In late years a partnership and companionship occupy your interest.

• OTHER MARCH 24 BIRTHDAYS

Fatty Arbuckle	1887
Clyde Barrow	1909
Richard Conte	1914
Thomas E. Dewey	1902
Byron Janis	1928
Steve McQueen	1930
Malcolm Muggeridge	1903

MARCH · 25 · You are torn between introverted treasures and extroverted pleasures. In youth you're taught to work for tangible results, but as your talents unfold, the imagery, electricity and aristocratic perfections demanded by your mature nature alter the traditional role anticipated in childhood. All your days, you base decisions upon youth's experiences. You conceal your emotional depth. You are a puzzlement to intimates and are often accused of covering your true opinions and feelings.

Art is an open field to you, and money can be made through your perseverance, discipline and stamina. Mid-life exposures are geared to specializing and establishing yourself as an authority. The affluence that you need to establish a tasteful life-style comes to you if you do not pursue it. Your wisdom is the magnet that attracts wealth and power to you.

Marriage or partnerships are desirable and profitable. However, you need your freedom to experiment with new enthusiasms, a sensual mate to share your ideals and to live up to the words that roll freely from your charming lips. You are tempted by unconventional interests and have extreme loyalty when involved in a traditional love commitment. Rules are your crutch, until you decide to break them.

Childhood made you want to run, although you were not deprived. Your ambitions were not clear until your mid-twenties. You attract experiences that deal with film, radio and computers, and you branch out in your workaholic forties. Changes of residence and close-to-the-vest financial planning are needed to produce results that win applause for a distinctive career late in life.

• OTHER MARCH 25 BIRTHDAYS

Ed Begley	1901
Anita Bryant	1940
Howard Cosell	1920
Eileen Ford	1922
Aretha Franklin	1942
Elton John	1947
James A. Lovell, Jr.	1928
Nancy Kelly	1921
David Lean	1908
Flannery O'Connor	1925
Simone Signoret	1921
Gloria Steinem	1935
Arturo Toscanini	1867

MARCH
·26·

If you want to sign the payroll checks, remember that the buck stops with you. Responsibility cannot be assumed in spurts. You have the charm, imagination and practical stamina to accumulate money, power and social expertise.

In youth you choose to get caught up in sensual diversions or unconventional adventures of other types, or you miss the love boat because you fear the thought of stepping onto the gangplank. You balance your impulsivity or fear of taking chances after thirty, and the intensity you feel when you become too busy or too bored is alleviated. It becomes easier for you to persist in your progressive plans after age thirty-six.

You are too impatient for success and refuse to do the detail work. You have been taught to aim high and go for the gold. In mid-life you reflect upon the disciplinarian of your childhood with the appreciation that comes with maturity. You are constructive and capable of planning, building and expanding upon business enterprises. You are too skeptical in a business-related friendship in your thirties, and you lose a potential windfall due to improper suspicions.

Family and the burdens that a domestic life-style incur take you away from your personal ambitions more than once during your mid-life. Your insecurity and sensual extremes put marriage to the test. You stay too long or leave your first love too soon. You must make an effort to maintain your staying power without destroying your youthful zest for living and loving.

Late years offer expansion of interests, travel and a chance to be helpful. You are remembered for your generosity.

• OTHER MARCH 26 BIRTHDAYS

Alan Arkin	1934
Pierre Boulez	1925
James Caan	1939
Robert Frost	1875
Sterling Hayden	1916
Duncan Hines	1880
Erica Jong	1942
Robert Taft, Jr.	1917
Leonard Nimoy	1931
Diana Ross	1944
William C. Westmoreland	1914
Tennessee Williams	1914

MARCH
·27·
Look at everyone through rose-colored glasses and note the positives. You grow a long way from your roots mid-life; practical realities include negatives that trigger disillusionment in your romantic soul. It's up to you to use your fine powers of communication to attract the notables that cross your path and warm to your empathetic personality. Youth offers people and experiences that open up your areas of self-expression. Friends are important to the family and give you a chance to build lifelong relationships and strong personal ideals. Late years provide opportunities to alter mental and emotional interests. Retirement years offer self-determination.

Your hot temper flares before you reach your teens. Youthful frustrations give you cause to feel misdirected or insecure. You have burdens and responsibilities that are too heavy for a youngster to carry, and your youthful optimism is turned to problem solving. Home and family ties are geared to mother or father as individuals, not as a team. You have a lifelong retrospect on your parents and your emotional reactions to your own spouse and children are influenced by your blind acceptance or extreme distrust of the traditions of your childhood.

After age thirty-seven you enthusiastically accept the teaching of a broad-scoped male friend or relative. You seek a mentor as you pass through each growth transition. You are not a loner and have a tendency to be concerned about appearances. Your tendency to waste time and energy on others gets you caught up in nested obligations in youth and you lose sight of your need to reach out to rehabilitate and counsel until late years.

• OTHER MARCH 27 BIRTHDAYS

David Janssen	1930
Budd Schulberg	1914
Gloria Swanson	1899
Sarah Vaughan	1924
Michael York	1942

MARCH
·28·

You're a bossy and adoring lover. If your fear of giving in to love is overcome by your desire for tenderness and affection, your late years will be perfect in every way. When you accept your untraditional role, exemplify your personal ideals and challenge your tendency to magnify personal projects, mid-life exposures to people and experiences give you options to live up to your unique potential. You are an innovator with a flair for the dramatic; an executive force for commercial success.

Stick with your original objectives—don't let go and become tactless, argumentative or inconsiderate when you have a taste of success. Take your restless emotions out of the survival war-making mode to pursue maintaining each objective that you obtain. You overthrow your own ambitions after they are realized.

In youth responsibilities and burdens teach you to pay attention to duty. You are delayed by lack of funds or denied the education offered to your peers. Friends and associates train your brain, and you are impatient for financial freedom. You need peace of mind and a serene environment and will marry to get intellectual stimulation. You are an investor in people and work to produce and package an opulent life-style.

You have a talent for dealing with eccentric or emotionally strained people. Your career application of patience and sensitivity does not extend to your intimate relationships. You expect a strong-willed and self-reliant mate to be able to withstand your inconsistencies. You are a dreamer and have spurts of laziness but will find your dreams realized as you grow older.

• OTHER MARCH 28 BIRTHDAYS

Nelson Algren	1909
Freddy Bartholomew	1924
Dirk Bogarde	1921
Maksim Gorky	1868
Ken Howard	1944
Frank Lovejoy	1914
Edmund Muskie	1914
Flora Robson	1902
Paul Whiteman	1891

MARCH

·**29**·

You gotta have faith—it can and will move mountains for you. Your vision and talent for attracting listeners, who put your statements into practice, make you capable of long-lasting leadership and acclaim. You are an extremist. Your emotions seep into everything you say and do. You need a support system as a child to avoid distorting your imagery. Your high nervous energy confuses loved ones, and childhood's changes and surprises do little to give you security. A female household member is an unforgettable influence upon your accomplishments as an adult.

Mid-life experiences are challenging, and you must balance your attentiveness to details with the broad and far-reaching philosophies that you encounter. You like a good debate, and play devil's advocate to the consternation of your employers or employees. You are troubled by a man who is too inhibiting or too assertive as you aim to make large profits. The only course of action for you is conservative. Hit-and-run real estate deals or stock market investments may come through but are lost quickly to follow-up hunches. You need a budget and a consistent effort to build security for late years.

You have the birthright to teach and set an example. The trials that cross your path in your forties are offered to set your mind to practical analysis. The far-out ideas that get you into trouble are based upon your elitist notion that rules and regulations are made for others, not intended for you. True, you are an exceptional therapist and have intuitive insights—but only for others. You are too moody and self-absorbed to balance your marriage or career until later years provide time to share.

• OTHER MARCH 29 BIRTHDAYS

Pearl Bailey	1918
Walt Frazier	1945
Eileen Heckart	1919
Eugene McCarthy	1916
Dennis O'Keefe	1908
Karen Ann Quinlan	1954
John Tyler	1790

MARCH

· **30** ·

You're a starter—not a finisher. You are happiest involved with lighthearted people, in beautiful surroundings and bringing optimism to a dreary world. The variety of games that interest you never quite come to a conclusion. You tend to buzz your way through experiences and rarely taste the honey. You meander on the path to success and do well in theater, fashion or as a writer for any marketplace. You are wise and naive—a man/woman child until your youthful domestic obligations give way to a conventional profession that serves a major humanitarian cause.

You are aimed at providing entertainment or service and are at your best when disassociated emotionally from your work. Your voice and your eyes are unforgettable. People comment upon your ability to light up a room when you're happy or darken it when you enter feeling sad. Mid-life requires cultivation of your multifaceted talents—a concentration for your inspirations. You must decide how to concentrate and not to subjugate your personality into real or imagined responsibilities to loved ones. You are best in your forties, when you realize that you must follow your feelings and your intuition is applied to understanding human nature. You become financially secure and "know" what to compromise and how to self-discipline to rest your mind. If financial security is elusive, you are too self-contained or too unselfish for your own good.

Late years offer the companionship, cultural expansion and travel that you remember desiring, but missed, in youth. You have been overworked in your concern for others. Why change now?

• OTHER MARCH 30 BIRTHDAYS

Warren Beatty	1937
McGeorge Bundy	1919
Vincent van Gogh	1853
Francisco Goya	1746
Richard Helms	1913
Frankie Laine	1913
Sean O'Casey	1880

MARCH **· 31 ·** You are a practical, intellectual seeker. When you find a job that you like, stick with it and expect to attract attention for your imaginative methods. You are not geared to commercial success when your impulsive gestures and uncontrolled ambitions get going. You'll never make it at the crap tables or at the track. Although you can analyze how to be a millionaire at twenty, you cannot deny your skepticism. When your doubts reach your intellect, your fine analysis and intuitive feelings drown in fears of poverty, loneliness and past memories of gullibility. You succeed when you plan, organize and work for traditional goals.

Early marriage serves your personality well. The duties and positions of trust that are part and parcel of family life have a stabilizing influence that you need. You want to be boss or you are too accommodating. Aim to assert yourself, and be cautious with a mate who needs to control you as much as you need to assert your controls. The male who influenced you in childhood set unrealistic leadership standards, and you attract unjust situations when in conflict with aggressive people. In impersonal situations, your innovations, inventions and independence are not threatened.

Late years bring out your artistic talents, and you finally get proof of the beliefs that have been uppermost in your mind. You've made more than one career change; now music and art provide a common ground for your late life experimentations. You are finally able to be less ambivalent about your responsibilities in relationship to your ego desires.

• OTHER MARCH 31 BIRTHDAYS

Herb Alpert	1935
Johann Sebastian Bach	1685
Richard Chamberlain	1935
Sidney Chaplin	1926
David Eisenhower	1948
Franz Josef Haydn	1732
Israel Horowitz	1939
Gordie Howe	1928
Shirley Jones	1934
Richard Kiley	1922
Henry Morgan	1915

APRIL

• 1 •

You hide your talents or blare them to the world—you are a secretive materialist and a saver. You are not the April Fool, but you are different. Childhood is a conventional, practical and down-to-earth upswing. You learn to plan, work and build for tangible results. Everything you acquire is earned. Your family and environment are a bit mundane for a person of your expressive talents and far-reaching ambitions. You experience a desire to belong and join the mainstream with a serious approach to building your own family and a career that offers travel or adventurous challenges.

You are honorable and excel when you take a backseat to manage the finances of others. Leadership is offered to you in business, and you prefer to take the controls in domestic relationships. Career and family are always priority aspects in your legalistic mind. You are able to do many things at the same time and have learned, by experience, to be multifaceted, spontaneous and speculative. Your childhood environment was conventional and changable. You learned how to make and appreciate money.

From a productive youth you enter a self-reliant mid-life and deal with uncertainty that constantly alters your point of view. Your forties include hobbies or family involvements that focus upon the water—sailing, swimming, socializing—and career progressions that force you to adapt yourself to challenges to your authority. You make the most of bad bargains and build security for your late years through cautious real estate or money market investments. Your power grows with age.

• OTHER APRIL 1 BIRTHDAYS

Wallace Beery	1886
Otto von Bismarck	1815
Eddie Duchin	1909
George Grizzard	1928
Ali MacGraw	1939
Jane Powell	1929
Sergei Rachmaninoff	1873
Debbie Reynolds	1932

APRIL

·2·

"There ought to be a law" to bring everyone up to your standards; then you would be able to get help as you remake the world. You are just, sympathetic and determined. However, you run into disharmony when your judgments are too emotionally personalized. Education is important and can make the difference between a life of physical labor or manicured fingernails. You are a serious adult and need a mate or partner to bolster your self-confidence. Your dignified exterior is only exceeded by your inner sensitivity.

In childhood the female family members bring humor, gaiety and buoyant personalities to ease your sense of responsibility. Mid-life productivity places you in second-string positions, and your success depends upon your ability to be tactful, adaptable, cooperative and attentive to the little things in life. You are exposed to positions and people that exact obedience. It is to your benefit to collect money, power and applause without being pushy. The key that opens the door to your opportunities is coated with diplomacy, and your ability to go unappreciated for a time—until your steadiness is noted—is essential to late life security and fun.

You are too self-concerned and often make hasty and caustic remarks that cause gentle persons in your path to recoil from being in your company. You are too friendly, giving and loving or too detached from intimacy. You are too easygoing or too strained. Later years offer associations with intellectual, well-traveled people and you reach out for enlightenment. You feed your mind and enjoy sharing a pleasant life-style.

• OTHER APRIL 2 BIRTHDAYS

Hans Christian Andersen	1805
Giovanni Casanova	1725
Buddy Ebsen	1908
Max Ernst	1891
Rita Gam	1928
Marvin Gaye	1939
Sir Alec Guinness	1914
Jack Webb	1920
Emile Zola	1840

APRIL
· 3 ·

Youth taught you to work with and for others, to be constructive. You developed determination, perseverance and a liking for tangible results and material security. At the same time your aristocratic tastes were developing, to be fulfilled in the future. You learned to stand back and look things over. The pattern for a sound foundation and your structure for future goals is based upon the ability to practice the system and the economy that you established prior to your thirtieth year.

Mid-life offers more enjoyment, and you suffer if you keep your nose to the grindstone. You leave mundane people and experiences to meet creatively expressive, entertaining and imaginative youthful personalities. You make people a major part of your life. The total picture that greets your late years is painted in your labors for your loves.

Love, and the crosses you bear to give and get it, inspire you to constantly find ways and means to self-improvement. You are restless and loyal. You are progressive and want to be a winner. If you think that you never get anything without making some sacrifice in return—you're right.

The need to be very individualistic, assertive and personally ambitious begins with childhood. You have choice and vacillate between selfish ambition and submission to the desires of your loved ones. You fear rejection and become intimidated by the assertive types of people you attract. Avoid becoming discouraged, and maintain your personal ambitions. You will find companionship, educational opportunities and enriching charitable experiences that you enjoy, at your doorstep, later in life.

• OTHER APRIL 3 BIRTHDAYS

Marlon Brando	1924
Doris Day	1924
Virgil "Gus" Grissom	1926
Leslie Howard	1893
Washington Irving	1783
George Jessel	1898
Henry Luce	1898
Marsha Mason	1942
Wayne Newton	1944
Jan Sterling	1923
William "Boss" Tweed	1823

APRIL

·4·

You've got all the ingredients necessary to make a big business career in show biz. Imagination, nobility of purpose and dedication to work for practical results put you in line to beat out the competition. Childhood introduces you to the challenges of the affluent and influential aspects of society. You have stamina, develop the insight to know what you want and are encouraged by the examples set by the executives and managerial types that surround you. You're more mature in your understanding of human frailty than the average youngster and are born with adult wisdom that makes you a precocious child.

Your youth is set in concrete structures and routines, and your teachers sing the praises of "practice makes perfect." You are surrounded by workers whose methods produce results—or else! Your mentors are pioneering and have the ability to cope with the progressive changes that they talk about and undertake. You are born to be a winner. If you feel like a loser, you're too detached from practicality in the romance of your work or too enclosed in sacrifice of your true personality, by your chosen love.

You may feel lonely or deprived of childhood companionship. The burden of helping siblings or parents is placed upon your tender shoulders to soon; however, you conquer your problems. You make valuable contacts and want prominence. You think about making a marriage for prestige and expect to build security with your mate. You are an asset to groups and major organizations. You enjoy showing off when you travel, change professions and are swept into a more pleasurable career in your late years.

- OTHER APRIL 4 BIRTHDAYS

Maya Angelou	1929
Elmer Bernstein	1922
Gil Hodges	1924
Frances Langford	1913
Arthur Murray	1895
Anthony Perkins	1932
Robert Sherwood	1896

APRIL
· **5** ·

You attract the unconventional and deal with inconsistency and surprising events with discipline nurtured in childhood. You take a mundane beginning and broaden your scope to appreciate the cultural advantages denied you as a child. You are enthusiastic, and through your love of living—not observing life—bring your dynamic and dramatic interpretations of what you see and sense to serve the needs of the masses. You are a healer, a counselor and a communicator. Youth sets the stage for a career in the arts, medicine or politics. Only your lack of independence or egocentricity can drain the energy from your ambitions. You are a swashbuckler and can tackle anything because you learn from experience.

You tend to spend money or see a fait accompli at the onset of a venture. You're finished with a project as soon as you plan your strategy. In youth that type of speculation creates problems. In midlife you deal with a fluctuating income by showing an astonishing talent for covering up your mistakes with winning ideas. Money is a problem in marriage, and you are in trouble if you try to drink your way out of family responsibilities. You recognize your self-indulgence. The result is a change of pace, and you begin to look before you leap.

In your forties you benefit from a real estate investment. You take on the burden of helping a male relative, and the test of faith in yourself builds your ego. At the middle stage of your life you finally take charge of your destiny. You realize that impulsivity and impatience have had a negative effect, and your late years bring success when you show tenacity of purpose.

• OTHER APRIL 5 BIRTHDAYS

Charles Bowles	1901
David Burpee	1893
Roger Corman	1926
Bette Davis	1908
Melvyn Douglas	1901
Frank Gorshin	1934
Merle Haggard	1937
Arthur Hailey	1920
Joseph Lister	1827
Michael Moriarty	1941
Gregory Peck	1916
Raphael	1483
Gale Storm	1922
Spencer Tracy	1900

APRIL

·6·

Which way to go? Decisions are the bane of your existence. You learn discipline in youth, responsibility in mid-life and use your talent for sharing your experiences in late years. To be practically decisive, you require knowledge before you get into new ventures. To secure your position, you need to apply yourself to your chosen ambition. Patience and the ability to put yourself in the other guy's shoes before you react to their comments are the answers to getting and maintaining the stability and peace of mind that you want.

Curb your temper. Your childhood need for female approval and the sharp criticism to which you felt you were subjected effect your lifelong impressions and create emotional confusion for you and your loved ones. You are tenacious in youth and form deep dependencies. You are centered upon getting your own way and lack adaptability if you do not receive encouragement, affection and approval. Your mother is a major force and a mirror of your self-esteem. You relate positively to a financially secure, outgoing, affectionale woman mid-life and want an opulent, comfortable family and home based upon your childhood structure.

Work is the key to your stability and provides you with the tools to be the sympathetic, generous and trustworthy guardian that you enjoy being. You want respect, take pride in your possessions and plan for your late years. You want and give protection; however, your personal judgments will bring on disappointment if you expect to take the easy way and refuse to set an example of the attitude that you expect from others.

• OTHER APRIL 6 BIRTHDAYS

Butch Cassidy	1866
Emperor Charlemagne	742
Harry Houdini	1874
Walter Huston	1884
André Previn	1929
Lowell Thomas	1892
Billy Dee Williams	1938

APRIL

·7·

It's quality, not quantity, that regulates your ambitions. You are a questioner, a visionary and a bit impractical. You know what you think is correct and expect others to live up to your aristocratic standards. In youth the mundane aspects of daily living provided a good training ground for mid-life professionalism. You need privacy and an outlet for your communications skills. As a power behind the scenes, you excel. It is not to your benefit to appear to be aggressive, self-serving or impatient.

Childhood does not offer people and experiences that help you fulfill your intellectual or spiritual requirements. Emotional problems and people who are emotionally based delay your progress. Women and the siblings in the family are too doting or too uncaring, and you are unable to come to grips with your own creative self-expression. You may be the oldest or the youngest—the only boy or girl—and have family focus on appearances rather than on the depths of your character. Your inquiring mind is not given free rein until the problems with friends, women and home are alleviated by the journeys you make in your thirties.

You wish to be inspirational and to serve the needs of those who are less fortunate as a mature adult. Later in life you give priority to your urge to uplift and soul search, and you surround yourself with purple and fine linen. Throughout life your dislike for the common-place puts you in more than one financial hole. You are helped by association with a tough-minded businessman. After age fifty you are above criticism, and delaying legal problems are eliminated.

• OTHER APRIL 7 BIRTHDAYS

Donald Barthelme	1928
Francis Ford Coppola	1939
Daniel Ellsberg	1931
Percy Faith	1908
David Frost	1939
James Garner	1928
Billie Holiday	1915
Janis Ian	1951
Edmund Brown, Jr.	1938
Walter Winchell	1897
William Wordsworth	1770

APRIL

· 8 ·

Power and money are one and the same to you. They are the core of your value system and rage a lifelong battle with your hunger for love. Things—gifts of jewelry and real property—are symbolic of your feelings for another, and you understand the giver who offers status symbols. Childhood influences are based upon materialism and the emotional responses that a tot needs are replaced by disciplines. You are not deprived. You are given friendship and practical nurturing and instilled with down-to-earth ambitions. You were born to turn a profit on your investments.

As a child, you aim to excel at everything from sports to academics. You attract talented friends and maintain school ties to late years. You believe in efficiency, organization and delegating authority while you promote your imaginative projects. You are a charmer and choose an intelligent, productive, socially adept mate to compliment your life-style. You listen to advice but rarely take it.

You are too intent upon following your plans and often get caught short when appointments are changed or others suggest playing it by ear. You dislike routine and find yourself instigating detailed procedures that exhaust your associates and dull creativity. You are a workaholic and a slavedriver for yourself and others. You will not take a vacation until you are drained—make yourself ill—and then you give yourself permission to rest. If that sounds like sick thinking, you're right; it is. Your neurotic tendency makes you an achiever.

Late years find you living near or on the water and keeping up with the times as you expand culturally.

• OTHER APRIL 8 BIRTHDAYS

Jacques Brel	1929
Ilke Chase	1905
Franco Corelli	1923
Betty Ford	1918
John Gavin	1935
Sonja Henie	1912
Jim "Catfish" Hunter	1946
Josef Krips	1902
Carmen McRae	1922

APRIL

·**9**·

You're good at philosophizing and telling others how to run their lives. Why not listen to yourself and accept love from the strangers that come your way? You are a romantic—in love with the world of people who respect your polish and skills, need your empathetic counseling and consistently steal you away from the intimate relationships you initiate.

Marriage or one-to-one long-lasting relationships test the mettle of your mate. You are generous to a fault and must take one deep commitment at a time. You have difficulty when you make emotional attachments in business or professional capacities and try to keep your nest feathered too. You may have been promiscuous or too sensually sheltered as a youth. You need money, stability and consistency as mid-life unfolds. Late years are protected by a woman of charm, wit and beauty who has seen humanity at its best and its worst. You inherit or marry the financial security you crave after age fifty.

Mid-life responsibilities put you into careers and situations that are unfulfilling, confining and tormenting. You incur expenses and assume leadership roles that make change in midstream impossible. The situations that arise are beyond your control, but you attract notables and authorities who help when you find it difficult to get financial assistance. Your timing may be off, but money is behind you and becomes available when you travel to expand your interests.

You're not a risk taker. You are programmed to the work ethic as a youngster and suffer emotionally when you change goals impulsively or stick unreasonably. Worry not—you attract love.

• OTHER APRIL 9 BIRTHDAYS

Jean-Paul Belmondo	1933
Ward Bond	1905
Antal Dorati	1906
J. William Fulbright	1905
Hugh Hefner	1926
Sol Hurok	1888
Mary Pickford	1894
Paul Robeson	1898
Brandon de Wilde	1942

APRIL

·10·

You are changable, independent and inventive. If you don't know what to say or do in any given situation, you'll keep talking until you see a glint of understanding in the eyes of the listener, and you'll take it from there. Childhood exposures and training incorporate orderliness, system and practical planning into your personality. Like it or not, you learn how to use elbow grease. Put your need to produce tangible results together with your creative abilities, active energy and cleverness— and you've got charisma. Not bad for a kid from mundane roots.

Your youth was unsettling and based traditionally. You learned to be a loner and never accepted the methods written in concrete by your teachers. You observed and kept your eyes and ears open for the chance to take the lead. Your ideas trigger inventions and investigations and are intended to serve the needs of others besides yourself. Your project for self-improvement is based upon your ability to communicate. If you don't display your wares, the world cannot beat a path to your door.

You try your hand at politics because you like to know the powers behind the scenes. You have the talent for getting help from friends, and you use your keen investigative mind, charm and executive efficiency to wheel and deal. You take a hobby to the point of business professionalism in late years and attract an idealistic supporter for your love of travel and mind-expanding adventures.

Love must combine with friendship to give you an emotional outlet and provide a sounding board for your ideas. An early marriage or a wedding after fifty work for your happiness. You are financially safe and drawn to writing in your old age.

• OTHER APRIL 10 BIRTHDAYS

George Arliss	1868
Chuck Connors	1921
Bernard Gimbel	1884
David Halberstam	1934
William Hazlitt	1778
Clare Booth Luce	1903
Tim McCoy	1891
Matthew Perry	1794
Joseph Pulitzer	1847
Omar Sharif	1932

APRIL

· 11 ·

Middle-class morality and its offshoot, self-limitation, may be your nemesis. You are too willing to take the prescribed route and will do anything to avoid criticism. Family plays an important part in your expectations for success. Mother has the leading role in your scenario, and you write yourself into the script to attract her applause. You expect to be called upon to participate and to receive help from your intimates. Childhood is a sociable period, youth inspires a suitable marriage and late years find you happiest at home. Your life can be as sheltered or as exciting as you wish to make it.

Nervousness is a problem. You are inclined to make mountains out of molehills. You need the companionship of a soul mate but you will be selective and feel concern for appearances. You are a nester and a nurturer who enjoys playing devil's advocate. Your peace of mind is based upon others living up to your personal ideals, yet you throw your family and close friends a curve just to watch them squirm.

In mid-life your ambitions are served by a protective, intelligent, monied woman. You speculate wisely and attract affluent and influential relationships thereafter. Family and loved ones make demands on you, and you make personal sacrifices that stunt your growth for a while. You're inclined to be less naive and more skeptical after you expand business interests in your forties. Your fifties find you locked into your judgments.

You have the capacity to be intolerant, want control and are disinterested in outsiders in your secure old age.

• OTHER APRIL 11 BIRTHDAYS

Dean Acheson	1893
Oleg Cassini	1913
Paul Douglas	1907
Joel Grey	1932
Ethel Kennedy	1928
Cameron Mitchell	1918

APRIL

· 12 ·

You're very sure of yourself and you should be authoritative. Youth provided you with practical tools and down-to-earth values. Mid-life offered you a stage for your self-expression. Late years brings you the love of your dreams. You're not slated for the mundane expectations of your birthright. You'll promote an aristocractic, selective, intellectual's life-style for yourself. Be patient!

Patience is not your mainstay. If you rush into moneymaking situations in youth, you slow your progress. Your fears of loneliness and poverty are rooted in the childhood squelching of your independence. You seek out prominent people and make friends among the academic or artistic community. You always imagine that there is more to be seen that meets the eye and are best suited to politics, government service, trial law or widespread communications industries. Education is very important to your mental health. It will be difficult, but you will develop a specialty and receive assistance from socially active people.

You are too bossy or too submissive in your love relationships. It's touch and go with marriage until you get over your dreams of perfection and settle down to accepting yourself and the mistakes you have made. You are paid well for your established talents, and if you think that you're not being given financial recognition for your expertise, you quit. You react similarly with intimates and detach emotionally if your ego is not fed. You change course in late years. Your personality mellows, a real estate deal provides a windfall and home is where your heart is nurtured as you pursue an active old age.

• OTHER APRIL 12 BIRTHDAYS

Montserrat Caballe	1933
David Cassidy	1950
Henry Clay	1777
Mia Danziger	1950
Ann Miller	1919
Tiny Tim	1930
Jane Withers	1926

APRIL
· 13 ·

Your childhood impressions linger throughout your lifetime, and you are wise beyond your years as a tot. You have leadership capacity and ambition. Work is your mainstay, and you are often rigid in the demands you make upon yourself and your peers. It is your sense of duty and loyalty that challenge your progress. Domestic relationships are never clear because you are a romantic and rarely see the people you love realistically. You have the wisdom to discriminate between wasteful interests and false idols, but you are always stretching for tomorrow. Think about today.

Your loves provide diversions from your practical goals. You relate to people who show approval, provide distractions or are inferior to your standards until you apply your powers of business selectivity to your romances. You are apt to marry more than once. After age thirty-seven you are mentally swayed by a member of the opposite sex who brings out the humanitarian and cultural aspects of your nature. Your scope broadens and you become alert to metaphysical questions although you do not involve yourself.

In your forties a supportive, business-minded woman assistant provides a helpmate for your ambitions, and you produce your best efforts in a pleasant and friendly atmosphere. You do well involved in market research or international advertising and publishing. You have a nose for knowing what the public wants and you are able to be reconstructive when others abandon progressive ideas. You are exceptionally astute when property and real estate values come into play but should never be confined to a small community marketplace.

Late years are centered around the home, but your plans are not rigid.

• OTHER APRIL 13 BIRTHDAYS

Samuel Beckett	1906
George Herbert	1593
Thomas Jefferson	1743
Howard Keel	1919
Margaret Price	1941
Eudora Welty	1909
F. W. Woolworth	1852

APRIL

· 1 4 ·

Love and sacrifice go hand in hand as you rush through your youth. You are restless, and you attract problems when you sign legal documents, commit to a routine job or take risks. Childhood is too earthy for your sensual, adventurous nature, and you leave or are pushed out of your nest. You travel and mentally catalog your experiences for future reference.

After your thirtieth year you are involved with helpless or hopeless younger people or take on a saddening challenge. You're a rule-bound taskmaster and disciplinarian inwardly, but you cannot live within the confines of convention. You swing from breaking with all tradition to obeying a stringent routine. Mid-life you attract unconventional experiences and break with your early teachings. You are dedicated to work that interests you but quit when you have mastered or comprehend a job. A career that keeps you unconfined and out of doors and that contains daily adventures is most likely to hold your attention. Home and family are important to your security, but stability is unobtainable without the help of a steadfast mate.

You age but you will never get old. Life after fifty brings you the opportunity to curb your impulsivity, and you take pains to complete your commitments. You attract recognition because you are unusual. Your past attracts publicity or promotional people. There is an element of mystery to you, and people are often unfair in their judgments of your actions or motives. You are an achiever when you are dedicated and a problem to yourself when you scatter your interests. Accidents are part of your destiny but you are not the injured party. Late years offer greatness.

• OTHER APRIL 14 BIRTHDAYS

Julie Christie	1941
Bradford Dillman	1930
François Duvalier	1907
Sir John Gielgud	1904
Mary Healy	1918
Loretta Lynn	1932
Frank Serpico	1936
Rod Steiger	1925
Annie Sullivan	1866

APRIL
· **15** ·

Position and appearances are important to your well-being, and no one is more critical of you than you are—except your mother. Early life is firmly guided by female opinions in the household, and nothing passes her detail-conscious eyes without a comment. You need affection from the opposite sex and attract the love that brings out your ambitions. Building an opulent life-style stretches you to earning capacities beyond your educational background. You learn the value of work in youth.

You are a collector of people, possessions and applause for your dedication to duty. You are willing to wait until you are prepared to "do things right" and are likely to believe in long engagements. Marriage is a stepping stone up the social ladder, and you select a mate with care. You learn that you cannot take risks and develop strong morals, ethics and standards that you apply to career areas that serve the needs of others.

You're capable of building a large organization or setting guidelines that improve working conditions for employees. You are inclined to work with family or contribute to community welfare. Midlife offers the opportunity to use your sense of fair play and you are called upon to use your creative, inventive, independent judgments as a mentor, teacher and friend.

If there is disappointment in love, it is balanced by achievement in business or profession. You are a pioneer and have steadfast determination to succeed. Plan for your retirement if you must slow your pace. You do not adjust to idleness and need a cause to serve or an activity to mastermind. You never lose your maverick instincts or innovative drives.

• OTHER APRIL 15 BIRTHDAYS

Alfred Bloomingdale	1916
Roy Clark	1933
Thomas Hobbes	1588
Henry James	1843
Elizabeth Montgomery	1933

APRIL

·16·

Childhood is not all fun and play. You are in a high-strung environment and are expected to shine as a personality kid or hide your self-expression. Mother and siblings or grandmother and mother join forces to set you socially apart from your peers. You become the class clown or neighborhood introvert. You experience one extreme or another until your thirties, when you establish your professionalism and expertise. Early years are revealing, inventive and intuitive when you realize that you are intended to be—or do—something special during your lifetime.

At times you are less than realistic. You want to relate only to your peers—people who are intelligent and triggered to elitist acts and attitudes. It is important to the family that you are well bred, and you are kept in tow as a youngster. In mid-life you exercise your authority with a heavy hand. You are concerned too much about fashion, fun and lightheartedness or you are a serious fuddy-duddy who is too old for your years.

Mid-life offers problems with lawyers or difficult-to-diagnose business and personal delays. At every turn you seem to be stymied or to get only a part of the success for which you have bargained. You must investigate carefully before you shake hands on a deal or become involved. You are best working alone and managing your own affairs. The aristocrat in you needs quality. You are eager for material self-improvement. But you must never cheat to get quantity or you will surely be caught.

Your late forties begin a fresh life-style. You attract prestige and foreign interests and maintain your self-confidence.

• OTHER APRIL 16 BIRTHDAYS

Edie Adams	1931
Polly Adler	1900
Kingsley Amis	1922
Lindsay Anderson	1923
Charlie Chaplin	1889
Milton Cross	1897
Anatole France	1844
Henry Mancini	1924
Herbie Mann	1930
Philip W. Pillsbury	1903
Lily Pons	1904
Peter Ustinov	1921
Bobby Vinton	1941
Shani Wallis	1933
Wilbur Wright	1867

APRIL

· 17 ·

You can make a Thanksgiving turkey last for a month or put a chapter eleven corporation back in the black. Mental stimulation soothes your practical, imaginative, confident personality. You have the stamina to beat out the competition and the character ingredients to succeed. You may not be from Missouri, but you are technical, methodical, expect to prove your points and have others do the same. Businesslike people and experiences cross your path, and you are capable of wheeling and dealing with the best.

If you have come face to face with poverty, take stock of yourself and you will realize that you have lacked material concentration and the resolve to put your personal ambitions to the forefront. The law, banking and photojournalism put your talents to the test. You dislike being tied down. When your responsibilities overrule your curiosity, you become dissatisfied. Too much attention to the rules and details of managing your affairs or too little focus upon the practical realities gets you into a rut. Mid-life financial progress is delayed by the illness or demands of an intimate female whose welfare requires your personal attention.

Marriage is not satisfactory unless your intellectual tastes are cultivated by your mate. Experience is your best teacher, and you may not marry until after age forty. You prefer older, aristocratic or affluent lovers and rarely find all your needs met in marriage. Sex and love cause complications for you.

A late-in-life inheritance is apt to have your usual legal tangles. You are secure, active and charity-minded after age sixty.

• OTHER APRIL 17 BIRTHDAYS

William Holden	1918
Nikita Krushchev	1894
J. P. Morgan	1837
Harry Reasoner	1923
Thornton Wilder	1897
St. Francis Xavier	1506

APRIL

·18·

Social service does not provide the financial freedom that your cultural tastes demand. You cannot give and take without experiencing financial instability. You want security, orderliness and to see tangible assets accumulate. The impulses that govern your personality—the freedom that you reach out to enjoy, the sensuality that controls and releases you—jeopardize the down-to-earth, everyday, practical values instilled in childhood.

You are destined to meld humanitarian, creative and commercial interests to attract people of polish, skill and nobility. Expect to go it alone to find your most choice opportunities and to meet adversaries in your changing occupations. Affluent and influential people surround you in your thirties, but your restlessness makes long-term relationships impossible and you do not hang on to investments. An exceptional man crosses your path mid-life, and your resolves are altered by his inspirations and departure. You begin again at forty.

Look before you leap into new jobs, loves and sacrifices. You have tremendous energy, but you spend money and your talents as if you had an unending supply. You are always surprised when you find that your checkbook doesn't balance or that you have committed your time to helping others fight for their beliefs.

Late years are less explosive. You have not received your due financially or found a soul mate because you are easily distracted from your personal ambitions. After age fifty you are less driven and you can begin to focus upon your own comforts. In later years your interests relate to your immediate surroundings.

• OTHER APRIL 18 BIRTHDAYS

CLARENCE DARROW	1857
HUNTINGTON HARTFORD	1911
HAYLEY MILLS	1946
CHARLEY PRIDE	1938
LEOPOLD STOKOWSKI	1882

APRIL
· 19 ·

Be yourself and stretch to meet challenges, and greet each day resolved to try something new. Far distant places offer you the opportunity for business and personal recognition. The innovative selling methods that cross your mind are destined to change common practice, and you are intended to break away from your traditional role. Family is protective. You are trained to be productive, but as a youth you scatter your interests and do not realize the potential that emerges in your thirties.

In childhood you are insecure socially and appear to be a clown or too serious. You may stutter or be round-shouldered as a way of showing your feelings of inadequacy. You find it difficult to express your true personality as a youth. You need stroking and recognition. You attract your audience as you widen your scope in mid-life.

Religion, community responsibility and family ties bring you to involvements with service organizations as you build your independent place in the scheme of your ambitions. You need a good education, and whether you are formally trained or gather knowledge from experience, people come to respect your wisdom. Marriage brings artistic or creative talents into your consciousness. You are cautious about money and do not speculate until you're sure that you have adequate funds to cover your obligations. Money is not an overall lifetime problem. You have earning capacity or the good sense to marry a secure person.

In some way you live a double life and enjoy appearing to be something that you are not. Late years are serene and well traveled if you are able to steer clear of emotional hang-ups.

• OTHER APRIL 19 BIRTHDAYS

Don Adams	1927
Jill St. John	1940
Jayne Mansfield	1933
Dudley Moore	1935
Hugh O'Brien	1930

APRIL

·20·

Domestic love is your mainstay, and along with the intimacy you crave, you attract responsibilities. Women, particularly the mother, have a forceful influence upon your personality. The sensitivity to yourself and the desire to collect friends, products, hobbies and support systems for your ideas stem from attitudes you established in childhood. Your need to control people and situations is based upon the lack of control you felt in youth.

You want to be independent and free of restraints, and yet you assume burdens that cause you to act out your insecurities in promiscuity or chameleonlike meaningless personality changes as a youth. You are always making decisions. Why? You have strong personal ideals and convictions—treasure them. You cannot expect partners or spouses to fill your intellectual and physical needs—but you do.

Mid-life irritations cause legal and domestic sparks to fly. You often stay too long at the fair, observing others enjoying the games, and miss the main attraction yourself. Then you get antsy and rush to make changes that are chancy. Patience and dedication will provide you with the skill to beat the boardwalk games of chance, and you'll have the fun of seeing the side shows.

In late years you do not allow your emotions to give you the shakes; your aim is true and the possessiveness, jealousy and lack of self-esteem that sapped energy or ambition early in life decline. As you grow older, your talent for music, which stems from a sense of the rhythm of all things, enhances business and personal relationships, and their progressions inspire you to balance your emotions and ambitions.

• OTHER APRIL 20 BIRTHDAYS

Nina Foch	1924
Lionel Hampton	1914
Jessica Lange	1949
Harold Lloyd	1893
Stanley Marcus	1905
Norman Norell	1900
Ryan O'Neal	1941
Robert F. Wagner	1910

APRIL
·21·

Words are the open sesame to your happiness and the fulfillment of your ambitions. The use of your self-expressive personality, wit and charm greases your path to the perfections you admire and want to own. Beauty and good taste are offered by the people and experiences that cross your path. Late years are secured to home and peaceful. Only lack of concentration or aimlessness can dull your success. Your childhood exposure to crabby or critical adults is dulled by your optimistic nature. You are an imaginative child and require direction for your innovative instincts for playacting. Dare to be different.

Be patient. You're destined to reach from the mundane to the elite as childhood passes into maturity. Home and business have equal priority in youth, and you derive benefits from a wide and divergent social scope. You establish a base and a partnership. A responsible, poised, attractive spouse, with common sense, who understands your spasmodic need for privacy, sees you through your lackadaisical or pointless restless moods.

You want and need to feel that you have control and enjoy being the expert or authority. Education is important for your mental health; contact with the earth or real estate soothes you, and contact with artistic or dramatic people relaxes you. You need diversification and to keep your emotions in tow.

After age thirty you seek and find the variety and travel you need to help you expand your ambitions. You easily gain financial success when you are willing to listen to advice before making major moves. In late years you remain investigative mentally but settle down to a comfortable life-style.

• OTHER APRIL 21 BIRTHDAYS

Charlotte Brontë	1816
Queen Elizabeth II	1926
Patti Lu Pone	1949
Silvano Mangano	1930
Elaine May	1932
John Muir	1838
Anthony Quinn	1915

APRIL

·22·

There's no rest for the workaholic. You are driven to lead a constructive and materially rewarding life. Childhood programming leads into interests in music, real estate and barnstorming problem-solving ideas that improve life for others. Method, practice and orderliness are ingrained in you, but your unchildlike wisdom makes you a precocious tot filled with misunderstood physical energy. You are opinionated and stubborn, and you baffle adults with your direct questions. You do not have a domestically tranquil childhood and head for the hills, join the military or rush off to an early marriage.

You have little compassion for people who are less capable than you are. You have vision, and leadership abilities. You either see the whole world as a marketplace for your charity or you project a self-absorbed facade. Time helps you find a cause or inspiration that attracts money to you. You undergo trials and disappointments until mid-life puts you in the right place at the right time to invest in progressive tools to expand and secure your future.

You are not the best bet for marriage. You have your own philosophy and appear to be traditional, to the confusion of others. After age fifty you are drawn to serve a public need or commit yourself to a humanitarian project that drains your energy and captures your mind, which in the past caused frustration and loneliness for your intimates. You are possessive and would not stay in a relationship that was not totally supportive.

Late years soften your heart to seek relaxation and warmth; however, rich or poor, your work remains your love.

• OTHER APRIL 22 BIRTHDAYS

Eddie Albert	1908
Glen Campbell	1938
Nikolai Lenin	1870
Yehudi Menuhin	1916
Jack Nicholson	1937
J. Robert Oppenheimer	1904
Charlotte Rae	1926

APRIL

·**2 3**·

If you can't have everything your way, don't call off the party. You'll cut off your nose to spite your face and lose your love, ambitions and good health if you do not feel that you have control. You are prone to worry over money ... a throwback to youthful dreams of specialized education put aside for a lack of funding. Mother or other female relatives have plans for you that do not relate to your untraditional ideas and talents. Youth is too restricting, and mid-life offers a break with conventions.

You learn from experience and apply the down-to-earth values instilled in you as a child to your maturity. You want a home, and have difficulty maintaining peaceful family relationships. You are emotionally intuitive, and your sympathy and understanding nature are taxed in marriage. A male child or protégée becomes a means to learning more about yourself in your desire to help him succeed.

The responsibilities you assume tie you down but they are a blessing in disguise and give you the stability you need to dig into your intellectual investigations. You are plagued by fears and challenges, which you intensify by playing devil's advocate. You are a talented diagnostician and instinctively know what makes people tick or how to get to the root of a problem. You get into hot water because you seek enlightenment. Throughout life you are a self-sufficient person who attracts clever, imaginative, artistic friends and enthusiasms.

In your early forties life begins to please you. You are set financially and retain a multiplicity of interests. Old age finds you far from your origins, living practically and enjoying life.

• OTHER APRIL 23 BIRTHDAYS

Janet Blair	1921
James Buchanan	1791
Sandra Dee	1942
Bernadette Devlin	1947
Stephen A. Douglas	1813
Roy Orbison	1936
Simone Simon	1914
Shirley Temple	1928

APRIL

·24·

Concentrate on one thing at a time and cool your impatience. Your life is intended to be lived in the fast lane—one revolution of the wheels at a time. Youth offers a chance to rub elbows with independent, inventive, ambitious people, and you learn to aim for creative, artistic and practical goals. You are dramatic and tend to enlarge your problems. Your mother is a strong influence and you base your self-esteem on her opinions or subtle reactions. You're ego is sound, and only a trace of the "poor me" attitude of childhood surfaces mid-life to trigger depression.

Taking orders from anyone but your spouse sets your dander up. You are a leader who strives for constant improvements in financial and domestic situations. Home is your haven, and you feel protective about your family, community and co-workers. You are the ruler of your roost and expect to be treated with adoration and concern. The paternal-maternal instinct is prominent in all your dealings, and you are a just guardian.

A hardworking, driving person influenced your early years and is a mentor in mid-life. You are too concerned about the opinions of outsiders and are better off when you trust yourself. A female places responsibility on your shoulders and curbs your freedom mid-life. Your strong sense of obligation makes it difficult to keep up the pace you set earlier. However, you are intended to give loving service and accept the changes that are inevitable.

In late years you want to expand your horizons. You are given the chance to counsel others and leave a lasting mark.

• OTHER APRIL 24 BIRTHDAYS

Shirley MacLaine	1934
Barbra Streisand	1942
Leonardo da Vinci	1452
Robert Penn Warren	1905

APRIL
· 25 ·

Success in love and career are tied to your heartstrings. Unhappiness in your early childhood and the inconsistency of your life-style prior to your thirteenth year are forever etched in your memory. It's difficult for you to maintain self-esteem until you try your wings. Once you have discovered that difficulties pass and you have the option to be your own person, you are able to capture the optimism in your soul.

Mother, siblings or grandparents hover over you as a tot, and your frustrations make you prone to hasty judgments. You attach yourself to a male influence and are swayed by his attention. You may spend your entire life benefiting or suffering from his teaching. In youth, career decisions are difficult, and you are a late bloomer until you polish a technical or scientific skill.

Your personal ideals are too elite for practicality, and until you establish a specialty in mid-life your expectations are not realized. You strive to leave a lasting image and cannot expect help from family or associates. You must go it alone and excel in the creative arts. You expect to be paid for your services, desire perfection from yourself, often find others to be too earthy for your tastes. After you reach age thirty-five you ally yourself with larger organizations and are able to support yourself and your responsibilities.

You attract leaners and enjoy participating in causes that benefit others. Your affections are interlaced with your career. Home is your place of beauty, imagination and fun. Your lover must be your best friend. You are a very private person. Late years give you opportunities to be understood and to be loved.

- OTHER APRIL 25 BIRTHDAYS

William Brennan	1906
Ella Fitzgerald	1918
Melissa Hayden	1928
Guglielmo Marconi	1874
Edward R. Murrow	1908
Al Pacino	1940

APRIL

·26·

Take the bull by the horns, look outside your immediate arena, don't be afraid of dropping your red mantle—and your success is assured. Plan your future passes and keep your eye on the gate that leads to your home pasture. You're really a lover, not a fighter, and you want a substantial mate, not an adversary in the bullring of life.

You have a touch of the dramatic and tend to reflect heavily on the past. Your domestic future is a prime target for your business ambitions. You find that the wherewithall becomes available while you invest yourself in order to build a harmonious, loving, opulent home life and an interest in community service. Your financial and domestic investments grow after a traditional childhood that offers little opportunity to stray from your roots. Education is important to you but funds are limited. You continue your education throughout your life as time becomes available.

Mid-life offers people and experiences that attract money, and you are a wise investor. You are executive in your abilities and never lose your desire for success. You maintain your practical property and plan for security in later life. You run into emotionally disturbed people who add to your responsibilities, but you are well equipped to use your constantly seeking mind to help them and overcome your own emotional problems.

In later life you get out of the domestic phase and go on to traveling and enlarging your social interests and obligations. Your musical talent finds a prominent place in your older years.

• OTHER APRIL 26 BIRTHDAYS

John James Audubon	1785
Carol Burnett	1934
Ferdinand Delacroix	1799
Bambi Linn	1926
Anita Loos	1893

APRIL
·27·

You are wise and have the prescience to attract recognition from notables. Prominent people sense that your creative ideas reach out to a marketplace that breaks cultural boundaries. In youth you're limited by conventional standards, but after age thirty you travel intellectually and physically. You independently promote yourself to project your personality to locations that are far from your roots.

You are the first in your family to break with traditions and you begin your own brand of domesticity when you marry. You are intended for a career that meets the public and serves artistic, spiritual or humanitarian needs. Others respond to your ideas because you are a willing friend and you expect empathetic consideration. You add a touch of originality, nobility and romance to the people you meet, and the scope of your private interests and career exceeds your expectations.

You were too unstructured, impulsive or sexual in youth or too rigid, rule bound or cerebral. You experimented inappropriately or feared taking chances that would take you out of your rut. One extreme or the other influenced your personality and governed the way in which you coped with the surprising people who crossed your path in youth.

You married as a virgin or tried to do everything at least once before you settled into domesticity. A male relative causes problems mid-life, and the teachings and devotion of a wise female childhood influence temper your stubborn hostility. Later years focus on your authority in your chosen field, and by eliminating material fears and being cooperative, you master your destiny.

• OTHER APRIL 27 BIRTHDAYS

Sandy Dennis	1937
Ulysses Simpson Grant	1822
Jack Klugman	1922
Snooky Lansen	1914
Samuel F. B. Morse	1791

APRIL

·28·

Are you too open to take superficial conversation as gospel or too focused upon looking for undercurrent meanings? You are secretive and should be inclined to cover your activities after your childhood and youthful experimentations. Childhood domestic inconsistencies teach you to seek out your peers mid-life and to be independent in your thoughts and actions all your days.

You are imaginative and make a novel out of the shortest story. When you enlarge upon life's vicissitudes, depression takes the upper hand. Your expectations for happiness are simplehearted, and you are exploitable in youth. In maturity you are suspicious and have difficulty cultivating lasting friendships or doing business without running into legal confrontations.

You want proof of intangibles, and although you are reasonably responsible and protective of your family and personal interests, you create intricate problems in romance and all areas that touch upon the communication of your feelings. You take on two loves—two hobbies—two business interests—searching for reassurance that you cannot be fooled.

Everyone fears rejection, but you get into financial binds, promiscuous escapades and change careers to avoid dependence and responsibility, only to create situations that draw attention to the things you want most to hide: You subject yourself to rebuffs. Stay out of the courts, be true to your spouse and concentrate on secure investments. In late years you are less self-absorbed, impulsive and dishonest with yourself. You apply patience and a dutiful attitude and learn to accept realities. Your leadership and innovations attract friends and teachers in your old age.

• OTHER APRIL 28 BIRTHDAYS

Robert Anderson	1917
Ann-Margret	1941
Lionel Barrymore	1878
Carolyn Jones	1933
James Monroe	1758
Ivan Nagy	1943

APRIL
·29·
Family traditions, pride or strong personal idealism set the stage for your ability to make money or to finance charitable public projects. Through hardworking, down-to-earth, practical people that you meet in youth, you develop your common sense and apply yourself to becoming someone special. You attract notable friends who excel as communicators. Gracious living is for you!

Marriage and partnerships serve you well if you do not personalize every little discord. Musical adaptability, mentally expansive travels and philosophies are part of your nature. You are high-strung, elite in your personal ideals and often absentmindedly lost in dreams of perfection. You are a collector and automatically attract friends, things and loves.

You are romantic and restless. Skepticism crops up at the wrong times and causes lovers' quarrels that are triggered by your jealousy, lack of self-esteem or misplaced humility. The world is not against you. You may be too unwilling to change with the times or learn by reflecting upon your past experiences. Your sense of responsibility, parental outlook and knack for learning or teaching are pluses from youth.

It pleases you to make others feel comfortable. You have a flair for entertaining, being entertained and showmanship. You are a director, a family or group leader, and you enjoy producing an entire extravaganza. Self-discipline, economy and a well-outlined life-style keep your obligations organized. You share more than the average amount of secret alliances and coverups. Late in life you alter your belief system and open your mind.

• OTHER APRIL 29 BIRTHDAYS

Keith Baxter	1933
Duke Ellington	1899
Tom Ewell	1909
Celeste Holme	1919
Rod McKuen	1933
Zubin Mehta	1936
Johnny Miller	1947

APRIL

· 30 ·

After a practical childhood you bring your unique communications talents to the attention of major conventional organizations. You respect security, perfection and practicality and want to deal with the larger issues. You digress from mother's expectations. Your priorities change with your earning capacity. Money represents your ticket to experiencing the things that indicate enjoyment and fulfillment. Mid-life ushers in a chance to use your capabilities and to achieve your wide-scoped goals.

You are too self-critical and often make mountains out of molehills. This personalized and belittling attitude relates to your maternal ties and the narrowness of her interests. As a tot, you identified with the nervousness, self-absorption or smothering love you saw or sensed was part of her personality. You may, in maturity, react with chronic problems—rashes, allergies, low energy—when you are placed in subordinate positions and are scrutinized too closely.

You appeal to the opposite sex and attract good luck through your charm, humor and youthful optimism. Marriage, education and financial-emotional obligations are destined to fill your expectations. Risks are not necessary and prove to be disasters when in mid-life you are tempted to experiment: Be professional.

During your childhood and mid-life, men relate to prosperity or inheritance and you do well working with organizations that are predominantly governed by males. The intellectual stimulation you receive balances your strong family programming. Life after fifty-five improves, and you travel for pleasure.

• OTHER APRIL 30 BIRTHDAYS

Eve Arden	1912
Corinne Calvert	1926
Cloris Leachman	1930
Franz Lehar	1870

MAY

· 1 ·

How many times can you change horses in midstream? You should know. Your life is as unconventionally burdensome as the salmon swimming upstream to spawn. To get your treasures, the fruits of your labors, situations arise that force you to let go of your loves, plans and projects.

In childhood, men are troublesome, finances undependable and your trust in a romance is wasted. In mid-life, you need courage to compete with proven methods as you bring innovations and inventions to your career. You are forced to be a loner and must keep busy or you get into trouble rebuilding your business repeatedly. Most of your education is gathered from experience and experimentation. You are a survivor and know how to be a workaholic when driven by a practical need.

You are talented, an untraditional investigator and your own best promoter. Partnerships prove to be beneficial after age forty, but only when the financial aspects are shared. You are apt to be a rulebreaker or too think-stuck in business. Creative leadership is your area of expertise. You want formal education and will have time to explore after age fifty-five. Mid-life requirements demand some sacrifices for family, and since you want to be the boss, the buck stops with you.

You are constantly trying to improve yourself and your circumstances. It is the people you select to nurture and love who cause you disillusionment and frustration. You have strong opinions and structures that are too limiting for intimates.

In late years family burdens decrease, and you are less restless. Life is secure and sometimes dull, but you find peace.

• OTHER MAY 1 BIRTHDAYS

Scott Carpenter	1925
Queen Isabella of Castille	1451
Mark Clark	1896
Judy Collins	1939
Danielle Darrieaux	1917
Glenn Ford	1916
Joseph Heller	1923
Jack Paar	1918
Kate Smith	1909

MAY

·2·

Youth offers you the opportunity to learn from experience and promote your talents—if you have the social graces to get out to be seen and heard. You receive help from feminine partnerships and blossom when you are lighthearted. A heavy, serious or unsmiling facade loses friends and loves to your silent moodiness. Escapism—drink, drugs or promiscuity—may seem the answer to your disillusionment when your dignity is shattered. Essentially you will strive to be influential and charitable and to have the wherewithal to live an easygoing life.

You are chastized for seeming to be aloof. True, you are a private person, perfecting good taste, finesse—a regal stance—but your personality compulsions make you swing to require the public attention of a movie star. You are secretive and a bit too childlike. Your destiny puts family and community warmth up front to compete with your need for artistic expression that pays off. Childhood domestic relationships were harmonious, and you look for a marriage that improves your status and provides security. Too often you are caught up in maintaining a beautiful facade and refuse to reach beneath superficial imagery. A woman exerts a strong business and personal influence on you mid-life.

You place your loves on a pedestal. When you bring them down to earth, you shatter the relationship if they cannot return to grace by showing signs of the elevations and self-development that you have acquired. Disappointments are more likely to arise if you are held down in marriage. You are self-sustaining in your career and suffer emotional impoverishment through love.

Late years bring changes, travel and agreeable alliances.

• OTHER MAY 2 BIRTHDAYS

Brian Aherne	1902
Bing Crosby	1904
Lorenz Hart	1895
Englebert Humperdinck	1936
King Hussein I	1935
Benjamin Spock	1903

MAY

· 3 ·

Take center stage and experience the joy of sharing your life with the people who admire a sunny outlook. You need cooperative partners and are at your best when you turn your artistic pursuits into conventional business ventures. As a child, impulsive gestures work for you, but in mid-life, scattering your interests lead you to lose the affluent and influential aspects that are offered in youth. Face the world with a smile, stick to your long-term goals and displace your pessimistic childhood programming with a less personalized attitude. You will find that your disappointment in people is the product of your own projections.

You do not get help in childhood and learn not to depend upon friends or relatives. Finances are shaky, and you are denied beauty in your surroundings by the pettiness and insensitivity of the people you love. Trouble comes your way if you spend before you earn or stubbornly refuse the advice and assistance of a hardworking woman who tries to organize your practical efforts before you're thirty-two.

In mid-life you try to escape from your realities and find that you cannot take risks without paying the piper. You are faced with the responsibility of caring for a male relative and are taxed financially and emotionally. A property investment pays off and you begin to cultivate your self-expression. You have a drive to get involved with medical or labor organizations. Your sense of justice is put to a test, and you retreat.

In late years you try traveling but decide to settle for mental stimulation and charity, close to home, for pleasure.

• OTHER MAY 3 BIRTHDAYS

Mary Astor	1906
Marcel Dupre	1886
Golda Meir	1898
Sugar Ray Robinson	1921
William Shakespeare	1564
Walter Slezak	1902
Frankie Valli	1937
Earl Wilson	1907

MAY

·4·

Expect the unexpected and you'll adapt to your destiny. You travel far from your roots and stretch your talents to educate, entertain or improve standards because you are gifted with the spirit of brotherly love. You have a need to be practical, structured and proper—to maintain traditions. You know that if you use common sense and dedicate yourself to work, you will produce the tangible results you want.

System and practice are your mid-life tools for getting and keeping the comfortable domestic life-style, material security and spiritual peace that you need. You are too self-centered or too concerned about the way in which your personal desires are perceived, by loved ones, to assert yourself. Impatience in youth may cause you to resist compromises that are necessary in your early family environment. You make thoughtless changes or resist observing the signs that indicate progress, and your time to move forward doesn't come until after age twenty-eight.

Men and self-insistent types of women are troublesome in business and personal interactions. A generous and sympathetic woman helps you to withstand the intimidation you feel as you strive to build a career or a business. You have the ability to make money and opportunities to be constructive with investments. Your marriage and loves demand that you be dutiful and honor your obligations. You find it difficult to accept inconsistencies, travel or any threat to your need for orderliness, budget balancing and reasonableness.

In later years you benefit from holistic medicine, financial investments and your salt-of-the-earth ability to be a saver.

• OTHER MAY 4 BIRTHDAYS

Audrey Hepburn	1929
Thomas Hupley	1825
Horace Mann	1796
St. Vincent de Paul	1576
Roberta Peters	1930
Howard de Silva	1909
Francis Spellman	1889

MAY
· 5 ·

Whistle "Don't Fence Me In" to your lovers and you'll let them know where you stand. You must be mentally and physically free to explore anything that sparks your curiosity. In childhood and youth changes are not methodical: they are unconventional and spontaneous. In mid-life your versatility, cleverness and adaptability are sustained by your high level of energy. You are capable of doing many things at one time, want luxury and attract entrepreneurs, advertising types or natural politicians . . . multifaceted people who trigger your enthusiasms.

You are at your best when you play it by ear. You are not inclined to dirty your hands, to be controlled by anyone or to maintain a routine. You have your own unorthodox philosophy that stems from broken relationships, unreliable financial situations and career changes that you experienced as a youth.

Mid-life continues to bring upheavals in business, love and domestic obligations. You are committed to a person or belief that becomes a cross to bear. You will learn from experience and must fight for your individualism. Men are helpful throughout your life and women never understand you. Friends—loves—challenges—come and go, but you are able to survive the rivalries and broken dreams that result from your untraditional maneuvers.

In your forties you become retiring and endeavor to use your abilities through group efforts. Near age fifty you hit the road and explore people and experiences that quench your intellectual thirst to investigate. You are at your best when you keep an open mind and do not fear the unknown.

Later years are spiritually fulfilling and self-revealing.

• OTHER MAY 5 BIRTHDAYS

James Beard	1903
Pat Carroll	1927
Oliver Cromwell	1599
Alice Faye	1915
Freeman Gosdin	1899
Karl Marx	1818
Bob Woodward	1943

MAY

· 6 ·

Love and marriage cannot be ignored as a prime motivation in your destiny—but you cannot tolerate the restraints to your creativity and individualism. You want to progress through education and social acceptance to a mid-life affluent life-style. Family ties are firm and laced to the strong personal ideals and the example set by the father. A marriage for prestige and/or money is more desirable to you than a blinding sensual attraction. You are a dominant innovator as a youth, and you attract impractical, supportive elitists to your table.

You'll never feel old, and you have a knack for stockpiling new enthusiasms that attract the younger generation to your overstuffed gourmet larder. You are inclined to put on weight in mid-life because you like to eat well, and you inspire an appreciation of comfort and opulence. However, you have the incongruous habit of fighting for bargains. Your commitments are long-lasting and demanding. Once you have observed and digested an unknown quantity, you incorporate it into your philosophy and reap unlimited rewards from mental and physical travels.

Late years are geared to social obligations and businesslike activities. You satisfy your need to make people feel welcome, entertained and protected. Your sense of justice and desire to be educated and teach reach out to humanitarian projects that attract public recognition. It is your pleasure and talent to play the roles of actor, director and producer. You have a loner quality—a delicate ego—that is witnessed only by your intimates and is hidden in a traditional facade or the expectations of your career. You are an eccentric do-gooder.

• OTHER MAY 6 BIRTHDAYS

Sigmund Freud	1856
Stewart Grainger	1913
Willie Mays	1931
Robert Peary	1856
Maximilian de Robespierre	1758
Toots Shore	1905
Rudolph Valentino	1895
Orson Welles	1915

MAY

· 7 ·

No one else understands your brand of excellence. To find the answers to your never-ending questions, you must be alone. The gift of intuitive reasoning is your mainstay. Give in to your emotions and the slide from your aristocratic pedestal reduces you to unbecoming humility and an overt show of pettiness. With your reserve, good taste and intellectual capacity, you can rise above the examples of personalized sensitivity you observed and experienced as a tot.

It is most important that you think out your domestic and career projects and problems in a noiseless, serene, off-the-beaten-path atmosphere. A room of your own, a place in the country or a waterside retreat represent your places of relaxation and peace.

Marriage is more appealing in youth than it is in mid-life. Family life-style, sex and the physical experiences offered to you as a youngster were unconventional, surprising and uncomfortable. You are a restless and insecure person until you meet educated, authoritative, investigative people who come into your life after twenty-eight, when you have fled the emotional drains of your birthplace. Travel and life experience change your assessment of yourself when finances are less apt to be secure in mid-life. You tend to stick to jobs or commitments for the sake of income and make efforts to improve circumstances for the people you love.

You are a giver, but fears of poverty haunt you. Friends are unable to fill the gaps of loneliness until you establish your authority or specialize your talents. Late years offer companionship, inheritance and an end to vexing complexities.

• OTHER MAY 7 BIRTHDAYS

Ann Baxter	1923
Johannes Brahms	1833
Teresa Brewer	1931
Robert Browning	1812
Gary Cooper	1901
Gabby Hayes	1885
Archibald MacLeish	1892
Darren McGavin	1922
Eva Peron	1919
Johnny Unitas	1933

MAY
· 8 ·

Money and power are the offshoots of your mid-life opportunities. People recognize your ability to relate to all types of people and experiences without prejudice. You are a ball of physical and mental energy that needs challenges, and if the adventures of the financial world don't come your way, you take your enthusiasm, untraditional ideas and stamina to greener pastures.

You have more personality than you show to the world and need self-expressive, humorous, friendly intimate relationships to fulfill your artistic interest and to encourage you to expose your talent. You're clever—a quick study—and learn early in life to seize unplanned opportunities and to throw your hat into the ring. Your coordination and ability to establish efficient means of practice are exceptional tools for playing a musical instrument, entering professional sports or juggling a multitude of communicators.

You are too talkative or too quiet. In childhood you were punished by the withdrawal of the personalities you loved or by too much superficial socializing. In maturity you open your mouth and stick your own foot in it or fail to kick up a verbal fuss when you should attract attention to yourself. Be careful not to be taken in by flattery, glitz or glitter and surface conversation. You are a sucker for a compliment, a listening ear for transitory fashions and game-playing. Use your mind.

Older women are lucky for you, and they encourage you to remain creatively active in late years. Your friends are your treasures as you realize that money isn't the end-all; career is.

• OTHER MAY 8 BIRTHDAYS

Thomas B. Costain	1885
Peter Benchley	1940
Melissa Gilbert	1964
Ricky Nelson	1940
Don Rickles	1926
Roberto Rossellini	1906
Fulton Sheen	1895
Toni Tennille	1943
Harry S. Truman	1884

MAY
·9·
Options come your way, but others dictate your destiny until mid-life. Your happiness is found in helping others improve themselves artistically, spiritually and materially. Youth is your time to gain experience, but due to the confines of the traditional expectations of your family and environment, you do not make the right choices for yourself. Changes come after age twenty-eight, and you attract notable people to your noble, often impractically romantic philosophy. Groups of people love you—personal love does not come easily.

Your values are your mainstay. Nurture them and you attract recognition for your wisdom, empathy and cultural expansiveness. You travel far from your birthright emotionally and physically. Money comes in through inheritance, personal supporters or your own clever wheeling and dealing when all seems to be lost. You always pull out of a hole and turn apparent failures into futuristic goals.

Your ambitions include a "good" marriage, building a solid family front and maintaining extensive and far-reaching social relationships. The mail, phone and telephone bring in associations with women of wealth and influence. You are not able to walk alone and should avoid becoming skeptical when given gifts or emotional responses. You are drawn to humanitarian service and are called upon to sacrifice for a loved one or a worthy cause.

Travel is a natural aspect in your true calling. You are best when left to your own devices and open to investigating broader horizons. In late life you rest and rule your roost.

• OTHER MAY 9 BIRTHDAYS

James Barrie	1860
Candice Bergen	1946
Albert Finney	1936
Pancho Gonzales	1928
Glenda Jackson	1936
Henry J. Kaiser	1882

MAY

· 10 ·

Take the initiative, give orders and use your fine mind to surround yourself with the intellects you admire. Childhood was too rigid, routined and proper for your innovative and independent nature. The work ethic that you absorbed stays with you all your days. You experienced unconventional relationships in youth and became a rule-breaker or a rule-maker. However, your protective, affectionate and determined personality holds on to domestic ties as you restlessly flee the nest due to the unacceptable behavior of parents or impatience to begin a uniquely different life-style.

Groups of people find you a comfortable leader, and you rise to the top of your craft if you are able to remain autonomous. You worry about everything and admire brains over beauty. You seek out associations that are influential and attract a "godfather" who sponsors you or protects your business ambitions. It is in your best interests to have a more conservative professional manage your funds. Somehow, your money dissolves as fast as you earn it when you are left without a guardian angel.

Mental health is a mainstay to your physical activities, and you are better off doctoring yourself. Your home is the place you return to after you travel. It is your little blue blanket and your private place of relaxation. Property investments bring you rewards, and you have difficulty building a firm financial foundation until you get up the guts to sink funds into real estate. You appear managerial but need a push to manage yourself.

Later years are better suited to enjoying love, gaining financial freedom and attracting the activities you most enjoy.

• OTHER MAY 10 BIRTHDAYS

Fred Astaire	1899
John Wilkes Booth	1838
Ella Grasso	1919
David O. Selznick	1902
Max Steiner	1888
Dmitri Tiompkin	1899
Nancy Walker	1922

MAY
· 11 ·

Know what you want before you begin selling yourself or your creative ventures. You must have a calling to bring your special point of view or personal ideals to the attention of others. You have the ability to present an image of better days or to do some flag waving to attract an audience and supporters who are dedicated to promoting your cause. Your best efforts are based upon a loving friendship or marriage, an easygoing life-style and a fanatical zeal to get your point across.

If you are too concerned with yourself or with superficial relationships and believe that what you see is what you get, you're not using your cleverness, adaptability and gambler's instinct. Perhaps you are too easily influenced by the words or facades that you assume to be the gospel truth. Dig beneath your own ways and means of attracting attention—are you too childlike or naive in your expectations for attaining star status?

How true to life or down to earth are the displays that are made to attract your attention? The examples of domesticity that you saw as a youngster caused you to daydream yourself into a different world. Your imagination runs rampant as an adult. It is in your own best interests to concentrate your mind and career activities to develop your interests past the investigation stage. Love relationhips confuse you because you do not stay in a singular relationship—everybody interests you. Diversions that satisfy curiosity ease your feelings of childhood rejection.

Plans for retirement are uncertain. You get involved in your neighborhood, relax and try to satisfy your desire for peace.

• OTHER MAY 11 BIRTHDAYS

Irving Berlin	1888
Salvador Dali	1904
Martha Graham	1894
Doug McClure	1938
Tyrone Power	1913
Mort Sahl	1927
Phil Silvers	1912
Valentino	1932

MAY **· 12 ·** Don't compare childhood memories with average folks; your youth is too unconventional. Your experiences carved your unique attitude and adult ambitions, which revolve around an imaginative, creative and sociable life-style. You are a loner who appears to be part of the crowd. Only intimates share your unique philosophy, while social contacts bolster your ambitions.

You understand the value of being fashionable, attractive and friendly. Few people see the importance of maintaining a manicured facade from your vantage point. You appear to abide by surface values, because in the depth of your philosophy you see the hunger in humanity to retain a childlike love of beauty.

You are aggressive and at the same time receptive. The opportunity to use your sensitivity courageously and wisely crops up in mid-life repeatedly. You're destined to undergo changes of heart, residence and point of view from childhood through mid-life. In later years you are applauded and rewarded for your efforts to help others see the color and sunshine in life.

In childhood you decide to get away from the traditions of the family. In your late twenties you select a career that exemplifies your personal beliefs, and you attract attention and criticism when you speak up. You are sincere, but your views may be scandalous. In mid-life you make sacrifices in order to uphold your ideals. Problems with family members are emotionally painful. You are often unfairly judged but attract fame for your struggles. Be cautious and serious about long-term goals.

Later life provides the security and relaxation you want.

• OTHER MAY 12 BIRTHDAYS

Burt Bacharach	1929
Yogi Berra	1925
George Carlin	1937
Lindsay Crouse	1948
Howard K. Smith	1914
Florence Nightingale	1820
Julius Rosenberg	1918
Tom Snyder	1936
Socrates	467 B.C.
Philip Wylie	1902

MAY
· 13 ·

You had to be wise beyond your years as a tot and didn't see pay dirt until you put your shoulder to the wheel and pushed to earn your keep. You take chances repeatedly, only to learn that gambles are fine for friends but they are devastating to you. Too bad that your best teacher is experience; some people learn by patiently observing the mistakes of others. In mid-life you work through emotionally taxing reconstructions of your ambitions. Later in life, when you are less concerned about material security, your cosmopolitan tastes are rewarded and many of your youthful romantic notions become realities.

Your determination, stamina and emotional security are tested continually. In youth you are exposed to people and experiences that open doors to artistry and the value of humanitarian service. You cannot help but grow far from your roots, but the influence of a forceful, squelching parent results in difficulty determining your own ego strengths. You try to please everyone before you make a decision to change goals or make a move. You confuse loved ones and rarely get exactly what you want in youth.

In mid-life you refuse to follow anyone's advice. You are stubborn. Your success is allied with large organizations that find the perfect spot for your managerial abilities. You are slotted to be a problem solver. You invest in real estate and find it difficult to move once established. You want to make embellishments to your life-style, but common sense dictates that you stay put and keep a low profile into retirement years. Inactivity is detrimental to your happiness: you work to the end.

• OTHER MAY 13 BIRTHDAYS

Beatrice Arthur	1926
Joe Louis	1914
Daphne du Maurier	1907
Stevie Wonder	1950

MAY
· 14 ·

Follow your intuition—your hunches—to attract success. Don't expect to follow in anyone's footsteps. You are the catalyst for change in the lives of the people you meet. Your special brand of enthusiasm is a trigger for spontaneity. Physical pleasures tease your palate, and the taste of each new experience you meet adds to your storehouse of knowledge. You learn and gain stature from throwing your hat into the ring and watching to see where and how it lands.

You have difficulty holding on to money and stabilizing your lifestyle until you reach your mid-forties. Promotional, theatrical, entrepreneurish business interests and ventures beckon you. In midlife you are better able to adjust to working with groups of people and find a lead position in a joint effort. Childhood programming taught you to work and use self-discipline. You rebel when your freedom is curtailed in youth, but rely heavily on the basic values instilled in you as an ambitious adult.

You are always surprised to discover the extent of the upheaval that your love relationships entail. You dive in headfirst and realize that you have trapped yourself. Sex and sensual curiosity bring out the extremist in you. No one solves your practical problems and promotes your projects as cleverly as you do. However, when intimates are involved, you must wait until late years to benefit from your brains, not your bravado.

Both mental and physical travels make your life an adventure. You must learn to take charge of each day as it comes.

· OTHER MAY 14 BIRTHDAYS

Bobby Darin	1936
Gabriel Fahrenheit	1686
Otto Klemperer	1885
Norman Luboff	1917
Patrice Munsel	1925

MAY
· **15** ·
You are independent, clever and talented. You are able to cope with offbeat people and experiences with a traditional twist. A strong, assertive family member stresses self-discipline, work and education in your youth. You want harmony, love and protection within your domestic environment, and you bend to clear-cut instructions. You become intimidated too easily as a child, rebel in youth and must learn to understand your unique ability to attract attention outside of the domestic community in mid-life.

As a youth, your expectations for happiness are based upon guidance and financial security through marriage and friendships. You are an unrealistic romantic who learns in mid-life that your diligent concentration is required. You are surrounded by high-strung, visionary, speculative people who desire your cooperation to achieve their ambitions for a large portion of your lifetime. Domestic and community responsibilities eventually bring your personal ideals and ability to assume positions of trust into the limelight.

Finances and business dealings are problematic because you are self-deluding. With a down-to-earth attitude, you are given fair compensation for your work efforts and are able to assume the burden of a female relative to whom you feel obligated. You are able to combine home and business commitments wisely.

In later years you retain your individuality and ability to be enthusiastic and youthful. You have always been wise and were seen as a precocious tot. Aging ripens your empathetic nature.

• OTHER MAY 15 BIRTHDAYS

Anna Maria Alberghetti	1936
Eddy Arnold	1918
Joseph Cotton	1905
Clifton Fadiman	1904
Trini Lopez	1937
James Mason	1909
Ken Venturi	1931

MAY

·16·

Look before you leap into partnerships or become a supporter of causes. You are a target for criticism. Your reputation and financial stability are jeopardized when you do not protect your privacy or uphold your aristocratic tastes. You are exposed to superficial and intellectual people who know how to make you feel humble. You learn to be yourself in mid-life, but before you take your talents into your own hands, you must first let go of the female influence of your childhood.

The loss of a male relative or business associate has a decided effect upon career decisions. You should travel for ambitions and to satisfy your curiosity. Home and family are important to you, although they do not detract from your individuality, creativity and unique style. You have a flair for self-promotion and a knack for attracting notables. Early life experiences have taught you to be adaptable to all situations and types of people.

You observed as a youth how easily fashionable or personable people were able to charm the skin off a snake. Late in life you put one face to the world and another to your intimate relationships. You are often disillusioned and disappointed in your loves and alliances. You have a fear of loneliness and emotional poverty that is based upon your dreams of perfection. You must learn to depend upon yourself and to see yourself realistically. Everyone will not like or admire you; don't try so hard to please people of divergent beliefs.

Later years demand that you live up to your personal standards. You meet frustrations but you're geared to success.

• OTHER MAY 16 BIRTHDAYS

Henry Fonda	1905
Woody Herman	1913
Lainie Kazan	1940
Liberace	1920
Margaret Sullavan	1911
Studs Terkel	1912

MAY

· 1 7 ·

You need intellectual challenges and opportunities to apply your exceptional executive, organizational skills to major creative or financial industries. If you expect to move mountains, you will. You are able to attract admirers and people who are eager to get on your bandwagon. Your childhood offers a diversification of experiences and personalities. A good education is your best bet, but your early life exposures give you hands-on lessons in survival techniques.

The practicality, stamina and dedication that were required in your childhood should set your career concentration in youth. It is your need for freedom and a feeling of restlessness that may make you indecisive. You make compromises, but after the age of thirty you benefit from affluent and influential friends and business associates.

Too bad you don't know when to give up on a bad bargain. You hang in to your romantic and material commitments past the time that they make you happy or increase your professional potential. You attract listeners and admirers throughout your lifetime. It is your exceptional ability to understand the tastes and fancies of marketable ideas and items that keeps a balance in your checkbook. Your family life is nurtured by your loving and protective outlook. You have an authoritative personality that interacts positively with subordinates. The only problems you have arise when your emotions rule your logic or you fail to make compromises to ensure your stability.

Later years show profits from real estate and a continued desire to counsel and relate to people. Expect to be a winner.

• OTHER MAY 17 BIRTHDAYS

Archibald Cox	1912
Sugar Ray Leonard	1955
Zinka Malinov	1906
Bob Merrill	1920
Maureen O'Sullivan	1911

MAY
·18·

After an untraditional youth, you organize your talents and set out to be of service to others. It is difficult for you to rest easily when you observe or feel that your family or intimates are suffering. As time goes on, you transfer your responsiveness to include the world. You grow far from your birthright and the practical personality patterns of your child-hood. Your best choice for a career lies in the creative arts. Your personal happiness is based upon the romantic in you.

Too much structured routine or too little orderliness in your daily routines, as a tot, train your to be an adult workaholic or an unre-strained underachiever. The extremes that you display are obvious to family and associates. You swing between self-limitations that are dictated by rule-bound rigidity or a distaste for established proce-dures. Your vacation time is governed by how exhausted you make yourself or how lazy you feel.

You like money. It is essential to your positive feelings of self-worth to see tangible results of your labors. You want to be a cultured person but repeatedly retreat into materialistic ambitions. Your loves are demanding, and you lose the momentum of your practical am-bitions in your desire to polish and hone your emotional commit-ments. You change your direction often and should avoid legal entanglements that result from your indecisiveness.

You grow far from family expectations and your birth environment. In mid-life and in later years, personalities who have developed a polish and skill of performance find you and applaud your talents. They recognize your ability to extend a helping hand and to give empathetic advice. You find serenity.

• OTHER MAY 18 BIRTHDAYS

Pierre Balmain	1914
Frank Capra	1897
Perry Como	1913
Dame Margot Fonteyn	1919
Reggie Jackson	1946
Jacob Javits	1904
Ezio Pinza	1895
Bertrand Russell	1872
Meredith Wilson	1902

MAY
· 19 ·

Vitality, uniqueness and progressive ambitions are the keys to your character. You are not Joe Average. You find your special spots as you adapt yourself to changing circumstances. In youth you may not be routinely attractive, but you've got that special something that sets you apart from the herd. Mid-life, your intellect blooms. Publicly, you seem to have a pedestrian life-style, but you live a very different private life. It is better for you to allow your self-image to surface. Until you do, you feel torn between doing "the right thing" and being yourself.

You are intended to be an innovator in your family traditions. You change in your thirties. You become expansive and have broad-scoped ambitions. You become a guide who attracts public appreciation, and you live your emotional relationships with the innocence of a babe. You are a combination of a romantic and a cynic. You set an example for others to follow when you stop trying to do what you imagine is expected and begin to express your pioneering ideas. You think that you need support: you don't.

You have stamina, resolve and constructive determination: the soul of the ballet dancer and the baseball player. All professions maintain a daily practice to achieve a tangible result. Lucky for you that you have a fine sense of humor, too. Your versatility brings out your unselfish philosophy, and your intuition gives you the ability to predict the timing for cultural expansions. You are a rare human being.

Any late-in-life disappointments result from your realization that you could have given less and retained more of yourself.

• OTHER MAY 19 BIRTHDAYS

Lady Nancy Astor	1879
David Hartman	1935
Nellie Melba	1861
Ho Chi Minh	1890
Peter Townshend	1945
Mike Wallace	1918
Malcolm X	1925

MAY
·**20**·
Your intuitive judgments take you into leadership positions, but you always seem to be sacrificing something you want to please your intimates or for the good of the group. You're clever; as a tot, you attract fast-moving experiences. Marriage is a good idea in youth but lacks luster for you later in life. Until your thirties you are changable.

Money is a concern in mid-life, and you are experimental and must gear yourself to face making decisions constantly. You can be gullible and naive. Problems arise from your desire to live a beautiful life surrounded by lighthearted, youthful, entertaining people. It's one side of the coin or the other for you; too superficial or too serious. You will learn to be more tolerant of yourself and others after you're fifty.

You want thinkers and workers in your life, and you won't tolerate interference to your freedom. You assume responsibilities and are parental in your desire to shape or control the people you choose for allies. The tests that face you come about when you accept face value as fact. It is in your best interest to get to the details before you involve yourself in business or personal commitments.

Habits are your crutches. They are a safe harbor, and you often miss the boat if you refuse to alter your course. Love may be very disillusioning until you relax and become adaptable when intimate. You require peace, rest and emotional control as you get older. You find a copemate-companion when you are calmer.

You're destined to learn to distinguish between phony values and practical realities. Your late years are the happiest.

• OTHER MAY 20 BIRTHDAYS

Honoré de Balzac	1799
Cher	1946
Moshe Dayan	1915
George Gobel	1920
Jimmy Henderson	1954
Dolley Madison	1768
James Stewart	1908
"Commander" Edward Whitehead	1908

MAY

·21·

You are a charmer and gifted with the ability to get your points across. You're a lover and want to be loved. As a tot, the influence of a dominating female alters your happy personality. You are too sensitive and self-depreciating as a youth, a result of too much focus upon material objectives. You need to express your talents through educational advantages, but petty problems delay your progress. Money and ambitions of others have a profound effect upon your nerves and self-esteem.

Partnerships with men are beneficial in mid-life. Late years have the added protection of inheritance or rewards from past work. You worry needlessly and are at your best when you reflect back to pat yourself on the back. Childhood and youth are a testing ground for your ability to take on burdens for others. Once you are past forty you appreciate your special ability to attract friends, gifts and applause. Most of your goals are accomplished when you put your personality in the forefront and allow yourself to be on the receiving end.

You were encouraged to be an achiever as a child. You strive to be influential and affluent. Let yourself be seen and participate in a variety of activities. The more you play, the more you will enjoy marriage, business and social contacts. Keeping up with the fashions, new places to travel, gimmicks and new products should interest you. If you find yourself hiding out or fearful of making changes, you are experiencing negativity.

Later in life your visualizations come to fruition. You attract admirers of the opposite sex and always will. You have the gift of youthfulness and will always remain young.

• OTHER MAY 21 BIRTHDAYS

Raymond Burr	1917
Peggy Cass	1925
Dennis Day	1917
Robert Montgomery	1904
Ara Parsegheon	1923
Harold Robbins	1916
Henri Rousseau	1844

MAY

·22·

You are a problem solver and will work to build a better mousetrap. As a child, your energy was not as much an asset as it becomes in your mid-life. High-energy children do not have the opportunity to be productive and see the results of their labors. Parents, especially the father, influenced your creativity and independent actions. After age twenty-eight you find it more comfortable to use your dynamic intuition, determination and practicality. Your greatest successes come through real estate, public service or building trades as your life unfolds.

You expand your interests early in life and grow far from your domestic environment. Mid-life demands that you take control and direct your energy to see the results of your personal ideals. It is in your best interests to be down to earth, empathetic and extremely honest in your business activities. When others fail to use their common sense, you "know" the right questions to ask to get answers that provide solutions.

Your destiny offers and demands that your intimate relationships and personal ambitions are your second priority. You have options to labor for a broader scope of humanity than the average person. Any overindulgences will be a distraction from your authority and are destructive. If your intuition indicates that you are in over your head, call upon professionals for advice. Gather details; never gamble and draw your own conclusions. You inspire new traditions for future generations.

Look forward to change. Accomplishments are important to you, and you are a severe critic and a teacher all your days.

• OTHER MAY 22 BIRTHDAYS

Marcel Breuer	1902
Judith Crist	1922
Arthur Conan Doyle	1859
Peter Nero	1934
Sir Laurence Olivier	1907
Vance Packard	1914
Michael Sarrazin	1940
Susan Strasberg	1938
Richard Wagner	1813

MAY

·2 3·

You never get lost in a crowd or stagnate. Life is one adventure after another. You learn to depend upon yourself as a tot and learn to detach your emotions from mental pursuits. You are born old ... too aware of the problems that take place in your domestic environment. To save yourself from the pain of total involvement, as a teen, you relate to projects, not individuals.

Before you are thirty your impatience makes you dissatisfied and prone to making hasty changes. You learn to be a clever survivor and relate to the opportunities offered at the moment. Politics, theater, advertising and all professions that allow you to use your adaptability, versatility and multifaceted personality should tempt you. You are at your best learning from experience and putting your ideas into form.

You are sensual and passionate. Your loves learn to weather the storms of your sometimes highhanded personality. However, your loyalty, generosity and attraction to razzmatazz keep your home fires burning brightly. Travel and unconventional opportunities may require that you speak more than one language. Try to plan for intellectual pursuits. Your life-style is based upon reacting quickly to new exposures and proceeding with new enthusiasms. You'll gain your ambitions quickly if you are mentally prepared.

A legal involvement adds to your good fortune, and a tie to one intimate relationship balances your proclivity for having uncertainty drop into your lap. You are conscious about paying your debts and have a tendency to worry about appearances inappropriately. In later years you welcome privacy and calm.

• OTHER MAY 23 BIRTHDAYS

Rosemary Clooney	1928
Joan Collins	1933
Douglas Fairbanks	1883
Herbert Marshall	1890
Anton Mesmer	1733
Artie Shaw	1910

MAY

·24·

You want the love and respect of your family and your peers. Yet you become anxious if your personal freedom is curtailed by responsibilities—the burdens that you take on impulsively. As a youth, you get involved in order to satisfy your curiosity. In mid-life it's the "right thing to do." Late years find you holding your loved ones near. Throughout your lifetime your immediate relationships hold the key to your success and happiness.

As a youngster, concerns about money and family interactions delay your independent progress. Impractical or unconventional people spark you to early maturity. Your teen years are unstable, emotionally sensitive and peopled with elitists who believe that rules are made for ordinary mortals—not for them. You may have to wait for the education that you crave. With or without the academic credits, you are a haven of sympathetic advice and sound reasoning.

If educational opportunities are not dropped into your lap, one way or another, you make progress. You are not ambitious for yourself alone and take care of intimates who are less businesslike. You have the capacity to rise above hardships. When necessary, you are thrifty and conservative. You never lose your capacity for dreaming or the possibility of fame.

Late years are planned for travel and a casual life-style. You apply your dramatic nature to everyday practicalities and pleasures. Your love of beauty, music and creature comforts is satisfied if you refuse gambles and concentrate on a career. Childhood dreams of fame may come true when you accept reality.

• OTHER MAY 24 BIRTHDAYS

George Washington Carver	1864
Chong	1939
Bob Dylan	1941
Henry Emerson Fosdick	1878
Elsa Maxwell	1883
Lili Palmer	1914
Mikhail Sholokhof	1905
Queen Victoria	1819

MAY

·25·

You must be known intimately to be understood and loved. You plan for the future by reflecting upon the past. You draw from unforgettable experiences in youth that instilled a fear of both emotional and financial poverty. Your childhood offers self-expressive, charming, sociable people who set out their talents and want attention.

You have a compulsion to get to the root of thoughts that cross your mind. You find it difficult, until your thirties, to establish self-esteem. You feel insecure until you are respected as an authority or an expert in your chosen field.

Until you reach your late twenties you make changes and learn from experience. After age thirty you meet quality-conscious people who are not conservative and live nonroutine lives. You need to have an intellectual appreciation and a sensual love to relinquish your privacy. Your lover must inspire your respect and accept your aloofness from mundane people or happenings. Marriage is not a simple emotional commitment to you. It is a mating that strives for perfection.

Photography, electronics and computer industries can use your discriminating tastes and investigative nature. Educational opportunities should be seized in youth or you will be a late bloomer and have a money crunch. As you gather mid-life professionalism, your reputation begins to precede you. You will attract whatever you need when you have established a reputation.

In late years, if you work with your loner self, you will never lack for money. You are not geared to benefit from legal actions or risky business deals. Keep faith in yourself.

• OTHER MAY 25 BIRTHDAYS

Dixie Carter	1939
Bennett Cerf	1898
Jeanne Crain	1925
Miles Davis	1926
Ralph Waldo Emerson	1803
Thomas Gainsborough	1727
Ron Nessen	1934
Dorothy Sarnoff	1919
Beverly Sills	1929
Marshal Tito	1892
Gene Tunney	1897
Leslie Uggams	1943

MAY

·26·

You may be "king of the hill" or the lowliest peasant. The choice is yours. Whether to live in the past or to visualize the future—how your mind does vacillate. A complete education that results in a practical job function boosts your potential to earn big bucks. However, a desire to have family and domestic roots tempts you to take on responsibilities in youth. Your natural diplomacy and ability to politic to maintain your comforts give you options for long-term commitments. It takes courage for you to assert your individuality or to stick with the intimates who have learned to depend upon you. You learn, as your destiny unfolds, to have true grit.

Childhood offers untraditional avenues, but you are surrounded by down-to-earth people who focus upon practicalities. You break through—you do not follow a conventional path. You break parental molds. The father or dominant male has a strong influence on your career decisions. You aim to please or displease the person who outshouts your creative ambitions. Until you reach your thirties, you vacillate as you try to receive recognition for your individuality.

Mid-life brings opportunities to meet powerful and influential people. You develop into an energetic doer. Your body, mind and intuition work together to produce practical results. You've learned to deal with the unexpected and to be curious about people, foreign countries and cultures.

You won't stop merchandising yourself in later years. Your sense of beauty, energy and businesslike approach defy old age.

• OTHER MAY 26 BIRTHDAYS

James Arness	1923
Aldo Gucci	1909
Al Jolson	1886
Peggy Lee	1920
Mrs. Miller	1897
Robert Morley	1908
Artie Shaw	1910
John Wayne	1907

MAY

· **27** ·

It's difficult for you to hang in doing one thing, but whatever you do, it will get you out of the kitchen and into the path of notable people. You're pegged for being eccentric in your traditions, and the quiet dedication you display, once invested in a career, sets you apart.

Childhood has you changing constantly, learning to survive unsettling experiences as you gain wisdom. People who ask questions, behave modestly and think of life in broad cultural terms add to your own curiosity. If you think that you are destined to write a book—if you haven't already done so—you're right. It is only a lack of determination to organize and and attention to structure and detail that will stop you from following a literary career.

Mid-life opportunities take you into domestic commitments. Although you are an ardent, romantic and generous lover, the close proximity of intimates and the burdens that they unintentionally add to your sensitive nature make marriage difficult. The world outside your neighborhood will always beckon you to take a leadership position. It will be your calling to find the greater good and serve artistically, charitably or instructionally. The legal, medical, spiritual, financial management and government professions are your roads to elevating yourself. Escapist diversions are your downfall.

You attract publicity when you don't want it. Secret fantasies, a desire to do it all and have it all in late years bring out your fascination for money. After age fifty you have the detachment to make millions, if you are able to withstand the work and loneliness that accompany commercial responsibilities.

• OTHER MAY 27 BIRTHDAYS

Amelia Bloomer	1818
Isadora Duncan	1878
Lou Gossett	1936
Jay Gould	1936
Dashiell Hammett	1911
Wild Bill Hickok	1837
Julia Ward Howe	1819
Henry Kissinger	1923
Vincent Price	1911
Sam Snead	1912
Cornelius Vanderbilt	1794
Herman Wouk	1915

MAY
·28·
Whatever you stick with will turn out to be a "first." You begin traditions. The trick is to get you to practice, work and use your determination realistically. You are too bound to rules and conventions, or you're decidedly improper.

Rigid structure in childhood and people capable of unemotional goodness trained you. Circumstances were not stable, and you tried to maintain an orderly routine surrounded by surprises and disorder. As an adult, you live by your own ideals and tend to focus upon your emotional relationships. Life will expose you to disappointments. Workaholic habits cause intimates anxiety. But you profess to find it difficult to accept limitation and see regulations as chains that bind you. As a result, you slip from one accomplishment to another, changing your concept of progress and rarely allowing your material success to form a foundation for inner security.

When you love, it is extraordinary. The recipient of your lavish affections must bend to your inclinations and be willing to share your dreams or represent your personal ideal. Mid-life experiences confirm your belief that more harm is done by stupid people than by people who intend to do harm. You are a debater and a detail catcher and are best working along with a supportive partner.

You have ample opportunity to travel to meet challenging new exposures after age fifty-five. Comfort, opulence and material success are assured by inheritance or a relationship with a male who alleviates commercial responsibilities. Your life-style and your mind stay sharp in late years. Your ambitions are rewarded.

• OTHER MAY 28 BIRTHDAYS

Carroll Baker	1935
Ian Fleming	1908
Gladys Knight	1944
William Pitt	1759
Dionne Quintuplets	1934
Madeline Le Roux	1946
Jim Thorpe	1888

200 · MAY BORN ARE

MAY

·29·

You're a multifaceted visionary: moody, nervous and self-absorbed. Childhood has insecurities and uncertainties that tie you closely to mother and sisters or female household members. You are the apple of their eyes or a pitiful Cinderella. For one reason or another you learned that you could attract attention with your charming ways or you could attract attention by escaping social obligations. Either area sees you the childish class clown or the overly mature, responsible schoolroom monitor—one extreme or another—talking too much or too little.

The oceans have meaning for you. In youth you may travel by sea, but throughout your life travel over water involves special rewards or problems. You're opinionated and attract unconventional alliances, and as you get older, your life-style reflects your inner philosophy. You are too imaginative; you do not dig deeply enough when you gather facts, or you create your own scenario. You'll get caught if you veer a bit from the truth or gamble. Friends will get you whatever you want and need.

You are geared to doing and seeing everything in extremes. Enemies become friends when you act as go-between; you have high-powered tact. There is a strong, maternal person who slows you down mid-life. That pressure lets up after you have achieved a measure of success. You rearrange your life. You have the opportunity to leave a lasting image by expressing your personal ideals. In film industries, data processing and commenting on the fashions, you have the flair to attract a loyal following.

When your ideas are presented publicly, you have power for great good or destruction. In late life you seek enlightenment.

- OTHER MAY 29 BIRTHDAYS

Isaac Albeniz	1860
Paul Ehrlich	1932
Bob Hope	1903
John F. Kennedy	1917
Pearl Lang	1922
Beatrice Lillie	1898
Herb Shriner	1918

MAY

· **30** ·

You are attractive, easily bored and enjoy being part of the influential, affluent crowd. In childhood examples were set to show you how to be self-expressive, professionally ambitious and constructive about money. You have difficulty with your sense of responsibility and prefer to be a chief who leaves the dirty work to the Indians.

Family and friends are important in childhood as advisers. Male-oriented businesses have more attraction for you. You have an inferiority complex, which often causes you to exaggerate in your casual conversation. A secretary, genteel associate or soft-spoken professional steers you into self-confidence after age forty. You'll find that your later years are your best years for work, love and authority. Money is only a problem if you play big shot or stick to a job that does not stimulate your talents.

Marriage is going to benefit your security and social position. Until you make your loyal commitment mid-life, you want companions who attract attention, are not too demanding and enjoy your generosity. Childhood exposures taught you to be a good detective, to earn money with as little perspiration as possible and to negotiate for bargains. You rarely admit to yourself that you are gaining stature and security. That little voice of doom that keeps cautioning you to expect that the bottom is going to fall out of everything is a waste of time. It's a childhood hang-up that stays on to threaten your stability.

You're clever; you test retirement before buying. You realize that you are not happy without new experiences and adventures. Late years retain the electricity of your youth.

• OTHER MAY 30 BIRTHDAYS

Tony Aylward	1939
Alexander Archipenko	1887
Frank Blair	1915
Mel Blanc	1908
Barbara Anne Eisenhower	1949
Benny Goodman	1909
Hugh Griffith	1912
Christine Jorgensen	1926
George London	1920
Cornelia Otis Skinner	1901
Clint Walker	1927

MAY

• 31 •

Whatever you choose to do with your opportunities to communicate to the public, with polished, noble, skilled work, you will be magnetic and dedicated. Your choices in childhood were stifled or stymied by the male parent's attitude toward your individuality, independence and originality. The untraditional exposures and changes that you met before you were twenty-eight had an effect upon your delicate or accentuated ego.

You go far from your roots and have talents for healing, counseling and acquiring wisdom. When you learn when to be aggressive and when to take a backseat, you'll handle your finances more appropriately. You are mentally directed and have a dislike for purely mundane people and experiences.

Sex and the physical senses are a strong force in your life experiences because you are a romantic. The concept that there is the perfect spouse, made for you alone, is a strong factor in your ambitions. You do not see yourself living without a soul mate.

If you were less intellectually, physically and financially active and accepted and gave love, for its own beauty, that would solve many of your emotionally triggered, difficult-to-diagnose health incidents. You have temper tantrums or emotional displays. Later life should not bring on impulsive or radical changes. Patience and sticking to a lifetime work—avoiding speculative commercial ideas—are the keys to holding on to what you've got.

In late years you want to travel and expand. You find you are met with disconnection or dissatisfaction. Make up your mind to get back to nature, be quiet and emulate Garbo to win.

• OTHER MAY 31 BIRTHDAYS

Fred Allen	1894
Don Ameche	1908
Clint Eastwood	1931
Henry Jackson	1912
Prince Rainier III of Monaco	1923
Joe Namath	1943
Norman Vincent Peale	1898
Alexander Pope	1688
Walt Whitman	1819

JUNE

· 1 ·

There is a focus upon family attachments and an equal focus upon conventional domestic uprootings in childhood. You're a product of people and experiences that teach you to question, investigate and stand alone. Spiritual, philosophical and authoritative associates add constantly challenging environments until you reach a plateau in your late twenties.

Money is a problem until mid-life when you accept yourself as a unique individual. Financial security fluctuates but is always available. Family ties linger as steady business relationships and as mellowing friendships. A dominant woman with superior stamina comes into your life in your mid-thirties and behaves as a support system for your ambitions. She is one of many females who help you to solve your problems throughout your lifetime.

Leaders need followers. You are a forceful planner who places mental analysis over heartfelt emotionalizing, when it comes to personal ambitions. The more work you do, the more work you will do.

Work is essential to bolstering your efficiency. When you can see and touch the results of your ideas, you stop procrastinating. Sex and the physical senses relate to your shifts and goal changes. Too much sensuality or too little concern for physical passions is reflected in the way in which you express yourself. You may be a sex symbol or an example of spiritual or brotherly love—one extreme or the other.

Long-term investments provide late life security. Your best years are less materially ambitious and more accepting.

• OTHER JUNE 1 BIRTHDAYS

Pat Boone	1934
Joan Caulfield	1922
Andy Griffith	1926
John Masefield	1878
Marilyn Monroe	1926
Frank Morgan	1890
Nelson Riddle	1921
Brigham Young	1801

JUNE

· 2 ·

You fine tune to every person you meet and delight if they serve you a large dollop of affection. As a tot, your emotional contacts were based upon practical attention to your needs. As a youth, you want love but limit your shows of affection to appreciative pats on the back for work well done.

Your family ties are tight and conventional. Your relationships are peaceful because you dislike upheaval and criticism. You are able to benefit from generous, sympathetic and responsible women from infancy to late years. The least challenging experiences of your life connect with early years.

You are years into your mid-life before you are able to deal with the emotions that accompany actions and reactions. You detest routine, orderliness and rules, or you use practical disciplines as a crutch. When you work for money, awards or physical fitness, you are able to keep your mind on tangibles. When you are determined to work, you feel that you are capable of controlling your emotions. When you are able to know when to focus upon material results and when to vacation from inner structure, you will cope with the people and experiences that open doors for your fulfillment of your destiny.

Your restlessness and unconcern for rule breaking cause a mid-life crisis. Moodiness and depression are brought about when you want material tokens of love, affection, emotional response; you get them and find that they do not fulfill your needs.

Be careful and decisive. Your intuition is exceptional, and through following your hunches you see financial profits. Partners and/or a mate will travel with you late in life.

• OTHER JUNE 2 BIRTHDAYS

Chuck Barris	1929
Jack Berry	1918
Charles Conrad, Jr.	1930
Pete Conrad	1930
Joanna Gleason	1950
Ben Grauer	1908
Marvin Hamlisch	1944
Hedda Hopper	1890
Stacy Keach	1941
Sally Kellerman	1938
Charlie Watts	1941
Johnny Weismuller	1904

JUNE

· **3** ·

You have the chameleon's ability to change facades. Early in life you are a product of your neighborhood but you are enticed to expanding your ambitions as you are exposed to people who have lived a more cultured life-style. You are attractive. Others see you as a peacock or an owl. You may dress up to attract attention one day and sit on a secluded perch as an all-knowing observer another day. Your social self requires flattery and supporters until you take a mature approach to your own talents and priorities.

Your manners and appearance open doors that would ordinarily be closed to you. You travel far from your birthright and in mid-life establish yourself, with the guidance of an older or cosmopolitan male mentor. Your interests are rooted in family or ethnic ideals, which leads you to humanitarian or charitable involvements. You are best equipped to work and thrive in a communications industry. You love or hate the demands that your social obligations entail. There is no in between to your youthful involvements or your fuddy-duddy distaste for superficial game playing.

Many of your interests prove to be disappointing because you scatter time, energy and money. You finally buckle down to hard work, discipline and face reality after age forty. Your abilities to produce, direct and personally involve yourself in everything that touches you emotionally prove to be your stabilizer.

Later years are less playful—more cautious financially—you become more forgiving. As an oldster, you learn how to use your unique philosophy. The optimistic child in you survives.

• OTHER JUNE 3 BIRTHDAYS

Josephine Baker	1906
Tony Curtis	1925
Jefferson Davis	1808
Colleen Dewhurst	1926
King George V of England	1865
Maurice Evans	1901
Allen Ginsberg	1926
Paulette Goddard	1911
Susan Hayward	1919
Jan Peerce	1904

JUNE

·**4**·

You are fair and work diligently to uphold the personal ideals instilled in you as a tot. Family expects that you will not be run of the mill and you aim to avoid the pain of petty criticisms by keeping harmony in your surroundings. Music, domestic comforts and pride in accomplishment are deep-rooted facets of your personality. You have a gift for philosophy, drama and assuming responsibility. A pioneering spirit moves you to break with family traditions—be different—and you suffer emotionally until you learn to be less personalized and to accept yourself for what you must become.

Money and power are only part of your destiny. You cannot manipulate for control or risk all for supremacy without losing emotional balance. You give the impression of a structured, dedicated, cool-hearted administrator who dotes on a good bargain. In reality you are a pussycat who has been clawed by the love bug. You are a hard taskmaster for yourself and for the imaginative, attractive, supportive people you enjoy having around to spark your self-improvement.

Your business or professional commitments are not as changable as your temperament. You can be too moody and self-depreciating or too good to be true. You build a life-style that improves as you invest yourself in work. A spouse can be an asset as a social partner and a financial buffer. You want to have intelligence, dependability and attractiveness in a mate. You profit by planning and promote yourself industriously.

Later years are busy, educational and progressive. You relax to reflect upon your observations but remain disciplined.

• OTHER JUNE 4 BIRTHDAYS

Fedora Barbieri	1919
Gene Barry	1922
Charles Collingwood	1917
Madame Chiang Kai-shek	1899
Judith Malina	1926
Robert Merrill	1919
Rosalind Russell	1908
Dennis Weaver	1924

JUNE

· 5 ·

You're not always a rock of dependability, sensible, responsible and constant. You find it unnecessary to follow the mundane order of regulations, propriety and traditions. You are regal and different, but you are not always able to keep your head above water financially. If money and position are inherited, you still have to contend with surprising upheavals and an unconventional destiny during your mid-life.

You have a more secure life-style in later years because you learn your lessons through experience. Childhood was not serene, and you felt the pinch of too many burdens and too little attention to your personal ambitions. An assertive parent dominated your individuality and you had to break out independently—travel mentally or physically—to be decisive about your career, friendships and place of residence. Once your creativity and leadership abilities surfaced, you took your destiny into your own hands.

The jobs you took or the lovers you accepted kept you financially afloat but were not up to your standards. There is a little child in you that craves the trimmings, adventures and challenges of constant new enthusiasms. You have charm, wit and intellectual capacities that you use in the multifaceted interests that you enjoy. When life gets dull—which is rare—you throw a few pebbles into the water to make some waves. Marriage can be fun, with a partner who allows your mind to roam free, praises your flair for beautiful fashions and doesn't stifle your desire for self-improvement. Home and an opulent life-style are your mainstays in later years.

• OTHER JUNE 5 BIRTHDAYS

Ruth Benedict	1887
William Boyd	1898
John Maynard Keynes	1883
Conrad Marca-Relli	1913
Bill Moyers	1934
Jean-Paul Sartre	1905

JUNE

· 6 ·

Expect to be protected and to be a protector. Your life-time is peopled by creative, wise and domestically con-cerned talkers. You want and provide love, peace and companionship. It is your strong sense of personal ide-alism that creates disharmony or conflicts in your relationships. It would be ideal for you if everyone you loved lived up to the standards that you set and the rules that you live by. You try too hard at everything you undertake. Your sense of justice is tested throughout your lifetime.

All forms of social service are your tools for feeling worthwhile. The creative arts delight you, because beauty and the symmetry of music, decorating and entertainment are combined in your aware-ness on a day-to-day basis. You strive to learn and to teach. Mid-life pleasures evolve around your community and the pride that you take in balancing your interests and developing discriminating tastes.

You can sell any product for a business that provides improvements for homes or the people who center interest on family living. You are happier helping others until later in life, when your hobby or secondary interest is complemented by a cultured woman. Her en-couragement is the push you need to express yourself as a writer, artist or critic.

You are drawn to interests that have emotional or humanitarian focus and stay with a business commitment until you feel it has been fulfilled. Powerful friends are always at hand and they respect your leadership, charm and sense of obligation. After age sixty you benefit from activity and should plan to travel.

• OTHER JUNE 6 BIRTHDAYS

Nathan Hale	1755
Aram Khachaturian	1903
Thomas Mann	1875
Maria Montez	1920
David P. Scott	1932
Alexander Pushkin	1799
Diego Velázquez	1599
Paul Dudley White	1886
Dalai Lama XIV	1935

JUNE

· 7 ·

You are an enigma: a loyal spouse and a bounding adventurer. You love to love and to be loved, but not at the risk of your privacy or your security. The older you get, the more introspective you become. The more introspective you become, the more you closet your true nature and show yourself only when you feel safe from material pressures.

Money and the action in the business community can exhaust your energy, to the extent that you often become reclusive. You are best when teaching or acting out your own philosophy. As a tot, you learned to stick to a good bargain and to move on quickly if your ambitions were stymied. If money is your only ambition or tangibles your sign of success, you become too skeptical. The quality or the perfection of your talents will elude you. You will be prone to moodiness or melancholy and drain your physical energy.

When you establish an expertise, you will attract the money, popularity and domestic tranquility that you need. You have a fear of loneliness and poverty that relates to your inability to have faith in yourself. In childhood you were too submissive, and when you did assert yourself, it was with a vengeance to be independent. You seem to vacillate in your decisions. It is difficult for you to speak up appropriately, and you take an aggressive stance when you have allowed yourself to be frustrated. In time you mellow to save yourself for exposure.

As an oldster, you are a shrewd analyst and a debater to be reckoned with. The control you seek and the selectivity you have worked for are not denied you. Life remains an exciting game.

• OTHER JUNE 7 BIRTHDAYS

Beau Brummell	1778
Paul Gauguin	1848
Tom Jones	1940
Empress Carlota of Mexico	1840
Peter Rodino	1909
George Szell	1897
Jessica Tandy	1909

JUNE

·**8**·

The power and the glory can be yours if you let go of your supersensitivity and grow a tough exterior. You meet surprising experiences as a youth, and Lady Luck deals you a good hand. If you learn how to finesse your queen, your jack-of-all-trades personality will win you a lifetime of grand slams.

Your life can be likened to a fast game of bridge. Youth deals out a full deck of opportunities. You pick up trump and losers. You can play the trump out first or hang on to your winning tricks too long. The choice is yours until you reach mid-life. Your teen years set the pace for appearances and in your thirties require that you make an analytic change of seats and partners. You have petty problems to overcome, but your brains win out and you look to high-ranking wheeler-dealers to support your power plays.

It is your talent and brains that earn money and trophies. A marriage partnership is not the answer you think it will be. However, you think that you need a support system, booster and permanent team player. You adjust your needs as you acquire self-esteem. Your commitments are long-term although they are not totally fulfilling. Your business changes are rewarding, and your career grows with your maturity when you allow opportunities to come to you. If you push too hard you face disappointments in your forties. You're happiest when working, maintaining friendships and demanding to be paid what you feel you are worth.

You tend to make mountains out of molehills. Let bygones be bygones. You have the ability to become rich and famous. Your talents reach across universal tastes and leave a lasting image.

• OTHER JUNE 8 BIRTHDAYS

William L. Calley, Jr.	1943
James Darren	1936
Robert Preston	1918
Robert Schumann	1810
Nancy Sinatra, Jr.	1940
Alexis Smith	1921
Frank Lloyd Wright	1869

JUNE
·**9**·

You'll take the high road to bypass the low road in your desire to simplify, relieve or eliminate responsibilities. As a tot, you had obligations and attracted attention. It is difficult for you to accept a compliment, or you are too easily fooled by flattery. Superficial chatter or lighthearted banter comes too easily or is impossible for you to handle. You want to have friends, and it is difficult for you to maintain an intimate friendship. As a result, you require tangible proof of your self-esteem.

A desire for money, community respect and authority over others is a strong motivation in your twenties. Adult toys are your little blue blanket: You hoard them or generously give them away. You are handed positions of responsibility and trust and find it difficult to trust your lovers. There is confusion in your mind that relates to marriage partnership and friendship partnership. Domestic relations in youth are problematic. You need recognition and approval. Love affairs may seem to be your answer, but you tie up with members of the opposite sex who are too young or too old. You demean yourself until you are prepared to be decisive and accountable. You are a late bloomer. You become less plastic—more discriminating—in your late thirties.

Money may be your undoing. In your late forties your personality and value system make a major transition. You become a public-spirited, intellectual, analytical romantic. You want cultural expansion and strive for education, polish and skillfulness. Emotional upheavals precede your awakening, but you are protected, peaceful and respected in late years.

• OTHER JUNE 9 BIRTHDAYS

S. N. BERMAN	1893
ROBERT CUMMINGS	1910
PATRICK HENRY	1735
ROBERT McNAMARA	1916
LES PAUL	1916
COLE PORTER	1893
HAPPY ROCKEFELLER	1926
CZAR PETER THE GREAT OF RUSSIA	1682
FRED WARING	1900

JUNE

·10·

You're born to be an icebreaker. The enthusiasm you have to share makes you a catalyst for change in the lives of the people you encounter. It's too bad you cannot stay in one mode long enough to dig out the depths of an experience, or you hang in—long past the usefulness of the exposure. You will learn when and what to change—but not until you are willing to remember and draw upon your past.

You are eager to leave your birthright to get out from under the conventional obligations that curtail your curiosity. You love the comforts and spend your youth looking to plant your roots. Your major efforts are aimed at creating a beautiful, harmonious, respectable life-style of your own choosing. Every time you think that you are settled, you are uprooted.

Love, sex, experimentation, gambling and just plain carelessness cause your downfalls. You work and persevere, then impulsively take the dice for one roll and find that you've lost your bankroll again. Your youthful struggles are finally rewarded after you recognize the need to concentrate on life's vicissitudes. Stop thinking— and fearing—that the stability of emotional and financial security is only born out of boredom. You are too busy or too bored—too exacting or too inconsistent—too adventurous or too think-stuck. One or the other will cause you to be nervous, selfish, discontented and an escapist.

You are ambitious. A marriage for money and position will keep you towing the mark. You have the ability to be aristrocratic, aloof and authoritative when you have satisfied your self-interests. You have pressures when you give all for love.

• OTHER JUNE 10 BIRTHDAYS

F. Lee Bailey	1933
Saul Bellow	1915
Judy Garland	1922
Jimmy Hendrix	1919
Frederick Loewe	1904
Hattie McDaniel	1895
Prince Philip	1921
Maurice Sendak	1928

JUNE

· 11 ·

You are inclined to overwork or have a distaste for the limitations of a regulated life-style. Affluent or influential, businesslike people cross your path early and set the stage for your elitist, often impractical childhood ambitions. You are limited emotionally or creatively by practical, down-to-earth realists, or you lack the routine disciplines and orderliness of an average childhood. Whichever extreme you experience, you must learn to live up to your personal standards and ideals.

It is far more important for you to express and sell your uniqueness than it is for you to make money your main objective. You attract listeners and followers who will provide you with financial banking, opportunities to travel and the technical facilities to leave a lasting image for future generations. You must have a strong belief—personal goals—and faith in yourself before you will achieve prominence. You will be given opportunities to attract public attention between twenty-eight and fifty-five years of age.

The company of comrades is rewarding when the emotions are detached. Friends cannot help you to make the multiple decisions that cross your mind. Your ideas are spontaneous, original and technically clever. Your eccentricity, combined with impulsivity, may be your downfall or your key to notoriety. You are unable to handle drugs, drinking and the like. It is important that you accept yourself as an elitist—a person who has ups and downs because of a desire to uplift or alter the expectations of the average person. In later years stay active; complete your obligations. Your voice must be heard above the crowd.

• OTHER JUNE 11 BIRTHDAYS

Jacques Cousteau	1910
Chad Everett	1936
Richard Loeb	1905
Vince Lombardi	1913
Rise Stevens	1913
Richard Strauss	1864
Gene Wilder	1934

JUNE

· 12 ·

Your imagination is vivid, and your ambitions depend upon your ability to communicate your visualizations. During your sleep cycles, problems are solved, and you awake sensing that your mind has organized itself to face a new day. You have music in your soul and a presence that attracts attention. The performing arts and the people who contribute to them are your best bet for social and business ambitions.

The sacrifices you make to become a practical success and the domination you feel in youth cause you to be submissive, lack eloquence or feel unattractive. Family is important in your formative years, and you are heavily indoctrinated with their personal ideals and traditions. You are protected but must assume obligations and work for your education.

You travel culturally and intellectually before you are thirty. You find it difficult to be a grown-up, to strive for self-improvements and to take yourself seriously. There are a variety of possibilities for you. If you choose to concentrate on domestic commitments, you are inclined to take on too many obligations. If you are self-concerned, you develop creatively, but your immaturity becomes a stumbling block. It's a temporary no-win situation that corrects itself when you become less concerned about appearances as you mature.

Communications industries treat you kindly. In later years you take control of your business and choose your associates carefully. You become tactful and sensitive to others. You don't have an easy time until you come to grips with your own anxieties and see yourself in cooperation with the realities of your life.

- OTHER JUNE 12 BIRTHDAYS

George Bush	1924
Vic Damone	1928
Anthony Eden	1897
Uta Hagen	1919
William Lundigan	1914
Jim Nabors	1932
David Rockefeller	1915

JUNE

· 1 3 ·

Your life pattern demands that you work and rework to achieve your ambitions. You're a fighter and will overcome all obstacles when you are dedicated, structured and realistic. You tend to be a naturalist and understand how to get down to basics when you must. You have responsibilities placed upon your shoulders as a youngster. Either a job, a daily practice session or your obligations to the family name involve you in an orderly routine that involves social contacts.

Your home, community and group relationships must be harmonious. Women cause problems or pleasures—alliances or partnerships—for a man; marriage is rarely satisfactory. The mother has a strong influence upon your childhood, and a deep love or hate lingers long into late years. There is a financial or emotional burden that brings about an upheaval mid-life, and the sensitivity related to the female parent eventually decreases.

One of your requirements is to give and expect to receive facts, not fancies. You are at your best dealing with down-to-earth people who give and expect a fair day's pay for a day of honest labor. When you become too set in your patterns, expect to be uprooted from any rigidity in your daily living habits and your expectations. You are in a destiny that requires outdated or bigoted beliefs to be pushed aside for fresh ideas and higher standards. You have the talent to revitalize outworn or dead issues.

In later years your property provides you with security and your finances are less likely to fluctuate. An inheritance or a desire to continue to work allows you to feel optimistic and less inclined to push yourself physically. Avoid getting into a rut.

• OTHER JUNE 13 BIRTHDAYS

Mark Van Doren	1894
Ralph Edwards	1913
Red Grange	1903
Ian Hunter	1900
Prince Aly Khan	1911
Paul Lynde	1926
Basil Rathbone	1892
Richard Thomas	1951
Mickey Walker	1901

JUNE
· 14 ·

You cannot learn from another's mistakes or avoid touching the fire to test just how hot, hot really is! You go from one frying pan on to another fire throughout your mid-life. Childhood associations—"the old neighborhood"—have a strong influence on your opinions and ambitions. You are temperamental, dramatic, secretive and inspire others to follow you in your personal enthusiasms. In politics, advertising, creative or performing arts, you are a revolutionary. When you are freed from dependency or submissiveness and follow your personal mission, you stop jeapardizing your own ambitions.

You are your own worst enemy when you travel with the pack. You are an evangelist with a passion for reform and have a talent to attract supporters. You are on the wrong street if you greet your thirties bound to a partnership or a contract. Change and the adventures of unknown challenges as a daily diet feed you into associations with influential and privileged personages. You are a promoter . . . your own best advertisement.

Sex and love are a problem in your lifetime. You give up too much of your mental freedom to intimate relationships. You have the ability to remain celibate or to become a slave to your passions. You swing back and forth, with disappointing results.

Men tend to be dominating or negative influences that cause you to worry or waste your individualism. You will never become old-fashioned or lose your ability to attract lovers. Jealous, conventional critics presume to judge you mid-life. You are limited for a while but fulfill your obligations and rise again.

After age fifty-five expect less activity and more security.

· OTHER JUNE 14 BIRTHDAYS

Che Guevara	1928
Burl Ives	1909
Dorothy McGuire	1919
Don Newcombe	1926
Pierre Salinger	1925
Harriet Beecher Stowe	1811

JUNE

·15·

You have to pick up the tempo of life outside your home as a youngster. When you make your compromises, to satisfy family expectations or obligations, you delay the start of your true destiny. Life begins at forty is your slogan. You require a broad scope of people, activities and interests. Your youth is influenced by the emotional upheavals in your surroundings, and you are called upon to be too wise for your years. You develop a detachment that saves you pain as you grow older. As a tot, you learned to be accommodating.

You are capable of submerging your own personality for your loyalties or coldly discharging your emotional commitments if you are not appreciated. You are tuned to the deepest feelings and emotional needs of your loved ones and humanity. You are philosophical or rigid. It is in your best interests to tell people that you are sacrificing or compromising to please them. If you do not speak up, others believe that you are comfortable. When they do not give you the same consideration that you give to them, you are devastated. Try to remember that charity begins at home and that another person cannot fulfill all your dreams.

Love and marriage are important to you, but if you lose your independence, disharmony results. You are exposed to situations that demand interaction; you impress others with your authority and will never be a loner. When pressured, you are manipulative.

Finances create problems throughout your lifetime. You are talented, self-assured and idealistic. Do not allow your emotions to overrule your logic. Late years pay off in travel, real estate investments and respect from your community.

• OTHER JUNE 15 BIRTHDAYS

Robert Russell Bennett	1894
Erik Erikson	1902
Erroll Garner	1921
Edvard Greig	1843
Malvina Hoffman	1887
Morris K. Udall	1922
Trini Lopez	1937
Max Rudolf	1902

JUNE
· 16 ·

You want to own comfortable treasures that feel and look luxurious. Your possessions are very important to you. When you think of marriage or sharing your privacy, you shudder. However, your fears of loneliness and emotional poverty make you moody and melancholy, and you feel that a tradeoff is necessary to your emotional security. If you have a job that allows you mental and physical freedom or an interest that involves your sense of responsibility, you decide that the commitment is too much of a burden. You are a maverick who should avoid divorce or any legal entanglements.

In childhood your creative, individualistic, active energy is thwarted by a dominating adult. You try too hard to please everyone and end up in conflict with yourself. It is important for you to decide upon a career early and to get an academic education or technical training in youth. As you mature, your highly intellectual, aristocratic, perfectionist nature surfaces.

The practical, down-to-earth, rule-bound people who surround you as you grow up cannot foresee where your quick and clever brain will take you. Your frustrations make you restless, promiscuous or inconsistent. Family material values and conventional standards make you uncomfortable later in life, and you may decide to keep your past a secret.

After age thirty your business and personal life undergo many changes. If you lack self-esteem generated by authority, you become uncertain or speculative and get involved with people or ventures that are disappointing and disillusioning. Have faith!

Later years are tranquil, and you locate near the seashore.

• OTHER JUNE 16 BIRTHDAYS

Jack Albertson	1910
Desmond Doyle	1932
Katharine Graham	1917
Stan Laurel	1890
Joyce Carol Oates	1938
Erich Segal	1937

JUNE
· 17 ·

You won't like the detail work, petty bickering or taking a backseat, but you will love the touch of class that money and power give you. When you squelch personal sensitivity and swallow a dollop of humility, you get lucky in your youth. You are a stickler for education and family unity and are prepared to adjust your personal comfort for the betterment of your domestic responsibilities. An early marriage enhances your chance to make your aspirations and ambitions a reality.

Childhood environments were filled with the hospitality of friends and family. In mid-life you attract big business and are exposed to affluent and influential people. In later life you reflect upon the mistakes that you made and enjoy the comforts you anticipated as a youth.

You are unaware of your potential and the appeal that you have. You are involved with talented, efficient, fast-paced executives and free-lancers. You should travel and encounter nonroutine, unconventional, surprising situations that satisfy your curiosity. You are at your best in a marriage or business partnership. You are inclined to hang back and let your sidekick or partner do the work. The results can be a long-term headache.

Your personal commitment and love are constant until you reach your fifties and decide that you might have missed something. Your escapist excursions, at any time in your life, prove to be shortsighted, childish and short-lived. You must avoid stagnating and becoming self-satisfied. Accept the transitions that your destiny offers without losing the clout that you have amassed. You have the power to enjoy your success.

· OTHER JUNE 17 BIRTHDAYS

Ralph Bellamy	1904
Paul Delaroche	1797
Red Foley	1910
John Hersey	1914
Dean Martin	1917
Alan Rich	1924
Peggy Seeger	1935
Igor Stravinsky	1882

JUNE

·**18**·

The far-reaching consequences of your ambitions are more important to you than the offshoot of money or possessions. You may scatter your time, energy and interests. However, you are economical or bargain conscious, whether you are dealing in hundreds or thousands of dollars. You are large-minded, efficient, self-assertive, and deeply involved or concerned with your family, group or community until your late twenties. Marriage is unconventional or able to withstand separateness. You have mental and physical traveling to do and cannot be cloistered by a selfish or materialistic mate.

You may be too giving or too self-determined. You are given too much or too little attention as a youth and do not develop confidence in your social self. You may be a fashion-conscious faddist or completely unconcerned about anything but the barest essentials in clothes, home decorating or career image. As an adult, you seek or relinquish the spotlight, depending upon how eloquent you feel you may be at the moment.

Your appearance is an asset. Your voice is memorable. You attract help from affluent, influential and magnetic people. Business judgment is good if you keep your emotional opinions bottled. You tend to call it quits or clam up when frustrated by a mixture of intellect and heart. Practical, original and expansive progressive ideas keep you busy, physically balanced and open to meeting people who do not keep you under their thumb. It is impossible for you to eat humble pie.

Later years are stabilized and inclined to relaxation rather than competitiveness. Companionship and changes are in store.

• OTHER JUNE 18 BIRTHDAYS

Richard Boone	1917
Sammy Cahn	1913
Louis Jourdan	1921
Kay Kyser	1897
Jeanette MacDonald	1902/3
E. G. Marshall	1910
Paul McCartney	1942
Sylvia Porter	1913
Tom Wicker	1926

JUNE

· 19 ·

Think your unique way through a problem or project and you'll get your way every time. Don't try to abide by precedents. After you reach thirty-two years of age you design patterns and present fashions that pioneer traditions. You live a very private personal life-style and show the world the picture you create. Sex, curiosity and impulsivity can be devastating to your ambitions. You get involved and cleverly play out the challenges. Somehow you rise above the confines of convention, remain aloof and survive the voices of critics.

You are inclined to change your behavior, lose your inferiority complex and overcome your aversion to being in the limelight. You are easily bored and overcommit your time and energy repeatedly. You cannot wait to change locations and fear the unknown experiences that a move entails. You are loyalty personified until you move on to new enthusiasms. You want money because it is society's symbol of success, and you can be stingy once you have it. Midlife, you are a victim and victimize others. You have a strong sense of individuality, detest nonproductive emotionalizing and should curb your temper.

You are intuitive and extend your ideas into the future. After age fifty-five the injustices that resulted from youthful experiments take a backseat. Any advice that was taken proves to be a mistake, but you always have more than one thing going for you—and past educational pursuits prove to be the keys to extricating yourself. Later in life your heart and your mind stop fighting each other. You value quality and professionalism. You shelve ego gratification and work to add polish to humanity.

• OTHER JUNE 19 BIRTHDAYS

Pier Angeli	1932
Charles Coburn	1877
Alan Cranston	1914
Martin Gabel	1912
Lou Gehrig	1903
Guy Lombardo	1902
Nancy Marchand	1928
Marisa Pavan	1932
Gena Rowlands	1936
Duchess of Windsor	1896

JUNE

·20·

Intimate relationships are your joy and your undoing. You are conscious of the little things in your surroundings and accumulate knowledge, friends and possessions. In childhood, home, family and traditions were regulated, and the values that were most respected related to money. You were instilled with a work ethic that serves you well in mid-life. In later years your scope of personalities and environments broadens. But before you reach the point when your common sense wins over your desire to be influential, you frequently change your personal values.

You desire alliances and comrades. There is a bravado in your soul that places you in life-or-death positions when your sympathy is aroused. In the face of danger you are highly motivated to do the right thing. At other times you may be a rule breaker and resent having to pay the piper for unconventional behavior. You become skeptical. Your honest efforts are often misunderstood, or you are apt to find it difficult to spot dishonesty in others. Your best bet is to maintain a constructive routine, avoid legal hassles and use your friendly personality to attract supporters.

You are able to earn money working closely with easygoing people. You need to be sharper in your first blush impressions. The difficulty lies in your emotional rather than intellectual assessments, and you find disappointment in your forties, when you realize that a decision made in your thirties was ill advised. If you check out involvements before you change your goals before age fifty, your late years are protected, varied and fulfilling.

• OTHER JUNE 20 BIRTHDAYS

Chet Atkins	1924
Errol Flynn	1909
Lillian Hellman	1905
Cindi Lauper	1953
Audie Murphy	1924
Helen Traubel	1899
André Watts	1946
Brian Wilson	1942

JUNE
·21·
If you open up a smile as your umbrella, you'll never have a rainy day. You are expressive and charming when you aren't feeling sorry for yourself. When you are socially secure, you enjoy being in the spotlight. Cultural advantages are offered to you in youth, and you should have a broader base for understanding yourself and others after age thirty-two. You attract noble and notable relationships, which expand your polish and skills. Your life and your loves bring more pleasure as you grow older.

Good luck is part of your birthright. You will miss golden opportunities if you place too much importance upon appearances and fail to read between the lines. In business and personal investments, legal questions or tax matters, a professional counselor is needed. You tend to scatter time and energy; when the time comes to pay attention to routine obligations, you lack the energy to follow through to a conclusion.

When you find yourself in a tangled web of realities, you dramatize your plight and imagine that you are the only person ever to experience a delaying deluge. When you make mistakes, you decide to change and curtail your interests. Then you become a fuddy-duddy, have inappropriate aversions and become jealous. You must avoid mood swings and unfriendliness. Your stock and trade is based upon your self-expression, not the influential supporters you think you need to achieve your ambitions.

You have sex appeal and need a home life. Once committed— to a marriage or partnership—you take pride and show interest. Later in life your empathetic nature surfaces. You use your talents, communications skills and buoyancy to help others.

• OTHER JUNE 21 BIRTHDAYS

Margaret Heckler	1931
Al Hirshfeld	1903
Judy Holliday	1922
Rockwell Kent	1882
Mary McCarthy	1912
Cosimo de' Medici	1519
Jane Russell	1921
Françoise Sagan	1935
Maureen Stapleton	1925
Martha Washington	1731

JUNE

· **22** ·

With your high energy you are free to build or destroy at will. In childhood you begin to assume the obligations that are part of your life pattern. Mother and family pay too much or too little attention to you. You are made to feel modest or humble, and can do little to alter the domestic financial picture until you reach your late teens. You want stability, authority and respect. You have ambitious goals and expectations that may be unrealistic for a youth.

You have power that may overwhelm you. You must use your physical and your mental capacities. A daily practice or study that coordinates using body and mind—for example, music lessons, dancing lessons, sports practice—introduces your innovations to a discipline. Your mid-life offers greater opportunity to express yourself and seed tangible results than early years of indecision, emotional sensitivity and family concerns.

Essentially you are a problem solver. As a tot, you could not put your dynamic talents to work and were frustrated and made to feel inferior. In maturity you set an example, capitalize on your ability to express what you have learned and take over projects that have stymied your predecessors.

You need analytic, friendly, independent mates or lovers. Early marriage with a person of similar ambitions helps you build your foundation for late years. After age forty you are a progressive and forceful leader with the potential to improve standards and leave a lasting mark. Be conventional in youth and you'll build castles in the air with your feet on the ground.

• OTHER JUNE 22 BIRTHDAYS

Bill Blass	1922
Gower Champion	1921
John Dillinger	1903
Katherine Dunham	1910
Julian Huxley	1887
Kris Kristofferson	1936
Anne Morrow Lindbergh	1906
Joseph Papp	1921
Freddie Prinz	1954
Billy Wilder	1906

JUNE

·23·

Expect the unexpected. You're clever, eager to learn and sure to receive help from your friends. You investigate, study and are a gifted communicator. Only selfishness or a lack of self-assertion can disable your ambitions. Curb your anger, and use your options wisely. You cannot please everyone. If you try to be too accommodating you will not satisfy anyone—least of all yourself. Develop your convictions. Be firm and sure.

Mid-life opportunities are ripe for your ideas, enthusiasms and forceful leadership. Your modesty may stop you from seeking the applause you deserve when you involve yourself helping the causes of needy young people or oldsters. Money may not always be available, but when it is, you're a giver. The comforts of your loved ones particularly and people who evoke your sympathy bring out your sense of responsibility, love of beauty and parental inclinations. You can commercialize on your managerial talents.

In youth you are surrounded by elitists and evangelistic visionaries. Financial success is less important than the perfection of their dreams. You never lose your childhood expectations and aspire to be in the public eye or to bring honor to your name. You are unable to independently commercialize on your artistic, musical or literary talents. You will find that you are a channel for others or find a partner who extends your ideas, but you cannot materialize on your intuitive, spiritual, extraordinary gifts as a loner. You attract publicity and fame.

Later years are secure if you have not taken financial flings. A female supporter and an argumentative male try to influence your unconventional ambitions. Don't be manipulated.

• OTHER JUNE 23 BIRTHDAYS

Larry Blyden	1925
Bob Fosse	1927
Empress Josephine of France	1763
Alfred Kinsey	1894
Wilma Rudolph	1940
Duke of Windsor	1894

JUNE

·24·

Your love of home and the women in your life bring out your protective instincts and awaken the sense of responsibility that you try to keep under wraps. Your thirst for freedom, to get away from the neighborhood, and the discomfort you feel away from a peaceful, loving, nurturing hearth drain you emotionally. The tugs and strains tap the thespian in your soul, and you run the gamut from utter joy to the deepest sorrow when you break away.

You are a student, an educator and a counselor—a refuge for people less able to provide for themselves than you are, who need your sympathy. Don't be naive and restless to get out to a broader scope before you are ready to pay your own bills. An early, quality education must be a priority. It is essential that you do not submerge your talents while submitting to the cause of the moment. You could lose your inspirational and intuitional gifts—and your ambitions— and become discouraged or discontented in youth. You may become old before your time.

You tend to take too much for granted and assume that you are intended to charm, pacify and parent all comers. You are a good judge of human nature, if people live up to your personal ideals. As a youngster, you felt lonely—unable to identify with tots and unable to take your place with adults. You were considered to be precocious—a little old lady or old man.

Peace of mind is more important than money in late years. Worry brings on physical stress. You will certainly fulfill your fears if you deplete your energy. Your patience pays off; if you do not reach out for cultural expanses in youth, as an oldster, you will. You grow wiser, wealthier and more romantic with time.

• OTHER JUNE 24 BIRTHDAYS

Henry Ward Beecher	1813
Norman Cousins	1915
Jack Dempsey	1895
Pete Hamill	1935
Phil Harris	1906
David Rose	1910

JUNE

·25·

You want all the comforts that family and group in- volvements provide without getting too close. Child- hood opportunities are limited intellectually and are based upon practical values. You find yourself becom- ing less open to sharing your feelings and your dreams. Your adult aloofness, secretiveness and close-mouthed facade is the product of your impressionable babyhood and your relationship with a inde- pendent, individualistic, strong male parent or guardian.

You want approval for your aristocratic, introspective questioning. You are intuitive and at your best when displaying your knowledge and expertise. Until you can speak from authority, you learn to use silence as a tool to receive input. You rarely show your hand unless you are fighting for your spiritual beliefs, companions or lovers. When you take a stand, you are a catalyst for change in the lives of the people your crusade touches.

You have a long memory for learning from reflection. In your quest for instant gratification you draw from the past and impatiently demand results. You are willing to be a "first," but require support when you go it alone. You respect and need freedom. You are im- pulsive when your leadership ability is sparked, and you pay the piper through personal sacrifices.

During your lifetime education is of major importance to you, but you make decisions that satisfy your material concerns. Until you are in your thirties, you get caught up in two loves, job choices or social circles. You are different and a loner in late years: challenged by your mind and your wanderlust.

• OTHER JUNE 25 BIRTHDAYS

George Abbott	1889
Walter Brennan	1894
Peter Lind Hayes	1915
June Lockhart	1925
Sidney Lumet	1924
James Meredith	1933
George Orwell	1903
Carly Simon	1945

JUNE

·26·

Your sense of balance is constantly tested. In love, money, sports, sex and marriage, you cannot go off the deep end. You want your comforts and status symbols. You pass your tests by avoiding your tendency to waste energy criticizing and by being courageous in the face of disbelievers, undeserved obligations or adversity.

Family social interactions or business practices open doors for your untraditional behavior and beliefs as an adult. Travel or exposure to cultures and individuals who are unconventional alters you and your expectations repeatedly as a youth. You are a survivor. You have ample opportunities during your lifetime to use cleverness, adaptability and determination to overcome your lack of confidence or lapses into self-depreciation.

Stability, common sense and concentrated effort will correct any problems that present themselves mid-life. Be tolerant of those less organized to produce results. You want partnership to cope with the myriad details that you observe. You require peace of mind but you will buck tradition and be forced to prove yourself. You are a gifted, interesting lover, friend, professional communicator. When you can hear yourself spouting hot air, you're losing touch with your personal ambitions.

If your youthful experimentations lead to uncertainty, use your family or group contacts and your mind to reassess your own capacities mid-life. Dependency is your downfall. Explorations and inventions that influence or expose the personal ideals of others can bring you fame and financial security in your fifties. Later years offer smooth sailing and safe emotional harbors.

• OTHER JUNE 26 BIRTHDAYS

Bernard Berenson	1865
Pearl S. Buck	1892
Peter Lorre	1904
Anna Moffo	1935
Eleanor Parker	1922
John Turner Sargent	1924
Stuart Symington	1901
Babe Zaharias	1914

JUNE

· 27 ·

You use your intellect and your emotions in your ambitions to teach, entertain and provide worthwhile products and services. You light up a room with your smile or sap the sun when you frown. Every aspect of your destiny deals with your magnetic and creative personality. The faith that you have in yourself, your self-esteem and your willingness to share your imaginative, lighthearted, fashionable ideas are the basis for your happiness and financial success.

If you do not have a large family, you will unconsciously attract and inspire the young and youthful like a magnet. Children, pets and lovers know that you are a soft touch, although you try to act impersonal. You may sacrifice personal ambitions at different times and for varied reasons, but you will find that you volunteered or worried yourself into burdening commitments. You make money and put it right back into circulation. You want a beautiful, romantic, unselfish world and must confront your compromises before you are able to put your personal philosophy to the test.

In mid-life you are surrounded by notables and are destined to reach a noble polish and skill in the performance of your career or duties. You must take care never to fall victim to glib talkers or superficial values. Midpoint in your life you are faced with health or financial problems relating to a woman from your past, which alters your material security. You bounce back but maintain a more self-protective attitude thereafter. Throughout your maturity you tend to be too forgiving or too intolerant. Late years reap benefits from public service.

- OTHER JUNE 27 BIRTHDAYS

Gary Crosby	1933
W. T. Grant	1876
Captain Kangaroo	1927
Helen Keller	1880
Willie Mosconi	1913

JUNE

·28·

You greet each day and each person who crosses your path as a new lesson to absorb. Conventions will never be your mainstay, and you are compulsive in your quest to satisfy your sensual and intellectual curiosities. If wishes come true, you'll never take second best. You want money and cooperative ventures and to hear the rhythm of life. However, when your dreamboat comes in, it no longer interests you; you jump ship, move on and make a fresh start. You need creative activity but do not do well when you are impulsive, too trusting or afraid of competition.

Childhood exposures and experiences offered confining family and community influences. As an adult, you want roots and an opulent life-style. Anything or any person who curtails your freedom or slows your creative juices by plodding through your life places you in an intolerable mental enclosure. The limitation makes you forget practicality and run for the hills. You rarely linger over the fruits of your labors.

You are often confusing: self-serving one day and totally dedicated to helping everyone else the next. Once you understand why something should work, you make it work for two. You attract a fortunate marriage—a copemate—and prosper. You are never too secure and may accumulate affluence and influential associates but maintain an inner fear of having the rug pulled out from under. If you cannot shake an inferiority complex that relates itself in a big-shot attitude, you may not find a helpful mentor until your late years. You meet with success.

You are smart and dislike boredom. When you have security in late life, you bask in the sunshine of your spiritual freedom.

• OTHER JUNE 28 BIRTHDAYS

Ashley Montagu	1906
Richard Rodgers	1902
Jean-Jacques Rousseau	1712
Sally Struthers	1948
John Wesley	1703

JUNE
·**29**·
Practicality is not your focus. Your talents attract admirers and honors. You leave a lasting image in the minds of your peers. Few people realize the impact that you have until they get caught by your easygoing style, homespun philosophy and uplifting personal ideals. You aim to preach or teach your gospel, and it is aimed to improve universal standards. You are a humanitarian worker or have a distaste for traditional extremes. It is your intention and expectation to surpass your birthright. You have the character ingredients and destiny opportunities to be unique in your time and space. The choices—how to capitalize on the opportunities of the moment—are up to you.

Your energy must be directed carefully. You tire easily and need a musical outlet or an understanding and dedicated lover. The rhythm of your life and the peace you feel relate to the expression of your talents and creative self-expression. You cannot abide rigid structure, and you rebel as a youth and an adult. Petty bickering will cause you to change jobs or professions with regularity until you are accepted for your individualism. You are torn between intuition and logic and have difficulty settling into one niche.

You are wise and are a natural emotional or physical healer. It is difficult for you to allow injustice to your fellows to pass without involvement. You do not protect your financial security or life-style position when your emotions are triggered. You spend your money and time mid-life and learn from the experiences. Your talents and magnetic attraction will always save your position. Later years require that you accept reality.

• OTHER JUNE 29 BIRTHDAYS

Leroy Anderson	1908
Joan Davis	1907
Nelson Eddy	1901
Harmon Killebrew	1936
Rafael Kubelik	1914
Frank Loesser	1910
William Mayo	1861
Slim Pickens	1919

JUNE

· 30 ·

You're pleased with yourself when you attract attention and may become too satisfied with your progress. Early years demand that you accept responsibility and take your place in the family. However, you grow far from your roots culturally and must meet challenges beyond your scope and control. You are mentally strong. However, you must overcome a childish habit of placing lovers or associates on pedestals. You need appreciation and give it to your peers.

When you realize that even the people you admire have feet of clay, your surprise and disbelief break down your emotional stamina. In your effort to avoid disappointment and disillusionment, you build a fear of failing and falling that may make you place yourself too far above the crowd. You are unable to be realistic, and you attempt to control or dominate. You are caught up in society's superficial trappings or dislike the outer image that most people create as they compromise to survive. You will work out your business or domestic problems mid-life.

You are influenced by all levels of love. Your heart goes out to all who need your generosity, empathy and unselfishness. Men enjoy your mental ability, and women are inspired by your unique philosophy. You like a bargain and have a head for business when you are interested. You have difficulty with indecisive and self-centered associates, but you try to teach or counsel them. You need to maintain a health regimen that includes plenty of sleep and privacy. You marry wisely or not at all. You have all the knowledge that you need, but you may not know how to use it. You should be the leader of the band if you work.

• OTHER JUNE 30 BIRTHDAYS

Nancy Dussault	1936
Glenda Farrell	1904
Susan Hayward	1919
Lena Horne	1917
Buddy Rich	1917

JULY · 1 · There are always too many or too few family ties to suit you. Your chances for success as an adult are based upon your individuality, assertiveness and inventiveness. As a child, when domestic disharmony spatters you with jealousy you are inclined to develop a secret plan. You invent your own world, and you set your strong will to stage your escape from troublesome females, friends and family relationships that are too close for comfort.

When you leave the nest you begin your climb to expertise in your profession and meet powerful people and experiences that offer promise of an extravagant, adventurous and idealistic life-style.

As a tot, you may find food more pleasurable than your intimate relationships. You may eat yourself into feeling better and forever fight fat. You learn to be a loner as a youngster. In mid-life you form binding and beneficial male friendships. The women in your life disturb your serenity. You need encouragement, although you appear to be mentally assertive, impatient and emotionally insensitive.

When you decide to instigate changes, you rarely show demonstrations of affection, although you are dedicated to your family and lover once you make a commitment. You are protective and must avoid pushing your personal beliefs on the people who trust you to share their burdens. Don't be lazy or smug—no matter how much you have in the bank or how successful you are, you will never lose a childhood fear of poverty and loneliness.

In later years you finally get to travel for the pleasure of cultural expansions and to receive well-earned recognition.

• OTHER JULY 1 BIRTHDAYS

Dan Aykroyd	1952
Leslie Caron	1931
Farley Granger	1925
Olivia de Havilland	1916
Charles Laughton	1899
George Sand	1804
Diana, Princess of Wales	1961
William Wyler	1902

JULY

·2·

As a youth, you have little opportunity to experiment or get into trouble, but when you finally do the unconventional, you cannot escape being noticed. The quest for education, good taste and expertise is part of your heritage; the quality, not the quantity, values are stressed. Spirituality wears many faces. You were born to inspire faith and to enlarge your scope of cultural experiences. If your lifetime judgments are based upon materialistic values, you will not have reached out of your "old neighborhood" to seek your potential.

You are a talented preacher, philosopher and universal communicator. You're not easily swayed from your comforts or personal ambitions. You want the outward display: diplomas, certificates, academic titles that show the world that you are entitled to speak with authority. Your admiring friends don't need them, and your enemies dispute them. You are a demanding perfectionist and choose your intimates from the intellectual crowd.

You want a working partner or a prestige mate when you marry. You've got something of value to give as a person, and you expect a spouse to equal you—or do better. Although you meet gentle, cooperative, supportive people mid-life, you are not geared to emotional responsiveness. You have the control to be completely honorable and collect whatever you plan to get.

You have opportunities to meet diplomats, politicians and detailers. If their abilities rub off on you, government service is a prime target for your career. You are not intended to make changes. Remain active, and find contentment in late years.

• OTHER JULY 2 BIRTHDAYS

Medgar Evers	1925
Barry Gray	1916
Ahmad Jamal	1930
Patrice Lamumba	1925
Thurgood Marshall	1908
Luci Baines Johnson Nugent	1947
Dan Rowan	1922
Alan Webb	1906

JULY

· 3 ·

In childhood you are exposed to situations and people who respect quality, exhibit control and require investigation. You may have conflicting influences and take it upon yourself to be independent before you are really able. You are surrounded by practical taskmasters and analytical aristocrats. You may be described as a problem child—a loner or abnormal.

Childhood may be lonely, but mid-life opens avenues to self-expressive, imaginative and attractive people who celebrate joy in living. You make progressive changes and are given opportunities to be inventive and different. It is up to you to be ready and willing to fight for your unique ideas. Don't lose your perspective by leaning upon anyone or accommodating a lover. It is in your best interests to seize the opportunities of your youth cycle by having the courage of your own convictions and focusing upon your personal objectives.

Your thirties to your fifties revolve around friends, up-to-date ideas and a chance to enjoy the lighter side of life. You combine your life experiences to become an introvert-extrovert in maturity. People who enjoy a joke, a game and using all types of communications devices and talents surround you. Allow yourself to play and develop your abilities to use words, appearances and social graces. You will overcome childhood material or financial limitations if you join business with pleasure.

In later years you will enjoy marriage more and find yourself in a satisfying position of authority or expertise. If you were unfulfilled intellectually in youth, an outstanding female will influence you and enlarge your scope after age fifty.

• OTHER JULY 3 BIRTHDAYS

Earl Butz	1909
Jean-Claude Duvalier	1951
Pete Fountain	1930
Leon Janacek	1854
Dorothy Kilgallen	1913
George Sanders	1906
Tom Stoppard	1937

JULY

·**4**·

In the early part of your life you cultivate your imagination, intuition and ability to project your goals into the future. You attract peer friendships that set you apart. They bring out the elitist or focus a spotlight on you. As you enter mid-life, you meet hardworking, dedicated and down-to-earth people who are constructive and organized to accumulate material rewards. You have the chance to maintain daily practices, organize finances and upgrade your life-style.

You don't mix business with pleasure. Your domestic and intimate relationships are strictly private. In your chosen career or business you have the electricity to inspire people outside your immediate family and friends, to support your personal ideals or talents. You may be a modest and retiring personality, disinclined to attract attention, or you may sparkle to encourage public attention before age thirty. Your diplomacy, cooperative approach and friendliness are an asset to your talents. Dynamic and powerful people are inclined to want to sponsor you or your products. You are an original. You excel when you work for yourself or as an autonomous executive.

Mid-life may be boring without a hobby or literary interest. You're inclined to play with words or be slow to mature; in some way your social self-esteem is delayed. You are a charmer and a born communicator, but you need flattery, tangible proof or reinforcement from a variety of lovers to take center stage.

Real estate, homes and all products that relate to the land are lucky for you, but you should invest in developing writing skills. Later years are active, comfortable and rooted.

• OTHER JULY 4 BIRTHDAYS

Louis Armstrong	1900
Abigail Van Buren	1918
George M. Cohan	1878
Calvin Coolidge	1872
Stephen Foster	1826
Virginia Graham	1913
Nathaniel Hawthorne	1804
Ann Landers	1918
Meyer Lansky	1902
Gertrude Lawrence	1901
Gina Lollobrigida	1927
Mitch Miller	1911
George Murphy	1902
Geraldo Rivera	1943
Tokyo Rose	1916
Eva Marie Saint	1924
Neil Simon	1927

JULY

· 5 ·

You are destined to be a performer—a showman—a people person. Your childhood exposes you to aristocratic, close-mouthed, investigative types of people. Your experiences teach you to follow your intuition and to sense when and how to keep a secret. You are eager to try everything and accept unconventional events with enthusiasm. By the time you reach your thirties, you combine the politician's adaptability and the professional's inflexible drive for perfection.

You are sensitive and tuned to observing the unconscious signals that people send out. Your closest emotional tie is to your mother. You learned as a tot to be modest and cooperative and to disguise your aggressive actions. However, you want embellishments, fanfare and changing challenges. Your childhood values did not prepare you for the untraditional happenings of your youth or mid-life. You are versatile, but must stay alert, responsive and speculative to overcome your tendency to let depression deplete your energy. Your forties are a far cry from the expectations of your teens.

You overcome early training, ridicule, and/or the hue and cry of ultraconservatives. You desire an advantageous partnership to remain as unconfined as possible within it and to promote your own philosophy. Your physical and mental energy increase as your individuality ripens. They are dynamic boosters for your chronic health problems, which are induced by emotional stress. You are shrewd and strive to get the most for your time and money.

In late years you tire of projections and keep track of things close to home. However, you keep a card up your sleeve.

• OTHER JULY 5 BIRTHDAYS

P. T. Barnum	1810
Jean Cocteau	1891
Julie Nixon Eisenhower	1948
David Farragut	1801
Henry Cabot Lodge, Jr.	1902
Georges Pompidou	1911

JULY

·6·

You are inclined to question established procedures and respond with an emotional commitment to work your heart out for "the cause." Whatever "the cause" may be, you stay with it until your late years bring you "the effect."

You are impatient. Childhood domestic responsibilities and financial circumstances curb your individuality. You surround yourself with inspirational talkers and group energies which bring out your very generous or very selfish attitudes. Men who relate to your early years, particularly the father, may be too authoritative, secretive or aloof or may not be reliable. Your self-motivation and inventiveness are challenged by youthful experiences, and you will desperately want approval. There is a tendency, as an adult, to allow yourself to be alternately dominated or dominating. A change before age forty opens doors to a fast-paced life-style that encourages you to discover a truer you.

A tranquil marriage, a career that makes a meaningful contribution and deep-seated friendships are high on your list of lifetime goals. Expressive and socially aware people add their interests in music, community welfare, and home improvements to your heavy sense of personal idealism. You enjoy upgrading and maintaining a consistently comfortable atmosphere. You take pride in your background, your family and your personal discrimination. Be tolerant of your opposites.

In later years you would be wise to realize that opposites are the desirable ingredients that provide the necessary grit to encourage change. You keep working. Be expansive and ready to teach and learn. Don't expect everyone to be just like you.

· OTHER JULY 6 BIRTHDAYS

Laverne Andrews	1915
Susan Ford	1957
Merv Griffin	1925
Dorothy Kirsten	1917
Janet Leigh	1927
Emperor Maximilian of Mexico	1832
Nancy Reagan	1923
Della Reese	1932
James Wyeth	1946

JULY

· 7 ·

Your perceptions are accurate and your experiences are extraordinary as a child. People are uneasy in your presence because you give the impression of seeing right through them. You are introspective, questioning, dreamy and intuitive. You are too emotionally adult for your years, and you do not relate socially as a tot. You may be too studious, retiring and analytic to be comfortable with the superficial joys and sorrows of your peers. Childhood and youth experiences are not conventional, and you learn to cleverly assess the untraditional and surprising events and people that you encounter. Lady Luck is your friend.

Opportunities for your material success walk into your back door in response to your professionalism or expertise. You're in the destiny of gamblers, promoters and entrepreneurs. Expect the unexpected; be adaptable and enthusiastic about challenges, and forgiving.

You have an empathetic, compassionate, generous approach to personal and charitable love when you think that your efforts are appreciated. If the recipient of your caring and sharing does not understand the sacrifices that you have made in the name of love, when crossed, you are an intimidating, coldblooded and selfish enemy. You are a candidate for stress problems before you're thirty if you do not take yourself and love less seriously.

In mid-life aim to make a few definite decisions and stick to them. Guard against becoming power hungry. You can overcome any obstacles and attract the money and help that you need. Marriage to a less polished spouse who is wise may result in a long-term commitment that is materially and creatively fulfilling.

• OTHER JULY 7 BIRTHDAYS

Pierre Cardin	1922
Marc Chagall	1887
George Cukor	1899
King Henry VIII of England	1491
Julius Hoffman	1895
Gustav Mahler	1860
Gian Carlo Menotti	1911
Ringo Starr	1940
Clinton Wilder	1920

JULY

· 8 ·

You will consistently encounter powerful, efficient and ambitious people after your thirtieth birthday. They are down-to-earth realists who relate their own stamina, drive and multitalents to you. The midsection of your life will bring you into the financial mainstream. You will have the option to go for the gold or to use your executive talents in the service of others.

Childhood experiences and exposures are aimed at quality, professionalism or spirituality. If you are realistic and your expectations are tuned and timed to your educational background, you will be prepared to seize the financial opportunities that come your way after age twenty-eight. If you concentrate on your material ambitions, you will reap a harvest. You may marry, inherit or build wealth and/ or power.

As a teenager, your personal desires will be challenged. You will have opportunities to break with tradition. You may sacrifice all for love or refuse to devote yourself to work for security alone. You want to look good and live well. You have difficulty if you gamble and/or force yourself to live up to the Joneses. You go to extremes and are criticized, often unfairly.

If you submit to intimidation from family—particularly the father—lovers or business associates, you will shelve your individual talents until your frustrations turn to anger. Your impatience will surface as a combustible and your luck will change mid-life. After age fifty-five your fears of never having enough or walking alone subside. You concentrate more on giving and receiving emotional fulfillment and less on minimizing your own anxieties. You are destined to need both love and money.

• OTHER JULY 8 BIRTHDAYS

Emperor Julius Caesar	102 B.C.
Billy Eckstine	1914
Faye Emerson	1917
Jean de la Fontaine	1621
Percy Grainger	1882
Walter Kerr	1913
Steve Lawrence	1935
John D. Rockefeller	1839
Nelson Rockefeller	1908
George Romney	1907
Ferdinand von Zeppelin	1838

JULY

· **9** ·

Early years are sprinkled with disappointing or disillusioning people and experiences. Your sixteenth year finds you feeling disconnected, misunderstood and humbled. Mother is your closest emotional tie, and you want to please her. You do your best and more often than not get only a little for the rewards that you anticipate. You are destined to attract notable people and to become a person who has polish and skills. You become less personalized and more empathetic as you go far from your roots between the ages of twenty-eight and fifty-six.

Values and goals may be confused during your youth. Every time you think you know where you're going and what you want, the options get taken away through no fault of your own. You will do well if you have developed a set of disciplines to lean on when delays get you down. An educational training should begin early, and a profession or technical skill should be perfected. During your lifetime you are intended to set an example and to make a contribution, not to be a loner or an escapist.

Childhood is less apt to bring you into the spotlight than are your later years. You attract a woman of means and stature who broadens your scope and inspires a direction as a second career—or after age fifty-six. But in mid-life you give more than you get, in spite of your magnetism and romantic appeal. The strong feelings that you show, the opinions that you voice and the wisdom that draws people to ask you for guidance don't show up as a special quality until you recognize that power and money cannot give you the self-esteem you need. Don't ever get lazy.

Later, home products and charity capture your interest.

• OTHER JULY 9 BIRTHDAYS

Edward Heath	1916
Elias Howe	1819
Samuel Eliot Morison	1887
Peter Paul Rubens	1577
O. J. Simpson	1947

JULY

· 10 ·

Home is where your heart is, but you're always on the go. You will have need for a well-developed sense of humor when your ability to be discriminating and competitive clash. If you take yourself too seriously, the peace, beauty and harmony that you crave will be lost and you will be left alone with your personal ideals.

Childhood family ties are close. You are exposed to authoritative people who expect professionalism. You learn the lessons of investigation, discipline and perfection. There is a power or money consciousness that prevails throughout your youth. Mid-life opens doors for you to excel as an original. Later years find you involved in group service projects. It is important for you to be realistic and to stand up for your personal standards, even at the cost of your material security.

You feel isolated and denied because people do not help you. If they came to your aid, you would feel guilty if you did not accommodate them when they needed help. Your timing for progressive changes is shattered when you volunteer too much. Timing is your nemesis and your champion. Pick your spots, but expect to advance rapidly and frequently between the ages of thirty and fifty-five. In maturity your innovations and mental agility put you in a class by yourself.

You're impatient, inventive and want to be a winner. After youthful tries at pleasing everyone, you finally take control, marry, and master your fears. You experienced emotional poverty, loneliness and a lack of intellectual companionship in youth; don't get think-stuck as an adult. Change is your only constant.

• OTHER JULY 10 BIRTHDAYS

Arthur Ashe	1943
David Brinkley	1920
Legs Diamond	1897
Arlo Guthrie	1947
Jean Kerr	1923
Marcel Proust	1871
James Whistler	1834

JULY

• 11 •

You are an inspiration to your peers and travel far from your roots before you recognize your own abilities to foresee the future. Childhood influences are spiritual or nonmaterialistic. You are restless, high-strung and difficult to understand. Parents cannot keep up with your indecisiveness and cannot relate to the ideas that flow through your rapidly moving mind. You become an experimenter, are impetuous and must learn by experiencing life and taking its challenges.

You are an extremist. Money will never satisfy you as much as cultural expansion. Elitists and people who have gained a polish and skill of performance are attracted to you. You are a gifted orator when expressing your personal ideals and code of ethics. Your reactions are swift and unconventional until your thirties, when you add self-discipline and determination to your varied talents. You are too busy or too bored in your teens and take on more than you can handle, which overwhelms you in your youth.

Lawyers, sensual pleasures and laziness give you grief. You are too self-concerned and often expect to get what you want without making any effort. You are sexy, like physical activity and are likely to marry or form partnerships with people who are from different cultures. In mid-life you grow wise and are called upon to counsel others. There is an electricity to your attraction, sensitivity and ability to get recognition for your eccentricities. Your personal need is for material security, but you are not comfortable getting your hands dirty or laboring.

Later years are useful, active and happier than imagined.

• OTHER JULY 11 BIRTHDAYS

John Quincy Adams	1767
Yul Brynner	1920
Tab Hunter	1931
Thomas Mitchell	1892
John Wanamaker	1838
E.B. White	1899

JULY

· 12 ·

A good education is a prime target for your communications talents. You can write, entertain or attract attention through a multitude of artistic interests. You are intellectually questioning and need to explore concepts and ideas. It is your early practical training and work ethic that can make or break the possibilities you have to live on the lighter side of life.

The mental stimulation that you required as a child was ignored and the material necessities were stressed. Properness, orderliness and conventionality were the guidelines for your youth. As a mature adult, your investigative mind must find a concentration and your workaholic tendencies are best curbed. You tend to be extremely honest and traditional or too uncomfortable with middle-class values and goals.

You practice what you preach to an extreme, or you are eager to escape from the habits that determine your financial security. You cause yourself to be self-protective and sacrifice your ability to gain through social contacts, charm and personal attractiveness until your forties. You rediscover yourself in mid-life, and make a job or career change.

The loss or demands of a male relative tie you to duties that tax your finances. You are helped by affluent and influential contacts as you climb back to mental, spiritual and material security. You set yourself apart and appear to be part of the mainstream after your late-in-life awakening. You reach a pinnacle where you must decide to be independent or continue to relate your ambitions to partnerships. Aim for peace of mind.

In late life you are happiest puttering in your own home.

• OTHER JULY 12 BIRTHDAYS

Milton Berle	1908
Van Cliburn	1934
Bill Cosby	1937
George Eastman	1854
Kirsten Flagstad	1895
Mark Hatfield	1922
Oscar Hammerstein II	1895
Cheryl Ladd	1951
Henry David Thoreau	1817
Andrew Wyeth	1917

JULY
· 1 3 ·
There will always be an element of sacrifice in your life. Your spiritual awareness is triggered as a child, and you develop your own brand of faith. You are a charmer and attract listeners but must work for anything you want or need. You are at your best serving, teaching or making others comfortable. You have strong personal ideals where children, family and community matters are involved.

Many of your burdens are really volunteer projects that enslave you. You are a dedicated worker and will face various conflicts that involve financial security for yourself or the people that you feel you are obligated to help. You are self-assured and ready to argue to put your set of conventions into practice.

Mid-life is protected if you are strictly honest with yourself. If you are lazy or incur insurmountable financial or emotional debts, you will have to change your life-style and work habits. As a tot, you were adored or unattended. You tend to become too sociable or antisocial, which scatters your energy. You are immature or too old for your years, and this inconsistency hampers your early progress.

You must concentrate upon an education, learn to control your emotions and focus on a specialty to realize your potential. As a youngster, you were surrounded by authoritative adults who inspired a drive in you for perfection. Until you are in your fifties you are too critical and have difficulty building self-esteem because you fail to accept human frailty. Later, after you let go of a bad bargain, you gain security through land dealings.

• OTHER JULY 13 BIRTHDAYS

Sidney Blackmer	1895
Cheech	1946
Father Flanagan	1886
Dave Garroway	1913
Charles Scribner, Jr.	1921
David Storey	1933

JULY

·14·

You are self-expressive, introspective and clever. However, you are too sensitive, possessive, detail conscious and personalized to enjoy your own delightfully surprising, adventurous, unconventional talents. Unchallenged by fear, you are the essence of freedom, enthusiasm and youthful sensuality.

The less you understand a place, a job or a person, the more inspired, fascinated and dedicated you become. The diversification of your talents—your ability to do many things at one time—are your mainstays . . . and your downfall. In youth you satisfy your ambitions and restlessly walk away. You want to explore the unknown and control each outcome. You crave change.

After age twenty-eight you switch career objectives and settle into a rigid, conventional pattern. You take responsibility too lightly or too seriously and have difficulty maintaining long-term relationships. The objects of your affections are cast by the wayside once you have uncovered their inner core. It is the element of mystery and the challenge of the chase that capture your interest. You are not slated to have one love in a lifetime.

Your tangible possessions represent stability to you. In order to avoid boredom or unexpected changes, you attempt to eliminate feeling unchallenged or overwhelmed by holding on to material things. In time you are owned by your possessions. Your business, home, pets, and so on represent your security blankets, and you collect objects, become cerebral or become intensely involved in sensual experiences until the end of your days.

You are intended to learn to live fearlessly, without escaping responsibilities. Later years are secured by caution.

• OTHER JULY 14 BIRTHDAYS

Polly Bergen	1930
Ingmar Bergman	1918
John Chancellor	1927
Douglas Edwards	1917
Gerald R. Ford	1913
Roosevelt Grier	1932
Woody Guthrie	1912
Arthur Laurents	1920
Dale Robertson	1923
Jerry Rubin	1938
Isaac Singer	1904
Irving Stone	1903

JULY

·15·

Where's the fire? You're not willing to wait for the appropriate timing or people to help you get the foundation that you want. Fortunately, you are an unforgettably sympathetic, nurturing, parental talent. Money is important to your ambitions. An appreciation of beauty, a desire to give and receive love and a respect for education are your mainstays. You have strong opinions about music, art, philosophy, spirituality and domestic life-styles. Whether lecturing or listening, you give your all.

On the down side, you are too impatient and expect instant gratification. You are strongly assertive or too submissive. Your childhood is not worry-free and includes problems with tactless, argumentative insensitives who created difficulties. Your strongest ties are family rooted, although you want to travel, live graciously and feel independent.

Mid-life you attract gifts and favors. Money is earned and enjoyed. You are a quick study and want your family to be intellectually progressive. You are likely to explode if you take yourself and the unconventional changes that you experience too seriously. Be decisive, and don't allow your loves to enslave you. You meet opportunities that open the door to freedom of choice. Stay alert to assess your options and make transitions.

Before you're fifty you will have the chance to develop your mental capacities and to learn not take things at face value or to worship false idols—which are your challenges in life. If you delude yourself and are given to ridicule, you will find contentment but not live up to your expectations. In late years you independently explore your enthusiasms and live comfortably.

• OTHER JULY 15 BIRTHDAYS

MoTHER CAbRiNi	1850
DoRoTHy FiElds	1905
IRis MuRdoch	1919
REMbRANdT vAN RijN	1606
LiNdA RONsTAdT	1945
JAN-MichAEl ViNcENT	1945

JULY

· 16 ·

It's the game plan that excites you and conquering the impossible that delights you—you've got a thirst for perfecting humanity in your soul. Education is the key to your success and happiness. As a tot, introspective, aristocratic, authoritative people guided your expectations. They were too emotionally responsive or too cold for you to receive your first impressions and to assess yourself practically. You expect too much from yourself and rarely feel total satisfaction when you are successful. You are an untraditional achiever as a youngster.

As a youth, you were too wise for your years. You may have taken challenges that should have been beyond your capacities and come out a winner. You receive only seventy-five percent of your goals, and through no fault of your own, the height of your ambitions eludes you. In part, you are to blame for your own dissatisfaction. You set impossible standards and accept dogma from people who have a title or speak as experts. You ignore your exceptional intuition in favor of the advice of others and deceive yourself or get involved with cunning partners. By the time you reach your thirties, you develop an exclusive philosophy that makes you a loner, aloof from mundane expectations but steeped in realistic work projects.

Your forties find you divided between focusing your intellectual growth and on your emotional responsibilities. Intimate relationships are the cause of your sorrow, and it is impossible for you to use your logic to find solutions. Later years offer you career changes, companionship and the chance to bring your aspirations and your intellectual capacity together.

• OTHER JULY 16 BIRTHDAYS

Roald Amundsen	1872
Margaret Court	1942
Mary Baker Eddy	1821
Alexander the Great	356 B.C.
Bess Myerson	1924
Ginger Rogers	1911
Barbara Stanwyck	1907
Patricia Wilde	1928

JULY

· 1 7 ·

You are penny wise and pound foolish due to your fine tastes and unaccountable fear of poverty. In childhood you were exposed to people who thought their way in and out of problems and left you to your own devices. You had to concentrate on yourself and learned how and when to keep silent. You're a planner and a worker. In youth you silently separate yourself from earthiness and the family that you love and build an inner life that prepares you to compete for affluence and power in mid-life.

You are a "good child" until you decide to break out and go it alone. The influence of the father was too strong or absent. You are too self-assured or too submissive and do not let go of family guidelines easily. When you test your body, mind and spirit in mid-life, you uncover your superlative stamina, courage and executive abilities. When you assume control, you are surprised at the influence your constructive energy generates. You are capable of building a firm domestic commitment and a thriving business venture and of expressing your unique creative talents.

In later years only your fear of asserting your individuality can spoil or delay achieving your ambitions. You break established patterns, take a stabilized attitude toward your work and find that your lover or mate is a burden you can handle. You are intelligent, inventive and competitive. It is imperative that you learn to accept the natural course of events that bring about progressive changes. You are inclined to want to be paid well for your efforts, and after age forty will stabilize your financial security if you work and refuse self-satisfaction.

• OTHER JULY 17 BIRTHDAYS

John Jacob Astor	1763
James Cagney	1899
DiaHann Carroll	1935
Phyllis Diller	1917
Erle Stanley Gardner	1889
John Paul Jones	1747
Art Linkletter	1912

JULY

· **18** ·

Youth's dissillusionments fade as you become less personalized and more charitable in mid-life. You are geared to set an example, to counsel and teach others as you mature. It's only the emotional disconnections of childhood and the early years of uncertainty that provide you with the fear of being caught penniless and alone. You have misguided judgments to overcome in mid-life. When you stop creating petty problems or interpreting the opinions of others as personal slights, you are able to achieve the perfection of your ambitions.

After age twenty-eight opportunities arise to use your charisma, empathy and artistic talents to reach a multitude of ready listeners. You have a common denominator personality that is acceptable to mass tastes, and you are a communicator. When you stop taking everything personally and share your wisdom, you will attract attention in a positive way. You must establish your own standards and values to put your goals into motion. Once you use your down-to-earth, practical training to make others comfortable or to entertain, you will reflect upon your childhood more kindly. You are intended to serve the public and should strive to avoid gullibility or becoming too skeptical. As a result of love, you will have to make some sacrifice.

It is in your best interests to be your own boss and to organize your financial interests in mid-life. You meet people and have experiences that open the doors to making money if you are willing to throw off all prejudices, to concentrate your energy and to specialize your interests. You are a romantic who will work and build an opulent family life-style with those who will share your blessings.

• OTHER JULY 18 BIRTHDAYS

Hume Cronyn	1911
John Glenn	1921
S. I. Hayakawa	1906
Gene Lockhart	1891
Harriet Hilliard Nelson	1912
Clifford Odets	1906
Red Skelton	1913
William M. Thackeray	1811

JULY
· 19 ·

You have the opportunity during your lifetime to be one of a kind and to share or shirk the responsibility of bringing innovations to the attention of the public. You take on the problems of the world or refuse positions of trust that group interactions impose upon your individual ambitions. Family opinions and standards make a lasting impression. Your programing as a youth was geared to getting involved, and as you grow to maturity, you protect your privacy. You maintain one face to the world and a separate identity to your intimates.

As a youngster, you need the attention and inspiration of one caring person to set you on the track of the right profession, career or business. You are capable of being a clinging vine and must avoid dependencies on lovers, family or teachers. You may forego personal happiness to serve or comfort those less capable of helping themselves or become an emotional supporter for talented artistes. In some way you are slated to use your creativity to bring yourself pleasure from pulling others up the ladder.

You need peace and beauty in your life. Discord at home or in a job is harmful to your well-being. After your forties you are less inclined to fight the organizations of people who challenge your ideas. You develop your patience to mingle amiably with groups and to tolerate their divergent opinions.

You are introduced to material accomplishments as a child and never lose your ability to upgrade yourself financially and influentially, but you are a victim of emotionalism. You learn to admire achievers and their rewards in youth but require a specialty if you intend to make your mark before later years.

• OTHER JULY 19 BIRTHDAYS

Vicki CARR	1942
SAMUEL COLT	1814
EDGAR DEGAS	1834
CHARLES MAYO	1865
GEORGE McGOVERN	1922
ILIE NASTASE	1946

JULY
·20·

Expect to travel far from your roots, to adapt to unconventional exposures and to spend your days learning to be a decisive diplomat. Your childhood is unconventional by traditional standards. You were too sheltered or given too much freedom as a youth. As a result, you are promiscuous or afraid to investigate sex and your physical senses. If life doesn't offer you adventures, you invent a few new tricks. You are too busy or too bored until you reach your thirties, when one intimate relationship captures you.

Good taste, quality consciousness and an aloofness from the expectations of the average person become part of your character. You are trained to think, analyze and look beneath the surface. It is in your best interests to get a good education and to grasp a profession. Although you know what is good for you, your impulsivity, curiosity and dislike of restraints create havoc within you. Obligations and responsibilities surround you as a teenager. You cannot become financially independent until you take charge of your own affairs. You may marry just to get away from a mentally or physically confining and emotionally insensitive family.

In mid-life you begin to see people as they really are and begin to look beneath the surface for intellectual companionship. Home and children are precious, and you make them a priority. You rely upon your talent to exercise subtle control over others and find it difficult to use reason, not emotions, when you exercise your options. You constantly evaluate your own potential, strive to help others and enjoy security late in life.

• OTHER JULY 20 BIRTHDAYS

Nelson Doubleday	1933
Sir Edmund Hillary	1919
Sally Ann Howe	1934
Elliot Richardson	1920
Natalie Wood	1938

JULY

·21·

You attract attention for your strong point of view and are willing to get into the thick of the fighting to back it up. You are a loner and invite success if you can structure your work and play by the rules. Practice what you preach and don't make your standards creatively self-limiting. Your home, friends and career are all in good taste—as you interpret quality. The world is your oyster, and you feel a need to travel that enriches your ability to express your variety of talents. It is the taskmaster within you that causes you emotional confusion.

As a tot, you are an imaginative, playful charmer. The practical attitude of traditional thinkers and doers who surround you in youth teach you to labor for your ambitions. However, you are slated to use your patience, determination and communications talents in the society of creatively expressive people. It is not your destiny to slave for survival, to willingly accept the inevitable or to remain aloof from responsibility to your community.

You dislike being mentally or physically confined, and you rush to the rescue when you think that unfair practices are stunting the growth or curtailing the freedoms of others. You have the charisma that attracts recognition, and you give voice to your talents or philosophy. You have learned—the hard way—to have the courage of your convictions. In mid-life you invite rewards, gifts and successful conclusions when you set an example of faith and dedication and share your outlook.

Late years find you married to an artistic, comforting partner, confronting your despairs or living a splendid old age.

• OTHER JULY 21 BIRTHDAYS

John Calvin	1509
Ernest Hemingway	1899
Al Hirschfeld	1903
Frances Parkinson Keyes	1885
Don Knotts	1924
Kay Starr	1922
Isaac Stern	1920
Robin Williams	1952

JULY

·22·

You are high-strung, misunderstood and uniquely sensitive as a tot. You sense that you are intended to rise above the crowd, and although you are generally unobtrusive, when fired with inspiration, you are a dynamic leader. Mid-life, your specialized talents push you into attention-getting situations, and you work tirelessly to design and pattern systems and upgrade material conditions for others. In old age you are remembered for past efforts and leave a lasting impression and material benefits for future generations. You have a karmic destiny.

Through your family ties, your own aspirations or the ambitions of your mate, you have exceptional opportunities to meet people and experiences that provide you with financial freedom and elitist social stature. You may have spiritual or material ups and downs, but these emotionally disconcerting time spans are in direct proportion to the depth and height of your desires. You will be called upon to absorb yourself for the betterment of family, lovers or humanity. You will sacrifice personal glory and push your physical stamina and practical dedication when the perfection of your ideals is in sight.

Children, the infirm and oldsters benefit from your reconstructive ideas. Mid-life offers comforting diversification of interests, but the demands that are made upon you leave little privacy or chance for revitalization of energy. Your strength is in your unique intellectual, technical, scientific or spiritual philosophy. Your tact, diplomacy, wisdom and patience are tested constantly due to increasing moral obligations. Life after age fifty-five increases your capacity to motivate and influence others.

• OTHER JULY 22 BIRTHDAYS

Licia Albanese	1913
Orson Bean	1928
Stephen Vincent Benet	1898
Robert Dole	1923
Rose Fitzgerald Kennedy	1890
Karl Menninger	1893
Oscar de la Renta	1932
Amy Vanderbilt	1908
Margaret Whiting	1924

JULY

·23·

You are clever, animated and regal. Essentially you are an idea person, gifted with physical agility, charm and poise. The spirit of adventure that you feel enables you to remain youthful—to live to old age charged with new enthusiasms. A routine life-style is not in the cards.

You are guided and protected by the experienced and professional people who cross your destiny. Be assured that any stubbornness or hesitation on your part to accept rapidly changing situations—and to adapt to the unexpected—will misdirect your exceptional intuition. It's up to you to expect to benefit from surprises or alterations of goals and to upgrade your ambitions. Never refuse to refresh your point of view or to become ungracious or unfriendly.

Between your twenty-eighth and fifty-fifth birthdays you will meet situations and people who tax your patience and self-esteem when you are on the brink of success. You are called upon to be tenacious and optimistic in time spans that give you additional responsibilities and financial obligations. If you direct your career to one concentration—you have many choices—success is assured in mid-life and security is not denied in old age.

Lawyers and accountants are the bane of your existence. It is in your best interests to stay clear of legal battles or complicated tax write-offs. You are restless and like to think big. Keep your multiple loves, plans and investigations on the up and up. Your insecurity should mellow as you grow older.

You have a comfortable old age if you put your faith in reality and educate yourself to test your intellectual capacity.

• OTHER JULY 23 BIRTHDAYS

Raymond Chandler	1888
Bert Convy	1934
Don Drysdale	1936
Gloria De Haven	1925
Emperor Haile Selassie of Ethiopia	1891
Michael Wilding	1912

JULY

·24·

There is a bit of earthiness and showmanship in us all, but you take the cake for combining common sense with a talent for creating a spectacular scenario out of your destiny. You expect life to have a dramatic meaning. You want to play the child and accept intimacy with only one person. "All the world's a stage" and you are the actor, writer, director and producer.

You want to be comfortable and tend to overeat, overact or overcompensate for imagined character deficiencies. You try too hard and force issues when you display your independence, creativity and innovative ideas. Your father or another male family member has a strong influence upon your self-image. It is in your own best interests to assert yourself with concern for your own safety.

You subconsciously look for approval from childhood relationships and are inclined to be headstrong when feeling frustrated. Aim to be discriminating and to make changes that support your ambitions after patient and reasonable investigations. You are dissatisfied with yourself as a youth and become too explorative, untraditional and uncompromising. In mid-life you see yourself as an equal in any situation and set forth to promote your personal ideals.

You are self-willed and opinionated but form love relationships or business partnerships based upon your conventional upbringing. Your youth is traditional and geared to the practical work ethic, a desire for professionalism and quality consciousness. In late years you are respected for keeping secrets; you remain aloof from mundane temptations and prosper.

• OTHER JULY 24 BIRTHDAYS

Bella Abzug	1918
Simón Bolívar	1783
Walter Brennan	1894
Ruth Buzzi	1936
Alexandre Dumas	1802
Amelia Earhart	1898

JULY

·25·

Between the unconventional people and experiences that cause you to be wise for your years and financial inconsistencies in youth, it's no wonder that you leave your nesting place for greener pastures. Your fears of loneliness and poverty and your desire for perfection are based upon the unreasonable actions and attitudes of grown-ups when you were a child. They were irrational. You spend your life attempting to rationalize or investigate your youthful first impressions.

You are restless, inquisitive and very bright. You are a fooler and rarely allow yourself to show your hand. You listen, analyze and reflect upon past experiences to intuitively settle upon solutions to immediate problems. Your loves are sensual, deep and enduring. Your beliefs are unconventional and challenge the imagination of traditional thinkers. You have a distaste for being indebted to anyone, and in mid-life you suffer from obligations incurred by a female relative.

You attract money and respect for your professionalism. Partnerships are beneficial only if they are based upon peer ideals. You are lost when confronted with nonabstract thinkers and seek solitude to ponder the uncertainty of your own beliefs. You will never find peace until you depend upon yourself and utilize your inner resources. You must avoid drugs or escapist devices, moodiness and submerging your unique personality in the name of romance or love. It is in your best interests to stay active in late years. Your mental gymnastics and the precedents you set are catalysts for change in the lives of others.

In late years your contributions to society are rewarded.

• OTHER JULY 25 BIRTHDAYS

Frank Church	1924
Jack Guilford	1913
Eric Hoffer	1902
Adnan Khashoggi	1935
Janet Margolin	1943
Maxfield Parrish	1870

JULY

26

You compete, make waves and scare yourself—but eventually you develop your self-confidence, stamina and ability to maintain long-term commitments. Self-control is the key to achieving your ambitions. In youth it's a toss-up between mental and physical interests. Money and power are reasons for entering the business world in youth, although you are happiest in your forties, content in love and managing your emotional relationships and obligations while balancing career and home life.

Family, group and community responsibilities, sympathies and objectives are foremost in your ambitions. You feel like a superstar when involved with a fast-paced, provocative and affluent society. You are intimidated and impressed by assertive or innovative competitors. When you find that they have feet of clay, you become the critic and intimidator. When unchallenged, you are submissive, lazy and selfish. You cannot settle for mediocrity and enter mid-life prepared to work for high stakes.

After age twenty-eight you plan for others, require cooperative partners and seek out capable advisers. You are less inclined to be a loner. You surround yourself with comforts, although you are never sure that your treasures will not be taken away without explanations or warning. There is a fear of losing control of people and situations that makes you pursue bargains long past the time when compromise is necessary for your security.

You hedge on your bets until your fifties, when you stop taking advantage of the foibles you intuitively identify in others. You are gifted with a higher intelligence, and efficiency to that dominates your late years. You never quit, and you win.

• OTHER JULY 26 BIRTHDAYS

Gracie Allen	1905
Salvador Allende	1908
Aldous Huxley	1894
Mick Jagger	1944
Jason Robards, Jr.	1922
Carl Jung	1875
Serge Koussevitzsky	1874
Stanley Kubrick	1928
George Bernard Shaw	1856
Jean Shepherd	1923

JULY

·27·

People of importance find you. You are secretive, sensitive and magnetic. In youth you are tutored by perfectionists who deny their emotional responses to achieve professionalism. Your mother is a forceful, generous, critical influence in childhood, and you strive to gain approval. You become ambitious and visualize yourself in powerful positions in which your talents extend to a broad scope of admirers.

It is in your best interests to specialize and get a good education. You are a romantic and are inclined to set unrealistic goals as a youth. You are never totally pleased with your performance until you pass your thirtieth year and travel professionally, which opens your eyes to how the people out of your realm of experience live. You become charitable, empathetic and concerned about the quality and skill of your performance. You are not disposed to get involved with anything petty or small in business or anyone who is small-minded in marriage.

In mid-life you have a "show me" approach to any problem, due to disappointments and disillusionments experienced in youth. You are self-conscious and require tangible proof of your worth. Marriage starts off with you in the subordinate position and changes as you require freedom and privacy and reflect upon family traditions. Your loyalty to your love and career remain steadfast, although you experience disappointing spans of time.

Late years are happiest if responsibilities do not rest upon your shoulders. Travel is appealing but proves to be unrewarding. You become a product of the multicultures that pass through your life. You travel far from your roots.

• OTHER JULY 27 BIRTHDAYS

Elizabeth Dole	1936
Anton Dolin	1904
Leo Durocher	1906
Peggy Fleming	1948
Bobbie Gentry	1944
Tony Tanner	1932
Isaac Watts	1674
Keenan Wynn	1916

JULY

· 28 ·

Go for the gold, stretch your capacities and you will win every time. If you just take the easy way out, you'll live a mundane, orderly life-style that is comparable to the effort you put into it. In youth you are shown power, affluence and stamina. It is up to you, and your ability to live up to your personal ideals sets the stage for your ambitions to flourish. You are intended to give service, entertain or provide comfort as you mellow with age. As a tot, you display musical-artistic talent, parental instincts and wisdom beyond your years.

You do not deserve the challenges that are placed in your path, but you have a great capacity to heal, counsel and serve humanity. You expect too much of others—particularly your family and loved ones. Others cannot live up to your personal standards or fulfill your personal needs. When you learn the lesson of live and let live, you will stop muttering "there ought to be a law" about everything that displeases you. When you find inner peace, you will stop blaming your intimates for disturbing your equilibrium or forcing you to escape their company. In mid-life, after forty, you cease to be overbearing and allow your sweet facade, protective instincts and active energy to reach your untraditional inner core.

You dramatize everything and subject yourself to unhappiness. You want to succeed at all costs and must avoid daydreaming your accomplishments. Be prepared to sacrifice freedom, independence and a few creative ideas to further your ambitions in later years. You cannot be a one-person army or deny past loyalties, once goals have been reached, to fulfill your destiny.

• OTHER JULY 28 BIRTHDAYS

Vida Blue	1949
Harry Bridges	1901
Joe E. Brown	1892
Peter Duchin	1937
Jacqueline Kennedy Onassis	1929
Beatrix Potter	1866
Rudy Vallee	1901

JULY

· 29 ·

You are a moody visionary, a romantic and an extremist. A specialized education, faith in a higher power and a supportive, loving, dependable helpmate are important to your happiness and dreams for success. As a youth, you are too experimental or afraid to try the unknown. You learn from experience and make restless changes until you reach your late twenties and find a mission that becomes all-consuming.

Life's surprises, changing environments and untraditional exposures rattle you as a tot. You are self-absorbed and intent upon reforming or uplifting others. You have a detail consciousness that is petty and wonderfully sensitive. The feelings that you have for service to humanity are often impractical but are inspirational to listeners. You attract a following and intimate peer relationships that feed your inquiring mind and relieve boredom in domestic situations. You are inclined to enmesh yourself in unfulfilled or dissillusioning loves and emotional discontent. You see yourself as king in your castle—and your castle encompasses all you survey.

You are persistent and wear down your opponents. Powerful people attract your attention, and you ally yourself with their causes to absorb their techniques. As you see it, a world of joy and peaceful unions would be nice. Although you extend yourself to expand culturally, you cannot force-feed the milk of human kindness or inbreed a spirit of brotherly love. If you are dismayed, be cautious in your use of escapist devices. In later years you are secure and less prone to diving or soaring emotionally. You teach and inspire to leave a lasting image.

- OTHER JULY 29 BIRTHDAYS

Theda Bara	1890
Melvin Belli	1907
Clara Bow	1905
Dag Hammarskjöld	1905
Peter Jennings	1938
Benito Mussolini	1883
William Powell	1892
Sigmund Romberg	1887
Booth Tarkington	1869
Paul Taylor	1930

JULY
· **30** ·

You are a practical perfectionist and assume that your leadership will be undisputed. You are self-expressive, and few people can hold a candle to your spectacular arguments, talents and workaholic extremes. You are open to ignore traditional expectations or you live by a code of ethics that is unyielding to progressive changes. You can write, entertain or perform surgery if you choose to concentrate on a specific. It is in your best interests to be less of a practical taskmaster and more of a skilled artist.

To get what you want from your lovers, friends and business associates, you will have to set an example. As a tot, your exposures were practical, orderly and materialistic. Everyone anticipated tangible results and expected that beauty, imagination and talent would be put to work. From youth to your late thirties, sacrifices are expected and given, but after age thirty-six your conventional and creative personality hits the open road to freedom.

Sex appeal is one of your assets, and you attract the flirtations that accompany your personal charm. Your loyalty, once committed in a relationship, should not be questioned. If it is, you feel like a martyr or waste your electric vitality and many talents. You want and offer trust in your maturity.

Money, awards, applause—all material treasures, including a happy home and family, can be yours. Children and pets love you, and you have all the charms of the Pied Piper. All you require late in life is an adherence to conventions, a willingness to work and a consistent philosophy. You are destined to do big things.

• OTHER JULY 30 BIRTHDAYS

Paul Anka	1941
Peter Bogdanovich	1939
Emily Brontë	1818
Henry Ford	1863
Eleanor Smeal	1939

JULY

· 31 ·

It would be a perfect world if everyone worked as diligently, competed as enthusiastically and, in general, had the imagination to dream your dreams. Your high material energy is a plus if you invest yourself physically and are willing to labor with a loving attitude. If you argue every aspect, are disorganized or lack concentration, your life will appear to offer one struggle for survival after another.

You are independent and can become too much of a loner if you are not inclined to relate to friends and neighbors. You are too expressive and naive or do not trust the spoken word or sincerity. You are too talkative or punish others with your silence. You are antisocial or too superficial. You exaggerate yourself or take everyone else literally. In short, you create problems when you lack subtlety. In your desire to win every round, you strain relationships.

In childhood material security should not stop you from getting an education or developing an expertise. You take pride in home, family and your reputation. You are concerned with the position and standings of your friends and business associates. Mid-life is filled with hard work. You can merchandise yourself or products in a big way. You are top banana in a group. The toughest assignment for you to handle is intimacy and love.

Partnerships are not considered cooperative ventures in your eyes, and you may dissipate your lover's passion when you insist upon having the upper hand. You should consider stepping aside once in a while, to cultivate a companion for your late years. You travel mid-life but do not stray far from home after age sixty.

• OTHER JULY 31 BIRTHDAYS

Hank Bauer	1922
Geraldine Chaplin	1944
Evonne Goolagong	1951
S. S. Kresge	1867
France Nuyen	1939
Casey Stengel	1891

AUGUST

· 1 ·

You are a trendsetter. In any creative position or field you are intended to be a pioneering, courageous leader. Your ideas are the seeds for progressive changes that spark inventions, designs and fashions. It is within your power to solve problems that stump traditional thinkers and to initiate constructive concepts. It is up to you to avoid laziness and dependency. You require only the self-assurance to have the courage of your convictions to become a dominant force in any assemblage. If you expect a written guarantee of success and refuse to accept a loner's stance, you will not achieve your potential. Be independent and dare to be different.

In youth you are exposed to affluent, influential and businesslike people and experiences. If your family drives a Chevy, you will aim to have a Caddy. You have opportunities to observe executives in action, to grasp the importance of status symbols and to become a self-made money and/or power person. If a lack of education or family background saps your ambitions, you are riding a donkey instead of a stallion in the fast lane.

In mid-life you can make miracles if you set your goal and concentrate on becoming the best in your ambitions. Sports, the arts, big business and governments look to the innovators. Only your secret fears of poverty, loneliness and unworthiness can impede your progress. Lawyers and the judicial system can slow you down. Your impossible demands for perfection from yourself and the world around you may bring you to feelings of inadequacy. It is in your best interests to adjust to human frailty and, in late life, to join forces with a cosmopolitan woman.

• OTHER AUGUST 1 BIRTHDAYS

William Clark	1770
Geoffrey Holder	1930
Francis Scott Key	1779
Jack Kramer	1921
Yves Saint Laurent	1936
Herman Melville	1819

AUGUST

· 2 ·

Your sense of responsibility and the burdens that you accept too readily or refuse unreasonably complicate your ambitions as a youth. People of means and power cross your path; you develop a businesslike awareness and set ambitious goals. As a tot, you are family oriented and stay close to your roots until they cling and bind your individuality. You strain under group, community or domestic duties until the peace that you require is totally shattered. You break with convention or become a slave in service to the emotional needs of others. You cannot be a "cosmic parent" and volunteer your time, money and love without losing your peace of mind.

In mid-life partnerships and intimate relationships are important to your career and happiness. You are a support system and a diplomat. You are at your best when assuming the role of a power behind the throne and collecting your recognition for being the glue that binds organizations and groups together. You are sensitive to details and see both sides of any question. It is difficult for you to make choices. You attract what you need by being receptive to the ideas of others. With poise and an outward display of humility, modesty and friendliness, you appear passive. In reality, by not intimidating, being consistent and calm, you have subtle control over impatient, aggressive, changable leaders. You excel at coexisting and labor relations or may be negative and allow your vulnerable emotions to turn you into an indecisive, petulant, secretive, petty troublemaker.

In late years you prefer to follow your personal ideals and team up with a kindred spirit. You are protected and secure.

• OTHER AUGUST 2 BIRTHDAYS

James Baldwin	1924
Paul Laxalt	1922
Myrna Loy	1905
Gary Merrill	1914
Helen Morgan	1900
Carroll O'Connor	1924
Peter O'Toole	1933
Jack L. Warner	1892

AUGUST

· 3 ·

You are the type of child that attracts attention. Elitists or people who believe that conventions were made for the other guy are part of your childhood. You expect to be or to do something special, and you are encouraged to rise above mundane expectations. It isn't your beauty or personality that stands out. It is the special quality of sunshine that shines in your eyes when you smile.

Throughout your lifetime you appeal to audiences, intimates and the child in every adult. You are a communicator. As a performer, writer, teacher, model—any career that allows you to be self-expressive—you can take center stage if you concentrate. You dispose of people or commitments that stunt your progress and are wise in the ways of social advancements.

You appear to have humility but your talents are noticed early. You may lack the incentive to work or take on an unconventional job load as child. Escapist temptations—sex, drugs, travel—slow you down and make you secretive until your thirties, when the advice of friends and a release from obligations get you on a conventional track. Restlessness and unconventional behavior are major threats to your overall success.

As a youth, you meet people and have experiences that teach you the value of organizational efficiency, commerce and physical stamina. You are gentle, loving and charming. But you are curious, impulsive and too clever for your own good—and you are ambitious. Mid-life, you find a marketplace and understand that art for art's sake will not support your love of beauty, game playing and domestic tranquillity. You are energetic to the end.

· OTHER AUGUST 3 BIRTHDAYS

Richard Adler	1921
Tony Bennett	1926
Jay North	1952
Dolores Del Rio	1905
John Thomas Scopes	1900
Martin Sheen	1940

AUGUST

· 4 ·

In mid-life your loyalty, balance and dependability mean much to the people and experiences that surround you. You are too practical and creatively self-limiting, or you throw common sense to the four winds and break away from the patterns you have cut for yourself. You are often penny wise and pound foolish.

The self-expressive, charming and socially adept personalities that entered your life in youth exposed you to ways and means of benefiting from friendly relationships. You get involved and gain information from club or group activities. The dramatic or congenial side of life is confined in your workaholic commitments, which are the outgrowth of your desire to be cautious or self-protective. You marry money and/or brains.

When you fall in love, you discover that your work suffers. When you become emotional, your broad-scoped philosophy narrows your ambitions. You like money, owning your own home and the peace of mind that accompanies security. It is in your best interests to deal in real estate, construction businesses and manufacturing. Landscaping, music, sports and sculpture are hobbies that can make you a rich oldster. You are inwardly rigid in your structure and rarely uncurtain the romance you feel to cuddle your loved ones spontaneously or demand the affection that you could enjoy. You are only weak where lovers are concerned. After the age of thirty older men are a great help to you in business or through inheritance. You may allow yourself to be too accommodating, but when you break away, you fear domination to the point of becoming too self-insistent and aggressive. In late years you must avoid getting in a rut or traveling too fast.

• OTHER AUGUST 4 BIRTHDAYS

William Henry Hudson	1841
Walter Paten	1839
Percy Bysshe Shelley	1792
William Shuman	1910

AUGUST

· 5 ·

You're a top-notch promoter and can make megabucks and hold on to your investments when you break with the traditional patterns set by your family. Your appearance enhances your ambitions. Your ability to plan, manage and work according to the lessons learned as a child stands you in good stead in mid-life You are a combination of common sense, practicality and the gambler's spontaneous gifts of intuitional lucky ideas.

It's your adaptability, imagination and love of pizzazz that make you a charmer—even when you are not inclined to be sociable. You talk with great imagination and conviction or clam up and cannot be expected to be friendly. Your face is the mirror of your moods . . . and you move rapidly and change hats frequently. You do many things at one time and have only to finish the projects that you begin to make money and enjoy life.

You should be married but are not the best fidelity risk, because you need freedom to explore anything that you have not seen, touched, tasted, smelled or heard. It is your clever wit, unconventional ideas and ability to understand all peoples that pulls your burned fingers out of the flames. You learn from experience, pass your experiences on to others and, throughout your lifetime, realize that you are a catalyst for change in the lives of traditional doers and thinkers. Politics, theater and advertising are excellent career choices for your sometimes mercenary but more often grandiose personality.

Near your fortieth birthday your intellectual abilities come into focus and you make a radical change in long-term goals. Later years are active, but you are not comfortable far from home.

• OTHER AUGUST 5 BIRTHDAYS

Conrad Aiken	1889
John Huston	1906
Richard Kleindienst	1923
Jack Lenor Larsen	1927
Guy de Maupassant	1850
George Reedy	1917
Robert Taylor	1911

AUGUST

· 6 ·

Money will not bring you the independence or love that you think it will automatically provide. You will work for it, marry it or inherit—but your life will include unconventional experiments, problems with assertive men and responsibilities to your family and community, with or without financial freedom.

Youthful changes, travels and gambles bring you to a mid-life in which you make sacrifices for love. You will have established a conventional pattern in marriage, career or business after your thirty-sixth birthday, but your youthful escapades are not forgotten easily and crop up to haunt your family or professional life. Lawyers and the judicial system are not kind to you. It is in your best interests to stay away from court battles. In other ways you are protected and comforted.

You have your own code of ethics and react with antagonism to criticism. Lovers, friends and business associates have your loyalty but, once crossed, you become a shrewd and unforgiving foe. You alternate between being the soul of diplomacy or a caustic criticizer. When you finally assert yourself, you are secretive, subtly controlling and tactless. Your emotions run amuck! Emotional upheavals leave you depressed and drained.

There is a strong maternal tie that causes you to personalize and criticize unrealistically. You rarely forget petty slights and make mountains out of molehills until you mellow. In mid-life you come to grips with your inner demons, but not without subjugating yourself to a lover or feeling humbled and worthless for a time. An artistic career offers fame. You require congeniality at home and in business later in life.

• OTHER AUGUST 6 BIRTHDAYS

Lucille Ball	1911
Billie Burke	1886
Robert Mitchum	1917
Louella Parsons	1881
Ella Raines	1921
Dutch Schultz	1902
Alfred Lord Tennyson	1809
Andy Warhol	1927

AUGUST

· 7 ·

A profession or specialty is a must for your most productive years between twenty-seven and fifty-six. You are a questioning, investigative and thought-provoking youngster, but the paternal-domestic focus upon material accumulation and/or power is devastating to your ego. You do not follow your exceptional intuition until you reach mid-life, when your aristocratic, spiritual, perfectionist inclinations establish you as an authority. You have an eye for money and power, which enables you to marry, work for or inherit its protection.

You are an original and must break with family tradition. That is easier said than done. You want an opulent home and to be a credit to your community—but you need privacy and cannot abide the intrusions that obligations to family, community and your business groups entail. You love beauty, have firm opinions and require logical proof to alter your course of thinking.

You are fastidious and would never wear another's clothing or lend yours. You cannot tolerate itchy sweaters, coarse pillows or people who are too earthy. You aren't unkind—you are keenly aware of anything that touches your individualism, personal ideals and standards. You become a loner when the mundane, ugly or illogical world closes in on you. A metaphysical or religious practice and the meditations that it entails soothe your emotions and awaken your inner promptings.

You get a payoff if you have altered your values, developed a spirit of brotherly love and begun to identify with ordinary people. Don't procrastinate: Settle on a plan for your retirement and invite a cultured companion to share your late years.

• OTHER AUGUST 7 BIRTHDAYS

Ralph Bunche	1904
Lana Cantrell	1944
Ann Harding	1902
Mata Hari	1876

AUGUST

· 8 ·

You like to dive into big projects, make a big splash and get your rewards. Petty, mentally sluggish or unimaginative people bore and annoy you. You choose to travel in the fast lane of the artistic, financial or government industries and dare to outthink others and initiate big deals. In childhood you impress others with your wisdom. In youth you feel disillusioned or disconnected from the family or neighborhood, but through your loneliness you build your personal psychology and inner faith. Poverty and the feelings of frustration that accompany it are not only connected with money. You experience emotional poverty, a hunger that causes you to become a loner.

Misplaced hopes and impractical dreams give way to common sense when you assume direction and take control and begin to work for big results in mid-life. After age twenty-seven you emerge from your cocoon to energize your connections with affluent and influential people who cross your path. The experiences arise to allow you to be independent, courageous and ambitious, while you live up to your obligations toward family, dependents and your instincts for professionalism.

You have underlying health, love, legal or financial problems that you overcome. You leave home to travel and improve culturally. Your loves are romances that survive to long-term marriage only if you do not dominate or go to the other extreme to submerge your personality. Money comes and goes. You are able to regain material balance once you decide to stick to one commitment. After age fifty you are more individualistic and alert.

In later years creativity is revitalized and you are progressive.

• OTHER AUGUST 8 BIRTHDAYS

Rory Calhoun	1922
Arthur Goldberg	1908
Dustin Hoffman	1937
Dino de Laurentiis	1919
Sylvia Sidney	1910
Connie Stevens	1938
Mel Tillis	1932
Esther Williams	1923

AUGUST

· 9 ·

You are philosophical, romantic and magnetic. In childhood you were exposed to people who were materially ambitious and experiences that offered you opportunities to develop a businesslike approach. Midlife, you travel far from your nurturing domestic background and expand your cultural, spiritual and intellectual capacities. Later in life you receive money through inheritance, royalties or legal entanglements that have been delayed. Throughout your lifetime you seek quality, polish and skills.

Nothing comes easily to you. You may be born with a silver spoon and realize that you are gifted with empathy, are driven by restlessness and cannot contain your dissatisfaction. You must work. You have the talent to counsel, heal, inspire, entertain or provide a service to the arts or the world of finance. You have a close connection to using the telephone and the mails.

Before you are forty you assume too much responsibility in a leadership position or submit to disappointing authority figures. You learn that when you are dependent on lovers or spouse, you vacillate in your personal decisions. You are better suited to staying single and enjoying the multitude of platonic friendships that you attract. If you marry you find happiness with an older or cosmopolitan person. Intimate relationships are tested, because you swing between selfishness and selflessness. Life with you is larded with emotional ups and downs that bring the problems of others into your home life.

Later years bring you success as a person. Money is less sought after and more secured. You have a lot to give and you share.

• OTHER AUGUST 9 BIRTHDAYS

Bob Cousy	1928
Jean Piaget	1896
Edouard Rothschild	1845
David Steinberg	1942
Herman Talmadge	1913

AUGUST

· 1 0 ·

Independence, sensitivity and intuitional business sense are terrific assets, but you are too self-protective to allow Lady Luck to romance you. As a tot, you were considered to be exceptionally wise, attractive or talented. There is always an element of disappointment in your midlife. You are impressionable and romantic and lack faith in yourself. You do not understand the promise for which others applaud you as a youngster and take your accolades too seriously in your thirties. Your family relationships remain an underlying legal or unspoken problem until you are in your late years.

In youth an older person gives you recognition and you have a taste of success. Through no fault of your own, unreasonable people or unexpected situations change material situations. You are alone— standing on your own decisions, innovations and ambitions. You make mistakes that you try to rectify by becoming your own boss. After age thirty-six, when you change objectives or begin to control your own career, the real learning process begins. You lose a male friend or protector. Your loves are misplaced. Finally, in your late mid-life years, you feel restless enough to uproot. You travel and make progressive moves that help you stabilize financially and compose yourself for your later years.

You meet a kindred spirit after the age of fifty. You do not attract reliable lovers, friends or business associates generally; neither are employees assets to your growth. You are meant to stand alone and must not dramatize the isolation that comes with success. You're a tiger in public and a pussycat who finds peace at home.

• OTHER AUGUST 10 BIRTHDAYS

Jimmy Dean	1928
Eddie Fisher	1928
Rhonda Fleming	1923
Herbert Hoover	1874
Martha Hyer	1934
Noah Beery, Jr.	1916
Norma Shearer	1900
Jane Wyatt	1912

AUGUST
· 11 ·

It's the message that you share with the world, not the money you repeatedly attract and lose, that enables you to leave a lasting image. You are sure that you were born to do something special, and you're right. Your dramatic concepts are brilliant, and you sparkle in an elitist society. In childhood family is important, but you have a desire to leave home early.

A youthful marriage, unreasonable obligations and extreme emotional reactions are part of your youth. Domestic burdens are too confining, or you volunteer your services and find that you do not have time or energy for yourself. You stay too long or leave too soon, but the commitments made before your thirty-seventh birthday do not support your intellectual capacity.

You are at your best when you are not out to impress anyone, when you forego status symbols and live quietly in order to concentrate on your chosen specialty. You are fortunate throughout your life and benefit from relationships with affluent and influential people. Your moods and interests are changable. Success always seems to be around the corner.

You find that you cannot be mercenary or too assertive and controlling—you must avoid being deluded by flatterers. When you follow your strong personal ideals, do not gamble and bring your best efforts to uplift acceptable standards, you receive recognition. Ask for fair pay. Too often you are unrealistic. Compromises are necessary in order to secure your domestic happiness. You destroy long-term relationships if your success comes before age thirty-six. If you are diplomatic and supportive into late years, your comfort is assured and you are cherished.

· OTHER AUGUST 11 BIRTHDAYS

Carrie Jacobs Bond	1862
Arlene Dahl	1924
Mike Douglas	1925
Jerzy Grotowski	1933
Allegra Kent	1938
Lloyd Nolan	1902

AUGUST

· 12 ·

Your charisma, love of the spectacular and unconventional methods of dealing with the traditional make you an oddity. Film, TV, computers and all mediums for imagery use your social, artistic and intuitional talents. When you believe in yourself and your impassioned messages, you are a convincing evangelist. If you scatter your interests or fail to alter your point of view as times change, you will fail to bring your grand schemes to their inspirational and promotional potential.

You are ambitious. Your childhood offered people and experiences that provided contracts for money and power plays. You will flirt with success and wait until you flirt with it again—finally your detailed, spiritually connected, physically attractive illusions come to reality. In youth you are impractical in a materialistic environment. Mid-life attracts opportunities that are not mundane or inharmonious with your personal ideals if you do not gamble and make an effort not to be cynical.

Your loves are considerably younger/older, more cosmopolitan or are simply able to deepen your insights, perspective and courage. You marry very young or very late to a mate or spouse who is a credit to you—or you experiment with a change of partners. You change career in mid-life but never lose your prosperous appearance. You prefer to have a facade—a show of money or class— enjoy serving charitable causes and take pride in and are closely protective of your parents and family.

In later years your imagination and past performances bring fulfillment. From youth, your voice is heard above the crowd.

• OTHER AUGUST 12 BIRTHDAYS

Diamond Jim Brady	1856
Cantinflas	1911
George Hamilton	1939
Christy Mathewson	1880
Cecil B. deMille	1881
Buck Owens	1929

AUGUST **· 1 3 ·** There's power to be wielded, money to be made and work to be done. Your life will never offer you musical talent without daily practice, or medals for competition in sports without daily dedication, or financially successful business organization without a detailed, routined, consistent administration. You are often a contradiction to yourself in your concern about proved methods and your insistence on using innovative ideas. You cannot abide unfairness, or you are unfair.

In childhood you have difficulty accepting your environments and the repression of your opportunities to be self-expressive. In youth you observed businesslike, wealthy and influential people. You become careful about money and may be considered too cheap or penny wise and pound foolish. You are stubborn and follow your feelings and intuition. Your ambitions prosper or fail based upon the creative limitations you placed upon yourself before your mid-thirties. You dislike superficiality or false boundaries, but you are a storyteller.

In midlife you have choice. If you accept what you see as unfair or dull and leave it as you found it, you lose your reconstructive opportunities. If you are dictatorial and unreasonable to the point of being emotionally unforgiving—therefore unreasonable—you will be a loner, constantly at war with conventions and saying or doing things that are considered improper. You open your mouth and stick your own foot in it.

You are an avid reader and late in life must keep up with the times. You are outspoken and entertaining and may charm your way out of difficult situations. You have a comfortable old age.

• OTHER AUGUST 13 BIRTHDAYS

Fidel Castro	1926
Alfred Hitchcock	1899
Bert Lahr	1895
Annie Oakley	1860
Buddy Rogers	1904
George Shearing	1919

AUGUST

· 14 ·

In youth you meet responsible, strong and ambitious people who set an example of planning, work, dedication and stability. But it is difficult for you to be realistic about money, and you use it to make an impression on others. You are drawn to offbeat, exceptional human beings who kindle your creative thinking. You find the ideal career when you combine your innovative ideas with freedom from traditional work schedules and spend your time promoting yourself and your schemes.

You must learn from experience. Love and sensuality teach you lessons. Problems arise from your lack of eloquence as a child and your exaggerated imagination as you get older. You are curious about everything and anything that inspires youthful enthusiasms. You are naive and superficial at times and become too serious and unpretentious in the other extreme. Your sense of the dramatic is always operating. Sensationalism may secure your good fortune and become a way of life for you.

You are adaptable, versatile, intuitive and reasoning, and you amass a storehouse of learning experiences before you are thirty-six. The opportunities that you have in youth are earthy and may not be as spontaneous as you would like them to be. In mid-life you are introduced to unconventional, speculative, freedom-loving people who give you opportunities to apply your practicality, managerial abilities and organizational skills.

Friends want to know you intimately, but you maintain an impersonal interaction with everyone but your mate, partner or spouse. Late in life you alter your course, travel less, find a loving, protective companion and continue to challenge yourself.

• OTHER AUGUST 14 BIRTHDAYS

John Galsworthy	1867
Buddy Greco	1926
John Ringling North	1903
Nehemiah Persoff	1920
Earl Weaver	1930

AUGUST

· 15 ·

The significant people and experiences in your youth relate to the power, money and/or aristocracy of your family. Their relationship, and particularly the impact that your mother exerts on your expectations, sets the stage for your entire life. You are sensitive, humbled by other siblings or rivals, and feel inferior or modest. You strive to be unobtrusive until your mid-thirties, when your talent for showmanship, responsibility and service to your family and community make you more discerning.

You have made judgments that are based upon a first impression, your limited experiences or the ideals certified to be true by your childish impression of family standards. You shatter traditions and learn from the sensations that you feel. You are destined to be protected financially and emotionally. Your talents may not surface until you mature. Your curiosity, impulsivity and adventurousness puzzle your conventional relatives, and your love of your home, philanthropy and artistic beauty delight the traditionalists.

You can independently commercialize on your merchandising, legal and theatrical talents mid to late life. You are slated to receive an inheritance, travel for business and expand culturally after age forty. You relate to a supportive male who cannot eliminate problems from your life but who regulates your work schedules and smooths emotional obligations. It is in your best interests to remain active, work and be responsible to your public image. Late in life you have the home you wanted as a tot and receive recognition for uplifting less fortunate people.

• OTHER AUGUST 15 BIRTHDAYS

Ethel Barrymore	1879
Emperor Napoleon Bonaparte	1769
Lillian Carter	1898
Julia Child	1912
Mike Connors	1921
Princess Anne of England	1950
Edna Ferber	1887
Tess Harper	1950
Jill Haworth	1945
Wendy Hiller	1912
T. E. Lawrence	1888
Louis Lehrman	1938
Phyllis Schlafly	1924
Sir Walter Scott	1771

AUGUST

·16·

The early and late years of your life have more variety and are the most fortunate. You are self-expressive, protected and surrounded by congeniality. During your mid-years it is difficult for you to achieve perfection of your desires or your work if your goals are purely materialistic. As a child, you are noted for your poise, intellect and physical balance. You may be athletic, businesslike or technically curious. It is difficult for you to accept answers without questioning. You are sharp.

The people and experiences that cross your path after your twenty-seventh birthday will help you to understand the impermanence of affluence and influence in our society. You will change your erroneous ideas and ideals through unexpected events or deceptive acts that delay or ruin expectations, upset your plans or spoil love relationships. When you reach your fifties, you will have self-esteem based upon your special brand of humor, optimism, faith and selflessness, developed in mid-life.

Throughout any adversity you may seem self-centered. You have natural aloofness that gives the impression that you are analytically self-involved. People imagine that you are uncovering complexities or that you are covering up your thoughts. You are difficult to see through—very regal—and then confuse everyone and yourself by becoming too earthy. In fact, you are very conscientious where home, family and community are concerned. However, you are understood only by lovers or intimates whom you choose to allow to disturb your privacy.

Later in life you should find peace of mind where your personal, material and humanitarian ambitions are concerned.

• OTHER AUGUST 16 BIRTHDAYS

Ann Blyth	1928
Robert Culp	1930
Betsy von Furstenberg	1931
Frank Gifford	1930
Anita Gillette	1936
Eydie Gorme	1932
Madonna	1958
George Meany	1894
Fess Parker	1927

AUGUST **· 17 ·** You are surrounded by demanding or selfless perfectionists as a youth and reach a height of professionalism after age twenty-eight. Whether you are educated academically, trained for a career or get sufficiently interested in a hobby to become an authority, affluent and influential people find you attractive. You may become obsessed with power and give it all up for love and, after time passes, reverse the procedure. Your purpose in the plan of life is to express your caring, charity and love to many—not to love on an intimate level.

The talents that you express and your magnetism are intended to entertain, uplift or heal. You will never have enough love, admirers or money to satisfy yourself if your philosophy does not extend outside your domestic community. It is your good fortune to be physically coordinated, courageous and conscious of material accomplishments. Your body and your mind join forces with your spirit when you approach mid-life. It is in your best interests not to be snobbish. You may be disillusioned by encounters with self-centered associates, but don't allow their lack of brotherly love to rub off on you.

Expect to travel, to broaden your scope and to grow wise. You were considered old beyond your years as a tot and solved adult problems in youth. Mid-life, you have a knack for practical efficiency, little patience for slowpokes and a "let's get down to brass tacks" approach. In late years you are inspirational.

If you find your love in youth, you're set for life. If not, your ambitions and life-style will make you work at marriage too.

· OTHER AUGUST 17 BIRTHDAYS

Davy Crockett	1786
Robert DeNiro	1943
Maureen O'Hara	1921
Francis Gary Powers	1929
Chita Rivera	1923
Mae West	1892
John Hay Whitney	1904

AUGUST

· 18 ·

You are a self-starter and a do-it-your-selfer when you are tomcatting, ambitious to take center stage. When you are intimidated by aggressive leadership or authority figures, you become as submissive as a kitten. It is your purpose in the plan of life to serve as an example. You have the opportunities to expand upon your talents and to teach, show or share your wisdom.

As a tot, you are creative, imaginative and sensitive to domestic, emotional interactions. You are inspired by material-minded people—too rich or too poor to ignore their obligations. In mid-life you get your efficiency, individuality and skills out to a major marketplace, audience or service organization. You are not comfortable doing anything small. The limitations that are set for less expansive, philosophical and humanitarian people are not intended for you.

In mid-life marriage, partnership or confining relationships are changed, concluded or disavowed. With a balanced ego, you are inventive, active and progressive. It is too difficult for you to be obliged to dependents and unable to travel freely mentally or physically. You have grown far from your place of birth and origins. The romantic in you has become somewhat jaded by your observations. You have developed a self-depreciating sense of humor that keeps you receptive and afloat.

When you commit yourself to a lasting love, your mate must be self-sufficient and intellectually, artistically and emotionally grown up. You are capable of reaching your deepest emotions in your dreams. You are continually working. Into late years, asleep, or awake, you are a broad-scoped problem solver.

- OTHER AUGUST 18 BIRTHDAYS

Emperor Franz Josef of Austria	1830
Rosalynn Carter	1927
Roberto Clemente	1934
Marshall Field	1834
Rafer Johnson	1937
Meriwether Lewis	1774
Roman Polanski	1933
Robert Redford	1937
Caspar Weinberger	1917
Shelley Winters	1922

AUGUST
· 19 ·

Take a leadership position in a creative, expanding service organization and your inventive abilities will be applauded. Don't be secretive, standoffish or uncommunicative. Speak up and ask your valuable questions and challenge the experts. You have a perfectionist's dilemma. You cannot find satisfaction in the realities. You must specialize, avoid self-doubt and persist.

People, including yourself, make mistakes, forget daily etiquette or lose their temper—simply because they are human. To build your self-esteem, you must learn to forgive yourself. To avoid becoming too skeptical or too gullible, you must accept the mundane practicalities that face people on a survival level.

As a youth, material accomplishments and the people who dared to make their financial or influential presence known surrounded you. You want the freedom that money and power imply. The ambitions, professionalism and authority that they expressed intimidated you. You have choice and the ability to overcome obstacles. Accept yourself as a tradition breaker—a loner. In mid-life you individualize and throw off the chains of self-depreciation—if you are wise enough to be true to your inventiveness, individuality and instincts for progress. If you channel your vacillating emotions— avoid egocentricity or submission to people who shout you down— you attract a happy marriage, recognition for your originality and rewards for your nobility of purpose. If you cannot accept yourself as an "original," you will face a moment of truth. There may be a scandal, and you will not be able to maintain your position.

In late years you develop a deeper faith and find peace.

• OTHER AUGUST 19 BIRTHDAYS

Madame du Barry	1746
Bernard Baruch	1870
Coco Chanel	1883
Malcolm Forbes	1919
Jill St. John	1940
Alfred Lunt	1893
Ogden Nash	1902
Debra Paget	1933
Willie Shoemaker	1931
Izaak Walton	1593
Orville Wright	1871

AUGUST **·20·** You are an asset to a group effort and a sensitive partner, and you embrace an unyielding set of personal standards. The sense of responsibility that you feel as an adult is nurtured in childhood, and you never lose your parental or judgmental attitude. You are a sympathetic, habitual volunteer and overload yourself with commitments until you cannot escape the ties that bind your independence. The diplomatic, easygoing, modest facade that you delight in displaying is your attempt to attract peace of mind.

In youth you meet people and have experiences that inspire self-discipline, leadership and a yen for the good life. You are a worker and a worrier. The exceptional intuition that is at your disposal is ready and waiting for you. Use it to blend your talents to your emotional needs. The conflicts that arise are products of your compulsions to fulfill real and imagined duties. During your lifetime it is a constant challenge to get in touch with your individuality and to follow your personal desires while sharing a loving relationship.

You are a student of human nature, but you should not rely upon your responsiveness alone. A good education will prepare you for a spurt of mid-life intellectual growth that puts the spotlight on your career, artistry or ability to purposefully socialize. Friendliness, charm and personality are major assets when you blossom after finding a mate. Early years are lonely. The older, less driven by ambitions you are, the more companionship, possibilities and contentment you enjoy.

Later life offers options to travel, experiment and promote your philosophy. You never lose your restless appetites.

• OTHER AUGUST 20 BIRTHDAYS

Carla Frasci	1936
Edgar A. Guest	1881
Benjamin Harrison	1833
Isaac Hayes	1942
Salvatore Quasimodo	1901
Jacqueline Susann	1921
Jack Teagarden	1905
Van Johnson	1916

AUGUST **·21·** As a youngster, you meet people and have experiences that make you want to be or to do something to set you apart from the ordinary. You may have too much or too little financial freedom, and your material standards are set at an ambitious level. You are a personality kid. It is obvious that you are slated to attract attention for your appearance, talents or personality. However, you manage to break with traditions and take the hard road to maturity. You are given too much or too little physical and mental freedom. Your rebellion and reversal of the family conventions set the stage for a dramatic and extreme lifestyle.

You do not learn from your experiences until you reach your thirties. In mid-life you deliver your lines with authority, costume yourself to the image you wish to expose and seek the limelight. You are lucky, imaginative and sociable. The greatest threats to your happiness and success are the problems that you invent or take on from lovers or friends. The worries that put a frown on your face and crease your brow detract from the exceptionally contagious smile, teasing humor and lightness of heart that bring sunshine to the saddest people on the sorriest day. You will never grow old, and you require time to play.

You are a gifted communicator. Words, current fads and fashions, artistic pursuits—and the people who make a game out of life—make you comfortable. You confuse yourself by being impulsive, irresponsible and bound by duties, obligations and a sense of protection for weak, naive, insecure associates. You develop a distrust for facades and are a skeptical listener.

In late years you begin to trust and change inner beliefs.

• OTHER AUGUST 21 BIRTHDAYS

Count Basie	1904
Wilt Chamberlain	1936
Mart Crowley	1936
Princess Margaret of England	1930
Patty McCormack	1945

AUGUST

·22·

Throughout your lifetime you peek through superficial impressions that satisfy average tastes and use common sense to solve the problems that stymie the experts. You speak with authority, assume responsibility and work until you drop when you are dedicated to a cause. You may be equally untraditional, disorganized and impractical if you are materially insecure, drowned in self-imposed details and feel creatively limited. You are a powerhouse of administrative energy, practical routines and physical stamina. As a youth, you look for bargains. In mid-life you are self-expressive, an outstanding master craftsperson and a constructive artisan. In later years you are free.

Real estate, home products and construction industries—all products of the earth—are fortunate associations for you. Marriages and partnerships are supportive, rewarding and stabilizing. You want power, attract the best resources and appoint yourself director or leader when a job is to be done. Your body is the house of your soul and as such should be well cared for. Physical fitness programs, sculpting and landscaping are hobbies that may turn into profitable business in later years.

Dare to work for high ideals and all-encompassing ambitions. Be practical: You cannot speculate with money or unclassified information. Ask a professional before signing contracts. You meet powerful people who may be too ethical or lack morals. Take your time before you change marriage partners, opinions or objectives. You travel and broaden culturally after age fifty. Your intuitional first thought provides the foundation for you to leave a lasting product or project for generations to come.

• OTHER AUGUST 22 BIRTHDAYS

Ray Bradbury	1920
Dr. Denton Cooley	1920
Claude Debussy	1862
Valerie Harper	1940
Dorothy Parker	1893
Cindy Williams	1947

AUGUST

·**23**·

You are ambitious and geared to have an untraditional life-style. Experience is your guide. You are clever and consume knowledge. It is your ability to diagnose the cause of problems that attracts gifts and applause. Inheritance or moneys due from past work will save you during financial ups and downs. Women and siblings cause childhood insecurities. Have faith in your ability to understand and direct people. You are multitalented.

Efficient, determined, courageous people encourage your youthful expectations. There is a businesslike atmosphere to your early years. As a tot, you are self-expressive and sensitive and have a retentive memory. In mid-life your physical agility, imagination and ability to work cooperatively attract marital harmony and professional recognition. In later years your love of good living, new enthusiasms and teaching your expertise prevail. You are lucky if you don't mix love and money.

Your challenge is to scatter your interests, energy and loves. Fears of poverty and the lack of positive visualizations that your negativism produces are the cause of failures. You are capable of escaping from responsibilities and holding on to childish attitudes. You tend to dramatize and see everything in living color. Be a realist and do not allow discouragement to stop you from socializing, dressing up and getting into the mainstream to attract business contacts and to enjoy pleasant pastimes. When you smile, you are a welcome addition to any crowd.

In late years you may be unable to accept the limitations of maturity, become stubborn and not realize that the pixie in you plays a youthful tune. You are incapable of getting "old."

· OTHER AUGUST 23 BIRTHDAYS

King Louis XVI of France	1754
Gene Kelly	1912
Edgar Lee Masters	1869
Vera Miles	1929
Keith Moon	1947
Tex Williams	1917

AUGUST **·24·** You are sensitive, detail conscious and want all the comforts of home. In youth your pettiness, jealous outbursts and overly humble manner create disharmony in your community. When you become cooperative and maintain friendships, your youthful relationships are helpful in mid-life. Love and a peaceful atmosphere at home or business are essential to your emotional and practical well-being. A helpmate, teacher or assertive friend is inspirational and helps you to make decisions. You intend to improve your material standards, have your own home and are willing to work in youth.

In your twenties you relate best to males due to your sensitivity to your mother as a tot. You are opinionated and play devil's advocate to get a rise out of everyone. It is difficult for you to be decisive or patient until you get in touch with your true feelings. As a child, your temper tantrums or violent dislikes were ignored. If you were encouraged to share your personal opinions, develop your intellectual strengths and build self-confidence, you would not make mountains out of your personal molehills or be too self-concerned.

You are too intent upon surviving before the war begins. In mid-life you assume responsibilities and begin to recognize your exceptional talents. You are a late bloomer and begin to receive recognition after age forty.

You have lived unconventionally and sensually and learned about life as you encountered changes and surprise. The people and experiences that you met in youth are stepping-stones to your concentration in later years. You have material protection.

• OTHER AUGUST 24 BIRTHDAYS

Aubrey Beardsley	1872
Richard Cushing	1895
Graham Sutherland	1903

AUGUST · **25** · You want the best of everything. In partnerships you want an intelligent, sensual, curious mate and professional, businesslike, courageous career associates. You need to use your brains and to invstigate technical, scientific, philosophical or metaphysical questions. You have or it is assumed that you have a strong sense of responsibility, intimacy and family pride. You are impatient and restless as a youth, and you mix your mental and emotional decisions. You may move from your childhood home, but you do not let go of your roots until your late twenties.

As a tot, you are close to family and your community obligations, although you are not schooled close to home. The encouragement, protection and position that they offer are exchanged for your independence. You want approval of the male in the household and are motivated to be a successful professional by the strong female influence in the immediate family. Your stamina develops, you practice and have options to begin a career when you break out from the confines to marry or enmesh yourself in deepening study to extend your ambitions.

You are temperamental, impulsive and sensually curious until you find an unusual person, whom you fear losing. You marry, and are loyal, once you have made a commitment. Marriage is important to you, but you require privacy and dislike getting involved in the practical, mundane daily domestic routines. You are aloof from superficial interests and intent upon having a "marriage made in heaven." Money comes and goes but should be spent for education and improving the quality of work and life.

Late years are quieter, the result of the first sixty.

· OTHER AUGUST 25 BIRTHDAYS

Leonard Bernstein	1918
Sean Connery	1930
Mel Ferrer	1917
Althea Gibson	1927
Ruby Keeler	1909
George Wallace	1919

AUGUST

·26·

You learn the ins and outs of money and community service, and develop ambitions that give you the power to be aloof from the ordinary and influential. As a tot, you are expected to be wise for your years. You are not given the options of a child and take on the obligations of adults. You sacrifice and submerge your personality to be destructive or serve the family philosophy, or you may marry a much older or younger person.

Your father exerts an influence on your self-image. He is too authoritative, too loving or absent in youth. You strive to be perfect in his eyes and feel that you are rejected by his criticism, impossible-to-believe accolades or desertion. Your disillusionments are caused by progressive changes that you find hard to accept. In mid-life you develop self-confidence after taking a few challenges, finding a supportive partner and assuming family, community, business burdens. You should marry early. Marriage is not comfortable until you reach mid-life—if ever. Your desire for power is satisfied if you ally yourself to an idealistic love and work at the relationship and a job.

Problems arise if your unselfishness is not recognized. If you are able to maintain a positive reality, you will not be deceived or disillusioned. The parental aspects of your nature are intended to reach out to universal problems. You want to serve the world and will run to help others and overlook the immediate emotional needs of your family. You have subtle strength and are a cruel adversary when confronted with hostility. You have inconsistent values and need to define them.

In late years you are secure, protected and comfortable.

- OTHER AUGUST 26 BIRTHDAYS

Prince Albert	1819
Ben Bradlee	1921
Ronny Graham	1919
Peggy Guggenheim	1898
Christopher Isherwood	1904
William French Smith	1917
Maxwell Taylor	1901

AUGUST **·27·** You are a self-made and magnetic. Although your mind and your emotions vie for supremacy, you are driven to deliver a quality and skill of the performance of your chosen career. You want love and to share your broad-scoped philosophy. You are compassionate, romantic and empathetic. It is difficult for you to assert your individualistic, inventive and untried ideas in youth. You forego comforts for education. You try too hard.

Patience is not your virtue on a day-to-day level. Big issues do not delay your progress, but where your intimate family relationships are concerned, you are a pussycat and vacillate in your decisions to follow your personal ideals. It is only when you are angry or frustrated in your ambitions that you take the bull by the horns and do the best thing for yourself.

As a tot, you are intimidated by aggressive people and are swayed by their expectations. You are fooled by quiet, modest, undemanding people who have a backbone of steel. In mid-life you do well as the creative leader of your own business or professional interests. Art, government and broad-scoped communications industries are inviting. Expect to get help and to attract interested investors for your multiple ideas. You have the ability to make a financial mark for yourself and the people who indicate that they have faith in you. It is your ability to inspire friends, lovers and admirers who are legalistic, aristocratic perfectionists that brings out your diplomacy, detail consciousness and showmanship.

In late years you work to extend your personal philosophy and to implement humanitarian or cultural expansions.

• OTHER AUGUST 27 BIRTHDAYS

Theodore Dreiser	1871
Samuel Goldwyn	1882
Lyndon B. Johnson	1908
Martha Raye	1916
Tommy Sands	1937
Tuesday Weld	1943

AUGUST **·28·** You are businesslike, efficient and well coordinated. You act when you get an idea and have the ability to inspire others with your positive energy. You have courage, assume executive authority and deal with supportive associates sensitively. You keep secrets, question everything and rarely let your intimates know exactly where they stand until you come to grips with your dreams of perfection. It is your tendency to be too skeptical or too gullible that delays your material ambitions in youth.

You travel culturally and meet people and have experiences that polish your tastes. The fears that make you moody and melancholy are brought about by falling in love too easily—accepting friends at face value or imagining that a business deal will go exactly as described at first blush. As you mature, you recognize the need to investigate, question and analyze before "marrying" a person or a concept or becoming another's blood brother.

In mid-life you catch up on your education, settle a score with your father and meet influential, cooperative people. You want companionship and are adaptable, accommodating and mentally congenial. You attract complimentary partners or supportive employees. Your youth and middle age require that you put body, mind and spirit together to attain your goals. If you work, you will receive tangible results for your efforts. Your intellectual capacities, which were neglected in youth while your personality was recognized, are put to commercial challenges. You receive good luck when your sex appeal is exploited.

In later years you may overeat, but you will never starve.

• OTHER AUGUST 28 BIRTHDAYS

Charles Boyer	1899
Ben Gazzara	1930
James Wong Howe	1899
Donald O'Connor	1925
Richard Tucker	1913

AUGUST

·**29**·

You are expansive, dramatic and romantic—high-strung and sensitive as an adult—and you want things your way. Your heart rules your head when you least expect to overthrow your conventional, culturally expansive and aspiring upbringing. You are intent upon a materially comfortable life-style, but you are willing to work for it—or to be a supportive partner to maintain it. The things that money can buy and the freedom that material power offers appeal to you as a youth, but you change your values in mid-life. You attract good luck in youth.

Before age forty you meet a futuristic, creative elitist who lives by a personal code of ethics and material standards. You go to emotional and practical extremes in your devotion to this relationship. You are intent upon attracting followers for their cause and are at your best in a partnership.

The course of your life is changed by the decisions you make, and you have trouble adjusting to the less secure circumstances. You succeed after a nine-year cycle of discouragement due to skeletons in the closet. You fall in love, but you do not relinquish your independence for a lover again.

Late years are quiet and promise privacy. A mid-life relationship should be preserved if it is threatened. You attract career or business recognition and learn to wheel and deal for traditional business opportunities. You receive offers and must wait to select the ideal opportunities. An award or prestige position is due to you in your fifties—if not sooner. You have a regal quality that never lets you down. Stay near home and protect and commercialize on the quality of your talent.

• OTHER AUGUST 29 BIRTHDAYS

Richard Attenborough	1923
Ingrid Bergman	1916
Elliott Gould	1938
Oliver Wendell Holmes	1809
Michael Jackson	1958
George Montgomery	1916
Dinah Washington	1924

AUGUST **30** You are self-expressive, organized and imaginative. In youth you are restless, break family traditions and learn that when you experiment, you are able to profit from your experiences. In mid-life you recognize your need to perform, polish and expand upon the services that you provide. You are a quality-conscious person. You travel and meet noble, generous and talented personalities. You are able to help, heal, entertain or educate, and when you systematize your specialty, you are paid well.

Marriage or partnerships are emotional hotbeds, but you have sex appeal and never lose your attraction to and for the opposite sex. Later in life others provide mental and practical companionship. You are not emotionally drained by intimate dependents, but your desire to be surrounded by inspirational or instructional groups fulfills your need for social relationships.

As a youngster, you set out to save the unfortunates of the world, to change traditions and to benefit from the influential and affluent. After age twenty-eight you are faced with decisions that alter your life focus and put you in the limelight.

People have high hopes for you, and you attract supporters. Money is available when you need it. If you use it wisely and unselfishly, you will receive a degree of the perfection that you strive to deliver and expect to receive. During your early lifetime you are surrounded by creative, elite or spiritual sensitives who feel that they have a special cause or mission. You have a chance to leave a lasting image through those contacts. Later years are more conventional and are protected.

- OTHER AUGUST 30 BIRTHDAYS

Elizabeth Ashley	1939
Joan Blondell	1912
Shirley Booth	1909
John Gunther	1901
Jean-Claude Killy	1943
Huey P. Long	1893
Fred MacMurray	1908
Raymond Massey	1896
Maria Montessori	1870
Regina Resnik	1922

AUGUST **·31·** You are a dogged, practice-until-you're-perfect fighter. In childhood you are surrounded by down-to-earth people who encourage you to fight for your ambitions. You learn to speak your mind, and may cut off your nose to spite your face until you learn to bend the rules when necessary. As time goes into mid-life, your sense of humor, imagination and outstanding personality get you into situations that encourage you to be less rigid in your beliefs. Trouble walks in the door when you are frustrated or angered by legal agreements or people who do not follow your ideology or break out from your immediate circle.

You are ambitious, have stamina and are willing to plan for your material growth and security. As a child, you were surrounded by businesslike, status-conscious, inventive executives, leaders or independents. You concentrate on overcoming obstacles that stand in the way of your progress. Your progressive mind, exceptional ability to communicate your ideas and the charm that you exert make your work a labor of love. You cannot afford vacations, speculations or to be impatient. You create problems for yourself when you overindulge in eating, playing or working. You are an extremist.

You have the ability to create new roads in merchandising, fashion, real estate and all areas of communications. You are a researcher—a performer and a pioneer for advancements for the good of the public.

Your spouse or lovers are in awe of you. You maintain your intimate relationships unless the rules are changed. In late years you are financially protected, well traveled and calmer.

• OTHER AUGUST 31 BIRTHDAYS

Richard Basehart	1919
Eldridge Cleaver	1935
James Coburn	1928
Arthur Godfrey	1903
Buddy Hackett	1924
Alan Jay Lerner	1918
Fredric March	1897
William Saroyan	1908
Dore Schary	1905
Ted Williams	1918

SEPTEMBER **·1·** In youth you develop individuality and independence, and you grow culturally. It is unusual for a tot to be as emotionally adult and selfishly childish as you are. The people and experiences that surround your youth take you artistically, academically or spiritually far from your birthright. You travel, meet magnetic personalities and benefit from exposure to generous communiciators who exemplify outstanding skill. You show courage and polish and expand your ambitions. If you are businesslike, do not ignore the responsibilities of establishment power or strive relentlessly for material goals, you can make your mark before you are thirty. If you are greedy or callous, you lose ground.

In mid-life you are surrounded by inventive, active, changeable trendsetters who will not settle for second best. It is difficult for you to stabilize relationships with instigators like yourself, but you spark them and they spark you into taking daring chances. You attract followers. People who are receptive to your impatient moves carry out the details. You are a pathfinder and are capable of breaking your own records—precedents that you set in your youth.

The leadership abilities that you have are based upon your unique ideas. It is in your best interests to be "different." When you are tempted to be dependent on other people or traditions, the results are disillusioning. You must maintain the courage of your convictions. When told that your concepts have no precedent, be firm and go it alone. It is within your character to alter family, community or universal customs.

Late years are secured by mid-life investments and values.

· OTHER SEPTEMBER 1 BIRTHDAYS

ENGELBERT HUMPERDINCK (COMPOSER)	1854
EdGAR RICE BURROUGHS	1875
YVONNE DE CARLO	1922
VITTORIO GASSMAN	1922
GEORGE MAHARIS	1933
Rocky MARCIANO	1924
WALTER REUTHER	1907
Lily Tomlin	1936
DAN WILSON	1900

SEPTEMBER **· 2 ·** As a tot, you learn to be diplomatic, to keep secrets and to rule with subtle control. Material things are important because you have a fear of poverty that often has little foundation. It is important that you develop a speciality in order to build your inner faith. You are encouraged to be cooperative, modest and detail conscious. The critical, authoritative, introspective analyzers who nervously surround you in youth detract from your self-assurance.

You appear to be aloof and refuse to dirty your hands or become too concerned with down-to-earth problems. You cover your uncertainties and do not allow others to know how lonely and emotionally impoverished you feel. You need intimate supporters to detract from your childhood feelings of separatism. The perfectionist demands that you make on yourself bring on late-in-life disillusionments. You marry for friendship and protection and to have someone make a fuss over you. You need to be needed.

You are not comfortable alone, but you find it difficult to bare your soul to anyone. You maintain a secret self that hides from the earthy realities and practicalities of daily routines. Personal sensitivity or being too gullible or too skeptical gets you into trouble, while tact, gentle awareness and persistence attract the things that you want and need. Until your late years legal matters, psychiatrists and a lack of faith in your own intellect create mundane problems. You need encouragement.

You allow yourself to be dominated, get lost in a group or place yourself in a position that allows another to outshine you. In late years you improve your self-image and remain active.

• OTHER SEPTEMBER 2 BIRTHDAYS

Cleveland Amory	1917
Richard Castellano	1934
Marge Champion	1920
Jimmy Connors	1952
Allen Drury	1918
Martha Mitchell	1918
Victor Spinetti	1933

SEPTEMBER

· **3** ·

A sense of responsibility to your family, home, profession, community—and to the problems of humanity—burdens you. It is your ability to find a ray of sunshine in any storm that attracts friends and lovers. You are a performer. The imaginative expressions of humor, beauty and love attract travel, gifts and admirers. As a tot, you are precocious. In youth you have sex appeal. Later in life your dramatic, versatile, charming personality is in demand.

You leave your roots, which were influenced by a powerful, philosophical man, but cannot let go of your feelings of obligation to uphold his ideals. You relate to older, cosmopolitan, culturally expansive members of the opposite sex. During your youth your attitude and ambitions are elevated beyond the traditional scope of your peers. You are self-expressive and retain your ability to give credit where credit is due. You are admired for your humility, individuality and friendliness.

In mid-life you attract attention, and help, by helping others. Problems arise when you volunteer too much and then resent the time or effort your commitments impose upon your time, money or emotions. It is difficult for you to avoid flirtations or scattering your interests. You enjoy playing devil's advocate, talking on the telephone and/or letter-writing. You are interested in people and have talents for accomplishing your ambitions when you deal with words. More than one marriage is possible before you are forty. After mid-life you change your goals and overcome your personal problems.

Late years are less structured and you enjoy your home life.

- OTHER SEPTEMBER 3 BIRTHDAYS

Kitty Carlisle Hart	1915
Anne Jackson	1926
Alan Ladd	1913
Valerie Perrine	1943

SEPTEMBER
·4·

You are a stickler for managing and organizing your financial affairs but never get the hang of learning from your experiences. You cannot manage the restlessness you feel as a youngster and leave your community to break with traditions. Basically you are down to earth and determined to be successful. It is the uncertainty and surprises of childhood that tax your methodical mind. Mid-life offers you the chance to meet people and experiences that recognize just how dependable you really are. As a child, you must be wiser than your years.

From your late twenties to your early fifties, you are productive and constructive. You are a habitual worker and practice your skills with a determination to see financial results. You want material success and to live comfortably. Real estate, farming, construction businesses, physical fitness programs and military service are stepping-stones for your technical applications. Manufacturing offers an opportunity for you to see a tangible result and a profit.

It is necessary for you to build consistently for the future and to put your physical energy to the test. Unused energy results in destructive activities. You can be very obedient or refuse to follow any pattern.

Love and work do not meld during your early years. It's one or the other. When you reach late years, you handle your self-imposed disciplines without imposing them on your family or lovers. You are devoted, trustworthy and sincere. However, your youthful follies may be a tough act to follow. You grow far from your place of birth and find life after age fifty rewarding.

• OTHER SEPTEMBER 4 BIRTHDAYS

Craig Claiborne	1920
Thomas Eagleton	1929
Henry Ford	1917
Mitzi Gaynor	1931
Czar Ivan the Terrible of Russia	1530

SEPTEMBER

·5·

The limitations placed upon your creativity and resourcefulness in childhood make you too practical or too disorganized as a youth. You alternate between using workaholic energy or refusing to dedicate yourself to down-to-earth labor. Basically you are clever and can handle a variety of interests simultaneously.

In mid-life you meet people and have experiences that challenge your curiosity. However, you require a conventional image while growing up. Your life changes after age thirty. You find yourself trying to escape from self-imposed confines. You need people, crowds and excitement. Your mind cannot be channeled indefinitely. You are an entrepreneur—a promoter—an inquisitive investigator who cannot be locked into traditional expectations. Your enthusiasms make you a catalyst in the lives of others. Due to touching upon your life, people who would not alter their conventional thinking find new freedoms. However, you bore easily and move on to new interests.

There is no doubt that you get into trouble before you find yourself comfortably settled into a career or marriage. Home and family are important, but your impulsivity places you in situations that are off the beaten track. You are a sensual personality and must experience all the unknown that life offers. During mid-life you must evaluate your options and make changes. You have the ability to be all things to all people, and all races, creeds and elements relate to you and your sociability. To be happy you must select to live one day at a time. Late years are more stable, and you become a do-gooder.

- OTHER SEPTEMBER 5 BIRTHDAYS

Johann Sebastian Bach	1735
Florence Eldridge	1901
King Louis XIV of France	1638
Jesse James	1847
Joan Kennedy	1936
Carol Lawrence	1932
Bob Newhart	1929
Arthur Nielsen	1897
Jack Valenti	1921
Paul Volcker	1927
Raquel Welch	1940
Darryl Zanuck	1902

SEPTEMBER

· 6 ·

Your vivid imagination can make or break your ambitions. Talk is a valuable commodity to you. You are charming and attract love and friendship with the opposite sex. You can be a nasty opponent when you choose to use your wit and wiles on unfriendlies, or you make friends in unusual places. It is your ability to put people, products and situations together at the opportune moment that is the key to your success.

In youth you are influenced by the women and siblings in your family. You reach out of your neighborhood to expand your thinking. You are aggressive, curious and adventurous; however, you assume obligations that enhance your ambitions. Your spouse or partners are assets. You have the ability to meet magnetic and accomplished people who take a liking to you. It is possible for you to make a commercial success or lose golden financial opportunities before you reach mid-life.

Your good fortune depends upon your social contacts and ability to concentrate on one goal at a time. When you scatter your energy, money and/or interests, the superficial aspects of your nature take over. You set your personal ideals first and expect everyone to live up to your standards. Your work, professionalism or career are your top priorities. Your ambitions are geared to an opulent home, beautiful people and gracious living. It is necessary to your well-being to have peace at all costs. You have a notable voice and are willing to teach your beliefs and to inspire others to excel.

Your parental nature provides service to your family and community. You are protected and will not go through life alone.

• OTHER SEPTEMBER 6 BIRTHDAYS

Taylor Caldwell	1900
Michael DeBakey	1908
Buddy Holly	1936
Daniel Inouye	1924
Elia Kazan	1909
Joseph Kennedy	1888
Peter Lawford	1923
Billy Rose	1899
Jo Ann Worley	1937

SEPTEMBER

7

You mellow like a fine wine and are attracted to research, science and the law. Your early years are not as fulfilling as the later part of your life; however, you are wise and magnetic and add polish as a youth. Your ideas are often impractical or inappropriate as you grow to maturity. Some aspects of your ambitions are disappointing due to your materialism.

You need a good education, a position of authority or an expertise to achieve your potential. It is not to your advantage to aim for power or money before you reach your thirties. Any attempts at commercialism will bring you only a modicum of the success that you anticipate.

You are influenced by the female relationship early in life. Your mother, a sensitive supporter or critic, is at the root of your emotional need for approval. You are an intellectual personality and require an aristocratic, analytical, refined partner or mate. Your first love may be disappointing, and you may feel disconnected from your ideal until you do some serious soul searching. The perfectionist aspects of your nature make it impossible for you to accept human frailty, and you strive for self-esteem or for compatibility with mundane realities.

After mid-life and into your late years, your reputation will build and money or rewards will be available. You are intuitive and begin to listen to your inner voice after age forty. The poise you show often belies your secretiveness. You learn to think before you speak as a youth. You think clearly as an oldster and eliminate superficiality from your life-style.

In late years you seek privacy, self-acceptance and peace.

• OTHER SEPTEMBER 7 BIRTHDAYS

KING BAUDOUIN   1930

SEPTEMBER **·8·** Your business judgment, executive ability and emotional control are dividends of your youth. You've come a long way from your roots and extended your capacities. The people and experiences that you met as a child drew out your compassion, empathy and ability to be discreet. You are a product of a broad scope of exposures and have traveled far from the old neighborhood. You have the character ingredients to be a businesslike, efficient, solid citizen. You will reap the financial rewards of your labors if you are aware of your individuality.

In youth you were called upon to be understanding of your elders. The leadership abilities, physical stamina and self-assertion that you are able to call upon may have been squelched by self-insistent, aggressive, authoritative males early in your life. You were frustrated in your individuality and did now show your creative abilities immediately. However, you are a natural leader, and in mid-life your healthy ego emerged.

From your late twenties until your fifties, you are exposed to affluent, influential and constructive people who have high expectations and broad-scoped goals. If you overcome your tendencies to vacillate in your decisions and are capable of making personalized, progressive changes, you will achieve expertise in handling your own affairs. You cannot expect help, submit to get-rich-quick schemes or allow yourself to be intimidated by fears of rejection. You do your homework and have self-expressive talents. Don't get bogged down by details, worry or become too impatient to enjoy each late-in-life accomplishment.

• OTHER SEPTEMBER 8 BIRTHDAYS

Frankie Avalon	1940
Sid Caesar	1922
Patsy Cline	1932
Denise Darcel	1925
Howard Dietz	1896
Antonín Dvořák	1841
Sam Nunn	1938
Claude Pepper	1900
Peter Sellers	1925

SEPTEMBER

· 9 ·

You are born with emotional maturity and find yourself capable of giving the shirt off your back all too frequently. It is extraordinary to be born with "knowledge." You understand the emotional ups and downs of the people in your surroundings and find it difficult to relate on a child-to-adult basis. Grown-ups wonder at your compassion, depth of comprehension and ability to be an empathetic leader. You are an "old soul" and are called upon to counsel, serve and improve standards for your family, neighbors and a broad scope of people you encounter.

In intimate relationships you are a considerate, generous and unselfish lover, parent and teacher. It is unfortunate that you tend to submerge your personality unnecessarily and breed resentment when you find that you are not appreciated or understood. When you overdo your emotional responses and find that you are taken for granted, you remove yourself from the pain and disillusionment. You are loving, loyal and trusting or withdrawn, self-pitying and bitter. The extremes of your emotional depths cause dramatic reactions and stress in your youth. In mid-life you navigate from a "right or wrong" set of personal ideals. Late in life you are a creative specialist.

You attract cultured, entertaining, magnetic personalities. They relate to your classic, universally acceptable tastes. You need a mission or a cause and belong in medicine, the arts, religious teaching— any field that reaches and benefits the public. Marriage is difficult. All emotional versus material aspects of your life demand compromises. In late years you remain self-assured, passionate and in a position of authority.

• OTHER SEPTEMBER 9 BIRTHDAYS

Granville Hicks	1901
Alfred Landon	1887
Sylvia Miles	1932
Max Reinhardt	1873
Cardinal Richelieu	1585
Cliff Robertson	1925
Leo Tolstoy	1828

SEPTEMBER
· 10 ·

Power, money and possessions are important to your happiness and feelings of self-esteem. You are an inventive, responsible and courageous original. It is your basic instinct to leave confining domestic circumstances as a youth to learn enough to lead others. You are a director—an innovator—an explorer. Your ambitions take you from your birthright and into the mainstream. The world is your oyster. Remember that grit is required to culture a pearl. You must develop a thick skin.

It is your curiosity and trusting nature that causes emotional problems in youth. As you mature, you realize that partnerships and compromises spoil your natural ability to make progressive changes. A fair amount of restlessness, speculation and education open your eyes to the possibilities of your unique ideas, personality and skillfulness. However, you must concentrate on yourself and have faith that you will be adequately paid for your investment in self-development. You have the ability to control yourself and capitalize on your intuition, freshness and good luck.

In mid-life you improve your reputation and fortune. You must remain active and be prepared to constantly reevaluate yourself. Rewards are open to you but are lost if you stagnate. Your mind works in mysterious ways, and you subconsciously set yourself up to conclude goals and set higher standards. The signals you send out are subtle. You create your own opportunities for advancement, and although you often feel isolated, you must walk alone. Do not be envious; be patient.

If you specialize early, your late years are secure and easy.

• OTHER SEPTEMBER 10 BIRTHDAYS

José Feliciano	1945
Leonard Lyons	1906
Roger Maris	1934
Edmund O'Brien	1915
Arnold Palmer	1929
Yma Sumac	1927
Fay Wray	1907

SEPTEMBER

· 11 ·

The insights that you take for granted are hot news flashes to average thinkers. You will never be part of the herd or self-satisfied. Your quest for perfection begins as a tot and grows. You have the ability to get lost in your imagination. As a child, you are not given the intellectual or emotional support that a youngster of your high nervous energy requires. Your mind is constantly deciding which idea to pursue or which turn in the road to follow. You are a secretive sensitive, a poetic elitist and a spiritual confusion until you settle into your niche.

Concentration is difficult without a supportive peer relationship to balance your nonmaterialistic tendencies. You are born to be a teacher and require discussions, sharing and bartering of ideas and ideals. Your personal magnetism attracts followers once you establish a specialty. You are diplomatic to a fault but have the capacity to detach from mundane obligations too. You can appear to be unfeeling when caught up in your evangelistic and zealous crusades. You may be too self-absorbed.

In intimate relationships you are emotionally responsive and need to be needed. You may find it impossible to accept the earthiness and inconsistency you find in others. When you are able to accept practical realities in mid-life, you are a proud, supportive and dedicated spouse and parent. It is within you to sacrifice your personal ambitions for the benefit of your loved ones. You are modest, cooperative and appreciative and persistently ambitious when stirred to action. You earn money but have difficulty stabilizing your finances. Late years are spent in learning and reflection. You are never self-satisfied.

• OTHER SEPTEMBER 11 BIRTHDAYS

Charles Evers	1922
O. Henry	1862
Tom Landry	1924
D.H. Lawrence	1885
Kristy McNichol	1962
Anne Seymour	1909

SEPTEMBER
· 12 ·

Your charm, personality, image and technical talents are the foundation of your ambitions. The spotlight shines on you and your social sensitivity. Friends and the contacts that your individualistic means of self-expression attract bring you financial good fortune. It is your extreme sense of obligation, strong opinions and unnecessary emotionalism that detract from your productive energy. In short, you would be an instant success if you would stop assuming burdens that should be shared.

In childhood the family is possessive and nurturing. You expand your horizons but never leave the morals, ethics and standards preached in youth. The responsibilities that you take on often overwhelm you. However, you are sympathetic, parental and have a sense of showmanship that inspires you to extend yourself. You want money, recognition, power, peace and love.

If you cannot have it all, you refuse to give up the ghost. Your optimism, imagination and persistence are undaunted by adversity. You delight in making others comfortable and will make a dishrag of yourself to provide service, entertainment or education for those people you imagine are less fortunate.

You are an outstanding leader and competitor when you are in balance. It is your poise, courage and personal philosophy that set you apart. When you have the presence of mind to search beneath surface values for the deeper or concealed meanings of conversations, contracts and handshakes, you will not be deluded. Too often appearances mislead you. Learn to accept change and to avoid getting think-stuck in self-pity.

In late years you are realistic, accepting and decisive.

• OTHER SEPTEMBER 12 BIRTHDAYS

Maurice Chevalier	1888
Alfred A. Knopf	1892
Frank McGee	1921
H. L. Mencken	1880
Jesse Owens	1913

SEPTEMBER **· 13 ·** Merchandising your military precision, sensuality and fighting spirit keeps your working constructively all your days. You have an attraction for notable and talented people as a youth. As you grow to maturity, your leadership, self-expression and practicality surface. As a youngster, you learn from experience. You are stubborn, impulsive and unconventional at your worst. At your best you are inquisitive, multifaceted and able to make your talents pay off. You get off to a good start, take a wrong turn and begin again in mid-life. You are capable of being an escapist. Problems arise when you are too busy or too bored. You are competitive, dedicated and organized to be materially aggressive after you make money and carelessly lose or misuse a sound basis for future security.

Your changing circumstances are not a matter of laziness or stupidity. You get into hectic or surprising situations and become rattled. After age thirty-five you adapt to a marriage that is stabilizing, supportive and expansive. You blossom under the guidance of an intelligent, youthful male who regulates your abilities and relaxes your unrealistic fears of the unknown. You feel less restrained and are freed to travel for pleasure and business.

After age forty your finances are secured by dividends, inheritance or past investments of time or cash. You have come far from your roots and are skillful and polished by exposures and experiences. You are a self-disciplined, home-loving, down-to-earth "class act." In late years work is its own reward.

You labor to leave tangible results, and you stay active.

• OTHER SEPTEMBER 13 BIRTHDAYS

Sherwood Anderson	1876
Jacqueline Bisset	1944
Scott Brady	1924
Claudette Colbert	1905
Leland Hayward	1902
Ruth McDevitt	1895
John Joseph Pershing	1860
Walter Reed	1851
Mel Torme	1925

SEPTEMBER
·14·

You are toilet trained with a whip in childhood and resent unreasonable rules, the limitations of outdated conventions or of traditional routines throughout your lifetime. The self-discipline that you exert upon yourself is creatively limiting. You take a vacation from narrow-mindedness as a life-style. It is difficult to get you on a cruise ship for relaxation. The twenty-eight-hour days and eighty-hour weeks that you spend setting an orderly, productive and constructive standard provide new enthusiasms, unconventional freedoms and adventures for others.

You have innovative, practical ideas and provide others with a catalyst for change. It is not your habit to personally reflect upon your past experiences to benefit yourself in the future. You try everything and keep trying to prove that established procedures may not hold true. Sex and the physical senses interest you. You may be promiscuous or too intellectual. But, in one extreme or the other, you test the fire to see how hot it is. Once you have answered your curiosity, decided that changes must be made, you are a promoter, a politician and a spark that lights kindling for bonfires.

Moderation is the key to your success. You are compulsive, restless and investigative. Too often you drown yourself in details and are too secretive to ask for help. You do many things at one time or get stuck in an obsession. Anything that is unknown to you is of interest, until you find the mental stimulation that captures, fascinates and justifies your existence.

You leave a world of friends and a footprint in your time.

• OTHER SEPTEMBER 14 BIRTHDAYS

Zoe Caldwell	1933
Milton Eisenhower	1899
Joey Heatherton	1944
Kay Medford	1920
Margaret Sanger	1883
Hal Wallis	1899

SEPTEMBER
· 15 ·
Your protective instincts, showmanship and ability to harmonize with opposites combine to make you attractive to many cultures. You are sympathetic, interpret the law as you see it and follow through on your commitments. However, you have an unconventional identification with leadership that sets you apart from the traditional facade that you expose. You twinkle on the outside and take responsibilities too seriously.

At some point in mid-life you exhibit unprecedented behavior and may make the headlines. You are magnetic and generally attract gifts, favors and close alliances. Money and possessions are important to your desire for an opulent home and to support the pride that you take in your family. You love beauty and music and strive to live with an absence of conflicts.

You are capable of down-and-dirty fighting for survival and will use your innate ability to understand human nature to stab at the ineptness in anyone you perceive to be an enemy. You plan your strategy and have the courage of your convictions. You have educated, nurtured and polished your performance since leaving your early environment. It is in your best interests to recognize when there is a need to change values or ambitions.

You tend to be too concerned about superficialities, rely on past agreements too heavily and get caught in the web of your vivid imagination. Beware of taking liberties with the truth or traditions when involved with an overly dependent woman.

From childhood you exaggerate problems, infidelities or obligations. You are a born skeptic and fear losing face. Your reputation, prestige and emotional control are late-year assets.

• OTHER SEPTEMBER 15 BIRTHDAYS

Agatha Christie	1890
Jackie Cooper	1922
James Fennimore Cooper	1789
Margaret Lockwood	1916
John Mitchell	1913
Jean Renoir	1894
William Howard Taft	1857

SEPTEMBER

· 16 ·

Petty people, legal dealings and delays in financial affairs may slow your progress, but you are destined to establish yourself as an authority late in life. You relate too closely to female relatives as a tot and are too sheltered or humbled to conceive of yourself as the original talent that you are.

In youth you meet people who have lived culturally expansive life-styles and who are skilled or polished personalities. You leave your place of birth for greener pastures but find disillusionment, disconnection or disappointments due to your own erroneous ideas. You marry for prestige, money or to avoid loneliness—or not at all. You require privacy and have an aloofness from mundane realities. It is in your best interests to get a good education, specialize and establish faith in yourself.

Mid-life experiences leave you short of your expectations. The perfection of your desires in career, love, marriage, money and/or reputation are affected negatively by partner or spouse. You have an inappropriate fear of loneliness and poverty that causes you to compromise or sacrifice for material goals. You achieve your ambitions and lose the end results through no fault of your own. However, you establish faith in yourself and the awareness that your greatest strength lies within. False values are dispersed, and self-confidence blooms when you do not allow yourself to be dominated by love or material possessiveness.

It's mind over matter in the latter stage of your life. You have a knack for coping and select aristocratic, bright people to surround you. Success is yours when your aim is for quality.

• OTHER SEPTEMBER 16 BIRTHDAYS

Lauren Bacall	1924
George Chakiris	1933
Peter Falk	1927
Anne Francis	1930
Allen Funt	1914
B.B. King	1925
Janis Paige	1922
Francis Parkman	1823
J.C. Penney	1875

SEPTEMBER **·17·** Yours not to reason why—but you do. Good fortune comes your way and you ask, why? Love and intellectual companionship are yours, and you doubt the reality. You like action, improvisation and independent people. The experiences that come your way expand your talents and emotional capacity and prepare you to take a leadership position in your chosen career. The expectations for your birthright are based upon your attitude toward doing business as usual in spite of emotional upheavals. You have the ability to plan, analyze and produce material results. Be an individual and expect the best. Your enemies are pessimism, submissiveness and inactivity.

In youth you travel, observe a broad scope of cultures and sort your own priorities. You bump into influential, financially secure, businesslike people and add to your storehouse of experiences. You develop communications abilities, persistence and human understanding. Assertive or authoritative males may shout you down. But after you reach your thirties you become secure in your self-image and refuse to allow others to mold you.

In mid-life your sensitivity, detail consciousness and perfectionist techniques are recognized. The rewards for your work alter your self-image. Due to improved stature, your personality mellows and you are less prone to debating issues and harboring resentments. You have sound executive judgment and work with equally energetic associates. Your courage is constantly tested in career and love. You have control.

In late years you advance intellectually and spiritually. You have options to become a wealthy and unique personality.

- OTHER SEPTEMBER 17 BIRTHDAYS

Anne Bancroft	1931
Warren Burger	1907
Queen Elizabeth I of England	1533
Ken Kesey	1935
Roddy McDowall	1928
John Ritter	1948
Hank Williams	1923

SEPTEMBER
· 18 ·

You are a "teacher's teacher" and are born to set an example of your personal philosophy. The people and experiences that you meet as a youngster train you to express your talents, and you are drawn to notables. Older, distinguished, worldly talents recognize the depth of wisdom that you command. With education and exposure, you travel far from your roots and submerge yourself in helping another. In youth you learn to face reality the hard way.

Initially you are emotionally generous, naively romantic and materially thoughtless. In your late twenties you become independent and businesslike. Your aloofness becomes an asset. It is too easy for you to feel the passions, responses and reactions of individuals in your surroundings. You must remove yourself mentally in order to sustain yourself. The potential that you have for counseling, healing and reasoning is a treasure and a strain. Your loyalties and ingenuity are constantly tested.

Travel, distortions and hard-driving materialists alter your destiny. You are conscious of finances and are a fine critic and investor. Your sympathies are often misplaced, but you develop a thicker skin as you enlarge your scope. It is best for you to be a loner and to move from one cultural expansion to another. You attract attention, burdens and disappointments in love. The fears that you have are not easily displaced. You must navigate on intuitional guidance, uphold your financial security and respect your perfectionist nature. It's not easy to relate to ordinary expectations with your exactitude, ego and viewpoint.

• OTHER SEPTEMBER 18 BIRTHDAYS

Eddie Anderson	1905
Robert Blake	1933
Rossano Brazzi	1916
Greta Garbo	1905

SEPTEMBER **·19·** Opportunity knocks and you are skeptical as a youth. Early years are insecure, and you are conscious of finances, food and futures. You are more aware of your body, physical stamina and outer appearances than the average youngster. The goings-on in your childhood cause you to keep personal activities secret and create a conventional image. It is difficult for you to accept yourself and circumstances. You have high ambitions that turn from materialism to inventiveness as you enter mid-life. It is your charisma, individuality and desire to expand your talents that open doors for late-life security.

You work hard to earn money and a reputation. You are capable of changing goals and succeeding in each attempt at professionalism. Once educated, you stick to your original plan until you feel the need to widen your horizons. In mid-life you attract celebrities or notables. Your obligations increase, and you are pressed to declare your loyalties. There are few pleasures or treasures for you without sacrifice or extreme self-assertion. The more you diversify your activities, the more pronounced your childhood nervous habits become. You need time to care for your body and to improve your mind.

Intimate relationships make demands upon your schedule, money and emotions. Your ambitions are far-reaching, and you rebel if you feel less respected or qualified than your peers. When your sense of justice is disturbed, take immediate action to renew your faith. The romantic in you cannot believe that life can be unfair. You become constructively involved in charitable or humanitarian interests as you grow older. You are a dreamer.

• OTHER SEPTEMBER 19 BIRTHDAYS

Brian Epstein	1934
Leon Jawarski	1905
David McCallum	1933
Joseph Pasternak	1901
"Colonel" Harland Sanders	1890
Duke Snider	1926
Ernest Truex	1889
Twiggy	1949

SEPTEMBER

·20·

Older, cultured, wiser talents and personalities open doors that expand your opportunities as a youth. You are a sympathetic, adaptable, friendly youngster. The powers of observation that help you express your talents in maturity are based upon a sense of isolation and emotional poverty experienced from your birthright. You question everything. However, you do not have people in your surroundings who have the time or energy to pay attention to your intellectual curiosity. Fear of being alone, even in a crowd, stays with you all your days.

You are trusting, sensitive and aware of the little things that disturb others. These qualities in your character, plus your quest for perfection, inspire others to be protective. Friends help you travel far from your roots to cultures that appreciate your commonsense, down-to-earth attitude toward work and discrimination. You lack patience for slowness, stupidity or superficiality.

In marriage you are a loyal partner. Lawyers, inconsistencies in the judicial system and petty delays create practical problems in mid-life. You have difficult-to-diagnose physical and business apprehensions for many years, until you apply yourself to mental rather than bodily work. As you gain wisdom, you extend your pride and love of home and family to community projects. The necessity to keep secrets and maintain an aloofness fades as you begin to accept yourself and receive recognition for your own ideas.

In late years you master your craft. You travel, improve finances and set an example. You come to grips with your illusions.

• OTHER SEPTEMBER 20 BIRTHDAYS

Sophia Loren	1934
Elliott Nugent	1899
Upton Sinclair	1878

SEPTEMBER

·21·

Your cup runneth over, if you are changable, individualistic and self-expressive. People are attracted to your charm, wit and up-to-date ideas. You are destined to be a free thinker, a traveler and have the persistence to bring your personal ideal to reality. Family ties bind you long into maturity. The standards, fears and sense of responsibility set in youth do not prepare you to make the decisions and sacrifices that face you in mid-life.

You are versatile, responsible and multitalented. Good luck does not pass you by. It's up to you to respect your individualized talents and to take care of yourself. Social contacts get you everywhere. A ready smile, imaginative word games and youthful interests set your stage. An optimistic personality is a must if you intend to achieve your potential.

If you are heavy with problems or too burdened to take time to play, your attitude repulses the types of people in your surroundings. If you are too involved with bolstering your loved ones, maintaining past values and ignoring progress, your opportunities to improve your career, finances and life-style pass you by. You are destined to walk on the sunny side of the street.

Your lover or spouse—all partnerships—influences your accomplishments. Avoid scattering your energy, money and emotional commitments. Seek out professionals—don't take a superficial approach to legal or business projects. In late years the visualizations and expectations that cross your mind as a youth should come to pass. Believe in yourself.

• OTHER SEPTEMBER 21 BIRTHDAYS

Dawn Addams	1930
Umberto Mastroianni	1910
Melvin Van Peebles	1932
H. G. Wells	1866

SEPTEMBER
·22·

You have the potential to leave a business, real estate, jewelry, or any written documents or practical products of value that will be appreciated by future generations. In your scope, you will constructively work for yourself. The results of your down-to-earth dedication to upgrade your lifestyle will not conclude when your contributions end. You begin your high-energy labors after your twenty-eighth birthday.

Prior to mid-life you experience unconventional, impulsive and sensually testing ups and downs. You find it difficult to learn from your experiences and continually gamble on your newest enthusiams or fear taking chances on unknowns. You travel from your neighborhood to meet people and experiences that deepen your philosophy and open doors to expand your expectations. Change, uncertainty and adventure cause you to alter your youthful goals.

You have extraordinary emotional developments that make you less selfish or prone to live untraditionally. You are less of a rule breaker. Circumstances help you to project and apply the wisdom that you accumulate as a youngster to let go of past programming. You become less of a romantic dreamer and apply common sense to daily living. Your mid-life decisions are based upon organizing your mind and body to do expedient or realistic things. Sacrifices or notable efforts of your talents are not forgotten. Youthful mistakes or sacrifices make you a transient lover. After age forty your "big shot" approach, fears of impoverishment and overly expressed sense of obligation ease off.

A mate is your supporter, adviser and friend to the end.

• OTHER SEPTEMBER 22 BIRTHDAYS

Debby Boone	1956
John Houseman	1902
Joni James	1930
Paul Muni	1895
Mark Phillips	1948
Erich von Stroheim	1885

SEPTEMBER **·23·** Trouble is not an unknown to you. But you throw off the worst of it, become less self-indulgent and discipline your emotional reactions as your life unfolds. Parents, finances or physical problems limit your freedom to explore your curiosities, and you are mentally rebellious in youth. You are a rule breaker and a sensualist, and you maintain a high-energy work level. Opportunities to meet celebrated or accomplished people broaden your scope of experiences, and you expand your tastes and aspirations until you are freed in mid-life.

You are multifaceted, practice your craft and have varied simultaneous interests. You need partnerships—lovers, mates or business associates—who are attracted to your lively, imaginative, self-expressive personality. You are never dull. It is part of your charm to tease and play while you expect tangible results from yourself and the people with whom you work, admire or love.

You are too speculative and changable to lead a financially or domestically stabilized, conservatively structured life-style. You appear to be sturdy, conservative and dignified at first blush, and want domestic security, you but need to be unencumbered to experiment, promote and produce the fruits of your investigations. You are confusingly lazy, worrisome and desirous of attachments—never allow boredom or outdated fashions to let you grow old. Youthful enthusiasms, carrying out ideas and physical sensuality keep you active and forever young.

Travel less in late years. The efforts you spend are unnecessary to your happiness and only break even financially.

- OTHER SEPTEMBER 23 BIRTHDAYS

Colin Blakeley	1930
Ray Charles	1932
Euripides	c. 484 B.C.
Walter Lippmann	1889
William Holmes McGuffey	1800
Walter Pidgeon	1897
Mickey Rooney	1920
Romy Schneider	1938

318 • SEPTEMBER BORN ARE

SEPTEMBER **·24·** In youth you are exposed to wiser philosophies "in the streets" than you can salvage while sacrificing for a demanding family or fulfilling obligations at home. Midlife offers protection from sympathetic women or parental males. Family or group financial involvements, opportunities for creative showmanship and experiences that open doors for your social growth and expanding talent as a teacher or communicator add to your security. Late years find you in a rut if you seek peace at the expense of your self-expression. When you are willing to get off your butt, speak up and exercise your control, you are the king/queen in your castle. Don't blame circumstances.

You are uneasy when work and love do not blend. Overindulgence, game playing and misplaced sympathy are the negative results of your emotional upheavals. It is your greatest pleasure to live graciously, to take pride in your home and family and to extend yourself to volunteer to serve your community. You know what you want and are at your best when you share your feelings before you get frustrated or angry. You will never have the expression of your personal ideals if you do not extend yourself to put the wheels in motion, live and let live and do not attempt to play out the role that you think is expected. Life is not a stage; you pay the piper for immaturity.

The child in you never grows up to accept ugliness, disharmony or hatred. You take people and life at face value or expect that the worst is lurking beneath every social contact. Your extremes range from naïveté to suspiciousness. Others cease to create problems after age fifty, and life does not change radically.

• OTHER SEPTEMBER 24 BIRTHDAYS

William Bundy	1917
Alan Colmes	1950
Cheryl Crawford	1902
F. Scott Fitzgerald	1896
Larry Gates	1915
Sheila MacRae	1924
Jim McKay	1921
Anthony Newley	1931
George Raft	1903
Lester Rawlins	1924

SEPTEMBER

·25·

If you make mountains out of molehills, you will never get an overview of incoming opportunities. Mother, the presiding female influence, or no maternal contact in your childhood cause you to be self-effacing, too receptive to criticism and too concerned about your own feelings in youth. You are spoiled or ignored. In mid-life you collect, synthesize and meet people and experiences that allow you to express yourself intellectually. You are an exacting, unconventional and enthusiastic family member, lover and judge of character.

You are an observer who strives for perfection and professionalism. You meet notable, magnetic and philosophical people. You travel far from your place of birth and exceed expectations, only to face last-minute disappointments in loves, business and/or legal agreements. After age forty you appreciate the value of investigation before making plans, investments or commitments.

Details are your forte. However, too much concern for petty administrative functions, small-minded people who offer personalized criticisms and allowing your individuality to be victimized by intimidation will deplete your energy and bring on debilitating or annoying chronic physical problems. You are easily depressed until you become emotionally selective, and logically discriminating and come out of your shell in mid-life.

After age forty you throw off self-imposed limitations. Later you overcome disillusionment, stay aloof, investigate before you become intimate and are recognized. You travel, enjoy privacy and speak, act, write—work— as an exclusive authority.

• OTHER SEPTEMBER 25 BIRTHDAYS

John Ericson	1927
William Faulkner	1897
Glen Gould	1932
Mark Hamill	1951
Juliet Prowse	1936
Phil Rizzuto	1918
Ian Tyson	1933
Barbara Walters	1931

SEPTEMBER
· 26 ·

After a lack of independence in youth, you aim for the mainstream in a pioneering, self-expressive and businesslike fashion mid-life. Partnerships, family and intimate relationships add to your success and happiness for a while. However, it is your lack of ego or compulsively individualistic attitude that causes you to overreact when, eventually, you are creatively limited. When you submit or control, you are the loser. After age thirty you become more self-concerned, cease to walk in domestic idealism or in another's limelight and go on to find uncompromising relationships.

You are wise and express universal sympathy. Music and all artistic art forms interest you. You have the life experience that inspires human understanding, which you convey to others. But you are too impatient with yourself, your peers and your ambitions.

Powerful, financially secure, courageous achievers cross your path from birth to your late fifties. The influential and affluent inspire and offer opportunities for you to become materially secure and to express your cooperative spirit. You provide comfort and instruction and inspire unity when you are burdened with the care of the young, old, animals or people unable to help themselves. Your personal philosophy, inclined to obedience or martyrdom originally, should mellow. Eventually you extend your ability—stretch your capacities—to delegate, execute, manage and achieve tangible results for the good of your family, career and the groups of people who attract your attention. At your worst you are frank, uplifting and loving.

Later your spirituality and image live after you are gone.

• OTHER SEPTEMBER 26 BIRTHDAYS

Johnny Appleseed	1775
T. S. Eliot	1888
George Gershwin	1898
Julie London	1926
Olivia Newton-John	1948
Patrick O'Neal	1927
Marty Robbins	1925
Dmitri Shostakovich	1906

SEPTEMBER **· 27 ·** There are few personal sacrifices that you are unwilling to make for love, charity or the general good. You are a stickler for detail, correctness and quality. Both mental and emotional companionship are necessary before you put aside your desire to contribute counsel, healing or technical expertise for marriage. Once you find a person of kindred philosophy, perfection of classic beauty, compassion and magnetic charm, you try to adapt your aspirations to an intimate relationship. However, the call to respond to humanitarian principles and to get out of a cloistered environment taxes your self-awareness and discipline.

In youth you come a long way in human understanding. As a mature adult, you meet magnetic, expansive, cultured people and have experiences that cause you to give everything the benefit of the doubt. When you feel positive, unswervingly energetic and boundlessly empathetic, it pleases you to expect the best and to give your all. In the negative, you suppress your personal talents, ambitions or growth in a feeling that you may give the shirt off your back and never miss it. You have a naive flair for the dramatic. Get involved to avoid loneliness in late years.

You are a passionate lover. Your generosity in sex, love or marriage relationships is boundless unless you think that denying yourself gratification is not appreciated. You are a formidable, unforgiving enemy once you think you have been deceived, cheated or treated coldly. Once you become self-insistent, unfeeling or manipulative, you are the extreme of egocentricity and the opposite of all your virtues. Avoid the extremes. In balance, you attract warm, enduring, unchallenging emotional satisfaction.

• OTHER SEPTEMBER 27 BIRTHDAYS

William Conrad	1920
Sam Ervin	1896
Claude Jarman, Jr.	1934
Catherine Marshall	1914
Jayne Meadows	1926
Arthur Penn	1922
Charles H. Percy	1919
George Raft	1896
Sada Thompson	1929

SEPTEMBER **·28·** You are an original, and you project ideas that reach a materialistic audience. Money and power hold too much or too little importance for you at different times in your life. In youth you expand your frontiers to learn and observe how the other half lives. You want companionship and find older or experienced lovers and friends. They extend the borders of your inventive imagination. You travel far from your origins through "big business," inheritance or artistic pursuits.

You progress and are encouraged to individualize. In mid-life you feel a need for quiet, peace and companionship. Love and the expectations that you have are disappointing. You anticipate a support system that is intimate and attracts independent, progressive innovators like yourself. You coordinate emotional and material ambitions with sensitivity, detachment and denial of one or the other. Your mate must relate to your practical purposes. You are a strong, courageous, hardworking loner.

A hobby or humanitarian contributions may take you away from the businesslike conditions that disturb your desire for an easygoing domestic life-style. It is difficult for you to do anything halfheartedly, and unwittingly you may turn the hobby into a major interest. You get involved with groups but find labor organizations and lawyers problematic. Your talents extend to fields of communications, government and medicine, where you tend to be controversial. Children uphold your personal ideals.

In later years you are receptive to current events, positive or negative reforms and walk on a tightrope to follow conventions or uphold traditions. You become more sociable.

• OTHER SEPTEMBER 28 BIRTHDAYS

Brigitte Bardot	1934
Al Capp	1909
Peter Finch	1916
Marcello Mastroianni	1924
William S. Paley	1901
Elmer Rice	1892
Ethel Rosenberg	1915
Ed Sullivan	1902

SEPTEMBER You are intended to leave a lasting work or image and
must forego materialism and a need for constant ap-
·29· proval in order to instigate your ideas. Your exceptional
intellectual capacities are untapped as a child and
smother under a materialistic domestic environment. As a youth,
older, culturally expansive, educated, authoritative guides force you
to exercise self-disciplines that inspire detail consciousness, artistic
awareness and a drive for perfection in the expression of your talents.
You dislike mundane realities, menial or manual work and prefer
the mind side of productivity.

The chance to leave your roots, educate yourself and release your
self-depreciating attitude comes early. You are a difficult child to
understand because your high nervous energy is displaced by a
careless attitude, petty jealousy and a brooding quality that seems
cold and calculating. Actually you are unsure of yourself, secretive
and experimental. You are a "don't miss a trick" sensitive and are
negatively affected by emotionally unstable, businesslike or changable childhood influences. In mid-life your personality problems are
resolved.

The love mates you select seem dependable, stable and secure.
They are not. You find disappointment in marriage and partnerships
until you relate to others with a down-to-earth look at yourself. You
have self-imposed limitations and overextend your commitments to
deplete your physical energy. Discover a far-reaching means of self-
expression. You will stop blaming circumstances and demand fair
pay for your extraordinary businesslike accomplishments. Late years
are warmly protected.

• OTHER SEPTEMBER 29 BIRTHDAYS

GENE AUTRY	1907
VIRGINIA BRUCE	1910
GREER GARSON	1908
BRYANT GUMBEL	1948
TREVOR HOWARD	1916
MADELINE KAHN	1942
STANLEY KRAMER	1913
JERRY LEE LEWIS	1935
HORATIO NELSON	1758
LIZABETH SCOTT	1922

SEPTEMBER

· 30 ·

You are extraordinarily family oriented, a compulsively parental friend and a social success when you choose to attract applause. The negative aspects of your character relate to your sense of responsibility and create a jealous love partner when a commitment is made. In youth you expect everyone to live up to your personal, exemplary, burden-bearing standards. When friends and intimates do not have the same intensity to provide comfort and nurturing that you exert, you are devastated. As you grow to mid-life successes, your need to assume control for the happiness and well-being of everyone who strikes you emotionally subsides. Later you enjoy ease and opulence, but work hard to express your talents.

You like being the star. You have a knack for showmanship and a flair for applying organization to your creative efforts. You are sociable, fashionable and enjoy a variety of interests. You have sex appeal and capitalize upon your looks or personality. You unwittingly make a game out of love relationships, and when beauty, fun and lightheartedness decline, you may flirt on. Obstacles seem to arise when you decide to settle down. It is your need for domestic tranquility, pride in your family and a fondness for children, pets or community participation that encourages you to marry or remain with one lover. You have a unique mental approach to the meaning of love.

Scattering your time and interests may be a cause for concern in your productive years. A cause or group commitment may reorder your priorities after age forty. Later years are spent near the water, far from the birthplace, and are not boring.

• OTHER SEPTEMBER 30 BIRTHDAYS

Truman Capote	1921
Angie Dickenson	1931
Hans Geiger	1882
Deborah Kerr	1921
Lester Maddox	1915
Johnny Mathis	1935

OCTOBER

• 1 •

You may enjoy working with others, but you are a born leader. In childhood you were given responsibilities or assumed that if you didn't take the lead, no one else would. It is within you to understand the emotional trials and tribulations that trouble or uplift—you feel the pain yourself or refuse to acknowledge another's suffering. You are a philosopher. Too often you submerge your personality in order to relieve the strain you see in your surroundings. Once you have been fooled or cheated, you refuse to forgive or forget a mistake. In youth you are too skeptically mature or too romantically naive for your years.

Mid-life opportunities are for independence. The people you encounter are progressive, active and inventive. They need followers— you are not inclined to take orders obediently. From your late twenties, minimally, until your late fifties, you are a loner in your chosen life-style. You cannot expect partners or lovers to think and solve problems the inventive way that you do. You find that you are different. It is in your best interests to have the courage of your convictions and to do what is best for yourself.

Power and the freedom that is enjoyed when you don't have to count every penny are yours—by hook or by crook. You have a natural understanding of what products are worth and put a price on your time and efforts. You expect to be compensated for your uniqueness, and you must keep in mind that you meet the same people on the way down that you insulted on the way up. Your loyalties and personal faith will be tested before you can relax.

Late years are progressive. But you must slow your pace.

• OTHER OCTOBER 1 BIRTHDAYS

Julie Andrews	1935
Faith Baldwin	1893
Tom Bosley	1927
James Earl Carter	1924
Lawrence Harvey	1928
Stanley Holloway	1890
Vladimir Horowitz	1904
Walter Matthau	1920
George Peppard	1928
William Rehnquist	1924
James Whitmore	1921
Roger Williams	1926
Sam Yorty	1908

OCTOBER

· 2 ·

You are the epitome of diplomacy or relentlessly tactless. Charm, humor and youthfulness are your saving graces. The independence that you asserted in youth was intermingled with your attraction for partnerships and group interactions. Until mid-life you are too self-assertive or too accommodating. In mid-life it is your ability to be firm while appearing to be cooperative that spurs your ambitions. The power, money and supporters you seek are available when you are subtle in your efforts to control, activate or communicate with others.

You are an assimilator of data, a collector of people and things. You were exposed to entertaining, lighthearted, imaginative personalities in youth and have observed their talents. You have the character that accumulates and receives input and may be a talker, a writer or enjoy the limelight as a critic or go-between. However, your impatience is not a virtue.

If you marry early, you are not inclined to cheat. Later, marriage and the demands of your ambitions are hard on domestic commitments. There is some confusion as to your being too careless or too careful with money. You are generous with loved ones and take pride in your family. You are a self-starter and work to be a winner. A home near the water stills your tensions.

There is too much or too little attention from the father in childhood. As a result, you are too self-assertive or too accommodating until you mature enough to realize that repeated vacillations have caused you frustration. A level-headed associate is there when you need to bounce off ideas and calm your changable mind. You begin again at age forty and accelerate.

• OTHER OCTOBER 2 BIRTHDAYS

Bud Abbott	1895
Lord Chesterfield	1694
Mohandas K. Gandhi	1869
Graham Greene	1904
Groucho Marx	1895
Rex Reed	1940

OCTOBER

· 3 ·

If there is beauty to be found, you will notice and enjoy. You are imaginative, fun-loving and attractive. You have a light in your eyes that entices the opposite sex and an unforgettable voice. Although you may appear to be a flirt, it is unlikely that you will do more than make a lighthearted game of the chase. Home, children and pets are dear to you. The creative arts—writing and speaking, in particular—come naturally.

Your body may be incorporated into your career because you have coordination of mind and body and the opportunity to be introduced to the advantages of maintaining routines. You systematize, train or practice and may become skilled in a career or hobby choice as a youth. Playing the piano, participating in sports or dancing may interest you.

You are surrounded by down-to-earth people who apply themselves to work for material results in an orderly life-style. In mid-life people are less inclined to save their pennies and are concerned with expressing their abilities. You learn to use your common sense early and strive for productivity.

You are too sensitive and must develop a thicker skin. You tend to emotionalize when you should apply logic. It is the pleasure you take in people and life's variety that gives you the good sense and optimism to bounce back when disappointments arise. You are congenial, traditional and will reap whatever you sow. If you cannot live within conventional guidelines, you have long periods of time in an upswing and equally long time spans going downhill. Money and security will be problematic in mid-life. Later you are loved, secure and active.

• OTHER OCTOBER 3 BIRTHDAYS

Gertrude Berg	1899
Chubby Checker	1941
Jack LaLanne	1914
Gore Vidal	1925
Thomas Wolfe	1900

OCTOBER

·4·

Owing to diversification of personalities that crossed your path and changing childhood experiences, you are unconventional, independent and creatively self-expressive. It is your intention to be constructive, and you expect to work to attain your ambitions. Real estate and all products of the earth are excellent areas for your financial investments and provide you with late-life security.

Early years are influenced by the mother in conjunction with siblings or mother and grandmother in combination. Too much or too little attention makes you socially self-conscious. You talk too much to attract attention or become too close-mouthed to allow others to enjoy your charm and talents. As you mature, you may be inclined to superficiality one moment and extremely serious the next. As time goes on, you take less delight in the games you play. You recognize the rewards that come your way when you apply your imagination and attention-getting looks or gifts to accomplishing material goals.

In youth you have had the opportunity to experience travel, sex and the physical pleasures. You have satisfied curiosities, and in your forties you buckle down, become more down to earth and devote time and energy to your career, love and domestic involvements. You take an interest in projects for the good of the community. You excel in labor relations, organizational leadership and managing your own affairs. You do battle when situations are irrational to your sense of orderliness. You respect convention or break tradition for useful purposes.

Later, if you have lived your plan, you are prosperous.

• OTHER OCTOBER 4 BIRTHDAYS

Felicia Farr	1932
Rutherford B. Hayes	1822
Charlton Heston	1924
Buster Keaton	1895
Jean Millet	1814
Frederic Remington	1861
Pancho Villa	1877

OCTOBER
· 5 ·
Life has an air of uncertainty. You are not intended to uphold traditions, other than those within your personal code of self-discipline. You shift between workaholic and lazaholic compulsions. You are honest to an extreme or cut corners. Youth and mid-life are very different. The family personal ideals, community obligations and childhood sense of responsibility influence you less after you pass the age of thirty. At fifty you may feel as though childhood values were just a dream and your reality is based upon living day to day.

You are capable of being all things to all people and have a youthful approach to your work and personal relationships. Your chief talents are derived from the experiences that you encounter. You grow by observing, testing and deducing—taking risks. It is impossible for you to live without constant new enthusiasms. You get involved with short-term jobs, adventures and interests that force you to adapt to new angles of approach.

You have the ability to love, work and play with the intensity of a teenager when you reach your late years. Maintain an open mind, consider yourself a trailblazer and recognize that you learned to exercise your individuality in youth. Your spiritual instincts will not lead you astray. It is your rigid childhood programming that limits your progress. It is not in your destiny to plan for tomorrow or to insist upon knowing exactly what the future will hold. Your most severe critic and confining enemy is yourself. Never stay in a rut.

You will earn your keep and pay a price for your freedom. In late years you overcome confusion, stay active and are useful.

• OTHER OCTOBER 5 BIRTHDAYS

CHESTER ALAN ARTHUR	1829
GLYNIS JOHNS	1923
JOSHUA LOGAN	1908
STEVE MILLER	1943
DONALD PLEASANCE	1919

OCTOBER

· 6 ·

Fears of going to the poorhouse in old age plague you. Worry not! You have a life protected by love, family and your showmanlike abilities. You develop your individuality in youth and make a few mistakes. Experience is your teacher until you reach your thirties, when you find keeping commitments less of a strain.

You cannot expect another to provide you with happiness or emotional security. It is in your best interests not to become a martyr or refuse to enjoy your freedom in youth. You are never sure when to sacrifice and when to expect others to live up to your personal standards. Your eye for symmetry, love of beauty and sense of rhythm are enhanced by a good education. If you want to live to old age with an opulent home, community respect and an adoring family, worry or self-pity will not attract them. You need to work to perfect your skill and hang in to establish your right to authority.

You should be cautious, question and investigate before you travel unnecessarily, make spontaneous decisions or involve yourself in a variety of love affairs. You are a sympathetic, parental, peace-loving problem-solver. Other people's problems are fodder for your grist mill. Too often you volunteer and get little or no thanks. Perhaps the reason you are not appreciated is that you take over instead of assisting, counseling or teaching.

In late years you focus upon teaching or learning. You enjoy your home life and watching people prosper. You are happiest providing comfort and entertainment, not criticism.

• OTHER OCTOBER 6 BIRTHDAYS

Janet Gaynor	1906
Thor Heyerdahl	1914
Jenny Lind	1820
Carole Lombard	1909
Anne Quayle	1820
George Westinghouse	1846

OCTOBER

· 7 ·

Early years are spent surrounded by ambitious people, and you are exposed to money, power and the freedom they can buy. You are intellectually gifted; a questioner, who is trained by unconventional, self-insistent, emotionally governed people. You do not get in touch with your introspective personality, spirituality or compulsion for perfection and privacy.

Your personal desires are not considered priorities, and you learn to adjust your ambitions for the good of the family. You are secretive, rebellious and uncomfortable. Responsibilities, obligations and standards are set for you to uphold. You are overloaded and do not know how to communicate your fears of loneliness and disconnection without causing domestic disharmony. It is difficult for you to lose the impulse to martyr or deny yourself that others benefit from until you reach your thirties, when you become impulsive and your financial picture changes.

You marry early, never leave the nest or divorce more than once due to inappropriate response to early environment. Mid-life does not give you opportunities to hold on to possessions or make material goals your sole ambition. You establish a specialty and attract what you need through your expertise or reputation. You develop poise and self-confidence, and do not fear loneliness. You are surrounded by people and feel aloof from the crowd. To enjoy and maintain a love relationship, you must find mental stimulation, a relaxing environment and freedom from mundane problems. You require time to live an interior life where peace, grace and solitude safeguard your ability to reason.

Late years are less dramatic. You are protected and calm.

- OTHER OCTOBER 7 BIRTHDAYS

June Allyson	1923
Sarah Churchill	1914
Andy Devine	1905
Alfred Drake	1914
Diana Lynn	1926
Vaughn Monroe	1912
James Whitcomb Riley	1849

OCTOBER

· 8 ·

The wonders of big business and the material rewards that accompany success in the mainstream tax your stamina. You travel far from your roots in youth to meet powerful, affluent and exacting people. Sacrifices, romantic dreams and a need for human understanding developed you emotionally. But your fears of loneliness and poverty made you secretive and disconnected from your domestic environments and relationships. You are uncomfortable with the practical realities and mundane expectations that busy the family as you grow up.

You find yourself an analytic loner surrounded by socially concerned, emotional, shallow—by your intellectual standards—materialists. You ask questions and do not get answers. No matter how much education, praise or established authority you receive, you never satisfy your own expectations. Until you accept human frailty and daily routine, you do not come down to earth. You see yourself as the little prince or princess—too gullible or skeptical.

In mid-life you face practical problems, struggle against opposition and come to grips with reality. You do not spare yourself, and you expect your vision, imagination and determination to pay off. You want the things that money can buy, and aim to attract a position of respect in a businesslike, courageous, enthusiastic manner. A progressive, expansive, executive life-style, where your lack of patience for petty people and details fits perfectly, is offered to you. You have too much or too little faith. Late years are content, if you rest. Take time to smell the roses.

• OTHER OCTOBER 8 BIRTHDAYS

Samuel Adams	1722
Rona Barrett	1936
Michelangelo Caravaggio	1573
Rev. Jesse Jackson	1941
Juán Perón	1895
Eddie Rickenbacker	1890

OCTOBER

· 9 ·

You are inclined to be philanthropic, strong-willed and intent upon amassing a broad education. In youth you encounter independent, inventive, ambitious loners who stay in your life until you reach maturity. In midlife your broadmindedness, changing interests and romantic nature emerge. You are interested in noble causes and attract magnetic, talented, culturally expansive people.

Childhood acquisitiveness diminishes, and you conclude emotional ties with youth as you reach your forties. Later years find you less aggressive, impulsive and ready to share intimate companionship. Family ties and interactions with kindred spirits are strong emotional links. You may lose connections, break day-to-day contact or divorce from commitments, but you are instilled with permanent integrity, uphold agreements and take pride in your domestic, business and community relationships.

You may need a swift kick to push you away from details and into businesslike efficiency. Too much curiosity and too little practical management delay your material progress when you have a partner, spouse or business associate to lean on. You try to escape mundane occupations and do well counseling, entertaining or serving the public through medical, government or religious work. You have earning skills that provide for your late-life security. Travel, upgrades and expansive thinking may drain your pocketbook. But you grow wiser with each investigation, have the broad philosophy to laugh at your own foibles and the strength of character to overcome setbacks. You are not shallow or selfish.

In late years you imagine that you could have done more.

- OTHER OCTOBER 9 BIRTHDAYS

Bruce Cotton	1899
E. Howard Hunt	1918
John Lennon	1940
Aimee Semple McPherson	1899

OCTOBER

· **10** ·

Expect to go it alone to do your best work. In youth you met innovative, aggressive self-starters. Exposure to mentally alert, active trendsetters reinforces your avant-gardist attitudes. You learn to be cooperative, modest and sensitive. It is difficult for you to take a leadership stance until you pass your twenties. You may be trained to be obedient, tactful and helpful, to follow rather than lead. You must exhibit patience.

The progressive energy that is hidden in you may be overshadowed and cause you to be sensitive and delicate and to feel too old for your years. You are considered to be different as a child, impatient as a maturing youth, assertive with subtle control in mid-life and known for your unique character in late years. It is likely that you are precocious. Your wisdom may have shocked, delighted and dealt with adult problems. In any chosen career or life-style you aspire to individuality. It requires courage, humility and the inner drive to be a winner. You have it all.

Stand on your own feet and have the courage of your own convictions. You discover that your ideas are fresh and others cannot relate or recall precedents. You are able to deal with conventional standards, too, and are able to earn money for your personal security. Domestic life includes travel and changes. You want love and suffer deeply when outside interests make a rift between your love and your talents. You have a quick temper or the composure of a saint. Your spouse and family learn to live with your practicality, intuition and decisive actions.

Late in life you have more companionship and protection.

• OTHER OCTOBER 10 BIRTHDAYS

Helen Hayes	1900
Jerry Orbach	1935
Adlai Stevenson III	1930
Tanya Tucker	1958
Guiseppe Verdi	1813
Ben Vereen	1946

OCTOBER

· 11 ·

Your dreams of creating an empire based upon your personal idealism have promise, although the money or power may not be available to you in youth. You are destined to leave a lasting image and must assert your individuality to accomplish your goals. A female relative is a problem when you try to do things on your own or find satisfaction in marriage. You attract a kindred spirit to love, but there is nervous tension in the intimate relationship. You are prone to tensions and impatience. Dominant males or aggressive leaders squelch your ideas, and you are too submissive, accommodating and lack aggressiveness as a young person.

In mid-life you need a supportive partner and have the diplomacy to keep relationships that are shaky on an even keel. You begin to fight for your beliefs and take on responsibilities that extend domestic bounds or your ordinary scope. There may be arguments, but you attract followers and supporters and back up material results for your cause. In spite of personal emotional upheavals, you have charisma and imagination and attract attention. The most rewarding years of your life begin at age forty.

It is necessary for you to specialize to achieve the fame that is offered in your destiny. The world of finance or practical reality is not your mainstay. You are a conceptualizer, a visionary, and you inspire others to extend themselves. Your intuition is high and your energy level is drained easily. Perseverance and determination are needed for you to achieve the dramatic results that your intensity of purpose demands.

Late years are financially secure and expansive.

• OTHER OCTOBER 11 BIRTHDAYS

Joseph Alsop	1910
Ron Leibman	1937
Charles Revson	1906
Jerome Robbins	1916
Eleanor Roosevelt	1884

OCTOBER

· 12 ·

You are a private person who needs an audience. Writing, entertaining and making social contacts bring you out to meet your destiny. You are sensitive to the little things in life and try to adapt your individuality to love and partnerships. You encounter practical, hardworking, home-loving people in youth. You develop common sense and recognize your need to separate emotional and business interests as you mature. Your interests extend domestic bounds and reach out to serve the public. In late years you develop a thick skin and refuse to submit to the opinions of others.

You are destined to make money and manage your own affairs. You are an excellent lecturer and have a flair for debating. Your love of beauty, fashion and humor makes you a charmer. When you establish a purpose and a plan of action, you finish your commitments. However, you tend to scatter interests, friendships and lovers until you have a long-term goal in mind. If you think that you are too prone to optimism and should be more cautious and self-protective, you may be right.

At times you are too humble, and at other times you are too critical. Find the balance before your late years to hold on to your material security. You attract dependent people and lean on authoritative manipulators. However, you are able to bounce back when the chips are down and recoup your losses when you depend upon your self-expression. Changes are progressive for you.

Don't fear getting caught up in petty details or allow small-minded people to swallow your innovative ideas. You have interesting friends, travel and broaden your scope in late years.

• OTHER OCTOBER 12 BIRTHDAYS

Dick Gregory	1932
Perle Mesta	1891
Jean Nidetch	1923
Luciano Pavarotti	1935

OCTOBER
· 13 ·

You are a responsible, dedicated, no-nonsense person with above-average stubborn streaks. Your beauty, charm and wit are displayed too prominently or hidden at will. It takes a conscious effort for you to grow up. You take people and life too superficially or too seriously for your own good. Your motives are misunderstood until you speak up or tone down. There is no doubt that you intellectually will fight for your beliefs or put on a good show exemplifying them. At times you are unreasonable.

You worry too much or look for approval when you should be enjoying the pleasure others have in your pleasant company. Friends will help, if you let them. Your outer personality appears sour, brooding or unattractive when you lack self-approval. You are a competitor, a worker and an honorable person. Try to be subtle when you need attention.

Early years teach you to be independent and to stand on your own two feet. Mid-life offers down-to-earth, practical, managerial people who expect you to use your common sense. You have a tendency to sacrifice for the wrong causes or handle yourself too emotionally. You do not see halfway measures in anything that you attempt to do. The changes that affect your progress lead you to greater material success. It is the upheaval and alterations in your schemes that dissipate your energy. You are a problem solver and take on the projects that have defeated others. Mid-life acceptance of practical realities sweeps away childhood misconceptions or ideals, and you break with tradition. Late years offer companionship and privileges.

• OTHER OCTOBER 13 BIRTHDAYS

Lenny Bruce	1925
Laraine Day	1920
Herblock	1909
Lillie Langtry	1852
Yves Montand	1921
Pamela Tiffin	1942
Burr Tillstrom	1917
Virgil	70 B.C.
Robert Walker	1914
Cornell Wilde	1918

OCTOBER

· **14** ·

Experience is your best teacher. You love an adventure, a gamble and a sensual experience. It is the discipline instilled in youth that serves you well in mid-life. After age thirty expect the unexpected. All you can do is organize, manage and reorganize to manage the unconventional people and experiences that confront you as your life unfolds.

Early years are family and community oriented. You meet responsible, sympathetic and public-spirited people. They are geared to serving, comforting and upgrading themselves and their loved ones. You are an individual—a leader—who is part of a team. You learn to handle your own decisions and dislike to be dominated. Marriage, obligations, learning and teaching become part of your expectations in youth. You compromise for peace, and try to maintain an even disposition. Work and the fruits of your labors are your mainstay.

You aim for physical fitness, mental application and financial security. You don't need millions but enjoy breaking your workaholic drives if you can afford to be lazy. You want to improve yourself and learn quickly. A love affair in mid-life may attract public attention, but you overcome any threats to your security. You are not a spendthrift, although you like display and are self-promoting or entrepreneurish when you feel restless. Narrow-minded people confuse you. Sensationalists have a fascination that belies your traditional pose. You become too busy or too bored throughout your mid-life.

In late years love is disillusioning. You look for new challenges and fear the unknown, or rush forward impulsively.

• OTHER OCTOBER 14 BIRTHDAYS

Dwight David Eisenhower	1890
Lillian Gish	1896
John W. Dean III	1938
Roger Moore	1927

OCTOBER

· **15** ·

Ambition spurs you on to financial success. People help you, and you consider the world your family. Your inventiveness, enthusiasm and ability to make others feel comfortable attract gifts, admirers and protection. You are generous, affectionate and impulsive. In youth you may lack material possessions, but you learn to appreciate quality, beauty and professionalism.

You are too sexually active or too virginal in youth. Your experiences do not prepare you to have the domestic tranquility that you admire or desire. Too much or too little freedom to experiment makes you wary of the unknown. Until late in mid-life the standards set by your family guide your appraisals and decisions. You expect everyone to live up to their ideals.

You have obligations and responsibilities to family that endure. A practical, determined woman works for your ambitions. You strive to have a gracious life-style and are willing to sacrifice, work and minister to the needs of those you love. It is not in your nature to be treated unfairly without fighting back. There are limits to your ability to compromise for peace.

You want to be popular, create an image and are self-promotional. You are at your best when married to a spouse who accepts you with all your outrageous inconsistencies. You need praise and support for your untraditional ambitions in order to feel loved. In finance and intimate relationships you drive a hard bargain, may be thrifty and prefer dependent relationships.

Late in life you recognize the tolerance in others and you become less dogmatic and judgmental. If you have been treated unjustly earlier in life, the score is settled.

• OTHER OCTOBER 15 BIRTHDAYS

Ina Claire	1895
John Kenneth Galbraith	1908
Lee Iacocca	1924
Linda Lavin	1937
Mervyn LeRoy	1900
Jean Peters	1926
Mario Puzo	1921
Arthur Schlesinger	1917
John L. Sullivan	1858
Robert Trout	1908
P. G. Wodehouse	1881

OCTOBER

·16·

Few people have the material power, analytical capacity and ability to make progressive changes that you have. You have the ability to make your own fortune. You meet people and have experiences in youth to show you the way. It is important to the outcome of your destiny that you get an education or specialize in a career to use your self-confidence wisely. Any speculations, legal manipulations or lack of investigation results in disappointment. When you read the fine print, do your homework and examine your motives for practicality, you will do big things. Use your showmanship, magnetism and ESP.

You are a perfectionist and rarely get the cooperation from others to produce the end results for which you plan and work. You experience delays, which are beyond your control, and achieve a partial amount of the success that you anticipate. Even a share of your ambitions is more than the average person can expect to accomplish. As you get older, your reputation grows, and you experience financial and personal success.

Technical, scientific or spiritual interests help you to establish your authority. Musical talents, domestic attachments and strong personal ideals bolster you. In youth you are innovative, and too impatient. You get into a rut when you are impractical or overly ambitious. You stunt your growth with irrational fears of going it alone and ending in a pauper's grave. You sacrifice your privacy to love affairs. You work with your hands when you should counsel or set an example.

Later in life you find kindred spirits and form attachments. You have the stamina to travel and enlarge your scope.

• OTHER OCTOBER 16 BIRTHDAYS

David Ben-Gurion	1886
Linda Darnell	1921
William O. Douglas	1898
Günter Grass	1927
Angela Lansbury	1925
Eugene O'Neill	1888
Noah Webster	1785
Oscar Wilde	1854

OCTOBER
· 17 ·

If you speak up in youth and assert your independence, you'll save yourself the trouble of making explanations or proving you are one of a kind in mid-life. You are a born aristocrat and find yourself surrounded by the practical realities of survival as a youngster. Any problems are concealed, and your domestic environment is not what it appears to be. Parents are not inclined to intellectual analysis and may be more socially or emotionally focused. You want to know the "why" of everything and are ignored or not answered in depth.

As you mature, your mental, cultural and educational curiosity surfaces. You become less of a loner and more of an achiever. You have a head for money management and are set in your ideas. Real estate, minerals or any products that relate to the earth are fortunate for you. You have an athlete's sense of balance and the ability to practice to bring body, mind and spirit together when taking a challenge.

Legal and/or marital problems arise before you fully mature. You are quiet and restless in youth—unsure of where to place your physical, sensual and intellectual curiosity. In mid-life you meet businesslike, influential people and have the opportunity to change locations and to build for the future. You have the ability to concentrate and can analyze to apply yourself mentally and to see tangible results of your efforts. Money and independence are yours when your attitude is positive.

You are competitive and philosophical, and you travel far from your place of birth to late-life security. You love quality and work for quantity. You strive for perfection and to own your dreams.

• OTHER OCTOBER 17 BIRTHDAYS

William A. Anders	1948
Jean Arthur	1908
Jimmy Breslin	1933
Spring Byington	1893
Montgomery Clift	1927
Rita Hayworth	1928
Marsha Hunt	1917
Margot Kidder	19??
Arthur Miller	1915
Tom Poston	1930

OCTOBER
· 18 ·

You are wild and wonderful, unforgettable, business-like and inventive. Your mood swings and your life-styles are changable and fast paced. Foreign interests play a major role in your point of view and ambitions. In youth you strain for accomplishments or refuse to be competitive. It's one extreme or the other until you come to realize that you have a false sense of values. In mid-life you meet people and have experiences that demand a polish and skill of your performance. You change your focus, broaden your philosophy and accept your reality. Owing to your actions, money and power limit your freedom. Added responsibilities control your days and alter your prerogatives.

An inheritance of money, property or influence from a male relative is fortunate and burdensome. You labor to extend your perceptions to upgrade tastes or products that reach a universal audience or marketplace. If medicine, politics, the arts or welfare work beckon you, you will expect them to pay off. You are not inclined to live an "art for art's sake" existence or to give your talents away. Organization, efficiency and executive leadership are part of your character. After your thirtieth birthday you are inclined to be more liberal. However, you are an outspoken critic when emotionally triggered and plan your arguments after careful investigation, analysis and logic.

Engagements, marriage, partnerships and love do not mix with the loner aspects in your nature. The older you get, the more you are willing to be accommodating. You are more selective, empathetic and romantic in late years and have greater success as a spouse. You are destined to contribute to society.

• OTHER OCTOBER 18 BIRTHDAYS

Chuck Berry	1926
Miriam Hopkins	1902
Mike Todd, Jr.	1929
Sidney Kingsley	1906
Lotte Lenya	1900
Melina Mercouri	1923
Lee Harvey Oswald	1939
George C. Scott	1927
Pierre Elliott Trudeau	1919

OCTOBER

· 19 ·

Your greatest treasure is your independence. Throughout your life outside influences will challenge your individuality. In youth you are wise beyond your years and develop empathy, compassion and charity. Due to exposure to people who are emotionally generous or universally philosophical, or parents who are considerably older than average, you are called upon to be unnaturally mature. You learn to make sacrifices and unselfish decisions. The carefree childhood enjoyed by your peers is denied to you. However, you are ambitious, active and filled with ideas. In youth and mid-life you are a game player in search of peace, and you resort to self-indulgences as a balance.

Escapist devices are temptations, but you suffer when you get caught or lose your momentum. A concentrated work effort is necessary to comfort you through the times you fear losing your security. Unnecessary fears of poverty drive you to sacrifice comfort for progressive changes. Travel is not always enjoyed and becomes a burden if it is tied in to business. You experience petty jealousies or injustices that cause you to cover your activities, to be financially secretive and to maintain a low profile. You want love and are often naive in your affections.

In marriage, family and domestic issues you have difficulty with your mother or sister. Burdens may deplete your resources. But you are capable of earning whatever you need, or you have funds available when you are willing to assume obligations. After your late twenties you stabilize. You are stubborn, set in your viewpoint and domesticated. You continue to strive to increase your income, improve your life-style and donate to your community.

• OTHER OCTOBER 19 BIRTHDAYS

Jack Anderson	1922
Peter Max	1937
Lewis Mumford	1895

OCTOBER
· **20** ·
Your tact, diplomacy and gentleness go a long way to contribute to your success. Love, partnerships and friends are your mainstays. It is your attention to the minute details that elude others that focuses attention on your talent to be the glue that holds families, organizations and productions together. After learning to stand on your own two feet in youth, working with others is a snap in mid-life. You are able to take a subtle leadership role and rarely reveal your personal ambitions.

You are a quick study and may have a photographic memory. Your ability to amass and coordinate data allows you to build a mental and physical library that stands you in good stead into late years. In youth you develop social graces, communications skills and a variety of areas for self-expression. You want an easygoing home life, are a cooperative mate and prefer to marry early. You plan and set the stage to encourage your interests in music, theater and people who add sparkle, wit and beauty to your life.

You are cooperative, sympathetic and not given to manual labor. You are a good manager, and strive to keep your temper, worries and impatience in check. You have a taste for instant gratification in youth, but as you develop your individuality, the strain to be a competitive, innovative winner subsides. You have a desire for approval from your father or your male authority figure as a tot. You are intimidated too easily or are too egocentric as a result. After age forty-six your own authority is established. You improve upon your original goals and relax.

Later years are calmer and may be dull by earlier standards.

• OTHER OCTOBER 20 BIRTHDAYS

Joyce Brothers	1928
Art Buchwald	1925
Arlene Francis	1908
Will Rogers, Jr.	1911
Bela Lugosi	1882
Wayne Morse	1900
Ellery Queen	1905

OCTOBER **·21·** You are friendly, sociable and sensitive. It is your greatest pleasure to surround yourself with beauty, to spread good news and to use imaginative means of self-expression. In youth you are close to your mother and may be spoiled or a chronic attention-getter. As you mature, your wit, talents and interest in trivia are material assets. You never lose your attention to the little things and have an eye for details. The arts, music and people with outstanding personalities interest you. In fact, you get a kick out of phoning to chat, dressing up to look attractive and just plain living each day.

You are optimistic to a fault, and your childlike delight is all too often squelched by businesslike necessities. You are a natural leader—a self-starter—and assume or are given positions of authority. You want love, children, pets, friends and to know everyone and everything. Work and constructive planning are part of your childhood programming. You are capable of practicing to achieve results, using your physical dexterity, determination and orderliness. Sports, bodily fitness and diet concern you. It is in your best interests to remember that your body is the house of your spirit, to maintain a health regimen and to avoid feasting on fad, fast or fattening foods.

You like games and may consider your credo to be: "He who has the most toys wins." In mid-life you must come to grips with your tendency to be shy, uncertain or modest or to humble yourself needlessly. When you learn to say no and still feel worthy, you are on your way to being yourself. In late years you are less temperamental, lose your inferiority complex and relax.

• OTHER OCTOBER 21 BIRTHDAYS

Samuel Taylor Coleridge	1772
Whitey Ford	1928
Dizzy Gillespie	1917
Manfred Mann	1940
Georg Solti	1912
Benjamin West	1738

OCTOBER

·22·

You are a stickler for orderliness, routines and material accomplishments. Flights of fancy, dramatics or superficiality should be applied to your career, hobbies or business. You tend to become too imaginative when your emotions are triggered and waste your energy talking too much or feigning antisocial behavior. Love relationships suffer when you punish others with your silence, extend the bounds of truth or refuse to read between the lines. You have exceptional powers of intuition. It is in your best interests to rise above childlike judgments, to concentrate your efforts and to take an optimistic approach.

In youth unconventional, entrepreneurish, freedom-loving people cross your path. Your experiences are nonroutine, changable and often surprising. Although you learn to accept untraditional aspects of life through experience, a work pattern based upon hands-on productivity and personal ideals is established. You are a dynamic workaholic and apply unorthodox methods to achieve tangible results, when others fail to see solutions.

You expect to take pride in your home, spouse, children, pets and community. Frequent quiet, serious moments are required for you to refurbish your energy. Your elemental nature is sweet, cooperative and easygoing. When your guidelines for a proper life are disturbed, you are rule-bound, bossy and will not be disputed. People who know you intimately should recognize an emotional breaking point when you exhibit intolerant, take-over behavior. If you do not save, invest or contribute, to leave a lasting benefit, you feel unfulfilled in late years.

• OTHER OCTOBER 22 BIRTHDAYS

Constance Bennett	1905
Catherine Deneuve	1943
Joan Fontaine	1917
Annette Funicello	1942
Timothy Leary	1920
Franz Liszt	1811
Giovanni Martinelli	1885
Dory Previn	1925
Joseph Welch	1890
N. C. Wyeth	1882

OCTOBER

·23·

Unusual places and people are attractive to you. You never get old, lose your engaging personality or stop demanding your freedom. You can sell, promote and charm your way into any career or love affair. You are a collector, and you strive for financial success. You have a few impulsive, boredom-induced compulsions that lead to setbacks. But if you can keep your emotions out of your business activities, you've got it made.

In youth you exhibit dedicated or traditional work habits. You have a down-to-earth family background and observe the common-sense material standards and practical economy that are expected of you. The restlessness that you feel is displaced by your versatility, curiosity and changable activities. After age thirty you are less inclined to conventional behavior, daily routines and assuming self-limiting obligations. You take on adventurous or speculative interests that help you learn about the less predictable aspects of people. All cultures, ethnic groups and foreigners relate to you. It is in your best interests to capitalize on your sex appeal, amusing ideas and quick thinking.

You are lucky, clever and destined to have an entertaining, challenging, mentally-physically stimulating life. However, you are inclined to self-indulgence and irresponsibility. When your enthusiasms and regular office hours conflict, you forget the big picture of your long-term goals until experience teaches you to use self-discipline. Your technical, social and salt-of-the-earth approach helps you to maintain your self-sufficiency and self-confidence. In mid-life you assume many burdens in the name of love. Later years are provided for and fascinating.

• OTHER OCTOBER 23 BIRTHDAYS

Sarah Bernhardt	1844
Johnny Carson	1925
Michael Crichton	1942
James Daly	1918
Diana Dors	1931
Pelé	1940
Chi Chi Rodriguez	1935

OCTOBER

·**24**·

You are domestically inclined, absorb information through your powers of observation and have a flair for financial or people manipulating. Real estate, banking and service businesses are fortunate career choices if you do not choose to express your love of beauty in an art form. You have a flair for dramatic interpretation and enlarge upon your emotional experiences. Overeating, drinking or self-indulgence in sensual pleasures are danger signals that indicate your feelings of frustration. You must remain active or you hurt yourself by wasting your energy.

You give your all for love or the perfection of your investigations and education. You alternate between aloofness and total involvements. In youth family requires personal sacrifices. You are restless and learn to avoid impulsive experimentations the hard way. You are too virginal or too promiscuous—too busy or too bored—too mental or too cerebral until mid-life.

You settle down to responsibilities and should marry young to instigate a life-style that is based upon your personal idealism. From your teen years to your forties, you learn or teach, assume obligations and provide comfort for loved ones. Musical, decorating and community service aspects are near to your heart. People appreciate your sympathetic, nurturing, hardworking approach. Even when you are at your lowest ebb, you remain friendly and helpful and are easily forgiven any thoughtless words or indifferent actions of the moment.

In later years your intellectual and introspective personality traits increase. You are firmly established.

• OTHER OCTOBER 24 BIRTHDAYS

Tito Gobbi	1915
Moss Hart	1904
Sera Jurinac	1921
William Penn	1644
Sonny Terry	1911
Bill Wyman	1941

OCTOBER ·25· In youth you meet the wheelers and dealers and observe how ambitious, purposeful, self-confident challengers operate. Family or domestic relationships are close knit but inharmonious. You are restless, intuitive and hide your feelings. You have legal or difficult-to-see or -diagnose problems surrounding you. You have an unusual childhood and in later years relate to inconsistencies and reflect upon your experiences as a guide to making mature decisions. Education is a necessity for your analytic, investigative, perfectionist nature. You may lack the thick skin required to be a loner in a socially materialistic crowd.

You feel like a fish out of water surrounded by businesslike, competitive, affluent youths. You are a late bloomer. Until you identify your expertise, you make attempts at different interests to keep yourself afloat. You do not organize or concentrate. Diversification and love interests keep you vascillating, idealistic and expectant. Until you become aware of your sensitivity to details, adaptability to changing conditions and environments and ability to sell yourself with authority, you bottle up your problems and suffer silently.

Partnerships in romantic relationships are difficult at best. You crave affection and an easygoing, independent private life. You are unconventional, adventurous and take your chances with foreigners or offbeat causes. You want the respect of your peers and the money due your professionalism. You have a droll sense of humor, insist upon having your way and are calculating into your comfortable, secure and private late years.

• OTHER OCTOBER 25 BIRTHDAYS

Georges Bizet	1838
Richard E. Byrd	1888
Anthony Franciosa	1928
Johann Strauss, Jr.	1825
Minnie Pearl	1912
Pablo Picasso	1881
Helen Reddy	1941

OCTOBER
·26·
You are creative, businesslike, talented and able to commercialize on yourself in a big way. You are involved with parents or the family image. You have universal appeal, harmonize with people and match your courage, stamina and physical agility with experts in youth. Your spirituality, personality and adaptability are tapped. You are surrounded by inventive, ambitious, impatient individualists. Perfection and introspection are demanded, and you fear losing love, friends and financial security in silence. You are a loner in a crowd.

You travel culturally and are wise beyond your years. You are inclined to relate to adults and to feel detached from childish frivolities. There is identification with notables, people who demand quality, skill and recognition for giving outstanding performances and having universal appeal. You meet people as authority figures. You are disillusioned, disappointed and disconnected from emotional responsiveness. Popularity or money decreases. Only the facade is recognized. You do not relate to human frailty or mundane realities. Standards are set too high, and you must reestablish midlife practical values.

Money can be earned, although a lack of education may interfere. Business relationships with friends cause problems and legalities. An older or insistent woman increases your difficulties. Just like the cavalry in a Western movie, a male saves the day. He gets you into a productive business and restores your security. You reestablish domestic comforts and self-esteem. Later years are wiser. You find companionship, inspiration to study and collect long overdue money or credit.

• OTHER OCTOBER 26 BIRTHDAYS

Lynn Anderson	1945
Jackie Coogan	1914
Eugene Ionesco	1912
Mahalia Jackson	1911
Rich Little	1935
Domenico Scarlatti	1685

OCTOBER

·27·

Recognition is given to you for public service, you are a respected humanitarian and set an example of determination and true grit in late years. In early years your physical stamina, competitiveness and material ambitions are challenged. Your courage is tested, and you are plagued with chronic personal problems and seem to carry the load for everyone in a highly competitive society.

You are passionate in your beliefs, a romantic, philosophical, loyal sensitive. You have difficulty in intimate relationships owing to concerns that take you away from home. Your domestic happiness is short-lived, with dry spells in between. Legal or technical intricacies cost you time, money and energy in mid-life. You have difficulty when you set another person on a pedestal. When he or she falls from grace, you must reestablish your ambitions. You walk in another's footsteps early in life, until, through erratic behavior, cooperativeness and genuine selflessness, your individuality commands respect.

Foreign travel and expansive philosophies broaden your scope. Healing, counseling and teaching help you to overcome personal losses. You are not overly concerned with money, but the power and freedom that affluence implies are important to your long-term goals. Family—the actions of your relatives—create some of your problems. You do not like to be dominated, are temperamental and react forcefully.

Leadership comes naturally. Stability is uncertain in later years. You respond to intellectual and emotionally stimulating golden age romances. Work may be your helpmate far from home.

• OTHER OCTOBER 27 BIRTHDAYS

Jack Carson	1910
Ruby Dee	1924
Leif Erickson	1911
Nanette Fabray	1922
Melba Moore	1945
Niccolò Paganini	1782
Emily Post	1872
Theodore Roosevelt	1858
Jonas Salk	1914
Isaac Singer	1811
Teresa Wright	1918

OCTOBER

·28·

In mid-life, after attracting attention for your individuality, making yourself a sought-after success, you travel far from your birthright. You attract unconventional relationships and may marry for intellectual stimulation, privacy or to perfect your early aspirations. You are inclined to halt your changeable ambitions for a peck on the cheek and a touch of intimacy from a loved one. Stubbornness, tenacity and inventiveness surface in your personality in childhood. You are impatient with trifles and prefer to deal with the major issues. You find it difficult to stay with an accomplishment after you initiate or instigate the concept and lose the opportunity to live by your laurels.

It is in your best interests to ignore back-biting, calm your restlessness and be tactful when self-assertive. You cannot have instant gratification. You may be full of ideas and a trendsetter. However, modesty provides subtle controls and you may get more flies with honey than with vinegar.

You are generous, empathetic and unselfish with loved ones and when it serves your material interests. When you realize that submerging your personality was not appreciated, you become a formidable adversary. You are a wonderful lover and exhibit the spirit of brotherly love in friendships. You want to see others succeed and are cooperative, diplomatic and sensitive to their needs. Money and awards are earned during your lifetime.

Later you have an intelligent partner, take supportive roles when it is prudent and lack a business education. You may not know how to add or subtract, but you can afford your desires.

• OTHER OCTOBER 28 BIRTHDAYS

Edith Head	1907
Elsa Lanchester	1902
Suzy Parker	1933
Joan Plowright	1929
Evelyn Waugh	1903

OCTOBER

·29·

You know the pitfalls, foibles and practical problems that accompany the object of your affections, but you blunder in, remain loyal and submit to personal sacrifices. You meet sociable, self-expressive and imaginative personalities in youth. You develop an eye for beauty, skillfulness and quality. You are a convincing salesperson when your talents and personal ideals are concerned. Leadership positions are offered by people who live by their own rules. In mid-life you may bring great honor or disdain upon yourself and your supporters.

As a tot, you want approval from your father. If he is absent, too austere or too doting, you do not establish appropriate habits of expressing your independence, assertiveness or aggressiveness. You are a "good child" until you break from submissiveness to become an extremist. Your loves, hates, joys, sorrows are experienced in living color. You are high-strung, nervous and constantly making decisions. You see all sides of an issue and have difficulty deciding whom to please: yourself or your intimates.

Home, family and companions are important to you. Friends and boosters support your ambitions. You need a clear-cut line of work, or a commitment, to slow your moodiness and to take your mind off yourself. You may become a fanatic or appear absentminded when obsessed with your desire for reform. You are a compelling, futuristic or critical speaker or performer.

Late years may be spent in service to humanity or learning humility. You are protected, need not fear fighting for survival and enjoy a friendship based upon brotherly love.

• OTHER OCTOBER 29 BIRTHDAYS

Fanny Brice	1891
Richard Dreyfuss	1947
John Keats	1795
Bill Mauldin	1921
Percy Westmore	1904

OCTOBER

· 30 ·

Your practical training, self-expressive personality, youthful charm and enthusiasm may make you a legend in your own time. Women serve your purposes well, while sensitive men enjoy your companionship and support your talents. You are inclined to be modest and gentle, and lack aggressiveness as a tot. You want to be the apple of mother's eye and may be spoiled or ignored. In youth and mid-life you want satisfaction and exert your charm, imaginative presentations and childlike youthfulness to overcome obstacles. You look delicate and work to become strong.

Others may think you naive or too rule-bound. But you sense that you must labor, practice and assign routines to gain strength to achieve your ambitions. You apply conventional methods to satisfy your desires. You need to concentrate and will get help from social relationships. The mail, phone and all means of communications are fortunate for you. A lost love in youth may alter the course of your ambitions and life's work.

You are at your best attracting attention as a loner. You take the spotlight when you are a free spirit and able to take on adventures. It is the results of your mundane birthright and down-to-earth honesty that attract late-life applause and financial security. After age fifty you travel, take on untraditional challenges and lose your fears and humbleness. You ask youself, "Who am I?" and stop playing cat and mouse.

At fourteen or seventy you are the eternal optimist. You see sunshine when others see rain. In late years your sparkle never fades, and the party begins when you arrive on the scene.

- OTHER OCTOBER 30 BIRTHDAYS

JoHN AdAms	1735
CHARLES ATLAS	1893
CHRISTOPHER Columbus	1451
Fred W. FRiendly	1915
RUTH CORdON	1896
RUTH Hussey	1914
EzRA Pound	1885
HENRy WinklER	1945

OCTOBER **· 31 ·** You are a lover, a competitor and an original. Imagination, inventiveness and optimism are your mainstays. In youth you meet untraditional, daring, mentally curious people. Your life is unpredictable, and you learn to cope with the unknown. Experience teaches you to be adaptable, self-promotional and mentally curious. Opportunities are offered that allow you to present original ideas to listening ears. You dare to have the courage of your own convictions. Your lifelong battle to have pride in yourself, your ideals upheld and to take actions to change the conditions that challenge your own beliefs begins before your are thirty.

In mid-life you find that your creative thoughts are not always appreciated. People prefer the old order, and your radical changes, fresh approach and personal aspirations fill your days with setbacks, defeats and a feeling of nonfulfillment. You are kind, generous and naive. As productive, practical and down to earth as you may be in some ways, you are not materialistic or financially businesslike. Your appearance is an asset. Your versatility, charm and social consciousness are characteristics that you display intermittently. You are too superficial or too serious until you become emotionally secure.

Marriage or an intimate relationship is necessary for your stability. You want children, pets and beauty in your surroundings. If you marry in youth, your sense of responsibility will be tried, but you benefit overall.

In late years you are beloved. If frustrated by finance and/or powerful people, you reflect upon foolish past actions.

• OTHER OCTOBER 31 BIRTHDAYS

Michael Collins	1930
Dale Evans	1912
Barbara Bel Geddes	1922
Lee Grant	1930
Chiang Kai-shek	1886
Michael Landon	1936
Alfred Nobel	1833
Jane Pauley	1950
Dan Rather	1931
Ethel Waters	1900
Christopher Wren	1632

NOVEMBER

· 1 ·

Decisions, decisions, decisions! From childhood to late years you weigh, measure and, dramatically, come to your inventive conclusions. You meet entertaining, attractive, versatile people as a tot, who recognize your individuality. You learn about fashion, fun and freedom of speech. Mixing business with pleasure in mid-life comes easily. You incorporate your subtle controls with a dollop of the modesty, humility and diplomacy you absorbed in youth. Until you reach your late twenties your independence is sheltered. Once you get going on your quest to establish and build your unique personality, there's no stopping you.

You need to be first—a winner—and make progressive changes in order to live up to your ambitions. Leaders, innovators and other pioneers recognize you as a conductor of your own band of followers. You are often lonely, frustrated and stubbornly self-defeating. However, each time you begin a project, you skillfully establish your reputation as a person set apart from the throng. After you channel yourself and concentrate on developing your skills and talents, your dependent notions become a thing of the past. You learn not to take no for an answer. You benefit from planning ahead before you contradict.

Finances and loves go to extremes. You prefer an easygoing lifestyle at home and action in career or outside interests. It is unlikely that as a youth you insisted on the education that you need in maturity. Mid-life finds you constantly seeking knowledge. In late years you are capable of managing your own material affairs, need public contact and are philanthropic.

• OTHER NOVEMBER 1 BIRTHDAYS

Victoria de los Angeles	1924
Stephen Crane	1871
Betsy Palmer	1926
Gary Player	1935
Grantland Rice	1880

NOVEMBER

·2·

You never get adequate compensation or the credit due for your concentrated hard work. You do receive love and cooperation and find yourself far from your roots late in life. Partners and mates support your inspirational ideas. You have a strong female influence as a tot and are receptive to working with or confiding in women. Sacrifices were asked of you in youth that cause your education to be delayed or you to be indecisive. You develop determination and a knack for dealing with details as you enter maturity. As a youth, you meet people who do not obey the rules and feel set above the crowd. You tend to feel restricted by your down-to-earth background.

During midlife you are not opposed to sharing or letting another take the spotlight. You want to associate with intelligent peers and have little patience for ignorance, slowness or disloyalty. Family and loved ones take all your emotional energy or none at all. You are tightfisted with money or careless. You give the reins to assistants or assume full charge. You may be domineering. The intensity of your extremes make you difficult to understand, and your friendships decrease in late years. If you remain modest, relax fears about money and invest for long-term results, security is assured.

Late years are more easygoing. You have fewer ups and downs, and after your late forties work is financially fruitful. An investment or inheritance is helpful in a trying time but does not change your standard of living or ambitions. You are sensitive, poetic, nervous and slightly absentminded and must avoid the physical strains that result from moodiness.

• OTHER NOVEMBER 2 BIRTHDAYS

Queen Marie Antoinette	1755
Daniel Boone	1734
Paul Ford	1901
Warren G. Harding	1865
Burt Lancaster	1913
James Knox Polk	1795
Ann Rutherford	1917

NOVEMBER

· 3 ·

Reflect upon your humble beginnings and dreams of fame as a youth when you stretch your self-expression to meet success in maturity. Your high nervous energy, daydreaming and sensitivity as a tot make you a difficult child. You are submissive or too independent and confuse yourself and parents. Father was too caring, authoritative or absent in childhood, and you seek approval for your ideas and try too hard to please until you recognize your individuality.

Your upbringing is untraditional, changable and nonroutine. You are not prepared for the experiences that you face alone. You become adaptable, apply yourself and learn to understand human nature. Mistakes in judgment are corrected with hard work, detail consciousness and your engaging personality. Concentration is the key to your success. When you diversify your many talents, you scatter energy, time and money in mid-life.

After you get the restlessness out of your system, lose your gullibility and travel through diversified life-styles, you are capable of overcoming your disappointments in love, finance and business dealings. Variety is truly the spice of your existence. You enjoy pleasing loved ones and appreciate beauty, humor and entertainment. Writing, speaking, music and all forms of communications are lucky for you. The phone and mail bring in life-altering information and are a mainstay of your social contacts. Business and pleasure combine in later years.

You are inclined to dramatics and overexcesses. Be cautious. You have a destiny that makes your dreams come true.

• OTHER NOVEMBER 3 BIRTHDAYS

Vincenzo Bellini	1801
Charles Bronson	1923
William Cullen Bryant	1794
Bob Feller	1918
Terrence McNally	1939

NOVEMBER

·4·

Home, family and the obligations and traditions that accompanied the love in your childhood are the mainstays of your reflections in late years. You are a diligent, down-to-earth, pragmatic person. Productivity is important to your emotional well-being. You are a technician and have physical dexterity. You use your hands in your work and may play the piano, engage in a professional sport or do well putting your vivid imagination to manufacturing an artistic product. You feel different as a tot and aspire to live up to your personal ideals.

Female influences are important in your life. They incite you to anger easily or are your main support for self-esteem. Approval from mother is eagerly sought in youth, and you are doted upon or ignored. As you mature, you become less self-conscious, but you never lose your focus upon the little details, your concern for the comfortless attention-getting people or your humility. You are economical when your desire for perfection is not involved. You are a planner, a saver and when pressed into self-imposed deadlines, a workaholic. It is your intention to be constructive and to produce tangible results.

Your personal philosophy is realistic and sets standards that are followed by admirers. You appear solid and sure but feel indecisive or critical. You introvert your problems or disillusionments. Love and partnership are not what you envisioned, but you adapt yourself because you or they are dependent. You are self-protective and quietly secure for old age, although money is unstable throughout your productive years. You need peace to establish or invent your own Shangri-la.

- OTHER NOVEMBER 4 BIRTHDAYS

Martin Balsam	1919
Art Carney	1918
Walter Cronkite	1916
Paul Douglas	1907
Cameron Mitchell	1918
Will Rogers	1879
Pauline Trigère	1912
Gig Young	1917

NOVEMBER

· **5** ·

You combine the introspective questions of your youth with your compulsion to try everything at least once. Through a concentrated effort you acquire a technical, scientific or spiritual expertise as you grow to maturity. Your loner years, filled with alternately adoring or ignoring family, produce a challenging and free-spirited personality in mid-life. Quiet, soft-spoken and sensual one moment and a nonstop, fabricating, antisocial being the next, you are destined for an unconventional, adventurous and experimental life-style.

You are an attention-getter, and your actions or interests make you a catalyst for change in other people's lives. Sex, travel and new enthusiasms interest you. You bore easily and rarely stay interested in one job, love or place too long. You scatter time, money and energy until you find the person who is comfortable with your often inexhaustible curiosity, physical explorations and unexpected changableness. You are clever, quick-witted and funny when you want to let down your hair. Too much seriousness or too much superficiality is not good for you.

You tackle a variety of business or financial interests and are your own best advertisement. Flatterers cause you problems. You must be experienced to be appreciated. You love a farm but are not geared to do the milking after once trying it. You are classy, aloof, earthy, partnership-oriented, individualistic, impatient, adaptable, perfecting, optimistic, careful and a quick study. Sound impossible? People will comment on your chameleonlike personality. You must exercise emotional self-control. In late years you play, work and enjoy land profits.

• OTHER NOVEMBER 5 BIRTHDAYS

Will Durant	1885
Art Garfunkel	1941
Vivien Leigh	1913
Donald Madden	1933
Jeb Stuart Magruder	1935
Joel McCrea	1906
Tatum O'Neal	1963
Roy Rogers	1912
Elke Sommer	1941

NOVEMBER

· 6 ·

You may be considered a child prodigy or just unusual. However, you know that you are special. In youth businesslike, ambitious, affluent people surround you. Whether your family has financial freedom or not, you do not learn how to conserve your money. You observe the planning, effort and courage that "big business" profits demand, but until you reach maturity you do not take actions based upon your fears of old age dependency or material insecurity.

You like to make a display and find that only structure, routine and common sense investments pay off. Mother or a rule-bound teacher limited your actions as a tot. You resent orderliness, traditions and practicality or are too rigid in your self-disciplines as a result of the relationship. In your forties too little relaxation or too many vacations have had an effect upon your domestic, business and personal happiness. You make an effort to reorganize your attitude toward your workaholic tendencies or laziness.

Peace, music and beauty are important in your life. The burden of parents, children and your willingness to volunteer to help strays or less capable people strains your energy, emotions and ego. You have a parental nature, a talent for producing group efforts and showmanship. You provide for the comfort of others before your own. An overflowing cupboard, good food cooking on the stove and goose-down-stuffed easy chairs make your home a refuge and retreat. You have come far from your place of birth, and it delights you to feel pride in your community.

You deserve and receive a well-earned rest in late years.

- OTHER NOVEMBER 6 BIRTHDAYS

Ray Conniff	1916
Sally Field	1946
Edsel Ford	1893
Gus Kahn	1886
Francis Lederer	1906
Mike Nichols	1931
John Philip Sousa	1854

NOVEMBER

· 7 ·

You are a stickler for details that improve the quality of your work, love relationships and intellectual investigations. Intuition is your mainstay. You are at your best when acting on your first impressions. You are a rule-breaker and a voice for untraditional thinkers. In youth you were surrounded by elitists who felt themselves more creative, spiritual or idealistic than average. It was expected that you would be a unique individualist, too... and you are.

Climb the highest mountain or reach the farthest shore and you still will not be satified with your accomplishments. It is in your best interests to have an education, specialty or field of concentration. You speak with authority and need a background that gives you credentials. Money is a source of trouble if your ambitions are materialistic. Delays, complications and family obligations tie you to fears of poverty. It is your intention to work to serve the public, and your long periods of isolation have humanitarian results.

It is difficult for you to adapt or compromise. You are your own severe critic. When you play devil's advocate, you are misunderstood. You have a unique approach to solving problems and will find supporters if you bother to explain.

In mid-life you are a loner on a crusade. You experience difficult-to-understand or -diagnose legal, technical or scientific problems. When you are introspective, associates cannot communicate with you. When you are crusading for your strong personal beliefs, you cannot be kept quiet. Late years are secure. But you ponder: could you have accomplished more?

• OTHER NOVEMBER 7 BIRTHDAYS

Captain James Cook	1728
Marie Curie	1867
Billy Graham	1918
Al Hirt	1922
Joni Mitchell	1943
Johnny Rivers	1942
Joan Sutherland	1926
Leon Trotsky	1879

NOVEMBER

· **8** ·

Family relationships and traditions stay with you. You may travel, be individualistic and establish your own financial security, but childhood domestic influences leave you with a permanent set of personal ideals and a firm backbone. You are high-strung, nervous and inspired to follow your star in youth. Money, power and the freedom to enjoy them are available to you between your twenty-eighth and fifty-sixth birthdays. In later years you reap what you have sown in your youth.

You are a survivor and learn not to depend upon others to obtain your personal ambitions. Rich or poor, as a tot, you feel special and have a dreamy quality that lights your way. In mid-life you rub shoulders with affluent, influential, businesslike people. You are a self-starter, self-confident and ready to take on all challengers to your ability to handle your own affairs. Efficiency, organization and fair leadership are your policies. You have emotional control where finance is concerned. You take on large projects and prefer to deal only with major issues. Patience is not a virtue when you are confronted with slowness or stupidity. You expect to be adequately paid for your talents.

You are an adaptable, easygoing, modest pussycat when you are in love. You manage your domestic or romantic responsibilities with the same courage, intensity and sacrifice that you give your material ambitions. When others disagree with your opinions, you are a stubborn adversary. Once you see the right of an argument, you become a dedicated, overzealous convert.

In late years you move, enjoy a mature love and are secure.

- OTHER NOVEMBER 8 BIRTHDAYS

Christian Barnard	1922
Bucky Harris	1896
June Havoc	1916
Katharine Hepburn	1909
Jerome Hines	1921
Margaret Mitchell	1900
Patti Page	1927

NOVEMBER
· 9 ·
Expect recognition in your youth, and to have the home problems that accompany a rising star. You aspire to fulfill your dreams and have extremes of depression and heights of joy. You are stimulated enough by your aspirations, cultural expansions and personal philosophical probings. You face conflicting opinions with unreasonable rationales— arguments—if you drink, take drugs, gamble or aim to escape your obligations. You break away from early irrational fears as you mature. In mid-life you are reborn. You reach out of your self-absorption to bring a polish, skill and improved quality of yourself to your ambitions.

Marriage and a stable family life-style are difficult, although you love your home, children and community. You have an exceptional storehouse of inborn information and imagine that you remember things that you have never experienced. You will leave a lasting image that people will remember after you are gone.

Social contact is the answer to your loneliness. In a crowd, with the warmth of surrounding family or with considerate partners, you feel a sense of isolation or disconnection. Love or recognition come to you from afar, in swarms of respect for your magnetic personality, owing to your adaptability or because you are broadminded, empathetic and volunteer to serve.

Legal dealings are not kind to you. The letter of the law does not consider your interpretation of brotherly love. You are too skeptical or too gullible and pay the piper. There are losses and profits, and you have the facility to live by your wits. In late years debts are paid. You are soul-satisfied, at peace.

• OTHER NOVEMBER 9 BIRTHDAYS

Spiro Agnew	1918
James Boswell	1740
Marie Dressler	1869
Hedy Lamarr	1915
Edna Oliver	1883
Sargent Shriver	1915
Tom Weiskopf	1942
Ed Wynn	1886

NOVEMBER

· 10 ·

You are smooth, sensitive and adaptable as a quiet, unassuming youth. Intimate relationships are profitable, emotionally and creatively rewarding. The opportunities you have to be inventive, personally ambitious and individually active are limited by your submissiveness to the male authority figures in childhood. You form a partnership or tie your aspirations to a peer. Diplomacy, tact and cooperation are required, and you feel frustration and angers that are difficult to repress.

In mid-life your originality surfaces. Money or financial interests are protected by admirers, lovers or the assistance of friends. You are stubborn, opinionated and often egocentric. You have a logical approach and use your mind when making decisions. You inject active energy and attract supporters for your progressive ideas. You travel and have extraordinary self-confidence. You influence a wide scope of people and their culture or concepts. You are an individual. Any surprising changes that you encounter are the product of your subconscious need to alter or upgrade your direction, companions or goals.

In mid-life your efficiently tackle many things at one time. It is unfortunate that you are extremely possessive and feel that you have the right to exclusivity in relationships. You want a mate, pride in your home, but do not want the emotional and practical details of domesticity to interfere with your mental pursuits... and you are self-insistent.

In late years you want to share your knowledge and work with an aspiring and kindred spirit. You have a challenge to follow elitist motives but lapse into material or sensual diversions.

• OTHER NOVEMBER 10 BIRTHDAYS

Richard Burton	1925
Tommy Dorsey	1905
Jane Froman	1917
J. P. Marquand	1893
MacKenzie Phillips	1959
Claude Rains	1890
Roy Scheider	1935
David Stockman	1946

NOVEMBER

· 11 ·

You have a knack for appearing to be down to earth, when in reality your visualizations and aspirations are often geared to specialized interests, impractical or costly. There is a "right" way and there is your way... both are the same. You have innovative ideas and personal ideals, which you follow and anticipate will be inspirational and attractive to others. It would not occur to you that you may be inconsiderate, snobbish or unrealistic. Your talents, magnetism and intuition are destined to leave a lasting impression. In this life you are faced with chronic details that relate to the law, economics and human frailty. You attract fame by helping or hurting the public.

In youth, people and experiences are conventional, materially oriented and applied to physical disciplines. You are expected to be emotionally understanding, wise or "street smart." It is necessary for you to sacrifice aspects of your childhood to appear to be or to actually perform with maturity. Mundane occupations are available, but you feel "special" and may elect religion, the military, theater arts or any job or means to getting yourself and future ambitions on an aristocratic level.

By mid-life you are either an uplifting leader, teacher and humanitarian public servant or you may take your exceptional ability to guide others into servitude or illegalities. You make your own rules but may put the right circumstances and people together to create new regulations based upon your judgments.

Your loves and hates are dramatic and intense. Companionship is desired but, to be enduring, must be with people that share your temperament and unique philosophy.

• OTHER NOVEMBER 11 BIRTHDAYS

Fyodor Dostoyevski	1821
Howard Fast	1914
Alger Hiss	1904
Lucky Luciano	1897
Pat O'Brien	1899
George Patton	1885
Robert Ryan	1909
Sam Spiegel	1901
Kurt Vonnegut	1922
Jonathan Winters	1925

NOVEMBER

· 12 ·

As a youth, you meet untraditional people and have experiences that add adaptability, cleverness and human understanding to your independent, personally idealistic and charming personality. You develop a specialized philosophy that enables you to walk with kings and talk about cabbages or work with laborers and talk about aristocrats. You are enthusiastic, diplomatic and inventive. Your youth is influenced by a doting and/or domineering male—or the lack of an assertive parent—and you leave the nest before you are able to control your feelings of submissiveness or egocentricity.

You can sell anything because you can sell yourself. You are at your best when mixing pleasure and business. The expression of your talents covers all means of communications. You are a good conversationalist, entertainer and party-giver or goer. The way you talk, dress, decorate your home or style your handwriting creates your image. It is your capacity to be welcomed by down-to-earth, conventional, hardworking people and to offer imaginative solutions to mundane problems that makes you different.

You want companionship and should marry an older or extremely mature person who gives you the space to feed your restless mind and active body and bolster your optimism. Trouble finds you if you flirt or take your responsibilities lightly. You find a cause or crusade that channels your concentration and offers you the opportunity to express your high ideals, social consciousness or artistic gifts. You want to be a success.

If you have planned wisely, you travel, maintain a lively life-style and enjoy domestic dividends later in life.

- OTHER NOVEMBER 12 BIRTHDAYS

Benvenuto Cellini	1500
Kim Hunter	1922
Grace Kelly	1929
Charles Manson	1934
Jack Oakie	1903
Stefanie Powers	1942
Al Schacht	1894
Elizabeth Cady Stanton	1815

NOVEMBER

· 13 ·

As often as you make plans and see them through to a rewarding result, the rug gets pulled out from your secure life-style. Each surprising upheaval—and the steps that you take to reconstruct your life—places you on a higher social or economic level. It's your fight to stay afloat that demands dedication, stamina and independence. However, you are able to commercialize on your talents and to attract friendships that place you in prominent positions to attract attention outside of your domestic environments.

You will not be limited by ordinary ambitions as a youth. Family is behind you, and the personal ideals that govern your childhood last through your lifetime. You are encouraged, by a domineering or neurotically sensitive maternal female, to be self-concerned and accommodating. You are spoiled or easily depressed until you see tangible results of your own work. You uphold traditions, assume obligations and aspire to have a comfortable, opulent home.

You may be a fanatic and too obsessed with your personal interests. These excursions into zealous enthusiasm often prove to be impractical, cloistering and expensive. You learn to be discerning, to calm your disenchantment or discontent in mid-life, when your peace of mind is disturbed.

Your stubborn attitudes and preoccupation with your ambitions make others think that you are not deeply touched or affectionate. You are often misunderstood and judged by your temperament and not your actions until you relax in late years. Travel, companionship and baubles are your golden age treasures.

• OTHER NOVEMBER 13 BIRTHDAYS

Linda Christian	1924
Jean Seberg	1938
Robert Sterling	1917
Robert Louis Stevenson	1850

NOVEMBER

·14·

You may fall victim to temptations of the flesh and sink to escape boredom or swim at the side of a lover. Take gambles: they pay off and keep you moving from one enthusiasm to another. Travel to appease your restlessness. Dare to challenge tradition and convention, and ignore street signs that read Dead End. You find rewards as a swashbuckler, personal comfort ignoring tradition and people who take you into their hearts at the turn of a cul-de-sac.

In youth you are set above the crowd and expect to uphold your personal ideals to contribute something of lasting value during your lifetime. You are reticent to speak your mind or go on overkill sharing imaginative thoughts. It is difficult for you to make personal friends, although you have a large scope of acquaintances. When you find a kindred spirit and feel that your intimate feelings will be wisely considered, you are childishly loyal.

Mother and siblings or grandmother and mother allied in your youth to make you feel too special or shut out. Until you reach maturity, find your love or achieve dramatic results of your work, you are socially self-conscious. You are charming, witty and attractive when you are not frustrated or angry. In payment for imagined or real broken promises, you refuse to speak or become antisocial. It is in your best interests to avoid escapist tactics—drugs, alcohol, too much sleep, too many baths—in your efforts to escape responsibility or dreary routines.

In mid-life you travel mentally and explore unknowns. You adapt to all types of people and conditions as you grow older.

• OTHER NOVEMBER 14 BIRTHDAYS

Aaron Copland	1900
Johnny Desmond	1921
Morton Downey	1902
Mamie Eisenhower	1896
Prince Charles of England	1948
Robert Fulton	1765
Barbara Hutton	1912
King Hussein of Jordan	1935
Brian Keith	1921
Veronica Lake	1919
Joseph McCarthy	1909
Claude Monet	1840
Leopold Mozart	1719
Jawaharlal Nehru	1889
Dick Powell	1904

NOVEMBER
· 15 ·
You want to have things your own way, but you assume responsibility for your family, your business associates and your community. You have pride in yourself and expect everyone to be as conscientious as you are. That does not mean to say that you are a stick-in-the-mud. You are domestic, parental and concerned with bringing music, harmony, beauty, love, enthusiasms, knowledge and comfort to others. All you crave is peace.

You want to do your work and to achieve tangible results for your planning. In youth you are surrounded by practical thinkers and material doers. Life is mundane and demands that you maintain traditions, practice economy and keep to an orderly routine. When you get out on your own, you may be too rigid and rule-bound and vacation only when exhausted by your own self-disciplines. You may go to the other extreme and laze into a disorganized life-style. The choice is yours. You will swing between the two until you consider yourself a pillar of the community, have others dependent upon you or hurt the ones that you love. You stabilize when dedicated to a single purpose.

You do not share authority easily or compromise your freedom willingly. You marry early, late in life or not at all. You are overtly set in your ways and open to change inwardly. Indecision may keep you unsure of your domestic commitments. You are conscious of justice and make efforts to use power and influence in the public interest. Material ambitions were established in your youth. You require proof to convince you of everything. Late years alter your beliefs, goals and skepticisms.

• OTHER NOVEMBER 15 BIRTHDAYS

Edward Asner	1929
Howard Baker	1925
Petula Clark	1934
Felix Frankfurter	1882
W. Averell Harriman	1891
Mantovani	1905
Curtis Le May	1906
Paul Simon	1942
Lewis Stone	1879

NOVEMBER
·16·
Money and recognition for your aristocratic, creative, futuristic ideas, talents or service does not come easily or when anticipated. In youth philosophical, religious or nonconforming people inspired your uplifting ambitions. You are an introspective dreamer, a perfectionist, a loner. You want a home and the comforts of loving relationships but do not always make the effort to get them. Peace, privacy and harmony are important to your well-being. You have the rhythm of life in your soul and should have a commercial or hobbyist's interest in music.

You are aloof from mundane practicalities and will uncharacteristically dirty your hands in the name of perfect work. Others, you feel, cannot do things as well as you can, and you get involved in doing when you should be supervising. You are too sure of your opinions and often base your ambitions on erroneous information or beliefs. Leases, contracts and legal agreements are disappointing or disillusioning.

You often bite off more than you can chew, delay and lose an opportunity due to skepticism or gullibility, or you may analyze until your moodiness or melancholy overtaxes your physical stamina. You must work for the accomplishment and let the profits come in through establishing a reputation for your expertise and authority. Until late years you have spiritual, emotional and financial ups and downs. But you have your love to keep you stabilized if you find a mate who lives up to your ideals.

You are restless. Learn to be discriminating. In later years you are respected by your peers, develop tolerance and are less argumentative. You find companionship in your interests.

• OTHER NOVEMBER 16 BIRTHDAYS

Eddie Condon	1905
W. C. Handy	1873
George S. Kaufman	1889
Mary Margaret McBride	1899
Burgess Meredith	1908
Lawrence Tibbett	1896

NOVEMBER
· **17** ·

Until you decide which course to take in your late twenties, you cannot escape making personal sacrifices in childhood and youth. You are surrounded by females who are impractical or who expect to be protected. You are expected to live up to and with the ideal family situations in mind. Money, education or housing problems may make your youth inharmonious. Family traditions, expectations and responsibilities delay your ambitions. You must be prepared to bury the old goals and move on.

After age thirty you move or shift your focus to change the course of your life. Friends are helpful. Foreign, legal or unconventional agreements are disappointing and disillusioning. Avoid going to court. The results that you expect initially return only a partial amount of the financial, career and domestic success and happiness that you anticipate. You are afraid of poverty and are an excellent money manager when there is enough to go around. You fear loneliness and realize that you must learn to enjoy reading, listening to music, studying or working alone. You are highly intelligent and secretive.

Your individuality, courage and businesslike approach attract responsibilities where money, material power and financial interests are concerned. Long-term real estate, antiques and modern art investments are profitable. You improve your feelings of self-worth, pride and comfort. You are in control of your ambitions. However, your problems are never crystal clear. They seem to be chronic. You work with quality-conscious, authorative, introspective loners. You perform a service to humanity and leave a lasting image.

• OTHER NOVEMBER 17 BIRTHDAYS

Mischa Auer	1905
Frank Fay	1897
Rock Hudson	1925
Lauren Hutton	1943
Gordon Lightfoot	1938
C. G. "Bebe" Rebozo	1912
Lee Strasberg	1901

NOVEMBER
· 18 ·

Money will never be a major problem, although your fears of poverty are very real in youth. You are surrounded by intuitive, creative, extraordinarily sensitive people who open doors to dreams of glory, fame or fortune. In mid-life you leave your place of birth, travel culturally and set an example of polish, skill and empathetic personal philosophy. You are very independent, courageous and materially-physically coordinated.

It is your ability to originate and put body, mind and spirit together—to see your ideas through to a tangible result—that sets you apart. If you are willing to accept human frailty and the earthy side of life, you can achieve anything you set out to do. You want a mate, partner, lover, friend to share the fruits of your personal ideals, magnetism and ability to get your talents to the attention of the public. Marriage is wanted, but not required for your success or comfort.

Freedom to be expansive and space to reach out to stretch your capacities is a must if you intend to achieve your potential. You make frequent changes, travel and get involved helping others. You give sound advice and are invited or leaned upon to counsel or teach. People sense your selflessness and will allow you to give them the shirt off your back. You would do well in politics, law or religion, and have an ambition to reform or liberalize without personalizing delays or failures.

In later years you have determination and persistence, and you approach large projects efficiently. Your friendliness, charm and communications talents are lifetime assets to your business abilities. You may find too much peace and not enough action.

• OTHER NOVEMBER 18 BIRTHDAYS

Imogene Coca	1908
Dorothy Collins	1926
Louis Daguerre	1789
George Gallup	1901
Edmund Halley	1656
Johnny Mercer	1909
Eugene Ormandy	1899
Ignacy Paderewski	1860
Alan Shepard	1923
Billy Sunday	1862
Brenda Vaccaro	1939

NOVEMBER
· 19 ·

You are unconventional and do not adhere to traditions, but it is never your intention to be offensive, brash or crude. You attract boosters and followers with your progressive ideas. It is not easy to understand how you find friendly supporters, because you emit a skeptical/gullible optimistic/woeful and pixie-ish/logical altogether deceiving character and personality.

You play devil's advocate, feign ignorance or disinterest or look to be enthralled, when actually you are trying to get a mental "fix." Once you have your philosophy, details and friendships come together to specialize your ambitions. You have tried to live up to your personal ideals. Your aspirations are unrealistic until you are able to live independently, and then you keep a different facade in public and live a private life.

You have changes of heart, ambitions and career options in midlife. You met charming, self-expressive, entertaining people in youth who are dreamers or visionaries. You are aware of choices but find that in following your personal preferences you lose powerful supporters. You need to serve or uplift public expectations, have multiple original ideas and constantly go from one plan to another. You are romantic and prone to injustices.

Your future security and material stability depend upon how loyal or disloyal you are to a friend, partner, employer or lover in your thirties. A decision to maintain beliefs or to fail to fight for your convictions is called for after you have established a pattern or gained recognition. You are extremely responsible and late in life work to better conditions for those who are less fortunate. You value home, but try to travel or satisfy your restlessness.

• OTHER NOVEMBER 19 BIRTHDAYS

Roy Campanella	1921
Dick Cavett	1936
Indira Gandhi	1917
Calvin Klein	1942
Martin Luther	1483
Clifton Webb	1893
Alan Young	1919

NOVEMBER

·20·

You may have to play the role of supporter to the "star" for many years—your productive years—to find that your best interests are served as the results of non-aggressive, diplomatic and cooperative approaches. Opportunities for partnerships are available to you, and you are too selfless or too self-protective, depending upon the actions of the moment.

You are frequently placed in situations in which you come under the protection of—or face problems for—competitive, down-to-earth, practical lovers, mates or partners. You may become over-burdened emotionally and show discomfort by arguing or lacking your customary modesty, humility and tact. It's time for a rest if you incautiously take over or stop being kindly when you are on home ground. You are strong, peace loving, want security and enjoy sharing ideas and social contact with males.

You are wise and old for your years as a tot. In mid-life you get your accumulation of details, data, cooperative friends and talents out to serve the public. You need to feel pride in home, family community and country. You accumulate information and do not always put it to work. You have difficulty with people who are not decisive or do not understand the philosophy of setting long-term goals. You are too charitable and may undertake responsibilities that tax you emotionally and financially. When you are drained and disillusioned by thankless results, you then take the opposite tack: you become selfish.

Later you begin to play, flirt, scatter interests. You feel youthful and refuse overloads of emotional or practical obligations. You want free time; a chance to do your best.

• OTHER NOVEMBER 20 BIRTHDAYS

Kaye Ballard	1926
Judy Canova	1916
Alistair Cooke	1908
Chester Gould	1900
Robert Kennedy	1925
Emilio Pucci	1914
Dick Smothers	1939
Norman Thomas	1884
Gene Tierney	1920
Judy Woodruff	1946

NOVEMBER

·21·

It is important that you do not aggressively commercialize your talents or act self-insistent in family or group interactions until after you reach your thirties. You are more practical and less inclined to feel yourself above the laws, standards and traditions of down-to-earth people in mid-life. You will meet promoters, unconventional opportunities and friends in youth who sway your ambitions. Father and people who are assertive intimidate or incite you to frustration and anger. You are alternately submissive and too changable. Fame, public acknowledgment or the ability to attract followers are part of your early life.

You are exposed to intense, self-absorbed elitists who recognize the delight you show in living through the expression of your gentle, sensitive, delicately appealing personality. Your creative talents include details that arouse sensuality or imagination. You are a flirt, a fashion trendsetter, a comforting idealist, an "original." Your individuality shines through your often impractical, dramatic—sometimes 'superficial—futuristic ideas. The choice is yours, but a professional career will bring out your potential to attract gifts and recognition and to travel for business or pleasure.

Friends and alliances will get you everywhere. Lovers or being "in love" may cause you to scatter your interests and lose your momentum. Marriage and career vie for supremacy in your life. In later life you have ambition, inventive notions and active energy. You enjoy your entire life if you use emotional control and economy during your years of magnetic public appeal.

• OTHER NOVEMBER 21 BIRTHDAYS

Abigail Adams	1744
Vivian Blaine	1924
Vito Genovese	1897
Goldie Hawn	1945
Juliet Mills	1941
Stan Musial	1920
Eleanor Powell	1912
Marlo Thomas	1943
Voltaire	1694

NOVEMBER
·22·

You will leave a lasting image of your concepts and tangible results of your work after you are gone. In youth you expected to be or to do something of value and to practice a skill or serve a worthwhile apprenticeship. A domineering father is a problem. After age thirty the personal idealism of early years added to your dedication and determination prove profitable. You attract people and experiences that put you in a position to do something realistic about solving problems that have proved difficult for the others to face or to apply practical solutions.

You want leadership and benefit from partnerships, marriage or alliances. You are a keenly sensitive mental person with a fighting spirit. Expect to have workaholic energy. You can be a fanatic when fired to promote your personal philosophy. You contend that following you will uplift quality, provide better ground rules or solidify details of futuristic concepts held by other leaders. You are capable of spreading propaganda, and when you evangelize may be the glue that holds a family, a community or a nation together. Personal sacrifice will be necessary during mid-life. You find greater comfort later in life.

You may be too self-sacrificing or too egotistical. Aim to investigate before spreading your news. You are capable of naïveté or astounding knowledge. Don't defy progress.

If you become disgusted with the way in which others receive your work or charity, you are prone to idleness or escapist devices. In your own neighborhood, the power to use your common sense, to uphold something worth saving, will be in your hands. The older you get, the more established and secure you become.

• OTHER NOVEMBER 22 BIRTHDAYS

Hoagy Carmichael	1899
George Eliot	1819
Charles de Gaulle	1890
Billie Jean King	1943
Geraldine Page	1924
Robert de la Salle	1643
Robert Vaughn	1932

NOVEMBER
·**23**·
You are youthful, imaginative and able to play many parts. You are filled with nervous energy as a tot and cannot stay put mentally or physically. Your mind is constantly flashing new ideas, and your hands get caught when you test to find out if fire is really hot... and you want to know, what does "hot" imply? You meet with obstacles to your dreams of happiness and perfection. Immaturity or too serious an approach to your work, playtime and career are the extremes of your problems. Learn to be subtle and less scattered or singular in your goals and personal intentions.

Money and responsibility join to create upheavals in your life. Friends, relatives, pets and children are dear to you. You are very independent, intense and surprising. You take gambles that make others shudder and are usually lucky. It is your greatest pleasure to play the host, and you enjoy entertaining and maintaining an attractive, organized, comfortable home. You require attractive, intelligent, sensitive people at work or when relaxing. You have a flair for dialects, languages and memorizing. You prefer to feel that you are of service and are generous, self-confident and adapt to circumstances or personal discomforts that dismay others.

The role of peacemaker is thrust upon you. Although you want to travel—enjoy adventures and new enthusiasms and feel restless all the time—people rely upon your ability to sense the basis for their problems. You have a nose for diagnosing and may not know why or how; however, you are in demand as a sensitive in late years. Your quick mind needs challenge, and you are secretive about your changing views as you grow older.

• OTHER NOVEMBER 23 BIRTHDAYS

Charles Berlitz	1914
Victor Jory	1903
Boris Karloff	1887
Billy the Kid	1859
Barry Landers	1932
Harpo Marx	1893
Franklin Pierce	1804

NOVEMBER

·24·

Forget about retiring. You are at your best working and achieving the tangible results of your ambitions. You may get lazy and overwhelmed with the details that you impose upon yourself. Take a well-earned vacation and get back to the grind if you want to achieve your potential. In youth you are inclined to see yourself as a savior. In mid-life you retain your ambition to help, comfort or improve living conditions and attitudes. You want love, orderliness and to take pride in yourself, your family and your community.

You are parental and volunteer your opinions. You enjoy producing, directing and advertising. Politics, theater and home products are exceptional areas for your commercial interest. Real estate brings in profits. The people and experience that you meet in youth expose you to the freedoms that money and influence offer.

You never lose your desire to have your hand in managing your own or the family finances. However, you do not put on a show of affluence. In fact, you are down to earth and practical where autos, clothes and fads are concerned. You have a conservative or traditional leaning and may be too rigid and self-limiting. You believe in education and self-improvements. It is your desire to see everyone live up to your personal standards.

Your observations, in late years, should incline you to be less dramatic or to avoid suffering physically from emotionalizing your reactions to the injustice that you see. Life after age fifty-five has a less demanding style, and you socialize or travel to pursue your personal interests.

- OTHER NOVEMBER 24 BIRTHDAYS

William F. Buckley	1925
Dale Carnegie	1888
Claudia Dreifus	1944
Howard Duff	1917
Geraldine Fitzgerald	1914
Scott Joplin	1868
Garson Kanin	1912
Henri de Toulouse-Lautrec	1864
Cathleen Nesbitt	1889
Zachary Taylor	1784
John V. Lindsay	1921

NOVEMBER
·25·

Base your decisions on past performance and experiences and you will satisfy your restlessness and avoid financial losses. There are difficult-to-see, -investigate or -diagnose problems that you must overcome. You are inclined to be unconventional, sensual and sensitive to the emotional responses of others. You travel mentally, creatively and financially from your place of birth. It is the philosophy you evolve, through a sense of isolation, that you come to depend upon when love, family, education or career opportunities become confused or too dependent upon your personal sacrifice.

Personal relationships are short-lived or disappointing. You are introspective and hide your feelings. However, you expect others to see through your aloofness, impersonal shows of concern or intellectual curiosity with overt affection. Only extremely sensual or extremely cerebral lovers will break through your facade. Politics, photography or any profession that brings about reforms, health or humanitarian improvements offers you opportunities to excel. You do well at any career that captures your concentration.

You exhaust yourself trying to meet your ideas of perfection. Security is always available; however, you are not paid your due and may become bitter if you allow jealousy to creep into business relationships. Your romantic entanglements create intense emotional upheavals. Work is your best medicine.

In late years you speak with authority, or listen to others. It is not your inclination to be tactless, crude or too earthy; however, you are blunt. You prosper, adapt and keep a low profile.

• OTHER NOVEMBER 25 BIRTHDAYS

Andrew Carnegie	1835
Helen Gahagan Douglas	1900
John Kennedy, Jr.	1960
Joe Di Maggio	1914
Ricardo Montalban	1920
Carrie Nation	1846

NOVEMBER **·26·** In youth you learn to depend upon yourself; however, you set ambitious goals and have access to money, power or people who set a materially aggressive example. Family or community obligations fall upon your shoulders, and you are conscious of the foibles and fallacies of close-knit or strongly idealistic relationships. You are too responsible or break from the ties that enclose your talents before you reach the age of thirty. Throughout your lifetime your family name, community spirit or compulsive emotional concern for others crops up to keep you at war with yourself.

You have a beautiful voice, physical dexterity or artistic talents that surface in youth. You are sensitive, detail conscious and expect to individualize to create or contribute something of value in your lifetime. It is in your best interests to get a practical education. Money and material accomplishments require organization, efficiency and courage. You are faced with managing to support your love of quantity, quality and comfort. You are sympathetic, generous and impractical when it comes to uplifting the expectations of others. You require privacy, an opulent home and a peaceful environment to pursue the perfection of your desires.

Love is important to your feeling of well-being. You are possessive and jealous, and take pride in your position and name. Woe be it to the person who causes you to be suspicious, cheats or deceives you. You force issues in your quest for truth and beauty. Remember that people in glass houses shouldn't throw stones. You cannot flirt and expect relationships of undying loyalty. In late years you travel, love the sea and find peace.

• OTHER NOVEMBER 26 BIRTHDAYS

Charles Brackett	1892
Robert Goulet	1933
Marian Mercer	1935
Charles Schulz	1922
George Segal	1924
Eric Sevareid	1912
Tina Turner	1939
Emlyn Williams	1905

NOVEMBER

·27·

You have an electrical mind and high nervous energy. In youth, family causes you to feel lonely and detached from stable relationships with other children and does not provide the emotional warmth that you crave. You are sensitive to family feelings and have a need for approval or affection from mother. She may be too doting, too self-involved or out of reach. It is your intelligence and ability to understand underlying problems that make you secretive and self-contained. You are a questioning, genteel, cooperative youngster. In time you become aloof from your emotions in order to avoid the pain of rejection.

Throughout your lifetime you grow culturally, travel and establish an understanding of human frailty. You are wise: born to rise above mundane expectations, to communicate with the public and to continually polish your skills and performance. Education is the key to your emotional stability and practical success. You crave knowledge, privacy and mental companionship.

You work with others and strive to perfect your ideas. It is in your best interests to specialize. However, you try to maintain diplomatic relationships and have a variety of distractions. You are intuitive. Religious or metaphysical interests capture your imagination, and you may find peace in a monastery, an ashram or escapist tactics. In spite of your desire to seek solitude, you are magnetic and attract audiences or company. Marriage or love is untraditional and difficult.

You are attractive to youthful imaginations and inspire the young or young at heart and leave a lasting image. Platonic relationships flourish in late years, and you are well guarded.

• OTHER NOVEMBER 27 BIRTHDAYS

JAMES AGEE	1909
JIMI HENDRIX	1942
CAROLINE KENNEDY	1957
BRUCE LEE	1940
DAVID MERRICK	1912

NOVEMBER

·28·

You are the critic's critic and always know how to improve upon anything. Ideas flow from you as a tot, and you are charming, talented and self-expressive. However, you are changable and restless. You have unexpressable energy that cannot emerge until you reach maturity. In mid-life your individuality puts you into the money and in a unique position. Partnerships are attractive to you, but too often you are drawn to aggressive, domineering or egocentric lovers or business associates. In late years travel and pleasures come more easily.

You tend to mix financial commitment, work and domestic or romantic affections, to the sacrifice of your individuality. You have high expectations and stamina, and strive to bring your elitist ideas to the public. You are a reformer in youth. You carry out the creative efforts of others or bring a sensitive interpretation to attract applause, publicity or the cheers of your peers. You take direction but bring your unorthodox twist to a team or group effort.

In mid-life you overcome childhood indecisions based upon impracticality or gullibility. Your need for approval no longer motivates your ambitions. You are less prone to suffering from self-imposed drives to beat out the competition or physical overexertions. You must work and assume the responsibilities that you accumulate to stabilize your material goals. You cannot marry without love or pretend that you have no emotional needs in order to gain power, money or position. Nothing is perfect.

It won't satisfy you in late years to keep changing. Your unique curiosity is never satisfied; however, you travel for fun.

• OTHER NOVEMBER 28 BIRTHDAYS

Brooks Atkinson	1894
Alexander Godunov	1949
Gloria Grahame	1925
Gary Hart	1937
José Iturbi	1895
Hope Lange	1933
Claude Levi-Strauss	1908

NOVEMBER

·29·

From a childhood based upon practical economy, tradition and conservative roots, you imagine a lifetime of uplifting service to your family, community or the world. You want money and security. You work until your maturity, before you take steps to ignore conventions and live up to your personal ideals. You want public attention and intimate love. It is in your best interests to live an orderly, empathetic and unselfish life-style. You have tendencies to dramatize, exaggerate or believe your own publicity.

It is the support of the people who believe in you that provides your success. You are the tool of your exceptional visionary, evangelistic and humanitarian personality gifts. You meet level-headed people who do not deny you security in youth. You are too wise and precocious for your years and make personal sacrifices as a tot. In late years you cannot ignore past loyalties or emotional ties to satisfy your ego. In mid-life you meet disappointment and receive credit for your outstanding talents in late years. You are most successful when you show humility, enjoy refining your work and do not wheel and deal for money or power.

You attract honors or self-deception. You are an unrealistic romantic or coolly philosophical. Your loves and hates are extreme, and you are a formidable enemy when crossed. You are a wonderful lover or detached from human emotions. Living with you is either heaven or hell . . . nothing in between.

Moodiness and dreams of an elusive Shangri-la may detract from enduring love. Your late years are filled with comforts.

• OTHER NOVEMBER 29 BIRTHDAYS

Louisa May Alcott	1832
Robert Devereux	1566
John Gary	1932
Adam Clayton Powell, Jr.	1908
Harold C. Schonberg	1915
Elmo Zumwalt	1920

NOVEMBER

· 30 ·

You are a clever maverick with a gift for attracting attention for your cause or philosophy. You are a master of self-expression; you can write, paint, entertain, lecture or find an organized means of selling yourself to the public. In youth you meet unconventional experiences and surprising people. You are exposed to promoters, sensual enthusiasts and people who have enthusiasm for testing their mettle. Until you reach maturity you are too independent or too accommodating as you strive to establish your unique identity. With your arrogance or submissiveness, you dazzle others with your brilliance or confuse them with your subtle powers of persuasion.

Women are very helpful or destructive in your youth. Your loves are deep and serve as a support for your ambitions. Men follow you or refuse your attempts at leadership with passionate disdain. In midlife your appeal is imaginative, dramatic and far-reaching. You are never closeted in society; rather, you charm others with your personality or your fashionable poise. You are a stylist, and your views may have dissenters, but they always attract an audience. Life is an ever-changing showcase for your wares. You provide for late-life security if you establish a concentration early.

You have sex appeal and should manage your personal affairs with a loyal, long-lasting associate. You prefer to talk your way through problems and let others assume responsibility for the details or practical outcome. You are an excellent figurehead and play your part until you get bored. Business and pleasure mix well for you. You attract confidence but rarely share your innermost thoughts. You are settled after age fifty-five, and happier.

• OTHER NOVEMBER 30 BIRTHDAYS

Shirley Chisholm	1924
Winston Churchill	1874
Dick Clark	1929
Richard Crenna	1927
Abbie Hoffman	1936
David Mamet	1947
Efrem Zimbalist, Jr.	1923
G. Gordon Liddy	1930
Allan Sherman	1924
Mark Twain	1835

DECEMBER

• 1 •

In youth, discipline, economy and practicality are stressed. The imaginative, charming, sociable people who surround you as a tot are down-to-earth, hard-working and determined. You are sensitive, shy and adaptable, eager to spend quiet times being cuddled, affectionate and close to mother. You fear mother's rejection and feel humble, ignored or unwanted in comparison to the people or necessities that attract her attention. You may have the opposite experience and be too spoiled or focused upon. Any extreme inclines you to self-pity and lack of self-esteem.

The foundation for your attention to detail, cooperative attitude and appreciation for intimate, loving partnerships is the product of overindulgence or neglect in childhood. In mid-life your originality, self-reliance and aggressiveness surface. You are a planner. With encouragement, your inventive methods pay off. You are different and must squelch conservatives.

You are in tune with the need for changes and originality in your career and love relationships. Patience is not your foremost virtue, and all too often you start actions that never get finished. However, if you have a close association to bolster your ego, it is easier for you to have the willpower and individuality to try out your ideas, to ignore critics and to be a winner in mid-life. If you are too critical to accept anyone in close association, your timing will be off, and progress delayed.

In late years you are given, have earned or assume positions of leadership. Experience mellows your frank appraisals and bluntness. Your material assets improve, and you are emotionally secure. You travel, enjoy friendships and work.

• OTHER DECEMBER 1 BIRTHDAYS

Woody Allen	1935
Alicia Markova	1910
Mary Martin	1914
Bette Midler	1945
Lou Rawls	1935
Cyril Ritchard	1896
Lee Trevino	1939

DECEMBER

·2·

During your lifetime congenial partners are your mainstay in personal and professional interests. Impatience is your problem in youth. You are too independent or too accommodating and make too many changes. You meet self-expressive, enthusiastic, unconventional sensualists as you grow up. Days are challenging: nonroutine, impulsive and frustrating. There is an air of restlessness in your surroundings, and you must be adaptable. Situations occur that are out of your realm and overwhelm you emotionally. You take on an easygoing, seemingly absentminded facade and cleverly approach your ambitions one day at a time.

It is within your nature to be affectionate, friendly and quiet. You prefer to be a lover, not a fighter, and become depressed easily. You are cooperative and receptive to progressive ideas if your personal standards are upheld when details are concluded. Music, rhythmical writing and dance may be pleasant hobbies or commercial moneymakers in mid-life. You capitalize on team or group efforts. In later years you prefer working alone to the dependency and delays that accompany sharing a work effort.

Teaching and enlightening delight you. You enjoy providing a service and solving the little problems that are easily overlooked. Be careful to avoid getting caught up in mountains of minutia or forecasting petty possibilities and losing sight of the end result. You are a considerate, appreciative collector of people and material things. Fill your dream home with your personal treasures to create your private haven, in later years.

- OTHER DECEMBER 2 BIRTHDAYS

Adolph Green	1915
Alexander Haig	1924
Julie Harris	1925
Randolph Hearst	1915
Edwin Meese	1931
Ezra Stone	1917

DECEMBER

· 3 ·

You are a youthful, attention-getting, communicative personality outside your home. Your beautiful smiling eyes twinkle when you are happy, and flirting is almost second nature. You have sex appeal, but you are not inclined to playing the field or cheating. You take the problems of humanity personally and attempt to find solutions at your own expense. Family, community and your domestic obligations are a major focus in early years. You stick to "bad bargains" repeatedly.

As a tot, you sacrifice your independence to maintain relationships. Music, education and comforts are important. The phone and mail are active. If frustrated, you are prone to overeating and emotionalizing. In youth you lay aside your desires in order to serve, provide for or solve serious family problems. When you realize that your sacrifice has not been appreciated or understood as a gift of brotherly love, empathy and compassion, you change from an attitude of complete loyalty to cutting off the past completely. Mother or a selfish woman is the cause.

You are too wise or too gullible in youth. Surrounded by sympathetic, parental, interfering relatives, you make your compromises to maintain stability at home or leave to find peace and harmonious relationships. You are naive and optimistic, and imagine that marriage to a much older or younger person will enable you to take yourself and life less seriously. You find that no one else can be responsible for your happiness, and in mid-life you become accountable for yourself. You never lose your broad-scoped philosophy. Later you are responsive to people you think need you or are less able to help themselves.

· OTHER DECEMBER 3 BIRTHDAYS

María Callas	1923
Larry Parks	1914
Gilbert Stuart	1755
Andy Williams	1930

DECEMBER

·4·

In youth you have limitations placed upon your independence, inventiveness and time to play. Father or the male influence squelches your self-assertion and originality. Later you rebel, and overreact by vacillating in your personal ambitions, while trying to attract approval. You are obedient or rebellious and make frequent changes or do nothing, until mid-life offers conventional people and experiences. You establish an expertise, authority or reputation in youth that is neglected or useless in later years, when material values, down-to-earth people and hands-on application are the motivating forces.

A real estate investment related to childhood pays off in mid-life. You are encouraged to concentrate on education, a technical skill or an intellectual specialty prior to your thirties. After you reach maturity you organize, manage and may have too much energy for your routine life-style. You are not a complainer and attempt to bite the bullet to maintain your self-discipline. Travel is more pleasant in late years, although you experience a large slice of social activity and changes prior to your fifties.

Love is offered and may entail burdens and sacrifices. Material investments or holdings, later in life, do not bring in a windfall. Money is not a serious problem in youth. In maturity life is not as luxurious or filled with attractive people; however, you are philosophical about disruptions of plans. You cope with disappointments and feel a calling to do the right thing. In late years have poise and curiosity. You remain secretive and inwardly aloof from mundane discomforts.

• OTHER DECEMBER 4 BIRTHDAYS

Pappy Boyington	1906
Deanna Durbin	1922
Francisco Franco	1892
Lillian Russell	1861
Robert Vesco	1935

DECEMBER
· 5 ·

You are a gambler with the right instincts to drive a hard bargain. In youth you meet beautiful, affluent and influential people. You are attractive to the opposite sex and can sell garden sprinkler systems to Puerto Rico's Rain Forest residents. Marriage may be for love (each time). However, you attract a loyal, brainy, practical, sensitive-to-you spouse who supports your ambitions. You promote yourself, your ideas and your willingness to attend to the management and details of your entrepreneurish projects. You have all the ingredients to live up to your mother's and your friends' expectations for success.

Your personal sensitivity and critical nervousness bring on chronic, annoying physical problems, lack of energy or depression. You are impatient, curious and cleverly learn from experience. Once you are exposed to a person, place or thing, you file it away in your exceptional memory and have the talent to bring your impressions to the attention of the public. Politics, theater and advertising are looking for a person of your continuing enthusiasms. You never grow old. You will reap whatever you sow. You thrive on change, adventure and the freedom to pursue your intellectual curiosity. You may overwhelm yourself.

Your major talent is the ability to be the catalyst for change in the lives of your family, business group, community or the world. You understand human nature and relate at a distance to people's intimate thoughts. You must avoid impulsivity, accidents due to hasty alterations of plans and having a long memory for petty slights. You are a master of method, exactitude and niceties when you want to be. In late years you are superb.

· OTHER DECEMBER 5 BIRTHDAYS

Martin Van Buren	1782
George Custer	1839
Walt Disney	1901
Grace Moore	1901
Jim Plunkett	1947
Otto Preminger	1906
Strom Thurmond	1902
Philip Wrigley	1894

DECEMBER

6

Temper! Temper! You can blow a fuse at the drop of a hat. You expect family, friends, lovers and business associates to live up to your youthful impressions of right and wrong. You have a tough time growing up, but when you do, you are deadly serious. You develop your tastes, loyalties and wisdom in youth. People who live graciously and have developed a quality consciousness and communications skills help you to expand culturally. You are uprooted in youth and travel far from home.

You feel neglected or catch the spotlight too much as a tot, cannot depend upon your outer personality as a youth and must bolster your social self-esteem in mid-life. You are a chatterbox, or you clam up when you are frustrated or angered. In maturity you gain insights into your compulsion to scatter interests or fear doing a variety of entertaining diversions. It is in your best interests to speak up, tell the truth and avoid imaginative jealousies, gullibility or skepticism. In youth you are considered to be antisocial or too gregarious.

In maturity you are gifted with a talent for using words, teaching and providing comfort or public service. You are parental and combine your brain and emotions when working or making decisions. You are often torn between logic and feelings. You have difficulty establishing enduring trust in intimate relationships and want to take pride in your loved ones. You are conscientious and intolerant of irresponsibility. Be discriminating, firm and remember to use your sense of humor often. Buy a home and fill it with the beauty and opulence you desire. In late years your sacrifices ease up and you find companionship.

- OTHER DECEMBER 6 BIRTHDAYS

Dave Brubeck	1920
Wally Cox	1924
Lynn Fontanne	1887
Ira Gershwin	1896
William S. Hart	1870
Horace	65 B.C.
Joyce Kilmer	1886
Agnes Moorehead	1906
Richard Speck	1941

DECEMBER
· 7 ·

Get an education, build your expertise and become the authority that you admire when you set out independently in youth. A specialty, profession or any specific concentration will attract material possessions and stability. You are an intellectual questioner and rely upon your practical upbringing in financial matters. You have decided opinions and may be too down to earth or blunt at times. Take time to think. You have a fine memory, a clever sense of humor and require privacy to investigate, analyze and draw your own conclusions.

You have self-discipline and are dedicated to producing tangible results. Take a vacation from your workaholic commitments or you will trap yourself and limit your creative imagination in mid-life. If your marriage lasts, thank your spouse. You are aloof from mundane realities at times and must be known intimately to be loved or understood. You are secretive, dislike physical changes and only speak when you are sure. Contacts are important to your career; find companionship.

It is in your best interests to take private time to rest, study and contemplate your navel. You are not at your best in a businesslike, wheeler-dealer, fast-talking atmosphere. Too much noise or superficial distractions make you irritable, moody and melancholy. Money and the knowledge that you seek are available in mid-life, and your reputation is assured in later years if you establish your credentials before you are fifty-four. Before you are thirty you may flounder due to a lack of education. Later you meet aristocratic, rational sticklers for detail who recognize your unique and original approach to a happy life.

- OTHER DECEMBER 7 BIRTHDAYS

Johnny Bench	1947
Giovanni Bernini	1598
Ellen Burstyn	1932
Rod Cameron	1912
Richard Warren Sears	1863
Eli Wallach	1915

DECEMBER **You will land on your feet financially no matter how
impractical your early ambitions seem to the family.
Entertaining, youthful, self-expressive people open doors
for you to use high nervous energy.** You have physical
stamina, coordination, courage and organizational efficiency. In
business, domestic and romantic relationships you are self-reliant
and you can handle many large commitments at one time.

In youth you are too unconventional or fearful of breaking traditions. When you are good, you are very, very good—and when
you are bad, you are horrid. You change as you grow to maturity
and often overwhelm yourself with untried ventures or challenge
your talents. The accumulation of money, influential friends and
leadership in your chosen field occupies your ambitions in mid-life.
You are goal oriented, ambitious and energetic. It is your impulsivity,
curiosity and desire to be free to try everything at least once that
trip you up or delay your success.

You like a display of your material accomplishments. You may be
mercenary or too flashy—ultraconservative or a reformer—too sure
or too insecure. Whichever tack you take for a time, the result is
clear-headed, socially responsible and true to the teachings of the
hard-driving, dependable, sometimes insensitive person who influenced your youth. In late years you reflect with appreciation upon
the structure, routine and determination that gave you a foundation.
As a child, you held resentments due to the curtailment of your
freedom. My, how much you have changed!

In late years you expand your philosophy and reputation.

- OTHER DECEMBER 8 BIRTHDAYS

Gregg Allman	1947
David Carradine	1906
Sammy Davis, Jr.	1925
Diego Rivera	1886
Maximilian Schell	1930
Tullio Serfin	1878
Jean Sibelius	1865
Adele Simpson	1903
James Thurber	1894
Eli Whitney	1765
Flip Wilson	1933

DECEMBER
·**9**·

The responsibilities that you undertake as a tot are based upon the personal ideals of your family. You are precocious, talented and magnetic. Before you reach your teens you develop a philosophy, and throughout your travels or during times of frustration or dependency, you have a mentor or masculine guide. Romance, love, and wisdom are your gifts. Your talents enable you to reach out to a large scope of people to serve a worthwhile purpose before your late years.

You have sound business judgment and work to establish a responsible life-style. Too much social consciousness or too many volunteer stints tax your emotional capacity. You are capable of making a dishrag out of yourself for the good of the family, your community or humankind. It is a thankless job if you comfort others by taking over their obligations. Inspire, teach and be helpful, but do not absolve them of their responsibility or you'll end up with a kick in the pants. When you reach mid-life, you will develop tolerance or be aware that you cannot be judge and jury if you face stupidity or self-destructive individuals.

Foreign lands or cultures benefit you financially and emotionally. You have empathy, compassion and charity to share and do well as a philanthropist, art dealer or counselor. You may find religion, metaphysics or welfare work satisfying. After age forty you set an example for others and cannot lead a selfish or cloistered existence. You feel a sense of responsibility to your roots, you take long journeys, sacrifice personal objectives and experience emotional upheavals in late years. You realize that nothing stays the same; things change.

• OTHER DECEMBER 9 BIRTHDAYS

Beau Bridges	1941
John Cassavetes	1929
Lee J. Cobb	1911
Broderick Crawford	1911
Kirk Douglas	1916
Douglas Fairbanks, Jr.	1909
Redd Foxx	1922
Hermione Gingold	1897
Emmett Kelly	1898
Dina Merrill	1925
Thomas P. O'Neill	1912
Donny Osmond	1957
Dick Van Patten	1928

DECEMBER

· 10 ·

Opportunities to bring your talents to the surface are offered to you in childhood. Purposeful, determined, hardworking people set a traditional example of Abraham Lincoln's comment, "My father taught me to work; he did not teach me to love." Mother or the female influence, in youth, is behind your sensitivity, aspirations and need for approval. She has subtle control of your self-esteem, and you are too well guarded, or lack a gentle touch from parents. You are self-conscious.

Men inspire and spark your inventiveness. You attract money, invest wisely and plan ahead. In maturity you are detail conscious, active and respond to cooperative partners. However, you are a trendsetter and must make progressive changes after a time. In mid-life you need mental stimulation, a friendly atmosphere and an orderly life-style. Marriage is stabilizing, provides a foundation and a conventional background for your ambitions. Every step you take to establish your authority brings you more involvement with the public, and your innovations are rewarded. If you are lazy, nothing happens.

Social contacts play a part in your nurturing process. Friends, phone, mail—all forms of communications—and the people who use their appearance, artistic gifts and words to an advantage set the stage for you to attract attention. You become aware of appearances, want to travel and to gain knowledge.

When you take risks, you can expect to be protected by your intuition. You have a sixth sense about new ventures and "know" what will attract supporters and when compromise is required. In late years you become more patient and explore new concepts.

• OTHER DECEMBER 10 BIRTHDAYS

Emily Dickinson	1830
Morton Gould	1913
Chet Huntley	1911
Dorothy Lamour	1914
Una Merkel	1903
Dennis Morgan	1920
Jonathan Swift	1667

DECEMBER
· 11 ·

Love, marriage and family are the supports for your innovative ambitions. In youth money, traditions and domestic expectations are in upheaval. You do not have a routine childhood. You are exposed to people who do not live conventionally and learn to cope with insecurity. Experience is your teacher, and you learn to understand human nature by observation, experimentation and social contacts.

Friends play an important part in ambitions. You develop communication skills, imagination and an affection for children, pets and youthful interests. Mother and sensitive females are there when you need them. In your youth domineering or selfish males challenge your individuality. Your enthusiasm is a lifetime asset and makes you a magnetic speaker. Your intensity of purpose attracts supporters. Stubbornness, impatience and self-importance cause delay and criticism. You are very conscious of the physical senses, sex and moral standards. Too much or too little sensual experimentation makes you promiscuous or a prude. You get involved in controversies. Legal problems drag out.

Your intentions to promote your personal ideals in order to uplift or alter opinion do not go unrecognized. You have the potential to leave a lasting impression on film, electrically supported communications mediums or in people's minds. Teaching or reforming the structure of another's thinking is dear to your heart. You may, when frustrated, be equally unfair or critical.

You take the lead in various interests. When you take pleasure sharing "your thing" and enjoy the work without placing a price on your sense of justice and fair play, you have power.

• OTHER DECEMBER 11 BIRTHDAYS

Fiorello La Guardia	1882
Brenda Lee	1944
Victor McLaglen	1883
Rita Moreno	1931
Alfred de Musset	1810
Carlo Ponti	1913
Gilbert Roland	1905
Aleksandr Solzhenitsyn	1918

DECEMBER · 12 · Don't base your ambitions on first impressions. You will have second thoughts. You will alter your perceptions during your nineteenth, twenty-eighth and fifty-fifth years. Each change requires a period of waiting before the new self-image takes hold. Your loyalties will be tested. You spread the word of brotherly love or show your intolerance.

In mid-life you are recognized for your individuality, creative self-expression and ability to set an example. You always have two career choices. Traditions that accompany "old neighborhood" philosophies stay with you to late years. As a tot, you are expected to be wise, compassionate and generous. You are not secluded from human frailty and meet a variety of people who understand hardship and cultural differences.

An ambitious, suspicious, conscientious woman subjects you to personal sacrifices and adult awareness beyond your youthful scope. You become worldly and remain a naive, impressionable, romantic. You have a gift for attracting friends, protection and listeners. Social contacts bring in business and pleasure. Music, telephones and languages have a special meaning for you in conjunction with your exceptional memory. Your youth and mid-life are dramatic, extravagant and filled with plans to explore a variety of intellectual pursuits. Later you are elegant.

In youth you assume the responsibilities that accompany acceptance of favors. Mid-life, you pay a price in changing loves, battered ego and emotional upheaval. When you fight the system, your ability to be paid, applauded and free to pursue new enthusiasms attracts problems. In late years the choice is yours.

- OTHER DECEMBER 12 BIRTHDAYS

Connie Francis	1938
Edward Koch	1924
John Osborne	1929
Edward G. Robinson	1893
Frank Sinatra	1915
Dionne Warwick	1940

DECEMBER

· 1 3 ·

In youth money is not plentiful. In mid-life it becomes available, but you cannot hold on to it for your ideal purposes. You dislike routine, try to be speculative and pull back when you scare yourself or losses occur. You are restless, individualistic and creatively expressive. Secretive alliances, involvements brought on by boredom or legal ties eventually cause regrets. You marry for material and emotional security or, pessimistically, refuse to take the plunge. In late years you are surrounded with the possessions you accumulate.

Men intimidate or expect you to take charge. You give an independent impression but need ego bolstering and constant approval. You have no patience with yourself or wishy-washy, indecisive people. You are intuitive, questioning and mentally curious. A technical, scientific or business expertise is a necessity to invite your concentration. Your intellectual capacities are rarely realized until mid-life. You are stubborn and temperamental, and attract a career by accumulating experience.

You want to go wherever you have not been and to own anything that you do not have. It is difficult for you to accept things as they are. You want to make changes or be in constant motion to progress your ambitions. You are competitive and carry on or manage practical affairs for others. Problem-solving is second nature, and you can transform a losing proposition into a moneymaker or a better marriage. You are the salt of the earth and must sacrifice some freedoms to preserve your reality.

You are contradictory: you choose your environment and suffer its limitations; bite the bullet or shoot off your mouth.

· OTHER DECEMBER 13 BIRTHDAYS

Marc Connelly	1890
John Davidson	1941
Dick Van Dyke	1925
Van Heflin	1910
Mary Todd Lincoln	1818
Carlos Montoya	1903
Drew Pearson	1897
Christopher Plummer	1929
Emperor Nero of Rome	A.D. 37
Lillian Roth	1910
George P. Shultz	1920

DECEMBER · 14 · You are multifaceted, impatient and self-promoting. Childhood is filled with adventures and unconventional experimentations, and lacks traditional routines. Father is too loving, too austere or unavailable. You have difficulty asserting your individuality or choose to be unorthodox. You are changable, restless and sensual. The women in your life cause you to vacillate in your decisions or to be too assertive. You try to please everyone and please no one—least of all yourself.

Youth is a time to marry, play, travel and do a variety of things at the same time. If you do not make a marriage commitment early, you will not settle down long enough in mid-life to establish a traditional home or domestic life-style. After age forty you follow your heart's desires—write, lecture, sell, entertain—and establish a philosophical approach to your ambitions. You make the acquaintance of affluent, influential, businesslike people in youth and maintain a desire for wealth, power and the freedom that money implies. You work to have it.

You have a reckless streak and may be promiscuous, nervous and tense. You are interested in health, physical fitness and increasing your stamina. You look to an older male mentor for spiritual or emotional strength as a rule. You get involved in new enthusiasms, must retain respect or become critical and pass on to untried ventures that capture your interest. Learn to be discriminating. You fall in love—with a new job, a car, a career, a date—too easily, on first impression. You get suckered into situations in which you think that you are selling and you are actually being conned. You travel in style in late years.

- OTHER DECEMBER 14 BIRTHDAYS

Morey Amsterdam	1914
Patty Duke	1946
Dan Dailey	1917
James H. Doolittle	1896
Spike Jones	1911
Abbe Lane	1935
Lee Remick	1935
Margaret Chase Smith	1897

DECEMBER **· 15 ·** You need freedom, action and a traditional home life. In that statement you can see the inconsistency of your nature. You are alternately optimistic and pessimistic— laughingly philosophical and drearily intellectual— childlike and venerable. Childhood made you too concerned with superficiality or inclined to be antisocial. You are the oldest, youngest, only boy or girl or an only child. The sun rose and set on you, or you were neglected, owing to the attachment for the mother to other siblings. You assume and cannot endure obligations.

You are a charmer and, if you choose, attract center stage with your witty or entertaining personality. You are a responsible person with concern for the protection of your home, family and community. You enjoy music, teaching and showmanship. Your ambitions are progressive, individualistic and attract leadership in your field. You understand human nature, persevere and will take advantage of your opponent. If flashed, money attracts emotional problems and jealousy. You want beauty, a gracious and opulent home and to give and receive all the comforts. If you take yourself or life too seriously, let your temper explode or escape through drugs, drink, and the like, your pressures will subside, but you will lose your precious gift of magnetism. Worry not! You earn money and provide service.

You need to be seen and heard without losing your freedom by assuming interfering constraints. Be open to new ideas and check out the bottom line for flaws in legal, business or social relationships. Be decisive. Don't delude yourself with immature impressions that start with, "Once upon a time..." Have faith.

• OTHER DECEMBER 15 BIRTHDAYS

Jeff Chandler	1918
Alexandre Eiffel	1882
Alan Freed	1921
J. Paul Getty	1892

DECEMBER

· 16 ·

Expect to be lucky in career and a bit disappointed, due to your dreams of outsmarting others or concocting the perfect plan, at the final outcome of love or business dealings. You are honest, blunt, practical, down to earth and traditional, except when you aren't. You switch between dedicated workaholic organized management of your affairs to superficial appraisals and a lack of common sense. You get caught in your own rules for living and may shut out the other half of the world.

There are hidden truths in your life that keep you aloof from ordinary society. Underlying problems, legal or financial, delay ambitions for an aristocratic, cultured, private life. Your fears of loneliness and poverty cause you to wheel and deal in the business community. You require privacy and quiet to do your best work. You are best letting profits and prestige come to you through your dedication to a specialty, profession or area of expertise. You are clever, magnetic and investigative. After age fifty-five, your rewards and security are assured.

In youth expressive, intelligent, attractive people brought in a variety of amusing or entertaining experiences. You are a seeker, a questioner, and cannot be caged by conventional concepts or light society. However, a practical family and basic necessities set your goals to producing tangible results. You are unable, in youth, to survive without hands-on earthy work. You enjoy changes, activity and a comfortable, welcoming home. Relationships in love are not enduring. You want a responsible mate but have difficulty making the right choice.

You are secure, relaxed and need less activity in later years.

- OTHER DECEMBER 16 BIRTHDAYS

Jane Austin	1775
Ludwig van Beethoven	1770
Noël Coward	1899
Margaret Mead	1901
Mary Stuart, Queen of Scots	1542
Leslie Stahl	1941
Liv Ullmann	1939

DECEMBER
·17·

You are fortunate and do your best as a wheeler dealer in your own business. Money comes and goes until you recognize your ability to deal in large businesses. Partnerships and marriage have material aspects that take you behind the scenes. You are a creative talent and often pick up the pieces when others need organization, efficiency and courage. In youth you are inclined to elitist ideas and get into impractical situations. You are nervous, intense and introspective. It's a toss-up between your emotional responses and your logic as a youth.

After age thirty you put body, mind and faith together. You are extremely sensual or cerebral. In youth you are impulsive or fearful in your sexual experimentations. You go to extremes when you fall in love. You need an intelligent, aristocratic, poised mate and a gracious life-style. You are not an open book, and people may think you eccentric. You prefer to be correct and ethical. It is important to you never to feel inferior.

You have a reasoning mind and require private thinking time. Noise and business activity have a place in your activities, but not when you are in the analytical, planning stages. You dislike working for others. In mid-life you detach from financial commitments that involve groups or require approval before you can take an action. There are flurries of material ups and downs, but you have a way of making your ideas, work and alliances pay off eventually. Legal problems, a snarled inheritance or difficult-to-diagnose problems may slow you down. You have a few unfair incidents, arguments and reversals, but you build security. Later you are tempted to gamble. Don't fool around.

• OTHER DECEMBER 17 BIRTHDAYS

Erskine Caldwell	1903
Arthur Fiedler	1894
Tommy Steele	1936
John Greenleaf Whittier	1807

DECEMBER · 18 · Money slips through your fingers because you often give it away. You are gifted with talent and personality, and attract attention. You have a flair for entertaining, humor and living comfortably. A secure, loving, exciting domestic life-style attracts you. In youth family traditions and responsibilities were important. You are an active, imaginative charmer and make social contacts that take you far from your roots. You leave the nest but never let go of your heritage.

You have the ability to be a wise counselor and a loyal lover and friend. You are tolerant, philosophical and romantic. Your nervous energy must have an outlet or you have difficulty getting a good night's sleep. Your mind is on the go, and you observe more than the average person as you travel, visit other cultures and become a refuge for those less fortunate.

You may be gullible, too easygoing or just assume that whatever you have and give away can be replenished with hard work. Your troubles come from other sources than those of your making. Lovers, business associates and friends involve you in situations that are deceiving. If you were more cautious, volunteered less and organized your material desires, you would hold on to your dreams.

Others indicate that they expect great things from you. You are an original and have a quality that sets you apart. You have a dislike for taking advice and show your independence. You are at home with large projects and have a knack for pulling the pieces of a family or group together. If you have determination you will get whatever you go after. You have a strong character.

• OTHER DECEMBER 18 BIRTHDAYS

Willy Brandt	1913
Abe Burrows	1910
Ramsey Clark	1927
Ty Cobb	1886
Christopher Fry	1907
Betty Grable	1916

DECEMBER

· 1 9 ·

Fortunate for you, your childhood was larded with practical people and you learned to be detail conscious. You are an idea person with a talent for reaching a broad scope of people. The steps that lead to material results are best left to the people who support your originality and love you for your empathetic philosophy. People accept your leadership. You cannot subscribe to standard conventions or life-styles. You intend to maintain an orderly public image and live according to your own rules privately.

It is in your best interests to be yourself under any conditions. You are a trendsetter. Set an example that less creative people may observe and follow. True, you feel like a loner. However, you have the common denominator in your personality that attracts love from admirers. The romantic, generous, enduring qualities in your character attract intimate lovers too. Love, marriage, material accomplishments and continued growth are aspects of your destiny. Only your lack of self-esteem, pettiness or paranoia causes depression or indecisiveness to delay your progress.

In mid-life the social contacts that you made in youth and your self-expressive personality attract rewards. Money, business and domestic problems are solved by your ability to change your concepts and directions. Impulsive actions stir up trouble if you are self-indulgent. You are loyal and have a long memory. Your past always catches up with the present.

In late years you are secure and recapture youthful optimism. You travel and expand your intellectual capacities.

· OTHER DECEMBER 19 BIRTHDAYS

Leonid Brezhnev	1906
James Garfield	1831
Edith Piaf	1915
David Susskind	1920
Cicely Tyson	1939

DECEMBER **·20·** Be patient. How many times you hear this said to you. In youth money, education and domestic stability are uncertain. You must take life one day at a time. Plans are broken, and until you pass into your thirties, your gentle desire for serenity and an easygoing life-style are uprooted. You absorb your experiences and learn about human nature as you progress into your thirties.

The authoritative, changable individualists of your youth, particularly your early male influence, make you too accommodating until you break out to assert your independence. You find that you attract partners or a spouse who has many of the qualities that caused you to be dependent. However, you are not easily intimidated in maturity, and you discipline yourself to be a cooperative, supportive, sensitive lover or friend. You make known your personal preferences and have great success with teamwork and one intimate kindred spirit.

After age forty your personal and emotional problems simmer down. You make fewer sacrifices and prefer quiet, modest, stable companions. Success and leadership in your field are attached to business, and you prefer an unassuming, less responsible, domestic life-style. You enjoy feeling protected and find contentment amassing knowledge, collecting interesting things and observing the little pleasures. Details, data and statistics that you accumulate automatically may be turned into a profitable venture.

A home in the country, away from demanding people, business and rigid schedules, is a comfort and a necessity. The people and experiences that benefit you in late years will find you.

• OTHER DECEMBER 20 BIRTHDAYS

Irene Dunne	1904
Harvey S. Firestone	1868
Sidney Hook	1902
Max Lerner	1902

DECEMBER
·21·

Your success or disappointment must be credited to your family background. The efforts made in your childhood to set an example or expand your cultural awareness made you wise beyond your years. As a tot, you are capable of sensing the emotions, ideas and expectations of adults. You are a creatively self-expressive, precocious, imaginative child and receive support or encouragement from a conscientious or ambitious parent. You make personal sacrifices and submerge your personality in youth, until as an adult, you change attitudes, to take your independence, emotional needs and individuality to heart.

Mid-life responsibilities are in your own hands, and you are inclined to recapture the lost freedoms of your youth until you reach age forty. You gain business or career opportunities and play a variety of amusing games as you expand your social contacts. The practicality, perseverance and sense of obligation to others that you absorbed as a youth turn your ambitions to less self-concerned interests. Idealists, politicians and business executives influence you. You reaffirm your personal morals, ethics and ideals. You begin to work to educate or support people and projects that make you take pride in yourself, your family and your community.

Love, money and charitable causes get your adrenaline flowing. You are proud of your independence and the influential position that you establish. You are impulsive, too forgiving or too cold at times. You are passionate in your aspirations. Hold on to intimate companionship. Late years are spent promoting brotherly love, and personal pleasure requires mid-life planning.

• OTHER DECEMBER 21 BIRTHDAYS

Benjamin Disraeli	1804
Jane Fonda	1937
Chris Evert Lloyd	1954
Michael Tilson Thomas	1944

DECEMBER

·22·

Don't depend upon seeing yourself mirrored in another's eyes, or how you are expected to live or spend your time, to understand your personal desires and capabilities. You really are intended to be a pioneer, to change traditions in your family, community or the nation. If you want to build a better mousetrap, you are on the right track.

Look inside yourself without considering the accommodating self-image you accept as a child seeking approval from your father. In youth you'll challenge his authority or stop being personally indecisive and submissive. You are impatient and break out to satisfy your independent, creative, courageous ambitions. You are filled with practical energy and have the tenacity to organize, administer and work to solve problems that have intimidated more compulsive workaholics.

Nervousness, stubbornness and too much or too little patience cause problems, particularly in youth. You are always in motion, attempting to inject your leadership, sensitivity to details and ability to shine as a supporter for less tactful hard-drivers into large-scale projects. It is your tendency to be a slavedriver that attracts criticism. Remember that most people rest when they take a vacation. You work at playing.

Honesty, integrity and common sense are your positive mainstays. In late years you have strong opinions, rarely see a problem that you feel is too big to handle and have the imagination for long-term accomplishments. Your self-limiting rules and tendency to be a one-man army tax you physically and emotionally. You will see many of your dreams come true.

• OTHER DECEMBER 22 BIRTHDAYS

Frank Corsaro	1924
Lady Bird Johnson	1912
André Kostelanetz	1901
Connie Mack	1862
Giacomo Puccini	1858
Gene Rayburn	1917

DECEMBER **·23·** Social contacts, self-expressive youthful people and a variety of interests capture you as a youth. Family traditions, domestic cares, home, a taste for showmanship, serving the public and a parental nature press you into surrendering personal ideals or assuming burdens for less fortunates in mid-life. Travel, investments and/or inherited money, legal problems and self-promotion keep you busy. Marriage, companionship, physical activity and adventures are not denied you. You gather influential friends and profitable experiences whenever you take on new enthusiasms. As you pass through people's lives, you change their perspective or position in the community.

In late years you seek privacy, relax your possessive attitudes and live culturally and physically far from your place of birth. You are capable of living unconventionally, taking successful risks, attracting lovers, accumulating wealth and/or power and feeling that everyone is out to get you while you prosper.

You are kind, considerate and accommodating when you relax your self-concern. Problems arise if you make mountains out of molehills and scare yourself into becoming smug and patronizing. You act like a spoiled child when you let your temper fly. You are a good politician, salesperson and entrepreneur. People are your ticket to keeping your ideas in motion. You cannot be perverse and hit back at your opposition if you expect to maintain your contacts. Make an effort to ignore hecklers.

Late years are confusing. You become a collector and have difficulty separating sympathetic intimates from pseudo-friends.

• OTHER DECEMBER 23 BIRTHDAYS

José Greco	1918
Harry Guardino	1925
Elizabeth Hartman	1941
Don McNeill	1907
Michel de Nostradamus	1503
J. Arthur Rank	1888
Vincent Sardi	1885

DECEMBER **·24·** Don't force issues; you are perceived as a self-sufficient, conscientious, magnanimous parental type. You attract all the comforts, influential contacts and financial wheeling and dealing that you will need. An inheritance, a family tradition or a service that invites recognition secures your position in youth. You expand upon your background. The approach you take is broad-scoped and intended to benefit large groups of people.

People who have achieved prominence accept you in their circle. They are elevated and expect you to produce a high-quality and professionally skilled performance. Your parental nature turns friends or business associates into family. You take responsibility to serve, provide comforts or make life more beautiful for the people you come to love or groups that depend upon you. You take offense too quickly and give your family, friends and loves cause enough to be critical of you.

You are detail conscious, practical and managerial. Members of the opposite sex are attracted to you and you benefit. You are too concerned with outer images or too antisocial. You extend the bounds of truth when frustrated or angry and allow your imagination free rein. Jealousy, unfriendliness and a loss of the pleasure in youthful pastimes are a result of your lack of social self-esteem. You are too naive or too skeptical when depressed and lose the love of intimates.

If you talk too much or refuse to communicate, these extremes cause you to lose the love you need. Mid-life offers people and experiences that open doors for showmanship, travel and beauty. Confinement is a detriment to your well-being.

• OTHER DECEMBER 24 BIRTHDAYS

Kit Carson	1809
Ava Gardner	1922
Howard Hughes	1905
Robert Joffrey	1930

DECEMBER
·25·

In youth you have unconventional experiences, break traditions and maintain your gentle approach. You are introspective, questioning and investigative. Family obligations are practical, down to earth and creatively limiting. You meet imaginative, self-expressive, supportive communicators who interpret your innovative ideas. Social contacts bring material results and protection. However, you are restless and a loner in your community and feel the need to help less fortunates or to work with partners for a while. Your life is a work of work. Success doesn't come quickly or easily.

In youth your tastes and personality are aristocratic. You are mentally aloof and physically at work. Common sense dictates that you organize, structure and plan your life. Your mind and spirit will atrophy if you do not leave your domestic environment, change your perspective and give yourself a chance to slay a dragon—fight a crusade—buck the system.

You are encouraged by intimates to study. Once you have determined to get an education, you learn about human nature from experience. You must overcome obstacles to travel mentally or physically into other cultures. People help to develop your enthusiasms and technical, scientific or spiritual talents and encourage you to try for perfection. You are secretive and prefer privacy. Anything that you need, including financial backers, you attract with your integrity of purpose, expertise and the reputation that ensues. Legal dealings bring disappointment, disillusionment and delays. No one can do your work for you. In late years you persevere and sacrifice personal comfort for another's welfare.

• OTHER DECEMBER 25 BIRTHDAYS

Clara Barton	1821
Humphrey Bogart	1899
Clark Clifford	1906
Conrad Hilton	1887
Tony Martin	1914
Sir Isaac Newton	1642
Little Richard	1935
Robert Ripley	1893
Helena Rubenstein	1870
Anwar Sadat	1918
Rod Serling	1924
Sissy Spacek	1949

DECEMBER

·26·

You discover your organizational capacities and talent for business after you sow your oats and achieve success. Money is scarce or not available to you as a youth. You may have to make your million by your wits. You are surrounded by people who feel special, above the crowd and more concerned with their own activities. It is difficult for you to play by the rules, get an education and a foothold on stability. You are apt to feel dissatisfied when you get what you want and then look for greener pastures. You experiment, learn by experiences and begin the many unconventional changes that uproot your career.

You get involved in situations that are too busy or too boring. Anything that you have not seen, heard, tasted, touched or smelled interests you. Foreign countries, different cultures and people of the opposite sex whom you cannot understand fascinate you until you learn about them ... then you move on. Too many sensual experiences, concentration on mental pursuits or fear of taking chances make you promiscuous or too virginal before you reach the age of thirty. A desire for domestic comforts, family pride or inability to conceive of disorganizing your life-style may keep you in one love relationship for a lifetime.

You attract social contacts, love and beauty. You are multifaceted and capable of a variety of communications skills. You have a flair for showmanship, music and physical dexterity. It is possible for you to incorporate all your talents into one career because you charm your way out of compromising commitments and get help from a down-to-earth woman. In late years you have companionship and security, and you travel for business and relaxation.

• OTHER DECEMBER 26 BIRTHDAYS

Steve Allen	1921
Albert A. Gore	1907
Alan King	1927
Henry Miller	1891
George Romney	1734
Mao Tse-tung	1893
Richard Widmark	1914
Rose Mary Woods	1917

DECEMBER
·27·

You have your own cockeyed philosophy and see the world through multicolored glasses. Your intellect is overshadowed by your creative talents, emotional obligations and the burdens that you assume for others. Your sense of humor, often self-depreciating, is a balance for your dreams of perfection. You are detail conscious, questioning and aloof from mundane work... if your family is not involved.

In youth the traditions, ambitions and welfare of the people you love detract from your personal ambitions. You have too much responsibility for a youngster and rebel before you reach age thirty. However, you never lose your desire for a home, family and close relationships. In mid-life your wisdom is sought by polished, skillful, culturally expansive people. As a tot, you were empathetic and understood the foibles of human beings and their emotional suffering. As an adult, you are extremely tolerant or, when drained of energy, too intolerant of humanity.

You are dramatic and optimistic, and attract the love of audiences or groups of people. You are magnetic when your positive attitude captures the imagination. You have ideas that benefit humanitarian or charitable interests, and counseling may occupy your time and energy. You must be free to travel to places where you are needed and cannot be tied to the home front. Medicine, welfare work and the arts are a few areas that attract you. Money and material treasures are yours if you are not lazy. If you choose to write, you will surprise yourself.

After age sixty foreign countries offer comfort and friendship.

• OTHER DECEMBER 27 BIRTHDAYS

Marlene Dietrich	1901
Sidney Greenstreet	1879
Oscar Levant	1906
Louis Pasteur	1822

DECEMBER

·28·

You may have two occupations at the same time and succeed at both when you are young. Youth is not your best time of life; mid-years bring in opportunities to establish your individuality. Your tastes, philosophy and style are established early, and you have difficulty changing viewpoints. Mother is a strong or weak influence, and you need affection, approval and to be sure that every detail in your life is attended to as an adult. Indecision is a problem. You do not feel self-assertive and lose your feelings of inadequacy until you are willing to admit your mistakes. You are inclined to be skeptical and critical.

Fears of loneliness and poverty detract from your ambitions and make you unwilling to make progressive changes. You have a loss of a dear one and quickly find things to occupy your time before you get a perspective on yourself as an individual. You are unjustly criticized and reject putting your ideas on the line until you are frustrated into action. Your intuition is your greatest tool. Your capacity for originality surfaces as you mature. Once you get started asserting yourself, you care little for traditions and are dogged in your attempts to market or give away your personal ideals.

You have a tendency to dream, but you are an organizer, a delegator of responsibilities and a controlled executive when you get off your butt. If you make mountains out of molehills and accumulate petty slights, your personal relationships get snarled. It is possible that you will achieve your objectives and move on before the rewards come in. Success fades if you do not have the patience to support your accomplishments. Be true to yourself.

• OTHER DECEMBER 28 BIRTHDAYS

Cliff Arquette	1905
Lew Ayres	1908
Earl "Fatha" Hines	1905
Yasmin Aly Khan	1949
Sam Levenson	1911
Woodrow Wilson	1856

DECEMBER
·29·

You attract public attention through your cooperative ventures with lovers and partners. Only curiosity about how you would relate to other people without a teammate changes your loyalty. Fame, money and happiness are possible in your lifetime. You will undoubtedly leave a lasting image.

You have high ideals, an elitist approach and eventually feel that the rules that are made for practical purposes are not necessary for you. Your enthusiasm, expectancy and extreme reactions attract supporters. Your dreams occupy your thoughts, and as a youth, you may seem to be impractical. The people you meet are imaginative, up to date and sociable. Friends are helpful, and you are a bit naive. A dependable lover sharpens your material ambitions.

Money is available if you let it come to you in response to your unique personality. If you strain after commercial investments or more than your share of a partnership, you will lose in the final accounting. It requires an authority or a leader to help you organize grand-scale activities and to build cautiously for the future. It is your tact, diplomacy and friendliness that add to a business arrangement. You are the power behind the throne and bring the flies to the honey.

You are a perfectionist and have artistocratic tastes. You expect to pay your debts and to have others live up to agreements and expectations. If you are fooled once, you become skeptical and have doubts thereafter. In any case, you are regal.

In late years you will find that another person cannot be responsible for your happiness. You own up and keep alert.

• OTHER DECEMBER 29 BIRTHDAYS

Thomas Bradley	1917
Pablo Casals	1876
Charles Goodyear	1800
Andrew Johnson	1808
Viveca Lindfors	1920
Mary Tyler Moore	1937
Jon Voight	1938

DECEMBER **30.** The luck of the Irish and their gift of gab are part of your charm. You love your comforts and social contacts, and you take pleasure in loving, living and languishing. You are idealistic and never lose the traditions, sense of obligation and feeling of family pride. True, you sacrifice your personal needs as a tot, grow up too soon and have wisdom beyond your years in youth. You develop strong loyalties, and if you are deceived you become unfeeling. In time you mellow and see your ability to sell your talents bring in financial and emotional rewards.

Your sex appeal is an asset and a liability. Few people give you credit for your versatility and ability to handle big projects until you reach mid-life. Travel, gifts and beauty seem to follow you. You expect quality from yourself and your associates. You have a knack for collecting or buying products that never seem to go out of fashion or lose their staying power. You succeed when you observe conventions and offer a service to the community.

You need love and affection in youth and grow to intellectual curiosity in mid-life. Flirting is just a game to you and does not affect your sense of duty. You will stay with one partner and build for the future, unless your generosity is unappreciated. You are ambitious to establish yourself and expect empathy, compassion and independence from a spouse or lover. You may marry an older or genuinely philosophical person and have a male mentor to guide you through rough spots.

Late years reorganize your life. Never allow selfishness or confusion to linger. Plan activities that keep you routined.

• OTHER DECEMBER 30 BIRTHDAYS

Rudyard Kipling	1865
Sandy Koufax	1935
Vincent Lopez	1895
Bert Parks	1914
Al Smith	1873
Marie Wilson	1917

DECEMBER
· 3 1 ·

Through your free, independent thinking, attractive personality, kindliness and ability to be all things to all people, you make others happy. You meet intelligent, cultured, authoritative people in youth who enjoy your down-to-earth approach, versatility and originality. You are too dependent or too ambitious and must be true to yourself before your work brings individualized rewards. Domineering men or aggressive people bring out your fighting spirit. If you are able to balance your personal convictions to team with others, you find your rightful place and build the relationship and security you want.

Once you get a taste for competition, you are in the race. In mid-life your dedication and organizational and managerial talents serve your purposes. You have vitality, determination and imagination. You are in a class by yourself and set an example that others remember before you reach your forties. Eventually your excellent memory becomes part of your career. You dig into a job with a constructive attitude and stay busy until you see results. System, orderliness and rules for this or that may make you too intolerant. However, you have the belief that anything will be resolved by talking it out, and you are not careless about social relationships.

You need beauty, cheerfulness and humor in your surroundings. You have your own way of handling things, and with concentration and economy you achieve your potential. Depression rarely gets the best of you if you take the time to reason things out and don't hold grudges. In late years, if you are single, you find worthwhile responsibilities, travel and keep working.

• OTHER DECEMBER 31 BIRTHDAYS

John Denver	1943
Anthony Hopkins	1937
Candy Jones	1925
George Marshall	1880
Henri Matisse	1869
Sarah Miles	1943
Odetta	1930
Jule Styne	1905